STATE AND SOCIETY IN CONFLICT

D1736091

PITT LATIN AMERICAN SERIES

GEORGE REID ANDREWS, GENERAL EDITOR

CATHERINE M. CONAGHAN, ASSOCIATE EDITOR

THIS BOOK IS A PROJECT OF THE

REGIONAL ADVISORY PANEL ON LATIN AMERICA OF THE

SOCIAL SCIENCE RESEARCH COUNCIL.

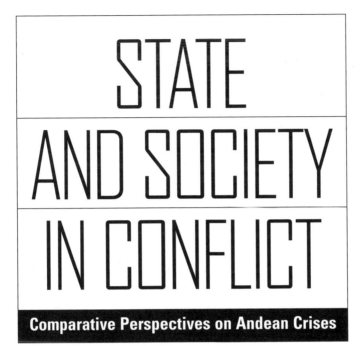

STATE
AND SOCIETY
IN CONFLICT

Comparative Perspectives on Andean Crises

EDITED BY

Paul W. Drake *and* Eric Hershberg

UNIVERSITY OF PITTSBURGH PRESS

Published by the University of Pittsburgh Press, Pittsburgh, Pa., 15260
Copyright © 2006, University of Pittsburgh Press
All rights reserved
Manufactured in the United States of America
Printed on acid-free paper
10 9 8 7 6 5 4 3 2 1

Library of Congress Cataloging-in-Publication Data

State and society in conflict : comparative perspectives on Andean crises
/ edited by Paul W. Drake and Eric Hershberg.
    p. cm. — (Pitt Latin American series)
  Includes bibliographical references and index.
  ISBN 0-8229-5922-4 (pbk. : alk. paper)
    1. Andes Region—Politics and government. 2. Andes Region—
Economic conditions. 3. Andes Region—Social conditions. 4. Social
conflict—Andes Region. I. Drake, Paul W., 1944- II. Hershberg, Eric. III.
Series.
  JL1866.S83 2006
  980.03'5—dc22

2006001960

To Susan and Judy

CONTENTS

ACKNOWLEDGMENTS

Collaborative volumes such as this one seldom result solely from the contributions of those whose writings are included in the published results, and that maxim holds especially true in the case of this endeavor. The book is a result of ongoing conversations and debates that began in late 2000, when members of the Social Science Research Council Regional Advisory Panel on Latin America, chaired at the time by Paul Drake and staffed by Eric Hershberg, concluded that there was something distinctive about what was taking place across the Andes and that this merited sustained attention by scholars from a variety of disciplines and perspectives. Victor Bulmer-Thomas, Carlos Ivan Degregori, Charles Hale, Evelyne Huber, Elizabeth Jelin, and Juan Pablo Perez Sainz contributed especially useful insights to that discussion, particularly with regard to the utility of situating the Andes as a distinctive region within Latin America.

Over the ensuing two years, several workshops were held to debate memorandums and draft papers addressing various aspects of the Andean crisis. More than three dozen documents were discussed at meetings in Chapel Hill, North Carolina (September 10–11, 2001); Quito, Ecuador (October 4–5, 2001); Princeton University (March 28–29, 2002); and Lima (June 7, 2002). Our sincere thanks to our hosts at each of those events: not only were Evelyne Huber and her colleagues at the University of North Carolina intellectual partners, they also accompanied us during that traumatic mid-September week of 2001, when workshop participants found ourselves stranded as well as stunned by events that continue to bring crisis to places far beyond the Andes. In Quito, our colleagues at FLACSO-Ecuador offered invaluable insights and a hospitable setting for debate, as did researchers at the Program on Latin American Studies at Princeton University and at the Instituto de Estudios Peruanos in Lima. It is impossible to thank all of the people who were instrumental in each of these institutions, but Arturo Escobar, Jonathan Hartlyn, and Lars Schoultz proved themselves friends as well as colleagues during those difficult days of September 2001. In Quito, Simón Pachano was a superb partner, and Francisco Carrión and Cesar Montufar offered hospitality as well as ideas. In Lima, Romeo Grompone assembled some of the best expertise available on the topic of decentralization, and in Princeton, Jeremy Adelman's support was crucial to the success of the meeting.

Among the many other people who contributed along the way, we are especially grateful to Luis Verdesoto, who accompanied us in most of these meetings and whose intellectual stimulus was crucial to fleshing out many of the key concepts, and to Fernando Rojas, who helped in many ways.

We are deeply indebted as well for the thoughtful contributions of Ana María Bejarano, Adrian Bonilla, Manuel Castillo, Catherine Conaghan, Jennifer Collins, Julio Cotler, Brian Crisp, Mauricio de Miranda, James Dunkerley, Steve Ellner, Jonas Frank, John French, Lesley Gill, Efraín González Ularte, Paul Gootenberg, Andrés Guerrero, Robert Kaufman, Francisco Leal, Jorge León, Margarita López-Maya, Nelson Manrique, Yasuhiko Matsuda, Enrique Mayer, Gabriel Ortíz de Zevallos, Simón Pachano, Eduardo Pizarro, Gonzalo Portocarrero, Karen Remmer, Silvia Rivera, Anibal Romero, Luis Salamanca, Barbara Stallings, Martín Tanaka, Kim Theidon, Carolina Trivelli, Luis Ugarteche, and Patricia Zarate.

For comments on drafts of the introduction, we thank Lisa Baldez, Craig Calhoun, Sujatha Fernandes, Marcial Godoy, Monique Segarra, Seteney Shami, and Peter Smith. Research assistance from Jennifer Collins and Dru Scribner was extremely helpful, and we benefited as well from able administrative support from Mara Goldwyn and Kate Levitt at the Social Science Research Council.

STATE AND SOCIETY IN CONFLICT

The Crisis of State-Society Relations in the Post-1980s Andes

PAUL W. DRAKE AND ERIC HERSHBERG

SINCE THE 1980S AND ACCELERATING THEREAFTER, THE FIVE Andean countries have been suffering a crisis of deteriorating relations between state and society. Conflicts between state and society have been escalating. Arousing international concerns, this crisis has been manifested in economic distress, social unrest, and above all, political corrosion. The outcome of this crisis could determine the quality and durability of the latest era of democracy in Latin America. Just as that current wave of democratization began its move forward in Ecuador and Peru at the end of the 1970s, so it could begin to recede in the same region in this new century. We do not mean to suggest that the economies, societies, and polities of contemporary Colombia, Venezuela, Peru, Bolivia, and Ecuador have been experiencing identical problems, or that the historical processes through which they have emerged have been the same. Nevertheless, a contagion of socioeconomic and political disintegration has been rampant in the neighborhood, partly because of the susceptibility of broadly similar nations to broadly similar foreign forces.

1

The recent crises have been linked inextricably with the insertion of the Andean region into an international context or regime favoring three interconnected codes of conduct.[1] Emanating principally from the hegemonic United States, these three frameworks have emphasized a security regime focused on drugs and external enemies identified by the United States, an economic regime centered on neoliberalism promoted by the United States, and a political regime prescribing competitive democracies endorsed by the United States. All three regimes have constrained the Andean governments, their sovereignty, and their maneuverability (Schoultz 1998; Smith 2000).

In the current crisis, the Andean countries have found it exceptionally difficult to adjust to these international norms, expectations, and demands. Particularly frustrating has been the attempt to balance liberal economic and political systems. In the Andes, market-friendly economies and voter-friendly political systems have been either poorly installed or breaking down. Moreover, the boundary conditions on state action imposed by externally sanctioned security, economic, and political models, even when they have not been fully accepted domestically, have inhibited the ability of already weak political institutions to implement effective public policies. Within these limitations, domestic elites have failed to forge a consensus about key aspects of governance and about crucial matters concerning resource allocation and development strategy. The result has been a failure to incorporate, represent, and respond to vast segments of the population for which the state is increasingly distant, if not alien. By contrast, the deficiencies of existing institutions have opened the way for some remarkably innovative democratic movements by ex-cluded groups.

Tensions between states and societies in the Andes have grown alongside enduring and accentuated patterns of social and economic exclusion. Indeed, from the onset of the debt crisis in the early eighties through 2005, uneven economic performance has failed to significantly reduce poverty and inequality, despite fairly good growth from 1990 to 1997 and 2000 to 2004. Given the frailty of political parties and the generalized lack of confidence in the capacity of existing institutions to respond to societal demands, the resulting discontent has been expressed in some instances through a retreat toward atomized individualism and decreasing interest in the public sphere. In other cases that alienation has erupted in sporadic outbursts of protest or in increased levels of popular mobilization through social movements, which have even toppled several governments; these movements frequently have assumed roles of interest articulation that social scientists typically associate with political parties. In still other episodes, the dissatisfaction has been manifested in powerful though often short-lived waves of support for individual leaders who, as outsiders to the prevailing order, promise to attack the roots of systemic dysfunction (which they usually attribute, not implausibly, to corruption of existing elites) and to restore hope and dignity to peoples who consider both to be in increasingly short supply.

Rocked by ungovernability, one country after another in the Andes has adopted semiauthoritarian mechanisms in an attempt to overcome political stalemate and the corresponding symptoms of decline, dissatisfaction, and disorder. The rise of personalist leaders who differ in many respects but who share impatience with constitutional niceties (e.g., Alberto Fujimori, Abdalá Bucaram, Hugo Chávez, Álvaro Uribe, Lucio Gutiérrez) is one example of this trend; the increasingly frequent intervention of the armed forces or security apparatus in the conduct of domestic affairs is another. Yet these phenomena have so far coincided with an inclination to maintain at least a foothold, however precarious, in the democratic camp. The result has been rickety hybrid regimes that lurch from crisis to crisis.

The Andean republics are not unique, for strains on governability have been felt throughout Latin America when market-oriented economics and structural adjustments have failed to deliver sustained growth and slash galling inequalities. Yet these tensions have been felt with special intensity in the Andes, where political institutions have long been fragile, as in the central Andes, or where they have been losing legitimacy, as in the northern Andes. Similar problems have been seen in other countries in the Americas—for example, in Paraguay, Argentina, and parts of Central America—but a particularly virulent virus seems to have been infecting the Andes. Systematic and comparative study of the factors that account for the consistent salience of crisis in that region should shed light on analogous problems throughout the hemisphere.

Unless the difficulties convulsing the Andes have been merely a series of coincidences, there should be some common threads that weave together and explain these parallel experiences with disintegration. From country to country, crisis is multifaceted and varied in content and consequence, as well as form and trajectory. Nevertheless, the crises plaguing the region have also exhibited common and interrelated features that may be employed as analytical constructs to better conceptualize contemporary problems facing Andean nations. Some of these facets have also surfaced in countries outside the region, but the particular ensemble in the Andes has been distinctive, acute, and roughly simultaneous.

Our analyses have both shaped the other chapters in this collection and been shaped by them. The guiding principle of this anthology is that the contemporary troubles in the Andes must be understood in a broader theoretical, historical, and comparative framework, not just as idiosyncratic turbulence in individual countries. All the authors make an exceptional effort to take a comparative perspective, whether geographical, chronological, or conceptual, and whether focused on one country or more. The order of their contributions follows the same outline as this introduction. Jeremy Adelman sets the stage with a deep history of the unfinished construction of states and nations in Colombia, Peru, and Venezuela. Then Ann Mason and Arlene Tickner present the current international framework enveloping the entire Andean region. John Sheahan covers the recent performance of all five Andean economies, followed by Eric Hershberg's analysis of contemporary policy dilemmas, employing a case study of Colombia. In the next two chapters, Donna Lee Van Cott and Deborah Yashar examine new forms of participation throughout the region, emphasizing indigenous movements in Bolivia and Ecuador. Finally, three chapters evaluate the roles of political institutions and governability, with Jo-Marie Burt concentrating on the state in Peru, Francisco Gutiérrez on the Congress in Colombia and Ecuador, and Miriam Kornblith on elections in Venezuela. Together, they afford the reader a good grasp of the regional issues and national variations in the Andes. Their potential ramifications for the rest of the hemisphere should also be clear.

Crises and Resolutions in the Twentieth Century

In the twentieth century, Latin America twice faced great crises and attempted resolutions of the relations between the state and society, once from the 1930s to the 1970s and a second time beginning in the 1980s and continuing to the present. Both crises began with economic disruptions that upset the existing contract between the state and society, opening the way to new models of development, growth, distribution, participation, and legitimate governance. The first crisis eventually led, although in some cases only after several decades and only partially, to more or less stable resolutions or new equilibriums; the second has not. For the Andes, Adelman in chapter 2 establishes that both crises battered incomplete states that had never consolidated vibrant ties with their societies (Rock 1994; Thorp 1998).

In Latin America, the 1930s catastrophe of debt and depression jolted the previous model of an open export economy presided over by an oligarchy, whether republican or dictatorial. In response, inclusionary popular nationalism challenged the prevailing exclusionary positivist outlook of a Europeanized upper class. At least rhetorically, this new national project extolled the common people as the essence and symbol of the nation. Their development was seen as the goal of the economy and their participation the source of legitimacy for governments. Influenced by the Mexican Revolution, intellectuals and politicians in the central Andes promoted visions of Indoamerica, a romantic and eclectic mestizo blend of Hispanic and indigenous traits and values, emphasizing Indian mythology. This *indigenista* ideology celebrating the Inca heritage was epitomized by the manifestos of the American Popular Revolutionary Alliance (APRA) in Peru and its charismatic leader Victor Raúl Haya de la Torre, followed by the National Revolutionary Movement (MNR) in Bolivia (Stein 1980; Klaren 1973; Baud 2003).

In the 1930s and 1940s, the equally nationalistic economic model that gradually took hold in much of Latin America emphasized anti-imperialism, inward-looking development, and import-substituting industrialization. That approach addressed not only the crisis of growth but also the crisis of distribution by constructing a limited welfare state. At the same time, populist mobilization of previously outcast groups from the middle and lower classes responded to the crisis of participation and social integration. In the paradigmatic cases, such as Mexico, Brazil, Chile, and Argentina, a compromise state supported and legitimated by the mass of the population answered the crisis of governability, although the military waited in the wings if populist politics threatened upper- and middle-class privileges. At least theoretically, these economic and political pieces fit together as a coherent resolution of the crisis, a response compatible with the state of development of the Latin American economy, society, and polity. However, in contrast with Mexico and the Southern Cone, in the Andes this resolution tended to come about later and in some cases was less profound.

For the elites, a key issue in these crises was the management of the popular classes, basically meaning workers and peasants, but also segments of the middle sectors. From the 1880s to the 1930s, oligarchic regimes ruled most of the hemisphere. At best, enlightened aristocrats guided narrow constitutional republics, as envisioned by Simón Bolívar. At worst, brutal military dictatorships held power. By contrast, in much of South America the era from the 1930s to the 1970s witnessed the incorporation of some subaltern groups into national political life, however unequally.

In the Andes, inclusionary if subordinate participation for some disadvantaged groups occurred through the rise of populist parties such as APRA in Peru and AD (Democratic Action) in Venezuela, through absorption by established parties such as the Liberals in Colombia, through a social revolution in Bolivia, and through corporatist state agencies directed by self-proclaimed quasi-revolutionary governments led by the armed forces in Peru and Ecuador. Techniques of incorporation included extension of the franchise to women and illiterates, enchantment by charismatic leaders, and co-optation by government bureaucracies and social programs. Without overstating successes, these myriad forms of participation eventually resulted, to different degrees but invariably partially and paternalistically, in political access for the lower and especially middle classes, in rights for popular organizations such as labor unions, in redistribution and welfare state programs such as social security, and in social restructuring such as land reforms (Collier and Collier 1991; Bergquist 1986).

In Latin America, this populist resolution of the crisis generated by the Great Depression transpired early in some countries—for example, in the 1930s with Lázaro Cárdenas in Mexico, Getúlio Vargas in Brazil, and the Popular Front in Chile—and late in others—for example, in the 1940s with Juan Perón in Argentina and Juan José Arévalo in Guatemala. In general, the Andean countries, with the exception of Colombia, reacted to the crisis in the 1930s with authoritarian repression of mass discontent and populist outbursts. Constrained by poverty, resolutions of the crisis spawned by the international disruptions of the Great Depression and then World War II came to most of the Andes late and only in piecemeal form. With the partial exception of Bolivia in the 1950s, economic nationalism, protected industrialization, and welfare measures were adopted only moderately, populism was weak or contained, and incorporation of the masses was incremental. The state remained unprofessionalized, corrupt, and, except in Colombia, incompetent. In other words, the resolution was quite spotty and conservative, characterized by half measures that would leave Andean countries fragmented, vulnerable, and poorly situated to confront the challenges presented by the debt crisis of the 1980s (Cardoso and Faletto 1971; Drake 1994).

In Colombia, the Liberals channeled the response to the 1930s crisis through the traditional parties. The Revolution on the March under the

Liberals carried out a series of tepid reforms and mild incorporation. The more audacious populist challenge from Jorge Eliécer Gaitán ended in his assassination and La Violencia in the 1940s and 1950s. At the end of the 1950s, the Pact of Sitges and its offspring the National Front clamped the lid on any threat to the two-party hegemony from populism or the Left until the 1980s. An elitist democracy predicated on "conversations among gentlemen" from the Liberal and Conservative Parties continued to postpone full incorporation of the masses. Clientelism overshadowed participation as the preferred means through which the dominant order secured a modicum of control and consent. The persistence of guerrilla enclaves in zones of the national territory that remained largely out of sight to authorities in Bogotá came to be taken for granted throughout much of this period and would only become costly for overall system survival once the overarching logic of the National Front was itself called into question beginning in the 1980s (Wilde 1978; Hartlyn 1988; Safford and Palacios 2001).

In Venezuela, the armed forces held the populist response at bay until Democratic Action took power briefly in the triennium from 1945 to 1948. Expelled thereafter, AD sacrificed its radical and popular impulses in exchange for power in the Pact of Punto Fijo at the end of the 1950s, although it retained labor support. From then through the 1970s, the two-party system that upheld the *estado del compromiso* (state of compromise) rebuffed any challenges from renegade populists and the Left. It would have little difficulty doing so for as long as it was possible for the state to maintain social peace by awarding handouts paid for by revenues from oil. Only once oil rents dwindled did the cost of failure to modernize or diversify the economy become clear: an elitist two-party system akin to that of Colombia generated stability and legitimacy through clientelist payoffs, but it created no other mechanisms for producing the resources needed to sustain that costly arrangement, nor did it give rise to participatory political or economic institutions capable of making difficult decisions or adapting to unforeseen shocks (Ellner 1993; Coronil 1997).

In the three less-developed central Andean countries, corporatist mechanisms were more commonly adopted to deal with the lower classes, as Yashar explains in chapter 7. In Peru, the popular response to the 1930s crisis mainly took the form of APRA, which was suppressed by the armed forces until a brief spin in government in 1945–1948, during the same springtime of democracy after World War II that benefited AD. Ejected by the military, APRA, like AD, had to give up most of its leftist and radical populist proclivities to have a shot at power. Ironically, the much-delayed period of state expansion and incorporation did not take place under an APRA government but instead under Juan Velasco Alvarado's revolutionary military experiment from 1968 to 1975. That military government did, however, incorporate many of APRA's reformist proposals. Nevertheless, the short-lived, top-down bureaucratic regime never carried mass mobilization and integration very far and failed to consolidate its project to the extent achieved by the Institutional Revolutionary Party (PRI) in Mexico or the MNR in Bolivia (Lowenthal 1975; McClintock and Lowenthal 1983; Klaren 1999).

In Bolivia, the oligarchy and the armed forces stamped out early populist outbreaks in the 1930s and 1940s, until the 1952 revolution ushered in the most radical episode of statist incorporation in the Andes. The National Revolutionary Movement mobilized the middle classes, workers, and peasants behind its nationalistic program to control natural resources, expand industry, and reform society, including drastic restructuring of land tenure. After the MNR turned to the right and then fell from power in 1964, the masses remained a force to contend with, but military domination, especially under General René Barrientos, succeeded in dividing peasants and workers, thereby successfully staving off challenges from the Left until democracy was restored in the 1980s. Extreme poverty continued to limit incorporation by populist leaders and marginalize most of the population, especially indigenous peoples (Dunkerly 1984; Klein 1992).

In Ecuador from the 1930s to the 1970s, the pseudopopulism of José María Velasco Ibarra constituted a personalist phenomenon that never incorporated the masses or installed an import-substituting industrialization model. To the contrary, his demagogy crowded out more progressive movements and preserved oligarchic control. A surprisingly democratic interlude from 1948 to 1963 failed to carry out fundamental reforms. In the 1970s, emboldened by a modest oil boom, the military carried out the only serious attempt at populist incorporation and reform, a pale imitation of the Peruvian experiment and one that accomplished little (Quintero 1980; Quintero and Silva 1995; Conaghan 1988; Isaacs 1993).

The second great twentieth-century crisis in Latin America, beginning in the 1980s and not yet ended, also started with a foreign debt debacle accompanied by general recession. Instead of popular nationalism as a unifying project, many countries turned to a new project of liberal modernization, loosely defined. The predominant economic response in the region has been neoliberalism, in various forms and degrees, in place of statist planning and redistribution. In contrast with the 1930s–1970s solution, that market-oriented model has addressed the crisis of growth but not of distribution. Instead of mass mobilization and incorporation, the order of the day from most elites has been political demobilization, social disarticulation, and individualism, accompanied by the atrophy of political parties. In lieu of mass democracy, classical populism, and corporatism, the ruling groups have generally embraced constrained liberal democracy, in which the market rather than the state is held out as the primary source of opportunities for improving one's life chances.

Conceivably, these responses could compose a congruent resolution of the crisis in Latin American countries with relatively advanced economies, urbanized social structures, large middle and working classes, and sturdy political institutions reinforced by effective states. One thinks of Chile, Uruguay, Brazil, Mexico, and Costa Rica as countries in which such a scenario is plausible, if not highly likely. However, these responses have not meshed or operated smoothly in the Andean countries, which have poor economies, fractured and relatively rural societies, and weaker political institutions.

Thus, whereas the crisis of the 1930s eventually yielded a model of development that thrived for a time in several countries, the crisis of the 1980s has produced a model that has so far been more unworkable in the Andes. In the 1980s and then again at the end of the 1990s, an economic downturn vitiated any national development project, undercut mass participation in political institutions (in those countries where participation existed even partially), undermined co-optive and corporatist instruments formerly available to the state, and corroded governability. Economic discontent sparked protests in an era of limited democratic openness.

During this second great crisis, one of the most perplexing issues for elites has been how to deal with groups that were never fully incorporated, such as indigenous peoples in the central Andes, and how to convince these and other previously incorporated groups, such as organized labor, to accept the neoliberal reduction of the state's role in the provision of employment opportunities and social services. The ability of the government to respond to popular sentiments has also been curtailed by security concerns imposed by the United States, which have provoked nationalist reactions against both economic and security demands from abroad. Mass pressures for inclusion—in participation and benefits, inputs and outputs—have been rising in an era when the state has lacked the will or capacity for amelioration. Demand has exceeded supply for access to and services from a strapped and shrinking public sector.

In this context of scarcity and exclusion, public outrage over corruption, which has long been ingrained in Andean political systems, has fueled disaffection with the state. Increasingly, discontented underprivileged groups have turned away from the state and traditional political parties because those institutions have been unable or unwilling to deliver much in an era of economic crisis and privatization. Instead, people have placed increased faith in direct action or in a variety of social movements, new political parties, independent personalities, and even guerrilla groups, many of which have little stake in the prevailing order. The extent of popular alienation is reflected in the success of so-called neopopulist leaders, whose personal charisma is deployed in place of the institutional channels represented by political parties but who project their influence without the mass mobilization, state intervention, and redistribution associated with classical populism from the 1930s through the 1960s. When personal appeal alone has proved unable to overcome institutional resistance to reform or to satisfy popular aspirations for change, leaders have reacted to popular disenchantment with new forms of covert authoritarianism and militarism, rendering already anemic democracies close to the category of repressive *democraduras* (hard democracies; O'Donnell and Schmitter 1986; Collins 2000; Stein and Monge 1988; Conaghan and Malloy 1994).

Conceptualizing Dimensions of the Current Crises

We consider four interconnected facets of the contemporary Andean crises: the lack of a consensual national development project, the absence of a viable alternative economic model, the prevalence of unregulated and unmediated forms of participation, and the generalized increase in challenges to political institutions and governablility. Analysis of these four features common to the Andean countries can further our ability to more productively conceptualize the post-1980s crises.[2]

Lack of a National Project

The five countries in the region have lacked lately a comprehensive, coherent, and consensual national project capable of inspiring diverse fractions of the elite to construct alliances that transcend conjunctural concerns (*lo coyuntural*), that aspire to fulfill some long-term notion of development, and that can motivate subaltern sectors to consent to the legitimacy of prevailing patterns of rule. At the same time, while the intrusion of external forces, primarily in the realm of economic management but also in the domain of domestic security, has impinged on sovereignty, clashes among competing internal forces have generated increasingly sharp disagreements over national identity, definitions of citizenship, and any collective vision or destiny. While flaring up in recent years, this disunity and contention over the meaning and mission of the nation has deep historical roots in the Andes, as traced by Adelman in chapter 2.

Since the 1980s, each of the Andean countries has exhibited a striking absence of a national project that could unite diverse segments of the elite and that at the same time could elicit the acquiescence, submission, or support of subaltern groups. Processes of truncated, segmented, or stunted modernization have failed to generate bases for enduring cohesion of either the upper or lower classes, both of which remain deeply fragmented. Divisions along sectoral, territorial, and ethnic lines have inhibited the emergence of unifying forces that might galvanize support for coherent projects of political reform or economic development. As mobilized ethnic groups have pushed for greater autonomy and a recasting of the very vision of the nation to one that is defined as plurinational, regional interests have railed against the centralized structure of the state, demanding decentralization and in some cases regional autonomy. By some accounts, the demands of the most militant ethnic or regional actors have called into question the territorial and cultural definitions of the nation itself (Van Cott 2000).

The internationally prescribed triumph of classical liberalism intellectually, economically, socially, and politically—the prevailing version of modernization—has not satisfied enough of the population to sustain regimes or governments, let alone their policies. The only new all-encompassing recipe that has emerged is the sketchy Bolivarian myth espoused by Hugo Chávez. That has not become a compelling, consensual model in Venezuela, let alone the rest of the Andes, although Ecuadorean President Lucio Gutiérrez initially tried to imitate some elements. However polarizing, Chávez's imagined nationhood has illustrated the void that needs to be filled.

At the same time, both external and internal forces represent powerful antagonists to the emergence of national projects and the preservation of state sovereignty. Externally, foreign economic institutions and investors have insisted on openness, a market-oriented mix of monetary, fiscal, and trade policies limiting government policy choice and flexibility. In the security domain, the externally fueled war on drugs has distorted national priorities, spurred militarization, exacerbated regionalism, pitted growers against the government, and fostered alliances among traffickers and guerrillas. At the same time, the hunger for drugs in the consuming countries has funneled funding to the narcotraffickers, so that the United States has occupied the awkward position of financing both sides in the drug wars, while undermining efforts by the United Nations and European countries to assist governments in the region to find some peaceful way out of the conflicts. Since 2001, the U.S. war on terrorism has further warped agendas in the Andean countries. In chapter 3, Mason and Tickner address the interaction between these external and internal impediments to regional and national integration and development (Gaitán et al. 1996; Ugarteche 1998; Bonilla 1993; Tokatlian 1995; Cotler 1999; Smith 1992; Thoumi 2004).

Absence of an Alternative Economic Model

Second—and simultaneously—the debt crisis, structural adjustments, the uneven pursuit of neoliberal reforms, and engagement with processes of globalization have eclipsed the old statist economic model associated with import-substituting industrialization, without producing a viable replacement or alternative strategy for achieving sustainable growth. Instead, from 1980 to 2005, economies overall in the Andean region have fallen short of expectations, with commonalities and contrasts highlighted in chapter 4 by Sheahan. While noting successes as well as failures, he tracks the destabilizing impact of international trends on the depression of the 1980s, the recovery in the 1990s, and the downturn in the latter part of that decade. Although often substantial, the improvements in the nineties proved insufficient to redress many of the losses in the eighties. Those gains in the 1990s failed to satisfy many hopes and rising expectations, which were then dashed by the recession at the end of the decade. After the turn of the century, the resurgence of growth, in and of itself, fell far short of assuaging sociopolitical discontent.

Even in the years when growth has occurred and social indicators have improved, vast segments of the population have not received or perceived the benefits. Spikes of growth without equitable distribution have not satisfied the expectations of the poor, who believe they have sacrificed for neoliberalism but reaped few rewards. In the minds of many residents of the Andes, particularly by the late nineties, their own economic situation has stagnated or regressed, traditionally high levels of poverty have

worsened, and inequalities have been aggravated. Because the incorporation into national life of the middle and working classes in earlier decades
was late and incomplete in the Andes, economic hardship and the decay
of state capacity since the 1980s have undercut many of the modest gains
achieved during the previous period, at the same time that they have
deepened social divisions among classes and ethnic groups, in particular
heightening the exclusion of indigenous peoples. Almost regardless of
national upswings in growth, the result has been mounting dissatisfaction
with and denunciations of neoliberalism, whether merely proposed or
actually implemented (Morales 1991; Gill 2000).

Economically, the dual predicaments of insufficient growth and poor
income distribution that became acute following the debt crisis of the
1980s have festered under globalization and neoliberalism. Unstable and
uneven growth, dire poverty, and glaring inequalities have disappointed
and roiled these societies. Structural adjustments have often been presented as the only solution compatible with the persistent need to generate resources needed to pay off debt and to reorient economies in a
manner consistent with the prevailing climate of globalization. However
logical, those reforms have yet to open promising and satisfactory
avenues for sustainable and equitable growth in most of the Andean
countries. Moreover, by destroying some of the existing productive
apparatus and slashing the scale of public sector institutions that provided stable employment to significant segments of the middle sectors,
they have worsened some distributional inequities, thus accentuating
popular anger.

Although the foreign debt has been more burdensome in some countries than in others (e.g., Ecuador compared with Colombia; see tables 1.1
and 1.2), it has hobbled all of them because outside investors tend to think
regionally. The resultant economic squeeze has constricted resources
required by elites to maintain social and economic control, by the rest of
the population to meet basic needs, by political parties to reward supporters with either clientelist payoffs or macroeconomic reforms, and by states
to cushion the most disadvantaged of their citizens from the hardships of
extreme poverty. When countries have failed to adopt orthodox policies
or have veered away from them, they have been sanctioned or threatened
with sanctions by international financial institutions or investors. In contrast, when elites have gone along with the preferred policies of the International Monetary Fund (IMF) and other external financial agencies
designed to reduce public sector deficits and service foreign debt, those

TABLE 1.1
TOTAL DEBT SERVICE AS A PERCENTAGE OF GROSS NATIONAL PRODUCT

	Venezuela	Colombia	Peru	Ecuador	Bolivia
1979	5.40	2.54	9.60	12.51	10.67
1980	8.66	2.87	10.92	9.04	13.13
1981	7.25	3.12	10.41	10.57	11.80
1982	7.64	3.95	8.56	16.73	19.58
1983	5.90	4.28	7.26	6.76	17.84
1984	7.80	4.42	6.39	9.46	21.28
1985	7.11	5.94	6.22	7.43	12.72
1986	8.44	6.71	4.19	11.13	6.87
1987	10.15	8.12	2.11	8.54	5.46
1988	9.24	8.76	3.16	11.35	8.58
1989	9.18	10.41	2.30	11.32	6.54
1990	10.58	10.18	1.87	11.12	8.33
1991	6.33	9.47	5.18	10.19	6.47
1992	5.65	8.50	2.88	8.14	5.42
1993	6.77	6.87	8.22	6.80	6.05
1994	6.52	7.04	2.64	6.48	6.00
1995	6.45	4.85	2.39	8.33	5.75
1996	6.54	5.80	5.40	7.42	5.74
1997	10.01	4.33	5.02	10.03	6.16
1998	6.26	4.68	4.42	9.04	5.59
1999	5.58	7.86	5.83	9.21	6.08

Source: World Bank 2002, table 4.17.
Note: Total debt service is the sum of principal repayments, and interest actually paid in foreign currency, goods, or services on long-term debt; interest paid on short-term debt; and repayments (repurchases and charges) to the International Monetary Fund.

policies have triggered widespread social outrage, often accompanied by paralyzing cycles of protest from public employees, consumers, urban and rural workers, peasants, and others determined to retain the last vestiges of the protectionist order that partially shielded them from the likelihood or fear of market-induced immiseration (Ugarteche 1990).

Even when the Andean countries have not reaped the promised harvest from stricter adherence to neoliberalism, they also have not been able to resort for long to the populist, inflationary policies of the past. As a result, they have found themselves trapped halfway between statist abstention and intervention, muddling through with government programs that have satisfied neither foreign capitalists nor domestic con-

TABLE 1.2
TOTAL DEBT SERVICE AS A PERCENTAGE OF EXPORTS OF GOODS AND SERVICES

	Venezuela	Colombia	Peru	Ecuador	Bolivia
1979	19.08	14.29	33.85	45.32	33.42
1980	27.15	16.05	44.51	33.89	34.95
1981	23.24	21.91	59.04	46.64	35.67
1982	29.52	29.56	48.65	78.43	59.22
1983	26.84	38.41	34.01	29.59	51.30
1984	25.17	30.07	29.80	37.69	63.23
1985	25.04	41.76	27.68	32.97	49.55
1986	45.35	32.14	21.07	43.11	36.63
1987	37.82	36.81	13.28	33.92	33.46
1988	43.70	44.23	9.44	39.76	53.96
1989	24.60	48.40	8.92	35.61	32.74
1990	23.25	40.88	10.81	32.50	38.63
1991	17.90	36.26	25.02	31.66	35.01
1992	19.46	38.82	20.33	25.67	36.37
1993	22.26	33.81	56.83	24.09	36.82
1994	19.10	45.29	17.64	21.12	28.93
1995	21.52	31.69	15.69	25.82	29.42
1996	16.77	37.25	34.40	21.71	30.73
1997	31.60	28.69	29.78	28.66	30.06
1998	27.58	30.76	27.46	28.98	30.24
1999	23.23	42.86	32.65	25.72	32.05

Source: World Bank 2002, table 4.17.
Noto: Total debt service is the sum of principal repayments, and interest actually paid in foreign currency, goods, or services on long-term debt; interest paid on short-term debt; and repayments (repurchases and charges) to the International Monetary Fund.

sumers. Caught between external demands to adopt neoliberalism and internal demands for social justice, the weak state has been unable to satisfy either. And as an increasing portion of the workforce has lost its ties to the formal economy, it has severed its connections to formal political institutions. As the state's internal base of support has withered along with the economic ties that linked it to societal actors, it has found itself crippled, unable to resist or accomplish the further steps toward state shrinkage demanded of it by external forces (Conaghan and Malloy 1994).

Indeed, by many economic and political measures, Washington Consensus policies have fared poorly in the Andes, despite some noteworthy accomplishments. By the onset of the economic decline at the end of the century, that recipe had certainly become increasingly unpopular. Even in years when growth spurted, critics complained about the neglect of social needs. Governments in Bolivia and Peru enjoyed dramatic successes imposing neoliberal reforms in moments of complete economic break-down, but despite initial achievements of price stability, fiscal balance, and growth, they could not overcome nagging poverty and inequality. Instead, temporary gains spawned rising but frustrated expectations. Sheahan notes that governments in Ecuador and Venezuela have never adopted the full package of neoliberal reforms, though opposition from both elites and popular sectors has brought down administrations that have attempted to do so in both countries. Prospects for achieving some middle way out of the crisis have been handcuffed by the international prevalence of the free market paradigm, on the one hand, and the deter-mined resistance of domestic actors, on the other hand (Thoumi and Grindle 1992).

Colombia has long seemed to be the exception to this general pattern, having exhibited greater independence and efficiency in economic policy making and selectivity in its ingestion of neoliberalism. But it has begun showing clear signs of movement toward the Andean norm, as a fiscal cri-sis compelled the country to seek IMF assistance in 1999. As Hershberg explains in chapter 5, the corresponding processes of privatization and rationalization have triggered devastating confrontations between neolib-erals in the Colombian government and organized actors and public opin-ion that spurn the official formula for coping with economic stress.

Beyond these questions of macroeconomic policy and acceptance or rejection of the prescriptions offered by contemporary neoclassical ortho-doxy lies an underlying challenge that no country in the Andes has yet been able to confront successfully. With the exception of isolated sectors encompassing a very small percentage of domestic entrepreneurs and even smaller portions of the workforce, Andean economies have pro-duced little that is both competitive on international markets and con-ducive to the creation of quality jobs and increased opportunities for prosperity. Those export commodities that have remained competitive employ few workers (e.g., oil in Venezuela, mining in Peru, soybeans in Bolivia) or employ large numbers of workers in intensely exploitative conditions. Interestingly, those sectors that would appear to offer hope for the future—tourism in Peru, nontraditional agricultural exports in several countries, handicrafts exports in Ecuador—tend to operate at highly local-ized levels. They may have the paradoxical impact of further undermin-ing prospects for shaping a national vision of development, reinforcing

instead localized identities and agendas, which may increasingly be articulated as in tension with those of the central state.

Unmediated Forms of Participation

Economic and other injustices have galvanized social movements and
spurred demands for economic and political change, which have been
expressed in increasingly unregulated and unmediated forms of participation. At least in contrast with some more prosperous and institutionalized countries in Latin America—which not coincidentally experienced
mass rural-urban migration at an earlier period than was the case in the
Andes—these frictions and conflicts have been exceptionally explosive.
One reason for the combustion has been that political parties and other
governing institutions are brittle, frequently having served historically to
co-opt rather than to represent significant sectors of the population.
Indeed, one feature common throughout most of the Andes has been the
diminished capacity of long-standing clientelist mechanisms to "deliver
the goods" to subaltern groups, whether they be located in urban or rural
settings (Mainwaring and Scully 1995; Crisp 2000).

The current trend toward unorthodox modes of participation in the
Andes has exposed the deficiencies of past populisms and incomplete
incorporations. In contrast with the Southern Cone, most of the Andes
never experienced full-blown assimilation of the masses through populist
means or their subsequent full-fledged expulsion from the political order
through the violence of bureaucratic authoritarian regimes. In other
words, although the uplifting of the pueblo never went as far in most of
the Andes as in the Southern Cone from the 1930s to the 1970s, neither did
enforced demobilization of the working class reach comparable proportions in the 1970s. In short, the lower sectors in most of the Andes were
not as positively integrated into the political arena or as ferociously
removed thereafter. Consequently, while they have not been as satisfied
with their existing level of accommodation, at least in several countries
they have been far less intimidated from expressing their discontent. The
result in the present context of crisis and governmental unresponsiveness
has been levels of uncontrolled popular mobilization that, in Bolivia,
Ecuador, and Venezuela particularly, have increased both democratic participation and tumultuous instability.

Massive dissatisfaction with the low levels of formal participation, representation, access, and incorporation has also derived from the types of
democracies adopted in the Andes. In all five countries, elites installed offi-

cially democratic systems that were intended to be procedural, managed from above, low intensity, and devoid of populism, mass mobilization, and socioeconomic redistribution. In this supposedly post-incorporation period, a restricted democracy without great popular participation or social reform has been the shared preference of both domestic and foreign ruling groups, with the latter, in particular, advocating a lean state that adheres to neoliberalism, honors the foreign debt, and prefers private to public solutions to matters of production, regulation, and service delivery. But such a sanitized, seemingly hollow democracy has proved unacceptable to a large percentage of the population, which has increasingly asserted itself through and around these democracies, after they were constructed from above. As a result, there now exists a mutual veto of sorts. The dominant classes have been able to block a participatory and distributionist state, while the subordinate classes have been able to disrupt an exclusionary and minimalist state (Burt and Mauceri 2003).

The normal channels for articulating, aggregating, and representing societal interests, in particular political parties, have lost cohesion and credibility throughout the Andes. Given the restraints of classic liberal economics and politics, wherein the market is far more pervasive than the state or its corporatist agencies, the traditional mechanisms of populist and clientelist parties and personalities have lost much of their ability to enroll, represent, or command large segments of the population. Some politicians have continued to offer clientelist and even populist promises on the hustings, but they have been unable to deliver once in office. Frustration with the ineptitude, venality, and vacuity of the traditional parties has led to a proliferation of smaller parties, but they have not proved very effective in Colombia, Venezuela, or Peru.

Creation of novel parties closer to their social base, as with the indigenous organizations in Ecuador and Bolivia, may hold out more hope of revitalization of the party system and expansion of democratic citizenship, particularly with their gains in the 2002 presidential elections, but so far they have remained incapable of governing the nation. As Yashar in chapter 7 and Van Cott in chapter 6 argue, by undermining traditional state and party mechanisms, neoliberalism has inadvertently provoked and cleared the way for new democratic forces, whose conquests have been stunning but whose full potential has yet to be realized (Ticona et al. 1995; Collins 2005).

The lifeblood of most Andean political parties has been clientelism. However, clientelism has been eroded in recent years by (1) the diminution of resources, as in Venezuela with the dwindling of oil revenues during the 1980s and 1990s and the skyrocketing of corruption; (2) the multiplication of claimants, as in Ecuador with the proliferation of social movements and identity politics; and (3) the competition among state and nonstate actors to exercise patron-client relations, as in the Colombian countryside with guerrillas, gangsters, drug lords, paramilitaries, local bosses, and foreign intruders, including nongovernmental organizations. At the same time, decentralization has multiplied the sites where clientelism can be practiced but where scarce resources sometimes lead to increasingly vicious battles. The erosion of political parties has further encouraged the emergence of seemingly anachronistic forms of *personalismo* or *caudillismo* (personalist strong men), especially in Peru, Venezuela, and Ecuador (Martz 1997; Menendez-Carrión 1986; Kornblith 1998; Romero 1986, 1994; Tanaka 1998) .

The inadequacies of political parties have motivated more people to rely on social movements—such as labor unions and indigenous organizations—even though most of these vehicles have been themselves poorly organized and funded. Focusing on prominent examples, Van Cott assesses the substantial gains by indigenous peoples and women against daunting odds. The legitimate demands of social movements have exceeded the resources of an indebted and impoverished state confined by its inability to raise revenue or to manage resources effectively, as well as by its adherence to neoliberal and elitist precepts. Even when economies have grown, governments have been unable to meet social demands. Therefore, a growing array of social movements and organizations have criticized neoliberalism, structural adjustment programs, privatization, government austerity, the IMF, debt payments to foreigners, and investments by foreigners. The protesters have accused these villains of producing recessions, raising the price of basic necessities, undercutting local industries and labor unions, hiking unemployment, and draining the government of resources for social services.

To an important extent, such social organizations have provided creative, necessary, and valuable channels for the expression of discontent and the entrance of new democratic actors. The upsurge of civil society to destabilize an unjust political system has the potential to deepen democracy. Yet in the absence of powerful and accountable political parties through which to channel these grievances, social movements have remained rather blunt instruments, frequently incapable of representing their constituents to the state in an institutionalized and enduring manner or of securing effective state responses to their claims. While some of these movements have treasured their autonomy from political parties, others have begun to develop linkages with parties or given birth to parties themselves, hopeful signs for strengthening democracy. At this juncture, however, the situation facing some Andean societies is that mobilization has exceeded new forms of institutionalization. While social actors seek to transform as well as disrupt the corrupt and exclusionary existing order, constructing citizenship requires both collective subjects conscious of their rights to articulate interests in the public sphere and a state that is simultaneously cognizant of the legitimacy of such demands and capable of coherent institutional responses (Huntington 1968).

Institutional Weakness and Challenges to Governablility

Finally, the first three factors have been exacerbated by institutional weaknesses that render governability extraordinarily difficult in the contemporary Andes. Part of the blame lies in a Bolivarian legacy of elitist and coercive republics managed by flimsy and corrupt states that have frequently been challenged by interventionist (though not always reactionary) militaries. In chapter 9, Gutiérrez dissects the unpopularity of the state by studying hostility toward the Congress in Colombia and Ecuador. There, as elsewhere in the Andes, reforms intended to increase the effectiveness or legitimacy of the state have sometimes sapped rather than strengthened state capacity, and they have often empowered rather than undermined potentially powerful antagonists to state authority. Never very strong, the central government has been challenged by international and transnational actors; by domestic regional and local competitors; by purveyors of violence among criminals, guerrillas, and paramilitaries; and by drug growers and traffickers. These contenders have called into question the capacity of the state to retain a monopoly on violence, and in so doing have undermined the very "stateness" of systems that aspire to rule in this troubled zone of the Americas.

The inadequacy of regular forms of political participation has enflamed the crisis of governability and of democracy. Instead of democratic consolidation, much of the region has been experiencing democratic disintegration. A mutual blockade between fragmented upper and lower classes has centered around an inactive and dysfunctional state. The hardly surprising result has been that disenchantment with democracy has been expanding along with levels of cynicism. To be sure, disenchantment is typical of new democracies, as expectations become less euphoric, more realistic, or even frustrated. Although discontent with the performance of democratic institutions has been spreading, diffuse support for democracy in some form has remained pervasive in the Andes, even in polarized Venezuela, as Kornblith documents in chapter 10.

This predilection toward democratic politics has been demonstrated by instances of high electoral turnouts, by episodes of popular resistance to what appear to be illegitimate seizures of political power (e.g., several recent upheavals in Ecuador, the eruption of opposition to Fujimori in Peru, the driving from the presidency of Gonzalo Sánchez de Lozada and Carlos Mesa in Bolivia, and clashes between the government and its adversaries in Venezuela) and by signs that even those who would change the rules of the political game radically (e.g., Fujimori in Peru, the armed forces in Ecuador, Chávez in Venezuela) perceive a need to clothe these reforms in the garb of constitutional democracy (Murillo 1993).

Increasing challenges to governability in these marginally institutionalized democracies threaten to precipitate a loss of legitimacy for the rules of the game. Such challenges place in peril the state itself and the principle that state authority must be based on the active and voluntary consent of the governed. According to Burt in chapter 8, struggles over and against the state have been intensifying in countries where the national government has never had much power, coherence, or scope, particularly in the central Andes. As neoliberalism has undercut the relevance of the state for the population, elitist, inefficient, and self serving political institutions have become increasingly intolerable to the public. This animosity has intensified as oligarchic governments have reacted to citizen activism with repression instead of democratic incorporation and reforms for long-excluded populations. States that serve their citizens so inadequately are unlikely to command much loyalty.

Atomized nodes of authority and resistance have confronted the central government. For example, regional authorities have become increasingly unwilling to heed directives from the capital city, particularly in Colombia and Ecuador. Guerrillas have continued to threaten state authority in Colombia and have begun spilling over into Venezuela and Ecuador. Although Peru has defeated its guerrilla antagonists, the manner in which it did so proved poisonous to the rule of law, and the state was hardly strengthened in the process. Moreover, Peruvian society will take decades to recover from the trauma of the violent confrontation between insurgents and the state and the accompanying violations of human rights. In Peru, Bolivia, and Colombia, many peasants have opposed U.S. and central government programs to eradicate coca crops. Along with persistent poverty and inequality, rising crime—whether common thugs or transnational syndicates—has added to the perception of social disintegration and governmental impotence. In reaction to the state's severely eroded ability to carry out even its most basic functions, such as maintaining order and imparting justice, many poor Andean communities—especially in far-flung rural areas but also in sprawling urban zones—have increasingly been taking justice into their own hands. Rarely in contemporary South America has the state confronted so many defectors or the rule of law so much defiance (Starn 1999; Arnson 2001).

Haunted by the specter of failing states, the Andean central governments have reacted to their diminishing authority in three main ways. First, they have tried to reinvigorate democracy by revitalizing institutions. In some cases, making governments more representative has rendered them less efficient, a classic tradeoff between participation and performance. Venezuela, Bolivia, and Colombia, for example, have responded with constitutional reform to decentralize authority and the delivery of state services to subnational levels. Ironically, reformist attempts to reconnect state and society have sometimes backfired. Despite some progress, administrative decentralization has at times spawned new crucibles of conflict and rivals against the central government and national parties, unleashing centrifugal forces and exacerbating regional, municipal, and ethnic divisions.

Similar cases of unanticipated consequences are evident in the experiences of constitutional and electoral reform in Colombia and Venezuela during the 1990s, described in chapter 9 by Gutiérrez and in chapter 10 by Kornblith. Although sometimes reducing the stifling presence of the two traditional parties, these measures unintentionally opened new avenues for corruption and clientelist practices. As Hershberg shows in chapter 5, comparable disappointments have been experienced in the wake of policy reforms that proved impossible to implement in practice (Verdesoto 2001). Second, these regimes have tried to reattach citizens to the state by bypassing institutions, primarily with personalist appeals, for example, under Fujimori in Peru and Chávez in Venezuela. Third, they have tried to impose order through creeping authoritarianism, while preserving democratic forms to appease their opponents and foreign observers.

Because of semiauthoritarian practices, some Andean regimes have become at best delegative democracies and at worst democraduras. Resort to arbitrary, unaccountable, and quasi-legal behavior based on coercion and use of the armed forces has been seen under presidents Fujimori in Peru, Hugo Banzer and Sánchez de Lozada in Bolivia, and Chávez in Venezuela. Incremental authoritarianism has also cropped up in impositions of states of emergency and military force to quell social protests in Ecuador and guerrillas in Colombia. In addition, the resort to undemocratic means without openly, formally discarding democracy has been evident in Chávez's constitutional reforms that further empower the presidency; the irregular changes of government in Ecuador in 1997, 2000, and 2005; the electoral shenanigans of Fujimori in Peru; and the abdication of large chunks of national territory to the guerrillas or the armed forces in Colombia. Whether loosening or tightening the reins of power, the state has become increasingly reliant on the military, thereby opening the door to more abuses of human rights, more alienation of civilians, and more distortions of democratic institutions. Governmental ineffectiveness, instability, and authoritarianism underlie the fundamental danger and fear in the Andes: that the current wave of democracy in Latin America might start to roll back there (Degregori and Paz 1993; O'Donnell 1994).

The Central Andes and the Northern Andes

The countries of the central and northern Andes all share the four dimensions of crisis discussed here, but their nature, mix, and intensity vary. First, the entire region suffers from the absence of a national project, unified populations committed to plausible and compelling strategies of development writ large. This common problem is most acute in the three central Andean countries, Peru, Bolivia, and Ecuador, which have long debated whether some notion of Indoamerica is a congealing or a dividing concept of nationalism. When it was first expressed earlier in the twentieth century, intellectuals propagated this worldview mainly as a rhetorical device to rally the common people against the Europeanized oligarchy. Now that the indigenous peoples themselves have begun voicing a more militant and ethnic *indigenismo*, it has become a counterhegemonic doctrine that generates conflict with the middle and upper classes, as well as some with mestizo sectors of the popular classes. In the northern Andes, Venezuela and Colombia, no mystical definition and discourse of national identity and destiny has ever taken hold, although Chávez has been trying unsuccessfully to concoct a Bolivarian legend to rally Venezuelans around a common dream.

Second, poverty and inequality historically have been more extreme in the central Andes, especially among indigenous peoples. Those economies are also heavily agricultural in nature, have tended toward greater degrees of instability, and have languished under more onerous burdens of external debt. As a result, they have been more subservient to foreign pressures to adhere to neoliberal doctrines. In contrast, the more independent northern Andes have experienced a decline from relatively well-to-do levels, by Latin American standards. Yet the past decade has witnessed a striking deterioration in virtually all economic indicators in Venezuela, and by the late 1990s Colombia had joined the poorest-performing economies in Latin America.

Third, modes of participation that outstrip the institutional capacity of regular channels of political involvement have been more prevalent in the central Andes, where feeble multiparty systems have prevailed, albeit occasionally including some individually strong parties, such as APRA in Peru and the MNR in Bolivia, although they have also shriveled from their heyday. With the partial and qualified exception of Bolivia, incorporation of the masses historically has been pallid and manipulative, particularly for indigenous peoples. Until recent years, corporatism has been a prevalent state strategy for managing subordinate groups (Rivera 1984; Van Cott 1995).

In the northern Andes, strong two-party systems prevailed from the 1950s to the 1990s, providing some minimal linkage of the masses to the state through clientelism. Elitist parties reached out to workers and peasants, but incorporation remained hierarchical and lukewarm. Yet by the end of the 1990s those political parties were losing support at an astonishing rate, as the resources for clientelist payoffs evaporated, and by the end of the decade the traditional two parties had virtually disappeared from the scene in Venezuela. Although losing ground, parties and party systems have retained the greatest vigor in Colombia and Bolivia, but they function not so much as mechanisms for articulating interests of their constituents but rather as ossified systems for gathering votes (Hartlyn 1988; Coppedge 1994; Ardaya and Verdesoto 1994).

Fourth, governability has also been more difficult historically in the central Andes, characterized by exceptionally weak states with authoritarian propensities, in which unstable governments have been subjected repeatedly to intervention by the armed forces. From the 1950s to the 1990s in the northern Andes, by contrast, democratic regimes ranked among the most stable and efficacious in Latin America. Colombia and Venezuela kept the military subservient to civilian control and remained immune from the dictatorial waves that swept the Southern Cone and

Central America. The northern Andes underwent democratization in the 1950s when the state and economy were expanding, while democracy came to the central Andes in the 1980s, when both the state and the economy were contracting. Even with the spiraling violence in Colombia and the implosion of the traditional parties in Venezuela recently, those regimes still appeared sturdier than their counterparts in the central Andes. Yet, in the last decade, the turn toward authoritarian practices and increasing reliance on the military and security forces has emerged everywhere, fueled in part, but by no means exclusively, by the drug war and other security demands emanating from Washington.

Challenges to state authority have arisen in all the Andean countries, but perhaps the gravest threat has come from guerrillas and paramilitaries operating in Colombia. Armed conflict reached its worst point in Peru during the 1980s and early 1990s (Degregori 1990; DESCO 1989; Portocarrero 1998) and more recently in Colombia, where it builds on a decades-old cycle of violence (Palacios 1995; Bergquist et al. 2000; Pizarro 1990, 1994; Roa and Galtung 1998). Colombia has also stood out for the power of drug traffickers and growers, who have also been significant in Bolivia and Peru, although relatively unimportant in Ecuador and Venezuela. Regional divisions and conflicts have also been obstinate in Colombia, followed by Ecuador, Peru, and Bolivia. Indigenous movements have been most advanced in Ecuador, followed by Bolivia, with surprisingly sparse activity in Peru and a minimal presence in Colombia and Venezuela. In the past few years, the exceptional strength of those indigenous movements and the extraordinary weakness of their national governments have spawned the most destabilizing conflicts between state and society in the central Andes, especially in Ecuador and Bolivia.

Countries in Crisis

These generalizations should not obscure huge variations in how the crises have manifested themselves in each of the five countries. Individual country experiences under the strain of the current crisis are briefly reviewed here and in more detail in other chapters.

Colombia

The debt crisis at first had limited impact on Colombia, though it suffered inevitably by the tendency of international investors to attribute guilt by geographic association. More recently, however, economic stagnation and the ensuing effort to impose IMF-style structural adjustment measures in Colombia have stoked popular disaffection with the regime. Nevertheless, the elitist party duopoly has continued to blunt popular movements or populism. More than elsewhere in the Andes, ruling groups have managed to ignore or co-opt mass discontent, containing most legitimate political activity within the two parties until the election of maverick President Alvaro Uribe in 2002. With both parties exhibiting unprecedented signs of fragmentation, clientelist practices have become all the more essential for their survival and increasingly constitute the sole basis for linking the state to stakeholders in Colombian society.

While the 1991 constitutional reforms were an ambitious attempt to revitalize Colombian democracy, their impact on the performance of political institutions has been highly uneven. In important respects, they have undercut the influence of the central government. In chapter 5, Hershberg analyzes how fiscal troubles are partly attributable to an explosion in spending by subnational governments, and in matters ranging from expenditures to security policy provincial governors have become increasingly resistant to orders from Bogotá.

Since the exhaustion of the National Front, Colombia has been plagued with intractable violence from multiple sources. Both the guerrillas and the paramilitaries have evaded state control, as have the drug lords and most social conflicts. Government attempts to negotiate with the guerrillas have borne little fruit. Then U.S. aid under Plan Colombia threatened to spread the fighting inside and outside the country, as did Uribe's determination to crack down on the "violent ones." Despite vigorous opposition to his neoliberal economic policies, public opinion backed Uribe enthusiastically. Unlike their counterparts in the central Andes, he and his neighbor Chávez maintained their personalist appeal. Whether Uribe's strong-arm measures could restore order and prosperity remained to be seen. According to some experts, Colombia had become the most decomposed and dangerous country in South America (Vásquez de Urrutia 1989; Thorp 1991; Ungar 1993; Zabaleta 1994; Rodríguez 1995; Posada-Carbó 1998; Gutiérrez 2000; Richani 2001; Alcántara Saez and Ibeas Miguel 2001).

Venezuela

In Venezuela, the debt crisis and the shrinkage of oil revenues in 1980s to the 1990s led to the depletion of the rentier state and the erosion of the two parties that had thrived on its largesse. Resentment against the corruption and arrogance of the party duopoly mounted from the 1980s to the 1990s, as poverty, unemployment, and inequality rose. Structural reforms—albeit thinly applied—failed to revive the economy, while the middle and working classes complained because the state lacked the resources to meet both its external debt obligations and its internal wage and social services obligations.

Venezuelan alienation from existing institutions surfaced in electoral abstention. As in Colombia, institutional reforms—elections of governors and mayors as well as decentralization—may have undercut the ties between the state and society more than fortified them. President Carlos Andrés Pérez's short-lived gambit to implement an IMF-designed structural reform diet sparked the coup attempt by Chávez in 1992, followed by his electoral rout of the two parties in 1999. Since then, President Chávez has been trying to fill the space vacated by the political parties with the sway of charismatic leadership.

Not unlike Fujimori, Chávez is an outsider who has carried out a quasi-constitutional coup against the political establishment and has succeeded in concentrating power in his own hands while encouraging a growing role for the armed forces. Rather than solving many of Venezuela's problems, his authoritarian style and a deteriorating economy have generated a backlash resulting in a failed coup d'état against him and a polarized opposition that has split the nation into two irreconcilable camps. Nevertheless, Kornblith reminds us in chapter 10 that the turbulent electoral showdown between the two antagonists had the potential to reaffirm as well as invalidate democratic practices. Buoyed by a gush of oil revenues, Chávez scored a landslide victory in the 2004 referendum, which seemed to provide a temporary solution for his government. That controversial but stunning election also suggested that the only Andean president to resist the security, economic, and political regimes fostered by the United States and to champion the poor had staying power (Wright 1990; Molina 1991; Naim 1993; Coppedge 1994; McCoy et al. 1995; Karl 1997; Salamanca 1997; Canache and Kulischek 1998; Crisp 2000; Canache 2001; Gott 2001; Ellner and Hellinger 2003).

Peru

At the beginning of the 1980s, democracy and debt came to Peru simultaneously. By the end of the decade, the country slid into a state of collapse, as examined in chapter 8 by Burt. After the shock of the debt crisis, the anachronistic populism of President Alan García (1985–1990) applied statist and nationalist policies that left the economy in ruins, wracked by hyperinflation. His attempt to reconnect the people to the government through charisma was discredited by incompetence and corruption. Meanwhile, Shining Path was gaining strength violently and rapidly, spilling from the countryside into the cities (Cotler 1987, 1989; Pasara and Parodi 1988; Thorp 1991; Graham 1992; Tuesta Soldvilla 1994; Seligmann 1995; Roberts 1997; Dietz 1998).

To impose order and defeat the guerrillas, President Alberto Fujimori (elected in 1990, in 1995, and supposedly in 2000) created a democradura through the self-coup of 1992 and the unleashing of the armed forces. At the same time, from 1990 through his ouster in 2001, he cultivated mass support with personalist appeals, targeted aid projects, and increasingly heavy-handed control of the mass media. While the imposition of structural adjustment policies managed to stabilize the economy and reignite growth in the 1990s, the economy fell into a tailspin by 2000–2001. Rising bankruptcies and unemployment fueled public discontent with a neoliberal model that required more spending on the foreign debt than on health and education (Degregori and Grompone 1991; Cameron 1994; Stokes 1995; González de Olarte 1996; Tuesta Soldvilla 1996, 1999; Cameron and Mauceri 1997; Stern 1999; Sheahan 1999; Gorriti 1999).

Fujimori's increasingly blatant authoritarianism and corruption combined with economic woes to bring him down at the start of the new millennium, leaving a vacuum of power, projects, and policies. The newly elected president in 2001, Alejandro Toledo, began presiding over civilian political institutions that were arguably even weaker than they were when Fujimori took over, because of the latter's dismantling, distorting, and disparaging of those entities. And like Fujimori, Toledo lacked the support of a major organized political party and was forced to rely for his success on the appeal of his personality and the good will of domestic and foreign investors. Amidst charges of corruption, his popularity plummeted as his privatizations encountered resistance and his promised social reforms sputtered, despite significant economic growth (Cotler and Grompone 2000; Wise 2003).

Bolivia

After a whirlwind of incompetent and kleptocratic military governments, Bolivia returned to democracy in 1982. From the mid-eighties to the mid-nineties, draconian structural adjustments recommended by the IMF brought foreign indebtedness under control, hyperinflation to a halt, and economic growth to new heights. In the mid-1990s, the Sánchez de Lozada administration implemented significant political reforms aimed at fostering greater participation in the political system, decentralization being perhaps the most important.

Despite laudable achievements, Bolivia remained the poorest country in South America. Structural adjustment measures included massive privatizations of the country's state-owned enterprises, including the government's huge mining interests. As a result, tens of thousands of workers were laid off, many of them displaced to the tropical lowlands where they eventually became involved in coca production for the drug trade. Privatization and economic restructuring served to effectively cripple what had once been one of the most powerful labor movements in the Andes. By 1999–2001, the Bolivian economy was also stagnating, unemployment was mushrooming, and inequalities were deepening. This decline in the Bolivian economy is attributed in part to the effects of the Banzer administration's efforts, strongly backed and financed by the United States, to eradicate illegal coca production. These measures spawned repeated conflicts between the government and campesino coca grower organizations.

The government's previous democratic reforms, primarily decentralization, did little to mask continued larceny and inefficiency. During 2000–2001, social protests and blockades in Bolivia exceeded those in Ecuador, denouncing the neoliberal model and its commitment to service the foreign debt. Although in chapter 7 Yashar notes how those upheavals exposed the loss of state control, they did not lead immediately to the fall of the government, partly because President Banzer still enjoyed the backing of the armed forces and the United States. His besieged administration became increasingly reliant on the police and the military, funded in part by the United States to fight coca production.

As the traditional political parties and their pacts lost support to previously excluded rural groups, Sánchez de Lozada was narrowly reelected president by a minority in 2002, promising to revive the economy and reduce poverty. When his neoliberal policies to raise taxes, prune spending, and favor foreign capital reignited mass mobilizations, led by indigenous and peasant nationalists, he reacted with armed force. That triggered even greater civil disobedience, driving him into exile in 2003. His successor, former vice president Carlos Mesa, resigned in 2005 when he could not contain even larger social uprisings demanding indigenous rights, social justice, curbs on neoliberalism, and constraints on foreign capitalists, particularly nationalization of natural resources.

Whether a new government could restore democratic stability, social peace, and economic hopes was problematic (Lora 1987; van Dijck 1998; Lehman 1999; Gill 2000; Crabtree and Whitehead 2001; Grindle and Domingo 2003).

Ecuador

Like Peru and Bolivia, Ecuador faced the debt catastrophe in the 1980s during democratization. The elitist political system that has emerged over the past twenty years has satisfied few Ecuadoreans as it has stumbled from crisis to crisis, discussed in chapter 9 by Gutiérrez. The failure of structural adjustments has led to backsliding and policy incoherence. The central government, whether elected from the Left or the Right, has found it impossible to reconcile demands from the IMF, the World Bank, the Inter-American Development Bank, and the Paris Club for austere structural reforms and hikes in taxes and utility rates as a precondition to debt bailouts with demands from domestic social groups for relief from poverty. Dollarization in 2000 was a desperate gamble to stem out-of-control currency devaluations and save Jamil Mahuad's teetering presidency, while Ecuador effectively went into default on the foreign debt. The protests against neoliberal formulas, globalization, the IMF, the World Bank, the debt, and domestic financial elites have been spearheaded by indigenous organizations, particularly the Confederation of Indigenous Nationalities of Ecuador, backed by nonindigenous social movements, trade unions, and students.

Trapped between external and internal demands, governments in Quito became increasingly unstable and short-lived. The military oversaw the unscheduled replacement of the populist president Abdalá Bucaram in 1997 and the neoliberal president Jamil Mahuad in 2000. Under pressure from the United States, the country has at least maintained a democratic facade. As economic travails and social eruptions mounted, fears rose that Plan Colombia would push drugs, guerrillas, violence, and refugees into Ecuador from its northern neighbor.

In 2002, army colonel Lucio Gutiérrez won the presidency with the backing of more assertive indigenous and labor movements because of his vow to curb corruption and poverty. Once in office, he reached agreements with the IMF on loans and with the White House on Plan Colombia. At home, however, his switch from populism to austere neoliberal policies, compounded by incompetence, scandals, and undemocratic behavior, alienated his indigenous allies, sparked social protests, slashed his popularity, and destroyed his presidency in 2005, despite economic growth. As in Bolivia, it looked unlikely that any presidents in Ecuador could finish their regular terms in office while torn between incompatible international and domestic pressures. (Ayala Mora 1986; Galarza Izquierdo 1992; Thoumi and Grindle 1992; León 1994; Pachano 1995, 1996; Kyle 2000; Selverston-Scher 2002; Gerlach 2002).

Prospects

In the opening years of the twenty-first century, the crises in the Andes ran deep, and no immediate solution was in sight. No inspiring, unifying national project loomed on the horizon. Notwithstanding temporary growth periods, economic disappointments and uncertainties continued to thwart policy makers and fuel protests. However legitimate and positive, frustrated and disruptive demands for participation and representation seemed likely to elicit authoritarian closings as well as democratic openings. If the previous tragedies of bureaucratic authoritarianism in the Southern Cone were any guide, there was reason to worry that the problem of governability might be solved by soldiers rather than solons. However, there was also reason to hope that new forms of popular mobilization might fortify civil society, citizenship, democratic accountability, and social justice. Indeed, the ability of the shaky democracies in the Andes to survive all the hardships and turmoil of the past two decades has been remarkable. Just as the resolution of the 1930s crisis was late and partial, so the outcome of the current crisis could be slow and unsatisfactory, incremental rather than apocalyptic. The results could have broad implications for security, neoliberalism, and democracy in the hemisphere.

Notes

1. Similar to hegemony theory, the concept of international regimes refers to sets of formal or informal international norms, rules, conventions, expectations, and procedures favored by dominant powers and widely accepted by developing countries. A common example is liberal economic principles. See Ruggie (1983), Kindleberger (1975), Keohane (1984), and Gilpin (1987).

2. In a classic book on the crises between the state and society during political development, Sidney Verba (1971) outlines crises resembling our conceptualization. Similar to our notion of a national project, his crises of identity and legitimacy refer to the citizens' normative acceptance of the rightness of the national government's political system, authority, and purpose. Reflecting our concern with the economic model,

his crisis of distribution speaks to the government's ability to produce equitable material well-being for its citizens. His crisis of participation is the same as ours, occurring when previously marginalized actors demand inclusion. Echoing our attention to governability, his crisis of penetration alludes to government efficacy and control. We thank Peter H. Smith for reminding us about this earlier study. See also Pye (1971). In a comparable analysis, Manuel Antonio Garretón (2003) argues that Latin America today has four great needs: devising a fresh collective national project to replace the outmoded populist syndrome, defining a new economic development model beyond neoliberalism, overcoming social inequalities and exclusions, and improving democratic institutions and participation.

Bibliography

Alcantara Saez, Manuel, and Juan Manuel Ibeas Miguel, eds. 2001. *Colombia ante los retos del siglo XXI: Desarrollo, democracia y paz.* Salamanca, Spain: Ediciones Universidad de Salamanca.

Angell, Alan, Pamela Lowden, and Rosemary Thorp, eds. 2001. *Decentralizing development: The political economy of institutional change in Colombia and Chile.* New York: Oxford University Press.

Archer, Ronald. 1995. Party strength and weakness in Colombia's besieged democracy. In Mainwaring and Scully 1995, 164–99.

Ardaya, Gloria, and Luis Verdesoto. 1994. *Racionalidades democráticas en construcción.* La Paz, Bolivia: ILDIS.

Arnson, Cynthia, ed. 2001. *The crisis of democratic governance in the Andes.* Washington, DC: Woodrow Wilson International Center for Scholars. Latin American Program.

Assies, Willem. 2004. Bolivia: A gasified democracy. *European Review of Latin American and Caribbean Studies* 76 (April): 25–44.

Ayala Mora, Enrique. 1986. *Los partidos políticos en el Ecuador: Síntesis histórico.* Quito, Ecuador: Ediciones de la Terra.

Baud, Michael. 2003. *Intelectuales y sus utopías: Indigenismo y la imaginación de América Latina.* Amsterdam: CEDLA.

Bergquist, Charles. 1986. *Labor in Latin America.* Stanford, CA: Stanford University Press.

Bergquist, Charles, et al., eds. 2000. *Colombia 1990–2000: Waging war and negotiating peace.* Wilmington, DE: Scholarly Resources.

Blanes, José. 2000. *Mallkus y alcaldes—Serie Documentos de Investigación.* La Paz, Bolivia: PIEB/CEBEM.

Bonilla, Adrian. 1993. *Las sorprendentes virtudes de lo perverso: Ecuador y narcotráfico en los 90.* Quito, Ecuador: FLACSO-Sede Ecuador.

Brysk, Alison. 2000. *From Tribal Village to Global Village: Indian rights and international relations in Latin America.* Stanford, CA: Stanford University Press.

Burt, Jo-Marie. 1997. Political violence and the grassroots in Lima, Peru. In *The New Politics of Inequality in Latin America: Rethinking participation and representation*, ed. Douglas A. Chalmers, Carlos M. Vila, Katherine Roberts Hite, Scott Martin, Kerianne Piester, and Monique Segarra, 281–309. New York: Oxford University Press.

Burt, Jo-Marie, and Philip Mauceri, eds. 2003. *Politics in the Andes: identity, conflict, and reform.* Pittsburgh, PA: University of Pittsburgh Press.

Buxton, Julia. 2001. *The failure of political reform in Venezuela*. Burlington, VT: Ashgate.

Cameron, Maxwell. 1994. *Democracy and authoritarianism in Peru*. New York: St. Martin's.

Cameron, Maxwell, and Philip Mauceri, eds. 1997. *The Peruvian labyrinth*. University Park: Pennsylvania State University Press.

Canache, Damarys. 2001. *Venezuela: Public opinion and protest in a fragile democracy*. Coral Gables, FL: North-South Center Press.

Canache, Damarys, and Michael Kulischeck. 1998. *Reinventing legitimacy: democracy and political change in Venezuela*. Westport, CT: Greenwood.

Cardoso, Fernando Henrique, and Enzo Faletto. 1971. *Dependency and development in Latin America*. Berkeley: University of California Press.

Carrasquero, Jose Vicente, et al., eds. 2001. *Venezuela en transición: Elecciones y democracia, 1998–2000*. Caracas, Venezuela: CDB Publicaciones.

Carrasquillo Barrera, Alberto. 1999. *Estabilidad y gradualismo: Ensayos sobre economía colombiana*. Bogotá, Colombia: TM Editores.

Collier, Ruth Berins, and David Collier. 1991. *Shaping the political arena: Critical junctures, the labor movement, and regime dynamics in Latin America*. Princeton, NJ: Princeton University Press.

Collins, Jennifer. 2000. Una transición desde las elites hacia una democracia participativa: Apuntes sobre el papel emergente de los movimientos sociales en el Ecuador. In *Los movimientos sociales en las democracias andinas*, ed. Julie Massal and Marcelo Bonilla, 55–71. Quito, Ecuador: FLACSO Sede Ecuador and IFEA.

———. 2005. Opening up electoral politics: Social movement parties in Ecuador and Bolivia. PhD diss., University of California, San Diego.

Conaghan, Catherine M. 1988. *Restructuring domination: Industrialists and the state in Ecuador*. Pittsburgh, PA: Pittsburgh University Press.

——— 1995. Politicians against parties: Discord and disconnection in Ecuador's party system. In Mainwaring and Scully 1995, 434–58.

———. 2001. Making and unmaking authoritarian Peru: Re-election, resistance, and regime transition. *North-South Agenda Papers* 47 (June), 1–35.

Conaghan, Catherine M., and James M. Malloy. 1994. *Unsettling statecraft: Democracy and neoliberalism in the central Andes*. Pittsburgh, PA: University of Pittsburgh Press.

Coppedge, Michael. 1994. *Strong parties and lame ducks: Presidential partyarchy and factionalism in Venezuela*. Stanford, CA: Stanford University Press.

Coronil, Fernando. 1997. *The magical state*. Chicago: Chicago University Press.

Cotler, Julio. 1987. *Para afirmar la democracia*. Lima, Peru: Instituto de Estudios Peruanos.

———. 1989. *Clases populares, crisis, y democracia en la América Latina*. Lima, Peur: Instituto de Estudios Peruanos.

———. 1995. Political parties and the problems of democratic consolidation in Peru. In Mainwaring and Scully 1995, 323–53.

———. 1999. *Drogas y política en el Peru: La conexión norteamericana*. Lima: Instituto de Estudios Peruanos.

Cotler, Julio, and Romeo Grompone, eds. 2000. *El Fujimorismo. Ascenso y caída de un régimen autoritario*. Lima, Peru: Instituto de Estudios Peruanos.

Crabtree, John, and Laurence Whitehead, eds. 2001. *Toward democratic viability: The Bolivian experience*. Oxford, UK: Palgrave.

Crandall, Russell. 2002. *Driven by drugs: U.S. policy toward Colombia*. Boulder, CO: Lynne Rienner.

Crisp, Brian. 2000. *Democratic institutional design: The powers and incentives of Venezuelan politicians and interest groups*. Stanford, CA: Stanford University Press.

Degregori, Carlos Iván. 1990. *Ayacucho 1969–1979: El surgimiento de Sendero Luminoso*. Lima, Peru: Instituto de Estudios Peruanos.

Degregori, Carlos Iván, and Romeo Grompone. 1991. *Elecciones 1990: Demonios y redentores en el Nuevo Peru*. Lima, Peru: Instituto de Estudios Peruanos.

Degregori, Carlos Iván, and C. Rivera Paz. 1993. *Peru 1980–1993: Fuerzas Armadas, subversión y democracia: Redefinición del papel militar en un contexto de violencia subversiva y colapso del régimen democrático*. Lima, Peru: Instituto de Estudios Peruanos.

De la Torre, Carlos. 2000. *Populist seduction in Latin America: The Ecuadorian experience*. Athens: Ohio University Press.

DESCO. 1989. *Violencia Política en el Peru*. Lima, Peru: DESCO.

Dietz, Henry. 1998. *Urban poverty, political participation, and the state: Lima, 1970–1990*. Pittsburgh, PA: University of Pittsburgh Press.

Drake, Paul W. 1994. International crises and popular movements in Latin America: Chile and Peru from the Great Depression to the Cold War. In Rock 1994, *Latin America*, 109–40.

Dunkerly, James. 1984. *Rebellion in the veins: Political struggle in Bolivia 1952–1982*. London: Verso.

Duque Giraldo, Horacio. 1997. *La descentralización y el desarrollo institucional en Colombia hoy: Un analisis a la descentralización*. Bogotá, Colombia: Escuela Superior de Administración Pública.

Echevarria Olozaga, Hernan. 2003. *La crisis colombiana de los años 90*. Bogotá, Colombia: Oveja Negra.

Edwards, Sebastian. 2001. *The economics and politics of transition to an open market economy: Colombia*. Paris: OECD.

Ellner, Steve. 1993. *Organized labor in Venezuela, 1958–1991*. Wilmington, DE: Scholarly Books.

Ellner, Steve, and Daniel Hellinger, eds. 2003. *Venezuelan politics in the Chávez era: Class, polarization, and conflict*. Boulder, CO: Lynne Rienner.

Ellner, Steve, and Miguel Tinker Salas, eds. 2005. Venezuelan exceptionalism revisited: The Unraveling of Venezuela's model democracy. *Latin American Perspectives* (March–April).

Escobar, Arturo, and Sonia Alvarez, eds. 1992. *The making of social movements in Latin America*. Boulder, CO: Westview.

Estrada Alvarez, Jairo. 2004. *Construcción del modelo neoliberal en Colombia, 1970–2004*. Bogotá, Colombia: Ediciones Aurora.

Fowks, Jacqueline. 2000. *Suma y resta de la realidad: Medios de comunicación y elecciones generales 2000 en el Perú*. Lima, Peru: Friedrich Ebert Stiftung.

Friedman, Elisabeth J. 2000. *Unfinished transitions: Women and the gendered development of democracy in Venezuela, 1936–1996*. University Park: Pennsylvania State University Press.

Gaitán, Pilar, et al., eds. 1996. *Democracia y reestructuración económica en América Latina*. Bogotá, Colombia: CEREC.

Galarza Izquierdo, Luis. 1992. *Partidocracia y descomposición de la clase política ecuatoriana*. Quito, Ecuador: CONUEP.

Gamarra, Eduardo, and James Malloy. 1995. The patrimonial dynamics of party politics in Bolivia. In Mainwaring and Scully 1995, 399–433.

Garay, S. Luis Jorge. 1999. *Globalización y crisis: Hegemonía o corresponsabilidad?* Bogotá, Colombia: TM Editores.

García Calderón, Ernesto. 2001. Peru's decade of living dangerously. *Journal of Democracy* 12 (2): 46–58.

Garretón, Manuel Antonio. 2003. *Incomplete democracy: Political democratization in Chile and Latin America.* Chapel Hill: University of North Carolina Press.

Gerlach, Alan. 2002. *Indians, oil, and politics: A recent history of Ecuador.* Wilmington, DE: Scholarly Resources.

Gill, Lesley. 2000. *Teetering on the rim: Global restructuring, daily life, and the armed retreat of the Bolivian state.* New York: Columbia University Press.

Gilpin, Robert. 1987. *The political economy of international relations.* Princeton, NJ: Princeton University Press.

González de Olarte, Efraín, ed. 1996. *The Peruvian economy and structural adjustment.* Miami, FL: North-South Center Press.

Gorriti, Gustavo. 1999. *The Shining Path: A history of the millenarian war in Peru.* Chapel Hill: University of North Carolina Press.

Gott, Richard. 2001. *In the shadow of the liberator: Hugo Chávez and the transformation of Venezuela.* New York: Verso.

Graham, Carol. 1992. *Peru's APRA: Parties, politics, and the elusive quest for democracy.* Boulder, CO: Lynne Rienner.

Grindle, Merilee S., and Pilar Domingo. 2003. *Proclaiming revolution: Bolivia in comparative perspective.* Cambridge, MA: Harvard University Press.

Hammergren, Linn A. 1998. *The politics of justice and justice reform in Latin America: The Peruvian case in comparative perspective.* Boulder, CO: Westview.

Hartlyn, Jonathan. 1988. *The politics of coalition rule in Colombia.* Cambridge and New York: Cambridge University Press.

Hoskin, Gary, and Gabriel Murillo. 2001. Colombia's perpetual quest for peace. *Journal of Democracy* 12 (2): 32–45.

Huntington, Samuel P. 1968. *Political order in changing societies.* New Haven, CT: Yale University Press.

Isaacs, Anita. 1993. *Military rule and transition in Ecuador, 1972–92.* Pittsburgh, PA: Pittsburgh University Press.

Kalmanovitz, Salomon. 2001. *Las instituciones y el desarrollo económico en Colombia.* Bogotá, Colombia: Editorial Norma.

Karl, Terry Lynn. 1997. *The paradox of plenty: Oil booms and petro-states.* Berkeley: University of California Press.

Kelly, Janet, and Carlos Romero. 2002. *The United States and Venezuela: Rethinking a relationship.* New York: Routledge.

Keohane, Robert O. 1984. *After hegemony: Cooperation and discord in the world political economy.* Princeton, NJ: Princeton University Press.

Kindleberger, Charles P. 1975. *The world in depression, 1929–1939.* Berkeley: University of California Press.

Klaren, Peter. 1973. *Modernization, dislocation, and aprismo: The origins of Perú's Aprista Party, 1870–1932.* Austin: University of Texas Press.

———. 1999. *Peru: society and nationhood in the Andes.* New York: Oxford University Press.

Klein, Herbert S. 1992. *Bolivia: The evolution of a multi-ethnic society.* 2nd ed. New York: Oxford University Press.

Kline, Harvey. 1999. *State building and conflict resolution in Colombia, 1986–1994.* Tuscaloosa: University of Alabama Press.

Kornblith, Miriam. 1998. *Venezuela en los noventa: Las crisis de la democracia.* Caracas, Venezuela: IESA.

Kornblith, Miriam, and Daniel Levine. 1995. Venezuela: The life and times of the party system. In Mainwaring and Scully 1995, 37–71.

Kyle, David. 2000. *Transnational peasants: Migration, networks, and ethnicity in Andean Ecuador.* Baltimore: Johns Hopkins University Press.

Langer, Erick D., ed. 2003. *Contemporary indigenous movements in Latin America.* Wilmington, DE: Scholarly Resources.

Lazarte, Jorge. 1989. *Movimiento obrero y procesos políticos en Bolivia: Historia de la COB, 1952–1987.* La Paz, Bolivia: Editorial Offset Boliviana.

Leal Buitrago, Francisco, ed. 1996. *Tras las huellas de la crisis política.* Bogotá, Colombia: Tercer Mundo.

Lehman, Kenneth D. 1999. *Bolivia and the United States: A limited partnership.* Athens: University of Georgia Press.

León, Jorge. 1994. *De campesinos a ciudadanos diferentes.* Quito, Ecuador: CEDIME.

Livingstone, Grace. 2003. *Inside Colombia: Drugs, democracy and war.* London: Latin America Bureau.

Lora, Guillermo. 1987. *Historia de los partidos politicos de Bolivia.* La Paz, Bolivia: Ediciones La Colmena.

Lowenthal, Abraham, ed. 1975. *The Peruvian experiment.* Princeton, NJ: Princeton University Press.

Lucero, José Antonio. 2001. Crisis and contention in Ecuador. *Journal of Democracy* 12 (2): 59–73.

Mainwaring, Scott, and Timothy Scully, eds. 1995. *Building democratic institutions: Party systems in Latin America.* Stanford, CA: Stanford University Press

Martínez, Maruja, and Nelson Manrique, eds. 1995. *Amor y Fuego: José María Arguedas, 25 Años Después.* Lima, Peru: Desco.

Martz, John. 1997. *The politics of clientelism: Democracy and the state in Colombia.* New Brunswick, NJ: Transaction.

Maybury-Lewis, David, ed. 2002. *The politics of ethnicity: Indigenous peoples in Latin American states.* Cambridge, MA: Harvard University Press, David Rockefeller Center for Latin American Studies.

McClintock, Cynthia, and Abraham Lowenthal, eds. 1983. *The Peruvian experiment reconsidered.* Princeton, NJ: Princeton University Press.

McClintock, Cynthia, and Fabián Vallas. 2002. *The United States and Peru: Cooperation—at a cost.* New York: Routledge.

McCoy, Jennifer L., et al., eds. 1995. *Venezuelan democracy under stress.* New Brunswick, NJ: Transaction.

McCoy, Jennifer L., and David J. Myers, eds. 2004. *The unraveling of representative democracy in Venezuela.* Baltimore: Johns Hopkins University Press.

Menendez-Carrión, Amparo. 1986. *La conquista del voto: De Velasco a Roldós.* Quito, Ecuador: Corporación Editora Nacional.

Molina, José Enrique. 1991. *El sistema electoral venezolano y sus consecuencias politícas.* Caracas, Venezuela: Vadell Hnos.

Morales, Juan Antonio. 1991. *Bolivia: Ajuste estructural, equidad y crecimiento*. La Paz, Bolivia: Baremo–Milenio.

Murillo C., Gabriel, ed. 1993. *Hacia la consolidación democrática andina*. Bogotá, Colombia: Departamento de Ciencia Politica, Universidad de los Andes.

Naim, Moises. 1993. *Paper tigers and minotaurs: The politics of Venezuela's economic reforms*. Washington, DC: Carnegie Endowment.

Ocampo, José Antonio. 2001. *Un futuro para Colombia*. Bogotá, Colombia: Alfaomega.

O'Donnell, Guillermo. 1994. Delegative Democracy. *Journal of Democracy* 5 (1): 55–69.

O'Donnell, Guillermo, and Philippe C. Schmitter. 1986. *Transitions from authoritarian rule: Tentative conclusions about uncertain democracies*. Baltimore: Johns Hopkins University Press.

Pachano, Simón. 1991. *Los diputados: una elite política*. Quito, Ecuador: Corporación Editora Nacional.

———. 1995. *La representación caótica*. Quito, Ecuador: FLACSO.

———. 1996. *Democracia sin sociedad*. Quito, Ecuador: ILDIS.

Palacios, Marco. 1995. *Entre la legitimidad y la violencia: Colombia, 1875–1994*. Bogotá, Colombia: Grupo Editorial Norma.

Pallares, Amalia. 2002. *From peasant struggles to Indian resistance: The Ecuadorian Andes in the late twentieth century*. Norman: University of Oklahoma Press.

Pasara, Luis, and Jorge Parodi. 1988. *Democracia, sociedad y gobierno en el Peru*. Lima, Peru: Centro de Estudios de Democracia y Sociedad.

Pizarro, Eduardo. 1990. *Insurgencia Crónica, movimiento guerillero y proceso de paz en Colombia*. New York: Consortium.

———. 1994. *Proceso de paz en Colombia*. San Germán, Puerto Rico: Interamerican University of Puerto Rico.

Portocarrero, Gonzalo. 1998. *Razones de sangre: Aproximaciones a la violencia política*. Lima, Peru: Pontífica Universidad Católica del Perú, Fondo Editorial.

Posada-Carbó, Eduardo, ed. 1998. *Colombia: The politics of reforming the state*. London: MacMillan.

Postero, Nancy Grey, and Leon Zamosc, eds. 2004. *The struggle for indigenous rights in Latin America*. Brighton, UK: Sussex Academic Press.

Pye, Lucian W. 1971. Identity and the political culture. In *Crises and sequences in political development*, ed. Leonard Binder et al., 101–34. Princeton, NJ: Princeton University Press.

Quintero, Rafael. 1980. *El mito del populismo en el Ecuador*. Quito, Ecuador: FLACSO.

Quintero, Rafael, and Erika Silva. 1995. *Ecuador: Una nación en ciernes*. 2nd ed. 3 vols. Quito, Ecuador: Editorial Universitaria.

Richani, Nazih. 2001. *Systems of violence: The political economy of war and peace in Colombia*. Albany: State University of New York Press.

Rivera, Silvia. 1984. *Oprimidos pero no vencidos: Luchas del campesinado aymara y quechua 1900–1980*. La Paz, Bolivia: HISBOL, 1984.

Roa, Hernando, and Johan Galtung. 1998. *Como construir la paz en Colombia*. Bogotá, Colombia: Escuela Superior de la Administracion Publica.

Roberts, Kenneth M. 1997. *Deepening democracy? The modern left and social movements in Chile and Peru*. Stanford, CA: Stanford University Press.

Rock, David. 1994. Introduction. In *Latin America in the 1940s: War and postwar transition*, ed. David Rock, 1–14. Berkeley: University of California Press.

Rodríguez Ortega, Julio Armando. 1995. *El Nuevo papel del constitucionalismo frente al estado y frente a los ciudadanos.* Bogotá, Colombia: Universidad Autonoma de Colombia.

Rojas Ortuste, Gonzalo, and Luis Verdesoto Custode. 1997. *La participación popular como reforma de la política: Evidencias de una cultura democrática boliviana.* La Paz, Bolivia: Ministerio de Desarrollo Humano, Secretaría Nacional de Participación Popular, Unidad de Investigación y Análisis.

Romero, Anibal. 1986. *La miseria del populismo: Mitos y realidades de la democracia en Venezuela.* Caracas, Venezuela: Ediciones Centauro.

———. 1994. *Decadencia y crisis de la democracia.* Caracas, Venezuela: Editorial Panapo.

———. 1997. *Decadencia; Disolución social y pronóstico político.* Caracas, Venezuela: Editorial Panapo.

Rospigliosi, Fernando. 2000a. *El arte del engaño: Las relaciones entre los militares y la prensa.* Lima, Peru: Tarea Asociación Gráfica Educativa.

———. 2000b. *Montesinos y las fuerzas armadas. Como controlo durante una década las instituciones militares.* Lima, Peru: Instituto de Estudios Peruanos.

Ruggie, John Gerard, ed. 1983. *The antinomies of interdependence: National welfare and the international division of labor.* New York: Columbia University Press.

Safford, Frank, and Marco Palacios. 2001. *Colombia: Fragmented land, divided society.* New York: Oxford University Press.

Sagasti, Francisco, et al. 1995. *Democracia y buen gobierno: Agenda Peru.* Lima, Peru: Apoyo.

Salamanca, Luis. 1997. *Crisis de la modernización y crisis de la democracia en Venezuela.* Caracas, Venezuela: ILDIS.

Sandoval Rodríguez, Isaac. 1993. *Los partidos políticos en Bolivia.* La Paz, Bolivia: UMSA.

Sawyer, Suzana. 2004. *Crude chronicles: Indigenous politics, multinational oil, and neoliberalism in Ecuador.* Durham, NC: Duke University Press.

Schonwalder, Gerd. 2003. *Linking civil society and the state: Urban popular movements, the left, and local government in Peru, 1980–1992.* University Park: Pennsylvania State University Press.

Schoultz, Lars. 1998. *Beneath the United States: A history of U.S. policy toward Latin America.* Cambridge, MA: Harvard University Press.

Seligmann, Linda J. 1995. *Between reform and revolution: Political struggles in the Peruvian Andes, 1969–1991.* Stanford, CA: Stanford University Press.

Selverston-Scher, Melina. 2002. *Ethnopolitics in Ecuador: Indigenous rights and the strengthening of democracy.* Boulder, CO: Lynne Rienner.

Sheahan, John. 1999. *Searching for a better society: The Peruvian economy from 1950.* University Park: Pennsylvania State University Press.

Smith, Peter H., ed. 1992. *Drug policy in the Americas.* Boulder, CO: Westview.

———. 2000. *Talons of the eagle.* Oxford: Oxford University Press.

Starn, Orin. 1999. *Nightwatch: The politics of protest in the Andes.* Durham, NC: Duke University Press.

Stein, Steve. 1980. *Populism in Peru: The emergence of the masses and the politics of social control.* Madison: University of Wisconsin Press.

Stein, Steve, and Carlos Monge. 1988. *La crisis del estado patrimonial en el Peru.* Lima, Peru: Instituto de Estudios Peruanos.

Stepan, Alfred, and Juan Linz, eds. 1978. *The breakdown of democratic regimes.* 4 vols. Baltimore: Johns Hopkins University Press.

Stern, Steve J., ed. 1999. *Shining and other paths: War and society in Peru, 1980–1995.* Durham, NC: Duke University Press.

Stokes, Susan C. 1995. *Cultures in conflict: Social movements and the state in Peru.* Berkeley: University of California Press.

Striffler, Steve. 2003. *In the shadows of state and capital: The United Fruit Company, popular struggle, and agrarian restructuring in Ecuador, 1900–1995.* Durham, NC: Duke University Press.

Tanaka, Martin. 1998. *Los espejismos de la democracia: El colapso del sistema de partidos en el Peru, 1980–1995, en perspectiva comparada.* Lima, Peru: Instituto de Estudios Peruanos.

Thorp, Rosemary. 1991. *Economic management and economic development in Peru and Colombia.* Pittsburgh, PA: University of Pittsburgh Press.

———. 1998. *Progress, poverty and exclusion: An economic history of Latin America in the 20th century.* Washington, DC: Inter-American Development Bank.

Thoumi, Francisco. 2004. *Illegal drugs, economy, and society in the Andes.* Baltimore: Johns Hopkins University Press.

Thoumi, Francisco, and Merilee Grindle. 1992. *La Política de la economía del ajuste: La actual experiencia ecuatoriana.* Quito, Ecuador: FLACSO-Sede Ecuador.

Ticona, Esteban, et al. 1995. *Votos y Wipalas: Campesinos y Pueblos Originarios en Democracia.* La Paz, Bolivia: CIPCA.

Tokatlian, Juan Gabriel. 1995. *Drogas, dilemas y dogmas: Estados Unidos y la narcocriminalidad organizada en Colombia.* Bogotá, Colombia: CEI-Tercer Mundo.

Trinkunas, Harold A. 2002. The crisis in Venezuelan civil-military relations: From Punto Fijo to the Fifth Republic. *Latin American Research Review* 37:1, 41–76.

Tuesta Soldvilla, Fernando, ed. 1994. *Partidos políticos y elecciones en el Peru (1978–1993).* San Jose, CA: CAPEL.

———., ed. 1996. *Los enigmas del poder: Fujimori, 1990–1996.* Lima, Peru: Fundación Friedrich Ebert.

———., ed. 1999. *El juego político: Fujimori, la oposición y las reglas.* Lima, Peru: Friedrich Ebert Stiftung.

Ugarteche, Oscar. 1990. *Deuda externa. Un camino sin salida.* Quito, Ecuador: Grupo de Trabajo sobre Deuda Externa y Desarrollo.

———. 1998. *La arqueología de la modernidad: El Peru entre la globalización y la exclusión.* Lima, Peru: Desco.

Ungar, Elisabeth, ed. 1993. *Gobernabilidad en Colombia: Retos y desafíos.* Bogotá, Colombia: Departamento de Ciencia Política, Universidad de los Andes.

Van Cott, Donna Lee, ed. 1995. *Indigenous peoples and democracy in Latin America.* New York: St. Martins.

———. 2000. *The friendly liquidation of the past.* Pittsburgh, PA: University of Pittsburgh Press.

van Dijck, Pitou, ed. 1998. *The Bolivian experiment: Structural adjustment and poverty alleviation.* Amsterdam: CEDLA.

Vásquez de Urrutia, Patrick. 1989. *La democracia en blanco y negro: Colombia en los años ochenta.* Bogotá, Colombia: CEREC.

Verba, Sidney. 1971. Sequences and development. In *Crises and sequences in political development,* ed. Leonard Binder et al., 283–316. Princeton, NJ: Princeton University Press.

Verdesoto Custode, Luis. 2001. *Descentralizar: Grados de autonomía para enriquecer a la democracia.* Quito, Ecuador: Ediciones Abya-Yala.

Warren, Kay B., and Jean E. Jackson, eds. 2002. *Indigenous movements, self-representation, and the state in Latin America.* Austin: University of Texas Press.

Weyland, Kurt. 2003. *The politics of market reform in fragile democracies: Argentina, Brazil, Peru, and Venezuela*. Princeton, NJ: Princeton University Press.

Wilde, Alexander. 1978. Conversations among gentlemen: Oligarchical democracy in Colombia. In *The breakdown of democratic regimes: Latin America*, ed. Juan Linz and Alfred Stepan, 28–81. Baltimore: Johns Hopkins University Press.

Wise, Carol. 2003. *Reinventing the state: Economic strategy and institutional change in Peru*. Ann Arbor: University of Michigan Press.

World Bank. *World development indicators, 2002*. Washington, DC: World Bank.

Wright, Winthrop R. 1990. *Café con leche: Race, class, and national image in Venezuela*. Austin: University of Texas Press.

Zabaleta Arias, Gerardo. 1994. *Partidos políticos y constituciones en Colombia*. Baranquilla, Colombia: Editorial Antillas.

Zamosc, Leon. 1994. Agrarian protest and the Indian movement in the Ecuador highlands. *Latin American Research Review* 29:3, 37–68.

———. 1995. *Estadística de las areas de predominio étnico de la sierra ecuatoriana: Población rural, indicadores cantonales y organizaciones de base*. Quito, Ecuador: Ediciones Abya-Yala.

2

Unfinished States

Historical Perspectives on the Andes

JEREMY ADELMAN

ANDEAN STATES ARE, MORE THAN MOST COUNTRIES, works in progress. Formed states are a species of political system in which subjects accept and are able to live by some set of basic ground rules and norms governing public affairs. Being finished need not imply an end to politics or history, but simply that a significant majority of a country's population acknowledges the legitimacy of ruling systems and especially the rules that determine how rules are supposed to change.

For historical reasons, this is not the case in the Andes. In Colombia, Peru, and Venezuela (the countries analyzed in this chapter), important swaths of societies either do not accept some underlying rules or could not live by them even if they did accept them. This is not a recent problem. Indeed, one of the principal difficulties facing Colombians, Peruvians, and Venezuelans is that they cannot easily turn to a golden (and often mythic) age of stateness. Each Andean republic bears the imprint of earlier struggles involving the definition of statehood from the nineteenth century, conflicts that have expressed themselves in different but still

unsettled outcomes to the present. This long-term historical process dis-
tinguishes the Andes from other regions in Latin America, from Mexico to
the Southern Cone, where consolidated models of order and development
(punctuated, to be sure, by moments of upheaval) prevailed for enough
time to remap the human landscape within each country and to furnish
these countries with the means to cope with the manifold pressures of
globalization, yawning inequities, or the misfortunes wrought by lousy
leadership.

The distinction between finished and unfinished states is partly
heuristic, partly real. Like so many analytic parsing acts, it is also in immediate need of qualifications. First, the main argument is not to say that
there has been no change in the Andes. Far from it. Rather, change has not
been the by-product of any forced or consensual enduring model of
development guided by an integrated ruling bloc capable of using public
levers legitimately for its purposes. Notwithstanding the oil boom
decades in Venezuela and the "guano" age in Peru, when elites forged
some "constructed" order with more or less support from popular sectors,
moments of order and development did not refashion Andean societies;
they appear much less consolidated and legitimate with the benefit of
hindsight and did not therefore resolve many of the basic problems they
inherited. This historical perspective contrasts with the idea of a crisis
wrought by globalization and the denouement of populism, which crip-
ples Latin American nation-states at a time when they are trying to build
the foundations of a new civic order. This combination is certainly part of
the drama of contemporary Latin American societies. But the sense of
contemporary crisis should not imply that it follows on the heels of peace-
able modernization or national-popular integration. In a sense, one might
speak of a long transgenerational crisis. But this vocabulary is only useful
for describing specific moments of breakdown in institutional orders,
because the notion of a genetic crisis may obscure some of the opportunities for and expressions of creative alternatives that are equally part of this
historical perspective—and, one might hope, the future.

While Andean societies share some features that contrast with other
regions in Latin America, there are significant differences among them as
well. In some senses, Colombians acknowledge the legitimacy of their
constitutional framework—what they bemoan is its inability to territorial-
ize itself. Neighboring Venezuela, by contrast, has a state with much more
scope but far less legitimacy. Peru has neither territoriality nor legitimacy.
All three are unfinished in different ways and for different reasons.

Accenting the unfinished condition of Andean states stresses the ongoing business of formation, which in the Andean cases remains an open-ended process—and deliberately contrasts with an approach that analyzes the idiographic features of each country and in some cases singles them out as instances of state failure. This is seen in the way some North American social scientists have dealt with Colombia's recent travails, which—deliberately or not—has served to justify a particular brand of foreign policy in Washington. Cast in comparative light, however, Colombia's political economy seems less exceptional, in need of a broader template of understanding that admits that the long-term history of state formation is a process that adapts to local circumstances and social forces while sharing some common structural features.[1]

Republican Legacies

Colombia, Peru, and Venezuela have obvious structural similarities: they were all once Spanish colonies with affine Iberian institutions, they were largely agrarian, and they were polyethnic communities of indigenous, African, European, and blended descents. But in this regard they were not so very different from other Iberian-American societies. Alone, these features do not explain the differences between this region and others, although they obviously established an important backcloth to postcolonial developments.

One important intrusion in the *longue durée* was the breakdown of Spanish rule and the ensuing struggles to fashion new systems of sovereign legality. The events beginning in 1810 wrought a conjunctural crisis with important structural consequences. The central and northern Andes, the Latin American region swept by the most violent struggle for independence in Latin America, led by the armies of Simón Bolívar, copes with some unresolved nineteenth-century struggles for republican statehood. Not everything that came to haunt the belt from Venezuela to Peru in the 1980s can be attributed to his unfinished efforts. But the great trials of state formation and the emergence of postcolonial elites set the stage for future possibilities for, as well as limitations to, the scope of democracy and the rule of law.

No ruling bloc—no matter how loose the coalition—took power after Spain's empire collapsed in the Andes. This, of course, was not unique to the Andes. In the power vacuum that opened up, colonists found it easier to agree on what they disliked—a restoration of the old order. But what was distinctive in the Andes was the depth of the polarization over independence. Unlike in Mexico, where Creole and peninsular potentates remained fairly loyal to the crown until the liberal revolt in Spain in 1820, and unlike in the River Plate, where Creoles were more uniformly disposed to part with the ancient regime, colonists from Caracas to La Paz were split—if not evenly, then enough to paralyze any effort for one side to call the shots. State formation in Mexico and Argentina faced difficulties, but Andean elites had a harder time making a new order cauterized to some shared mythic national project.[2]

With each battle, the victors tried to cobble together ruling systems to fill the vacuum opened up in the metropole. To Bolívar's constant chagrin, freeing the colonies meant liberating them to debate—and in turn fight over—the new republics. His effort to create a confederation stretching across the Andean regions freed by his armies threatened the latent centrifugal energies that made his army so potent against Spain. Nueva Granada was supposed to become the analogue of the United States in South America. But instead, provincial assemblies repudiated the confederation with almost the same ferocity and anticentralist sentiment as they had brought to their struggle against Bourbon restorationism. Instead of a unitary vision, what triumphed were constitutional charters drafted in the name of new peoples, Venezuelans, Peruvians, and finally Colombians. Nor was there much more agreement about what each of these new, imagined identities might mean for anyone living in Maracaibo, Arequipa, or Pasto, where provincialism locked horns with early nationalism.

By the end of the wars against Spain, soldiers were turning their guns away from Spanish regulars and toward each other. Civil wars replaced wars of liberation. Peru heaved up five constitutions in its first sixteen years of independence. Bolivia countered with ten of its own before the century was out. In this setting, there was not much room for optimism. Writing from Quito in 1829, shortly before his death, Bolívar reflected on some of his handiwork. The Liberator shifted the blame for the catastrophic results of independence to the neophyte citizenry: "the passions of a people who, although they had broken their chains, were devoid of the concepts of right and duty, and could only avoid enslavement (to Spain) by becoming tyrannical themselves" (Bolívar 1951, 742).

The difficulty in creating republican amalgamations had several legacies for the twentieth century. The wars created sui generis military politics that did not create unifying forces along the lines of the Brazilian, Chilean, Paraguayan, or even more ambitiously, Prussian molds. Armies were, rather, decentralized, and casual fighting forces were dragged into battle to fight not foreign enemies but neighboring war machines. What became called caudillismo in Spanish America was especially acute in the

Andes: rule by provincial warlords whose main appeal to subject populations was protection from marauders and tax collectors from anemic central states. This meant that chronic war mobilized the region's people into new political formations, especially local militias with vertical ties to caudillos, without aggregating into a constitutional synthesis. Bolívar's young collaborator and founder of Colombian historiography, José Manuel Restrepo, bemoaned the fate of republican war machines. Rather than harmonize a new national sovereignty, warlords nurtured loyalties to political leaders who defined themselves against the capitals of republics while trumpeting the language of political citizenship, relying on elections and plebiscites to legitimate the ties between local rulers and ruled (Restrepo 1970).[3]

Fractured militaries and fragmented sovereignties might not have shaped politics so decisively had a social bloc occupied the space vacated by Spanish mercantilist merchants and the colonial epigones. But ending three centuries of Spanish rule opened up a scramble for resources. In large measure, British capital moved in to serve as mediators with the Atlantic markets for capital and commodities. Across the nineteenth century, the Andean elites and markets were therefore internationalized before they could consolidate a base of national capital operating in national markets and as a core for a ruling bloc. Aggravating social tensions was the scramble for land, especially where definitions of property rights folded into broader issues of membership in political communities—local, provincial, and national.

State builders struggled not just to create viable public authorities to govern a new citizenry, but also to promote possessive individualists, especially in the communalist hinterlands. New property laws aimed to enclose commons and disrupt what were often seen as hermetic self-sufficient communities of Indian and black peasantries, who were themselves still mobilized from the independence wars. Resistance to enclosure and proletarianization of peasantries often reinforced the struggle against central authorities. Whatever the district or mode of production, weak states and fractured elites enhanced the scope of plebeian sectors to manipulate the process of commodification to their advantage.

One recent study of the Peruvian community of Tarma shows how inter-elite feuds, split along national, provincial, and local lines, weakened efforts to enforce a new labor code to restore or create a servile order. Villagers and their leaders learned to manipulate rival claimants for their labor power and thus blunt the formation of a stable, modernizing economic system. There were, of course, limits to popular power and divide-

and-rule tactics. Planters and merchants had access to financial instruments and to state authorities that could be marshaled in the last instance
to drive hard bargains. Until very late in the nineteenth century, the
Andes did not give way to a monolithic capitalist transformation and the
emergence of a social class able to rule nation-states. Rather, there was an
extended stalemate punctuated by frequent spasms of violence over local
social and political control (Wilson 2003, Mallon 1983).

By the end of the nineteenth century, some semblance of stability crept
across the Andes. It helped that world markets for South American staples grew; foreign capital, especially British investment, moved into the
region; and something like an oligarchy emerged. In reality, the term
highly exaggerated the unanimity of social vision and purpose of the
region's elites, whose cracks were papered over with layers of foreign
rents and revenues. Ascendant elites forged pacts among provinces and
between local and central governments. While never quite fused together,
ruling coalitions emerged and agreed to play by some common ground
rules. Colombian Conservatives, for instance, installed a regime called the
Regeneración, which lasted, albeit not without some bloody interrup-
tions, until 1930. Its architects, Rafael Nuñez and Miguel Antonio Caro,
tried to pacify the country with a new constitution (1886) and language
manuals to project a philology and a historiography that construed
Colombia as a uniform, continuous entity tied to its Hispanic and Catholic
origins. The myth of a shared, deep-rooted past was supposed to be a
balm for a strife-ridden republic.

Venezuela's Cipriano Castro ushered in decades of dictatorial stability
in 1899, and passed the torch to a dynasty of generals from the border
province of Táchira, beginning with Juan Vicente Gómez in 1908. All this
stability was highly contingent, but less on the appeal of Belle Epoque
tastes than on the nitty-gritty business of amalgamating politicos and par-
liaments in the capitals with caudillos and their clients in the provinces
(Deas 1992).

Rather than providing an integrated model of social, political, and economic change along the lines of the Mexican *porfiriato*, Argentina's *orden
conservador* (to use Natalio Botana's bons mots), or Brazil's Belle Epoque
(as these visions radiated out to the hinterlands they lost a certain amount
of gas), the Andean constitutions operated more as patinas of national
synthesis over a substrate that was still churning with unresolved conflicts over property and politics. José Carlos Mariátegui captured the
hybrid nature of Andean capitalism, which blended the coercion of colonial extractive traditions with unfettered markets and a republican consti-

tutional fabric wrapped around personal clientelist networks. Time made it harder, not easier, to uncouple feudalism and provincialism from successor modes of production and models of statehood (Mariátegui 1971).

The weaknesses of the ruling arrangements revealed themselves in chronic subnational levels of collective violence that occasionally bubbled to the national surface when clientelist pacts broke down. Colombia's conservative hegemony was wracked by deep violent clashes, and in many provinces did not integrate Liberals into the civic, parliamentary fold. Peruvian leaders never transcended the coastal-highland divide, and even President Augusto B. Leguía's long regime (the *oncenio*), while making room for a broader spectrum with the game of making social pacts, still fell far short of his centralizing aspirations. Venezuela's durable dictatorship was predicated on the military-civic alliance's ability to share spoils more than to share loyalties beyond a *gamonal* (bandit) clique. Each conformed to its own logic and bore the hallmarks of local circumstances and structure. But what they shared was the incompletion of the state-building projects unfurled with the end of Spanish rule.

As a result, Andean republics faced bouts of upheaval, especially at moments of presidential succession (a useful litmus test for any regime's consolidation), when the ground rules fell apart and coalition fragments jostled for an edge within the next administration. As Andean republics turned the corner into the twentieth century, they had ruling alliances but not particularly strong states capable of administering (or enforcing) school systems, taxes, or conscription laws. Andean regimes were too weak to portray themselves as suprapartisan entities capable of legitimately upholding the rights of citizens above the particularisms of region, class, or ethnicity. If the national idyll existed at all, it could not be said to have been the brainchild of state elites or of *letrados* (intellectuals) with access to the capillaries of public institutions to project their imagined communities on the ground.

Breakdown or Breakup?

The persistence of partially integrated states with incomplete powers to deliver public goods might imply that they were especially brittle and vulnerable to major overhaul. However, just because constitutional systems were not fully institutionalized does not necessarily mean that they were prone to *bouleversement*. State weakness, as Theda Skocpol (1994) notes, is neither a sufficient nor necessary condition for revolution. Indeed, in many ways, revolutions have transpired where strong states

are conjuncturally crippled.[4] The incompletion of the state-building project and the unresolved disputes over property relations in the countryside
actually gave these arrangements some powers to endure through a
sequence of crises—especially those wrought by the Great Depression
and the populist upheavals that swept through much of Latin America in
the 1930s. What is inherited, even the obstacles to progress (following
Albert Hirschman's classic observation),[5] is not necessarily doomed, but
can acquire strength, and be revitalized, by new developments. Rather
than dismissing legacies as retardants to change, our stories emphasize
their ability to shape development in unintended ways. Specifically, cast
in an Andean context, the loosely integrated states contended with com-
pound problems that added up to a breakdown in the 1930s. But in part
because they were so elastic and relatively unfinished, they adapted, so
that the breakdown did not lead their breakup in favor of something else.
In the skein of older institutions, there emerged something new. Newness,
however, did not resolve old dilemmas.

It is common among Latin American historians to argue that the 1920s
shook, and the 1930s shattered, the oligarchic regimes of the nineteenth
century and opened up a new phase in the region's history. Of late, some
have probed at the alleged discontinuities. But few reject the notion that
some fundaments broke down and something new emerged in their
wake: the collapse of the old orders and the pressure to integrate popular
sectors into the constitutional fabric gave rise to what has loosely been
described as the populist era in Latin American history, better known for
some of its leading figures, for whom a charismatic appeal served as a solvent for a vertical realignment of mobilized workers, peasants, and disenchanted members of the elites and middle classes.

In the Andes, the prospects for a different model of social and political
integration surfaced, culminating in a pivotal conjuncture after the Second World War. However, just as the nineteenth century did not see fully
consolidated liberal states, in the Andes, pressures to devise new principles and practices of citizenship to resolve a deepening problem of legitimacy did not end in populist states either. They remained syncretic
structures, part liberal, part populist, and still very much unformed and
unable to universalize the rule of law within their territorial limits, not
least because they were still held together by the solvent of clientelism.
How they integrated these disparate features varied according to underlying social and economic structures and the contingencies of the conflicts
of the late 1940s and early 1950s. Whatever can be said of the important variations of Andean politics, what Venezuela, Peru, and Colombia

shared was the persistence of unresolved tension over the principles of statehood and not a shift to a new institutional model of settling collective distributional conflict.

Petroleum Politics

In Venezuela, a rentier regime emerged from the entrails of dictatorship but never fully resolved the tensions of incomplete statehood. Juan Vicente Gómez ruled Venezuela for almost three decades with an iron fist and a patronage network that dispensed rents to clients in all corners of the republic. Such longevity and persistence might have created a new order, but when a hand-chosen successor tried to depersonalize the regime in 1929, it quickly unraveled and Gómez stepped back in to keep the country from cascading into nineteenth-century-style instability. Gómez, at 76 years old, finally died in office in 1935. A sequence of generals from Gómez's home province of Táchira muddled through the rest of the 1930s, adopting some piecemeal reforms and refining the use of the radio as a means to create a national movement behind the regime. General Isaias Medina Angarita—another *tachirense* (from the province of Tachira) officer—came to power in 1941 and began the process of opening the political game and bargaining within the ruling clique to new civilian actors. He even created an ephemeral official party, and in its wake legalized the Venezuelan Communist Party (which complied with Comintern orders to Latin American satellites and rallied behind the official coalition). Medina also allowed the formation of several other parties, such as Democratic Action (AD), and the conservative Catholic Comité de Organización Política Electoral Independiente (COPEI).

What might have appeared as a conjuncture with enough fluidity to break up older structures of rulership and reliance on patronage pacts among fractions of elites and their clienteles, did not, however, give way to a Venezuelan version of the Mexican Institutional Revolutionary Party (PRI) or of Argentina's Peronism—a party system organized around a dominant integrative movement. Venezuelan electoral mobilization quickly filled the space once dominated by caudillos, but in the main it adopted similar patron-client habits and folded them into civilian movements. Moreover, the parties did not dispense with personalized styles of conduct: two leaders, AD's Rómulo Betancourt and COPEI's Rafael Caldera, would shape Venezuela's modern democracy. In a contingency that laid the groundwork for a political structure that finally collapsed in 1998, a military coup unseated the reformist Medina in October 1945. It featured an unholy alliance of falangists, young officers led by Marcos Pérez Jiménez who trumpeted the argot of anticommunism and hemispheric security, and AD, which feared Medina's rival appeal.

The coup, as chance would have it, came a day after October 17, 1945, when Argentine trade unionists forced the military to release its former secretary of labor, Colonel Juan Perón. But the Venezuelan coup could not have been more different: it toppled one of the most progressive and open governments in Venezuelan history. While AD took the reins of power (monitored by its erstwhile military co-plotters) from 1945 to 1948, it could not scrub away the stains of its complicity. Nor could the Communist Left or the trade union movement provide the laborist ballast for the regime; instead each entered a period of factionalism and internal dispute. This brief and chaotic three-year spell of civilian rule soon imploded in another coup, this one masterminded by the bonapartist General Jiménez, who decided to do things his way until he himself was overthrown in 1957 (Ellner 1980).

If civilians could not dismantle Venezuela's caudillo state, they embraced the mild nationalism that governed oil policy and the system of rents that the elites used to lubricate their party machinery. By 1930, Venezuela was the world's largest oil exporter, and 98 percent of the business was in the hands of three firms: Royal Dutch Shell, Gulf, and Standard Oil. The latter in particular would play a decisive role in the next half century—Nelson Rockefeller personally shared his pan-American dreams with democratic and military regimes alike. As oil rents grew at a steady pace, they buoyed a treasury that ploughed the returns into public works and contracts. But they also had a malign effect: rents drove up an exchange rate that in turn made consumer imports easier and exports of commodities other than oil harder, infecting Venezuela with a "Dutch disease."

Whereas much of Latin America shifted to an import substitution industrialization strategy, Venezuela's model of development folded the impetus to promote manufacturing within a persistent reliance on export rents. This in turn had two consequences. First, as before, Venezuela's ruling bloc was highly internationalized. Second, aside from the oil workers (whose leadership locked arms with AD), the trade union movement did not have a strong industrial base with which to swell rank-and-file members and thus did not have the muscle to pose a laborist threat to the postwar alignments. Without either actor, efforts to create a new regime could not succeed.

The stresses of continuity soon became clear. While Pérez Jiménez expanded the public works program and tried to gather foreign firms, the state, and national capitalists into a coherent alliance, the logic of the oil boom diminished the importance of the private sector—and thus the role of autonomous social class or civic movements. The result was a paradox: oil created resources that could be poured into urban works (such as the modernization of Caracas) and the beginnings of a welfare system, but it made the country even more dependent on a single staple. So when oil prices dipped in the 1957 recession, and the middle classes and poor in the Caracas barrios began to ventilate their disenchantment, the Pérez Jiménez regime began to falter.

By January 1958, the barrios were in full revolt and the military, led by Admiral Wolfgang Larrázabal, forced Pérez Jiménez out and promised elections by the end of the year. The mainstream civilian parties, fearing an unpredictable transition, decided to apply a lesson learned from the failed transition of 1945. Before the elections were held, Betancourt and Caldera devised a plan, called the Punto Fijo Pact. Punto Fijo had many important nuances, but in essence it aimed to keep democratic participation within bounds, make it difficult for minor parties (although some had signed the deal, not including the Communist Party) to participate in power, and practically to ensure that AD or COPEI would triumph in elections—thereby also obviating a role for the military as ballast for the status quo.

The events of January 1958 were ripe with apparent possibilities, but the model of rentier capitalism and the weakness of organized opposition to the regime obstructed the type of mobilization that might have led to a more integrated state with deep taproots of legitimacy. To some extent the problems reflected fissures in the opposition. The Communist Party was especially important in the barrio cells that stoked the unrest. But when the dictator fell, the party leadership swung behind the military clique responsible for his ouster and backed Larrázabal's ticket—feeling that Betancourt's AD would sweep to power and consolidate a grip on popular constituencies. As it turned out, in part because the party was stuck with a military ally while Venezuelans were calling for a more dramatic change in regime, AD romped to victory and used its political appeal through the 1960s to make life hell for the Left.

It did not help that the example of the Cuban Revolution compelled many radicals into adopting guerrilla tactics. Convinced that there was no ousting Betancourt at the voting booths, they made easy eventual prey for the Venezuelan military. In particular, after a guerrilla uprising in May 1962, Betancourt ordered that the very Communist cells in the barrios that helped him in 1958 be smashed. Militants were rounded up and the Communist Party was banned. The trade union and peasant movements, wracked by internal discord, were purged of radicals, and Betancourt cronies rose to unrivaled prominence. Thus, what was a possibility in 1958, a popular-based radical movement able to organize in the absence of trade unions, vanished from the political scene just as the Punto Fijo regime congealed.

To some extent, ferment persisted, especially on university campuses—the Universidad Central de Venezuela was a chronic source of opposition to the regime—but bereft of popular allies mobilized into militant cells such as the Peronist resistance or the Socialist miners in Chile, student demonstrations were mainly episodic. When the Communist Party was finally legalized again in 1969, it had lost much of its base. Undaunted, inspired by the electoral example of Salvador Allende, Venezuela's radical shards tried to form a common front and posted some impressive results. But the Left could not overcome its internal divisions, nor could it dislodge the patronage system that bound the mainstream trade union movement uneasily to the dominant party (Ellner 1993, 5–24).

What this created, even though AD would start swapping power with COPEI in 1969 (until 1998), was an active electoral system that had great trouble accommodating reforms that did not reinforce the power of the ruling parties. To make matters worse, the oil-based economy created massive rents, especially when petroleum prices soared sevenfold from 1970 to 1974, that bathed the treasury in spoils and financed projects that altered the face of Venezuelan capitalism but not its fundamental structure. When AD reclaimed the presidency in 1974 under the Betancourt protégé Carlos Andrés Pérez, wastage and corruption were widespread but mystified in the bookkeeping of the new national oil holding company Petroven (later renamed PDVSA) and Pérez's florid style and Third Worldist bromides.

For a time, the government tried to promote domestic demand and local industries, with the endorsement of a clutch of capitalists called the Twelve Apostles whose public sector contracts swelled as the oil money poured in. But cozying up to one group of insiders alienated others. A coterie of Maracaibo financiers, advocates of open markets and exports, disliked Pérez's interventionist convictions and promises to workers. When the export proceeds were not enough to embolden the loyalty of elites, Pérez went hunting for foreign loans from commercial banks. It would only become apparent several years later that while the oil money and bank loans flowed in, Venezuelan capitalists were leaking their capital out to offshore banks recycling oil rents into capital flight (Karl 1997, 130–33, 150–53).

The shriveling alliance behind the Punto Fijo regime became more and more dependent on oil rents and thus more and more contingent on world oil prices. When deep recession hit the Atlantic economies in the late 1970s and oil prices plunged, the Venezuelan treasury ran dry. To make matters worse, international interest rates spiked under the anti-inflationary policies of Ronald Reagan and Margaret Thatcher. By the early 1980s, sagging oil prices and soaring interest rates squeezed the capacity for populist largesse. Trade unionists launched strike waves, capital fled, until eventually, the government let the currency float on Black Friday, February 18, 1983. For the rest of the decade, COPEI and AD governments alike tried to run the following gauntlet: opening the Punto Fijo arrangement to greater civic participation and partners while imposing austerity policies that simply emboldened the opposition to the regime as a whole.

When Carlos Andrés Pérez returned to power in early 1989 on a wave of populist promises, he promptly declared severe austerity measures. The accumulation of grievances and the depletion of popular legitimacy of the regime unleashed a spasm of violence. There ensued weeks of rioting and looting, leaving hundreds dead and entire neighborhoods in ruins (López Maya 2003). Shorn of oil rents, Pérez's *paquetazos* (austerity packages) stripped the final vestments of legitimacy from the Punto Fijo regime. The inability to develop an alternative program or to apply International Monetary Fund (IMF) neuralgia meant that Pérez got no support from any segment of an increasingly polarized society.

To make matters worse, the whole party system disappeared into the same ether as the economy. The once-mighty AD was now fracturing, and the legislature was in perpetual gridlock. Opposition festered in the military and finally erupted in several coup attempts in early 1992, led by young army officers. They were easily crushed, and the marginality of the leaders led many to dismiss this military unrest as a recidivist holdover. This was an overconfident and premature appraisal, born of post–Cold War faith in the ineluctable triumph of democratic liberalism, with fatal consequences for the regime. It certainly did not dissuade the IMF from prescribing more of its medicine, and in mid-1992 it urged the besieged Pérez to implement a second, more severe phase of structural adjustment. Desperate for some relief, and thinking that the IMF would reward good faith efforts, he complied again.

This time, the whole political system heaved—his party and the opposition launched impeachment proceedings and forced Pérez from power in May 1993.[6] By then, corruption talk had evolved into the tag word for stigmatizing public authorities for doing what they had been doing for decades. In the name of cleansing the state, corruption talk began destroying it altogether. The seventy-eight-year old Rafael Caldera returned to power in 1994 and tried to rekindle the Punto Fijo state with a coalition of seventeen feuding parties—now with an impenetrable Congress, historically low oil prices, and a quarter of the country's foreign exchange earnings earmarked for debt-service payments. Five weeks after taking office, Venezuela's financial system collapsed, and Caldera's economy minister, Julio Sosa Rodríguez, did what came increasingly naturally for Latin American leaders whose domestic economies were imploding: he flew to New York for help. In the end, the government recirculated funds raised from foreign loans, privatization, and tax revenues to bail out domestic banks: in one staggering year, $5.6 billion, fully 12 percent of the country's gross domestic product, was spent to prop up ten "intervened" banks. Caldera served out his term as the last president of the expended Punto Fijo regime.[7]

As the regime sank, the vacuum created opportunities for political dark horses and oddball discourses. As it turned out, the 1992 coup attempt was fateful. Its leaders, among them Lieutenant Hugo Chávez, accused the system as a whole of corruption and called for special tribunals for the malfeasants. They also upbraided the government's economic policies for betraying a sacred contract with the people. After the surrender in 1992, the government allowed Chávez to address the country by television to explain the defeat—thinking that this would rein in his followers. While the wily Chávez certainly told his fellow soldiers that it was time to rub the camouflage from their faces, he used the occasion to speak for the first time directly to rapt television viewers. Matters worsened when former (and soon to be again) President Caldera televised his own speech to the Senate, explaining that the actions of the plotters were the result of years of frustration and while not excusable were certainly understandable. Meanwhile, the new U.S. government of Bill Clinton, desperate to establish credentials as a defender of democracy, warned that the Venezuelan military would face severe sanctions if it tried to take power again. This finger wagging did not go down well among Venezuelan nationalists in the military and made many rulers in Caracas wince. What was remarkable in retrospect was how the rhetoric of national populism evolved into a discourse that announced the demise of the postwar regime (Gott 2000, Trinkunas 2002).

In the name of rekindling a Bolivarian mission, Chávez promised to build a national state that he claimed had never existed. If Chávez could not take the system by force, in 1998 he did by consent. That year, 56 percent of voters cast their ballots for him, while the previously hegemonic AD and COPEI scraped only a handful. Chávez called for deep and radical reform, starting with a new constitution, approved in 1999 by an assembly stacked with his followers. In 2000, an even bulkier majority (59 percent) reelected Chávez for a new six-year term to govern with a more centralized and presidentialist constitution. This charter made military involvements in civilian affairs easier (dispensing with the 1961 charter's prohibition on the military's deliberative role), consistent with the view that saving the nation requires a heroic bond between the army and the people.

Within two years of his election, Chávez cleansed the Venezuelan polity of political parties and redesigned it to be governed by a movement that transcends partisanship with little mediation between rulers and ruled. The challenge of the former was to incarnate and express the popular will and of the latter to articulate it through plebiscites and honor it by submitting particular aspirations to the will of whole. Such lofty ideas, squeezed from choice passages of Simón Bolívar, ran roughshod over those who wanted to contest the martial Chávez's sui generis notions of a homogeneous national folk—and soon had Chávez at odds with detractors in all quarters. Venezuelan society polarized over Chávez and the state he prophetically aimed to deliver into existence.

Mariátegui's Ghosts

Unlike Venezuela, Peru inherited a tradition of mass mobilization before the Great Depression shattered the financial and trading nexus of the export economies. In the cities, anarchist and syndicalist leaders planted seeds of labor radicalism, and some factions of the middle class became a bulwark for President Leguía. But more importantly, the highlands never ceased to be the basis of peasant resistance to spreading capitalist relations in the countryside and centralization of Lima's authority in the provinces. The persistence of opposition in the highlands limited the power of dictators and democrats alike. Such opposition was strong enough, ironically, to motivate elites to thwart any populist synthesis. So, while the levels of partisan activity were higher in Peru, the country remained deadlocked over the principles of political and social integration. The nineteenth-century structures of *gamonalismo* (bossism), which braided extralegal systems of extraction from rural folk with quasi-legal systems of boss rule, persisted, with the common-enough phenomenon of the local capitalist doubling as caudillo, which is why the Peruvian thinker Mariátegui insisted that the conventional sequence or stages (from feudalism to capitalism or tradition to modernity) of history did not apply to Peru's syncretic amalgam (Manrique 1991).

The struggles for a different institutional system punched through some changes that distinguish Peru from Venezuela. Urban middle classes succeeded in winning legislation and decrees for white-collar employees, and by the late 1930s such benefits were spread to blue-collar workers (Parker 1998, Drinot 2003). But the idea that national laws would govern the principles of social relations stopped at city limits. Unlike in Mexico, where rural mobilization pushed a revolutionary regime to accommodate some degree of popular citizenship, Peru's indigenous highlanders never aggregated into a force majeure. While Mexico's revolution inspired Peru's populist movement led by Victor Raúl Haya de la Torre, the American Popular Revolutionary Alliance (APRA) never made deep rural inroads and could never forge the alliance with native capitalists that populists in Argentina, Brazil, or Mexico did. If anything, the combination of APRA on the coast and the menace of peasant opposition in the highlands drove the fragments of a conservative bourgeoisie in cahoots with provincial caudillos to rally behind regimes that promised to keep revolution at bay. Thus, like Venezuela, Peru never saw a full-blown populist movement take power. But unlike in Venezuela, the sources of contention pushed the republic closer to the edge of insurgency—and its nemesis, a counter-revolution.

Peru and Venezuela, in spite of their differences, moved in uncanny lockstep to quite different positions. In the 1930s, as in Venezuela, an old guard hung on to power while the economic order collapsed and the new one slowed in emerging. After a massacre of *apristas* (followers of APRA) near Trujillo in 1932, a succession of generals occupied the presidency, vowing to maintain stability at all costs. And, as in Venezuela, the absence of a thriving industrial base meant that manufacturing did not generate social classes, manufacturers, or industrial workers interested in or capable of becoming the core of a new social alignment. When the aristocratic banker Manuel Prado won the elections of 1939, he vowed to keep the country on its track. Luckily for him, World War II revived the prices of Peru's old export staples, and the Peruvian Communist Party rallied to his side as Peru's savior from fascism (and as an ally in keeping the party's main rival for rank-and-file support, APRA, from power). The Left, therefore, split deeply, and lost its democratizing potential.

The conjunctural crisis of the war and its aftermath could not shake the structural underpinnings of the Peruvian political economy. But there was a brief moment of potential discontinuity, cut short by a defensive reaction. The old guard tried to live by voting conventions—but could not honor them beyond the breach. In 1945 Peruvian elections, as elsewhere in much of Latin America, gave way to a new electoral coalition. The victory of an alliance of parties around APRA (temporarily renamed the People's Party) appeared to poise Peru for a transformation. But the structural impediments would not give way so easily. The flirtation with open elections and pluralist politics was short-lived.

The APRA coalition promised political cleanliness, but it did not advocate the formation of autonomous workers' and peasants' associations and could not rely on the backing of a capitalist fraction that saw nationalism as its passport to a new economic order. What was more, the rhetoric was brazen enough to horrify the ancient elites. In the end, APRA seceded from the coalition to become a spoiler, mounting a succession of insurrections against the government. *Apristas*, instead of inscribing popular power, weakened a civilian administration and set the stage for coup plotters. Thus, without a viable social bloc to support it, the regime wobbled until the military stepped in and toppled it in 1948 (Bertram 1991, 426–32).

The basic deadlock endured through a sequence of regime changes. The new ruler, General Manuel Odría, like Pérez Jiménez in Venezuela, tried to modify the structure of Peruvian society while stanching political unrest. Populists were banished. Haya de la Torre spent six isolated years encased in the Colombian embassy. Odría's package aimed to prevent Peru from sliding into APRA hands, promote exports (which grew by 7 percent annually from 1950 to 1967), and cobble together a social alliance of domestic capital and increasingly prominent international investors with middling sectors who shared the mining rents. This model aggravated a latent disparity between the coast, which consumed the rents, and the interior, which produced them. It was especially the neglected agrarian sector of the sierra that suffered. Farmers who could not make it flocked to cities and filled the swelling shantytowns. Others revived an old tradition of land invasions and emboldened local leaders to make the case for the countryside in the capital.

When it became clear that General Odría was incapable of containing trouble, and as his style irritated the sensibilities of a ruling bloc that saw itself as part of a broader hemispheric modernizing and democratizing movement, he was dumped. Peru entered the 1960s, like Venezuela, grappling with the challenge of how to prevent disenchanted sectors from flocking to *fidelistas* by creating institutional mechanisms to resolve collective conflicts—but bereft of the legitimacy or resources (Venezuela's oil rents were far greater) to make their rhetorical commitments to change at all credible. Even APRA waned as the prospective movement for deeper and more inclusionary social change. While the party survived the repressive years, its leader, Haya de la Torre, toned down much of the radical nationalistic rhetoric so that APRA could become a keystone of a viable coalition.

Coalition politics meant that the civilian alignments were chronically unstable, with incessant jockeying among partners. It also meant that, while APRA joined the constitutional fabric in power, it gradually lost touch with its original bases, especially among the working classes, that wanted to change the structure of power. Moreover, though APRA had filed down its sharp edges, it was still unacceptable to conservative elites. So when Haya de la Torre appeared to have edged out his competitors in elections in 1962, the military intervened again and staged elections a year later, and this time Fernando Belaúnde took power by a narrow margin. APRA, burned by its inability to constitute itself as the national party, decided to make life miserable for any other party that might eclipse it at the polls, even if this meant joining up with archenemies, the military and the conservative right.

While elites and their clienteles and partners hung on to power and oversaw incremental changes, much of the country slid into informal participation in market life and partial affiliation with politics. The Belaúnde years exemplified many of the difficulties facing civilian Andean governments in the 1960s: promoting exports and trying to address underlying structural problems while keeping more radical alternatives—and movements—in check. But the underlying weakness of the domestic sector, and agriculture above all, worsened, sending more rural migrants to cities, where they joined the rank and file of what would soon be called the informal sector. Unrest that had begun in the 1950s in the valley of La Convención, near Cuzco, seeped into the central sierra.

On Belaúnde's inauguration day (July 23, 1963) thirty-five hundred *comuneros* (rural workers) seized an estate in Junín, sparking a wave of invasions and pitched battles between peasants and hacendados, attracting the attention of left-wing splinter movements inspired by the example of the Sierra Maestra in Cuba. The Peruvian Rangers wiped out the insurgency. But they could not solve Belaúnde's more fundamental problems. Deep reforms stalled, export returns began to run out of steam, and the expensive public works schemes drained the treasury. So, beholden to the interests of foreign and domestic capital and bereft of any support in Congress, Belaúnde could not get any serious tax reform, perhaps the single biggest obstacle to financing a greater role for the public sector in Peru, on the books. Inflation soon took off and aggravated the distributive tensions between social classes.[8]

If Venezuela appeared to have settled on a working constitutional system with a little help from oil rents, Peru backslid into a social and political crisis. No faction was powerful enough to rule, but each was powerful enough to deprive any alternative alliance of legitimacy. By 1968, civilian rulers were incapable of handling Peru's mounting problems, while the military and conservative elites refused to accommodate the only sort of reforms that would rekindle the relations between civilian rulers and the ruled. In the countryside, armed farmers seized estates, and the prospect of an imminent, if inorganic, revolution began to spread. The military stepped in once more. Under General Juan Velasco Alvarado, the military regime tried to channel reform under the slogan of Peru's Second Independence (suggesting that the first round did not resolve underlying strivings for sovereignty).

Within days, the generals seized the vast possessions of the International Petroleum Corporation, a subsidiary of Standard Oil of New Jersey. Then they turned on the mining companies. In part, the idea was to assert symbolically the autonomy of the regime from foreign capital. Another motive was to take over the ground rents directly and plough them into the costs of social change. By far the most aggressive and important of social reforms was the redistribution of land, seen at the time as a synonym for agrarian reform. In what was dubbed by its authors Plan Inca, officers and agronomists fanned out across the sierra to reshuffle the land tenure system, with amazing results in some pockets in a very short time. Many observers felt that the crisis had culminated in a regime that forced a national synthesis on recalcitrants.

This model had to rely on too few, and ultimately weak, institutions to realize its aspirations. It relied upon an exaggerated estimate of the rents that had been drained from the republic. What is more, agrarian reform created more enemies to the regime than loyalists. Solving the national question through an authoritarian model only deferred the inevitable problem of how to include all Peruvian citizens in the country's political life while upholding the rule of law. Fundamentally, the military never gave up its mistrust of autonomous mobilized civic activity and was hostile to the formation of peasant leagues. For their part, rural activists were almost genetically allergic to occupants of state power. Thus for all the change that occurred between 1969 and 1975, Velasco never forged anything resembling the *agrarista* (agrarian) base that gave Mexico's PRI such command over the corporatist regime. But if his successors backed off reform and began negotiations for a return to civilian rule, they closed their fiscal books by embarking on systematic, large-scale borrowing from international banks. By the time Belaúnde returned to the presidency in 1980, Peru was up to its neck in debt. By the time his administration slumped to defeat in 1985, debt-service payments (what borrowers pay simply to cover interest and service costs) exceeded the country's total exports.

An economic catastrophe was not the only mess that the military and Belaúnde bequeathed to the *aprista* Alan García. The atrophy of the state across much of the central and southern highlands meant that essential security vanished, making room for a guerrilla movement, called Shining Path (named after a student movement inspired by the Sendero Luminoso de José Carlos Mariátegui, the founder of the Peruvian Communist Party). What is important to note about the guerrilla insurgency, and the narcotic economy that emerged simultaneously, is how marginal they were. Whatever importance or strength they enjoyed reflected the state's inability to enforce its own basic rules on the ruled. The atrophy of the Peruvian state enabled Shining Path to expand beyond Ayacucho and Huancavelica to coastal cities, eventually moving into the coca frontier of the Amazon watershed. Universities, trade unions, barrio associations, and peasant leagues—the very civic fiber that García would have needed to build his national-popular cause and pull Peru from its vortex—were becoming battlegrounds in a civil war (Gorriti 1999). As violence escalated, the economy went into a tailspin. Led by the famous writer Mario Vargas Llosa, the only viable alternative to García and his hyperinflationary platform began to coalesce into a new alliance called Movimiento Libertad. Mass rallies, pot clanging, and a virulent press campaign hounded García to his final days. When APRA finished its term in 1990, it was a shadow of its former self. García fled into exile, pursued by charges of corruption and malfeasance.

At this point Peru appeared to be, as political scientists would say, ungovernable. This did not dissuade the famed novelist, who could not resist the temptation to transform his loose civic alliance into a political movement to carry him to power. Telling Peruvian voters that they had to get in touch with market realities, Vargas Llosa crusaded across the country. Most voters wondered what country Vargas Llosa lived in after a decade of economic austerity and export promotion that only yielded more inflation and fewer jobs and sucked the remaining resources from the state. Out of nowhere emerged a political novice best known for his television program for farmers, Alberto Fujimori, with rather vague promises of jobs and political probity. His party, called Cambio 90, leaped past Peru's traditional parties and eventually eclipsed Vargas Llosa's alliance. Vargas Llosa, genuinely shocked that Peruvians could not see the world his way, renounced his citizenship and left the country (Guillermo-prieto 2001, 155–77).

To say that Fujimori was something of a mystery would be banal. He seized upon the weakness of the state not to build a new legitimate order but to take what remained of state institutions—especially the military and intelligence structures—and refashion them into a mafioso state (to use Julio Cotler's term). The sheer scale of the economic problems, the guerrilla war, and the utter collapse of faith in public authority gave Fujimori a degree of autonomy that he used to his own advantage as well as the advantage of a small group of magnates who recognized the conjunctural promise of turning the construction of a new order into their order.

Paradoxically, when Fujimori came to power, many wondered whether he would be able to rule at all, especially as his movement did not carry significant loyalists in Congress. For almost two years, he was locked in a battle with surviving APRA representatives, as well as Vargas Llosa's followers. In a shocking move, Fujimori mounted a self–coup d'état in April 1992, closing down Congress and the Supreme Court, demolishing the checks and balances of the constitutional system, ruling by decree, and then promising Peruvians that he would revise the constitution to fit Peruvians' desire for more "effective" government. The only way to rule Peru, claimed Fujimori, was to act, not deliberate, and thus rule technocratically with a minimum of checks and balances. He in effect installed a governable undemocratic regime, only to use his unfettered access to public resources to hollow them out to his—and his cronies'—personal advantage (Cotler 2000).

What appeared to give Fujimori so much power to restructure the Peruvian political economy—a propensity to autocratic rule and preference for clientelist systems of representation—proved to be conditions for his dramatic and lurid demise. Televised spectacles of videotaped corruption kicked the legs out from under his clients' support for Fujimori and his henchmen; he eventually fled to Japan in disgrace. The vacuum that ensued resembled in many ways the one that had brought him to power. With older systems of political representation in shambles and the economy reeling, the stage was set for newcomers from the margins with only threadbare constituencies.

The heir to Fujimori was the little-known Alejandro Toledo, a former shoeshine boy turned economist. Toledo promised to scrub clean the political system and nurture "capitalism with a human face." But he assumed power at a time in which the Peruvian state had been stripped of much of its capacity to manage the crisis. His cabinet became a revolving door of ministers, and the countryside still seethed with unrest, discontent, and occasional violent eruptions. To be sure, there were valiant efforts to dismantle the vestiges of Fujimori's rule, a campaign to round up the most corrupt officials, and a vaunted Truth and Reconciliation Commission—which issued a detailed catalogue of about twenty years of human rights atrocities accompanied by a clarion call to the country to reconsider the very social and political conditions that gave rise to violence in the first place. But Toledo's government never resolved the underlying conditions that depleted its capacity to deliver on its many promises, in large part because it was the product of a long crisis of the state itself.

Violence and Politics in Colombia

If Peru and Venezuela cannot boast of much continuity in their political regimes, Colombia can. It can also boast one of Latin America's oldest constitutional traditions with some legitimate taproots. Paradoxically, however, it has been wracked by spasms of violence and civil warfare that have kept legions of social scientists toiling away in the vibrant, if gruesome, subfield of *violentología*. The combination of constitutional continuity and political turbulence makes Colombia more similar to its neighbors than is often appreciated. The inability to create public institutions capable of universalizing the rule of law within the state's territorial limits was, like the country's constitutional system itself, a holdover of incomplete efforts at state building in the nineteenth century. So, while *violentólogos* have tended to dwell on Colombia's idiographic features, it does share some important legacies with its neighbors.

A shared legacy is not the same as a shared destiny; unfinished states are, like their "finished" counterparts, not all alike. Colombia is struggling with two entwined issues. The first is the way state leaders handled the incompletion of their institutions. As elsewhere, central authorities struck deals with local caudillos to paint a semblance of national authority. The difference in Colombia was that local bosses belonged to political parties that enjoyed more or less regional preeminence. Negotiations between national and subnational authorities got caught up in the partisan bickering and bargaining between Conservative and Liberal parties whose genesis dated back to the mid-nineteenth century.

The second issue is the way in which agrarian tensions were resolved. Colombia's open frontier, scattered throughout the republic, provided a constant safety valve for peasant producers looking for an escape from the power of landlords and tax collectors. When the peasants were militarized, their defiance of authorities could cut several ways. They could be defenders of squatters, like the guards of the Colonia Agrícola de Sumapaz, or they could be the agents of a stateless plantocracy, like the desperados of the Magdalena del Medio throughout the twentieth century. Either way, the battle for land titles on Colombia's multiple frontiers revealed how little the state could cope with rural conflict, so rather than frontiers operating as the democratic hearth (as in North America), they checked the territorialization of the nation-state. At worst, the struggle for land and the struggle for local political control entwined to yield a Colombian version of gamonalismo, which made violence the means to sort out social and political alignments (LeGrand 1984).

The 1930s brought an end to a long cycle of coffee expansion and Conservative rule. The Depression opened the way for a more integrationist moment in Colombian history, not unlike those in Mexico, Brazil, and Chile. Peasants on and within the frontier went on the offensive. In 1936, railway and port workers led the formation of the first labor federation, sometimes with the support of the Communist Party and sometimes in cahoots with more radical Liberals who took President Alfonso López Pumarejo's 1934 declaration of a Revolution on the March too literally for his own tastes. Either way, the battle to expand social citizenship and agrarian transformation heated up. From 1945 to 1947, River Transport Workers struck repeatedly for higher wages and rejected the government's law validating only enterprise unions. In late 1946, oil workers in Barrancabermeja walked out of Standard Oil's refineries. This was the largest strike in Colombian history and prompted a declaration of a state of emergency. Finally, in May 1947, Colombia got its first general strike. The countryside also teemed with estate occupations and squatters. For a moment, splintered unions and scattered agrarian movements appeared poised to transcend the cities and valleys of their inception to aggregate into the makings of a national-popular alliance (Urrutia 1969, 191–95).

If a high degree of mobilization in Colombia seemed to prepare the country for a major turn, partisan struggles fractured the drive for a populist synthesis. Instead of implementing a new model, Colombia plunged into civil war. Like Peru and Venezuela, Colombia entered the decisive juncture from 1945 to 1948 and came close to a populist transformation. And like Peru and Venezuela, the turn faltered. Colombia too eventually saw its sequence of coups d'état try to put the country back on an institutional track, but unlike in the other Andean republics, partisan carnage left two hundred thousand people dead.

The details of how the prospective populist turn was not made are fairly well known. The party that might have transmogrified into an agrarian-laborist flag carrier, the Liberals, splintered; in 1946, the Conservative Mariano Ospina Pérez took power on a slender plurality of votes, and, in the wake of massive demonstrations, the firebrand Liberal leader who might have institutionalized a new order, Jorge Eliécer Gaitán, was gunned down in the streets of Bogotá on April 9, 1948. What ensued was a sui generis war baptized simply La Violencia, until even Conservatives were appalled enough at the recursive bloodletting and conspired with Liberals to ask the military to take over directly. Rather than a populist republican like Gaitán, Colombia got a dictator like Odría and Jiménez—which is to say a martial leader whose ability to don the presidential sash depended on the support of established civic-political forces. The new president of Colombia was General Gustavo Rojas Pinilla, and he embarked on a triadic policy of negotiating with Liberal guerrilla leaders, combating recalcitrants, and modernizing the economy (Palacios 1995, 199–211).[9]

Strikingly, neither the mobilization of the 1940s nor the violence of the 1950s nor the dictatorship that was supposed to restore order created institutional mechanisms to transcend the underlying source of fragmentation and fratricide. This was not for lack of effort. Indeed, Rojas Pinilla himself began to maneuver around the traditional parties, their traditional leaders, and their social supporters, who were justifiably worried that the general was crafting himself into a Perón. Accordingly, the two parties that had once lunged at each other's throats agreed to a plan. The Liberal leader, Alberto Lleras Restrepo, hammered out a deal with Laureano Gómez, the mastodonic Conservative, to restore civilian rule—and the hegemony of the old biarchy—under the banner of a National Front. In this sense there were important resemblances to Venezuela's Punto Fijo agreement.

There was one important nuance: instead of a bipolar system, the National Front created a bipartisan one. The accord did the following: the presidency alternated between the two ancient parties until 1974, after which the executive would be thrown open to real elections; "millimetric" parity applied to positions for both parties throughout the bureaucracy; and a two-thirds vote in Congress, not a simple majority, was necessary for legislation to pass. Like the Punto Fijo in Venezuela, here was an arrangement to fix not just a government but a regime, through power sharing and exclusion of outliers. The regime not only succeeded in patching up—if not erasing—the differences between the parties but also crippled oppositional civic movements. The labor movement remained as divided and weak as ever, and the peasantry had to channel its demands to the official Agrarian Reform Institute. In this context, the two-party regime earned the confidence of Colombia's elites, who plowed capital into farms, mines, and factories. Indeed, Colombia was not immune to some of the foreign exchange and inflation problems that crippled the rest of Latin America, but growth and the emergence of an industrial bour-geoisie, especially in Medellín, was impressive. Under the National Front, new and old fragments of Colombia's elites reconstituted into something that Colombia had long lacked: a unified dominant bloc.

The National Front regime tamed electoral life without taming political life. Making the system work at the national level required redoubling local-level clientelist networks of party bosses who organized the local electorates into voting blocs for the two mainstream parties. In return for casting the right ballots, clients got modest patronage payments in the form of housing, irrigation, and protection services. Clientelism may have stabilized a national order, but the scramble among bosses for spoils and support at the local level was frequently unruly if not savage.

The legacy of violence also shifted in another way. As the 1960s unfolded, partisan vertical cleavages gave way to a more horizontal form of conflict. In the words of Gonzalo Sánchez, the strategy of demilitariz-ing bipartisan politics led to a militarization of social polarization. Some Communist survivors went to the hills and folded into the remaining guerrilla units that were not vanquished or demilitarized by the dictator-ship. Indeed, from 1958 to 1966, La Violencia persisted, though differently. Some of the opposition blurred the line between banditry and political insurgency. Pedro Antonio Marín, so-called Tiro Fijo (Sure Shot), carved his Independent Republic of Marquetalia out of the highlands above Bogotá. Tiro Fijo and other guerrilla leaders also picked up Maoists from the ranks of the disenchanted Communist Party, as well as neophyte gue-varistas. Together, they formed the Revolutionary Armed Forces of Colombia (FARC) in 1966. The cuadrillas (protagonists) of the 1960s insurrection enlisted discontented peasants, fleeing communists, and social bandits (who were encouraged by state weakness) and were thus thorny reminders that pacted transitions are not sufficient conditions for institutionalizing relations between citizens and the state (Sánchez 1991, 55; 1983).

In the end, the final blow to the National Front came from its own success. While defusing old partisan friction, it did little to legitimate elections as civic rituals for citizens to choose their representatives freely. Ironically, it was the former dictator, Rojas Pinilla, a born-again democrat, who exposed the charade of the alternating elections—and who unintentionally opened the way for a new round of militarized politics. His party, the National Popular Alliance, posted some impressive—and therefore uncomfortable—results at the polls. The more the party succeeded, the more it illustrated the pointlessness of political citizenship. The 1970 elections registered the party's high-water mark. A mere 40 percent of voters cast ballots for the National Front ticket, and radios announced the imminent victory of Rojas Pinilla. But the next morning official tallies gave the victory to the Conservative Misael Pastrana. Many followers of Rojas Pinilla denounced the National Front regime and picked up guns—becoming in a few years the main guerrilla force, the Movimiento 19 de Abril (M-19, named after the date in which their victory was overturned). It announced its presence in 1974 by stealing Simón Bolívar's sword from the National Museum, decrying the elites' betrayal of the Liberator's aspirations, not unlike Hugo Chávez's subsequent claim to historic legitimacy. The guerrillas, by the 1980s, went from the political margins to being crucial political actors, even if they refused to play by official rules (Chernick and Jiménez 1993).

By the 1980s, political violence was so widespread that the remnants of the National Front parties all agreed that the system had to be more inclusive. A sharp turning point came in November 1985, when 35 M-19 assailants stormed the Judicial Palace in Bogotá and took the Supreme Court hostage. Embarrassed by the security lapse, the army attacked the building. Their overconfidence and overkill led to a firefight, leaving twelve justices and hundreds of employees dead. The awful carnage prompted politicos and the guerrillas to change their tack. The Conservative Belisario Betancur (1982–1986), Liberal Virgilio Barco (1986–1990), and Liberal César Gaviria (1990–1994) confronted the political mess with peace overtures. The three differed politically, but all hoped, through delicate negotiations, to demilitarize not just elections but politics as a whole.

In 1985, the FARC and the Ejército para la Liberación Nacional (National

Liberation Army) sponsored civilian branches, the Unión Patriótica (UP) and A Luchar (To Struggle), respectively. After some tough negotiations, the members of the M-19 laid down their arms just before Barco completed his term. In a matter of months, these guerrillas reassumed the civilian mantle they had discarded after the 1970 elections and became an immediately potent force in Colombian electoral politics. In 1986, the UP won fourteen congressional seats. Two years later, when Colombia had its first direct elections for municipal offices (in an effort to curb the power of local political bosses), the UP took many town councils and mayoralties. To boot, the Colombian trade union movement cohered in 1986 to create a Unitary Workers' Central (CUT) to bring some unity to reverse decades of fractures and frailty. Gaviria followed with his own initiatives, integrating several other smaller groups into the electoral spectrum and finally repudiating the remnants of the National Front order by convoking a constitutional assembly. The Left got more than a quarter of the votes cast for the assembly and played a major role in redesigning the structure of the Colombian state (Villamizar 1997).

Peace did not put an end to war—it simply changed its nature. First, peace rested on political reinsertion with whichever party was willing to strike a deal. This was not a broad social model of insertion with several— or all—groups simultaneously. The result was that many agents, particularly those with the least vested interest in acknowledging the legitimacy of the regime they were entering, were left in the field as potential spoilers. Second, the constitutional blueprint was in many ways a remarkable document with enormous promise, but in decentralizing the Colombian state even more, it gave the local-level patronage networks greater autonomy. And as political violence evolved, local bosses forged ties with armed agents who offered more than just protection services; they operated as outright militias contracted to wipe out dissenters, especially on the Left and in the incipient CUT.

From local-level gamonal systems emerged parastatal actors inhabiting the nebulous frontier of legality to become death squads mowing down civic movements. Hundreds of CUT activists were wiped out. The electoral Left also got chopped down. Assassins killed three UP presidential candidates and proceeded to execute fifteen hundred UP militants, all of them elected officeholders, including senators, congressmen, and congresswomen. The guerrilla stragglers remained in the hills and eventually made arrangements with coca producers to generate the rents to sustain their struggles. So too did the parastatal death squads. By the late 1980s, the booming cocaine trade was fueling the escalating political economy of

violence. In a confusing mélange, drug traffickers and right-wing paramilitary units reinforced each other, relying on drug money to fund counterrevolution, while deploying private militias to protect the drug
economy from law enforcers. By the end of the decade, the democratic
Left was in ruins. Violence therefore forced the legal political spectrum
back into the bipartisan shell from which it had been struggling to evolve
(Sánchez 2001, 26–27).

This kind of retrogression made it even more difficult to break the
political and social stalemate—even though civic leaders, intellectuals,
and politicos of all stripes agreed that a fundamental overhaul was necessary. Indeed, in the face of demands for political change (possibly even
because there was so much need for reform), coca capitalism not only co-
opted left and right militarized spoilers, it seeped into the formal political
arena as well. Given the nexus of local clientelism and local capitalists,
this was not at all surprising. In the trade-off between political loyalty for
pork barrel contracts, caudillos redoubled their strength by sheltering
new circuits of capital from drugs. It was a matter of time before coca capital filtered up through the system to the top echelons of the state.

In June 1994, days after his defeat by the Liberal Ernesto Samper, Conservative Andrés Pastrana accused the president-elect of taking campaign
contributions from coca capitalists in Cali. A member of the police intelligence service released an audiocassette of conversations between Samper's campaign brass and donors. It was not a very clear recording, but
subsequent testimony revealed that the Cali traffickers had funneled
around $6 million into Samper's campaign coffers starting in April 1994.
The contribution was probably decisive, because at the time Samper and
Pastrana were running neck and neck in opinion polls. Twice, in 1995 and
1996, the House of Representatives voted on motions to launch impeachment proceedings against Samper but did not muster the necessary
majority.

Paradoxically, it was the Samper administration that finally managed
to bust up the Cali consortia and put several prominent traffickers behind
bars. But this did not deter the Clinton administration from picking out
Samper as a target for Washington's own war on drugs. The foiled
impeachment proceedings justified Washington's decision to slap sanctions on Colombia for failing to cooperate with the war on drugs. While
many Colombians wanted Samper impeached, the last thing they wanted
was for Colombia as a whole to pay a price for someone else's war. Yet
punitive measures spurred capital flight and a deep recession, possibly
the worst economic malaise of the century. Samper hobbled through the
rest of his term as a pariah. The Colombian government therefore sur-

vived, but it could scarcely govern.[10]

Pastrana may have gotten his revenge against Samper when he came to power in 1998. But he had to negotiate with right-wing squads, guerrillas, and coca capitalists, who were all stronger than ever, from the weakest possible bargaining position. In retrospect, his own peace efforts, and eventually the vaunted Plan Colombia, appear to have had the odds stacked against them, since they required wielding state powers that he did not have. By the time Pastrana launched his initiative, indeed in reaction to previous peace overtures, several right-wing militia groups formed a national network called the Self-Defense Units of Colombia, decrying concessions to guerrillas, fighting those (and other subversives) that the official army could not. Eventually network leaders claimed the same rights to participate in peace talks as the guerrillas. With the rents from the coca trade, therefore, the spoilers could mow down bystanders with impunity while talking about peace.

On the night of September 29, 2001, a night patrol of Colombia's Special Forces spotted guerrilla movements along the hillside of the Sierra Nevada de Santa Marta, near the Caribbean coast. It turned out to be one of the fronts of the FARC escaping to higher ground with twenty hostages. Among the captives was Consuelo Araujonoguera (known as La Cacica), the popular former minister of culture and personal friend to President Pastrana. Commanders gave orders to engage the FARC. In the ensuing battle, several hostages escaped and the surviving guerrillas withdrew into darkness, leaving behind a forest scattered with cadavers, including La Cacica's, whose face was obliterated by bullets. The next day, Colombians began to grieve over the loss of another beloved citizen, gave up hopes for peace, and wondered whether anyone ruled at all. As the president joined the funeral wake, the crowd of thirty thousand mourners waved white handkerchiefs, chanting to the stricken Pastrana, "There is no government!" (*Cambio* 2001).

Andean societies carried their nineteenth-century legacies into the twentieth in various ways, and states that relied on shifting clientelist systems to embolden elite fealty to national rule had to cope with the rising demands for political and social citizenship from popular sectors. When the terms of citizenship began to broaden and deepen, the institutions that were called upon to envelop these new (and sometimes not so new) vindications were still unfinished. Ironically, the old regimes had to be strong and integrated enough to found the institutional networks of their own successor systems. Long-term continuities reflected less the underlying strength of older systems than the great difficulties in creating new ones.

If this was the common challenge of Andean societies, the contingent ways in which these conflicts evolved created different permutations. The opportunities to create new integrative orders once the Great Depression shook the pillars of the old regimes were clearly seized, but not in ways that enabled successor regimes to transcend inherited problems. Thus the civilian regimes, Punto Fijo in Venezuela, National Front in Colombia, and the long Belaúnde shadow in Peru, aimed less to dismantle the inherited legacies of the past than to recalibrate them for a new phase of export-led growth. These new orders rested on active parties but constricted participation. The forces of perseverance endured not so much because of their intrinsic legitimacy, although they could claim undeniable conjunctural appeal compared to the military governments or guerrillas, but because they appeared at the time to be so effective in combining electoral mobilization and incremental reform while leaving the fundaments of peripheral capitalism largely intact.

What ensued was therefore the exhaustion of systems that could neither shoulder the burdens of social, cultural, and political changes nor give way to something new. By the 1990s, Andean societies were contending with a variant of political development that is quite different from the rest of Latin America. If transitions to democracy—or latterly consolidations of democracy—were the order of the day in the Southern Cone, Brazil, and even Mexico, what was in doubt in the Andes was less democracy than the underlying institutional girders that enable it to exist at all.

Notes

1. The literature on state formation is now vast and complex, if relentlessly Eurocentric. See Tilly (1990) and Brewer (1989) for examples. Of course these authors have not been arguing that the historic sequelae are normative. But the recent outpouring of work on failed states has implied, sometimes explicitly, that the missing preconditions involved a consolidated fiscal-military order at a foundational stage to transcend warlords, sheikhs, or absolutists. On failed states, see Stohl (2000) and Rotberg (2002). For alarm about Andean contagion, see McLean (2002).

2. The origins of this contrast are the theme of Adelman (forthcoming).

3. On the nexus of caudillos and war, see Dunkerley (1992, 155–58). A suggestive treatment of the notion of citizens in arms is Sabato (2001, 1312–13).

4. The debate about revolutions remains lively. See Skocpol's overview (1994, 3–22). In the end I am quite skeptical about the prospects for some general theory of revolution, though I admit that comparative patterns and typologies can be developed. In this respect I am sympathetic with Alan Knight's recent contrast of the Mexican and Bolivian revolutions (2003, 54–90).

5. The insight goes through much of Hirschman's work, though it was first crystallized in *The Strategy of Economic Development* (1958, 9).

6. The charges were that Pérez had misused funds meant to cover Nicaraguan President Violeta Chamorro's defenses.

7. For a detailed report on Venezuela's financial problems, see *Latin American Weekly Report* (1994).

8. Pedro-Pablo Kuczynski, a manager of the Central Reserve Bank, later recalled the impossibility of squaring the circle of paying for modest reforms while promoting Peru's exports by printing money (1977, 77; see also chap. 7 for a revealing portrayal of the limits to tax reform).

9. For a fascinating testimonial of the rural insurgency, see Isaza (1994).

10. The probity of the procedures themselves became a matter of considerable dispute, as many of the congressmen who voted were themselves on traffickers' payrolls. A Citizens' Oversight Commission turned in findings after the last impeachment vote, finding reason to believe that Samper did in fact know about the illicit contributions. It is not known whether in fact the Drug Enforcement Agency or Central Intelligence Agency was behind the tape's release (*New York Times* 1996; *El Espectador* 1997; Dugas 2001, 157–74).

Bibliography

Jeremy Adelman. Forthcoming. *The shattered meridian: Empire and revolution in the Iberian Atlantic*. Princeton, NJ: Princeton University Press.

Bertram, Geoffrey. 1991. Peru, 1930–1960. In *Cambridge history of Latin America*, ed. Leslie Bethell, 8:385–449. Cambridge: Cambridge University Press.

Bolívar, Simón. 1951. A panoramic view of Spanish America. In *Selected writings of Bolívar*, ed. Bierck, Harold A., 1:742. New York: Colonial Press.

Brewer, John. 1989. *The sinews of power: War, money and the English state, 1688–1783*. New York: Knopf.

Cambio. 2001. Quién manda aqui? October 12.

Chernick, Marc W., and Michael F. Jiménez. 1993. Popular liberalism, radical democracy, and Marxism: Leftist politics in contemporary Colombia, 1974–1991. In *The Latin American left*, ed. Barry Carr and Steve Ellner, 61–81. Boulder, CO: Westview.

Cotler, Julio. 2000. La gobernabilidad en el Perú. In *El fujimorismo: Ascenso y caída de un régimen autoritario*, ed. Julio Cotler and Romeo Grompone, 13–67. Lima, Peru: Instituto de Estudios Peruanos.

Deas, Malcolm. 1992. Miguel Antonio Caro and friends: Grammar and power in Colombia. *History Workshop Journal* 34 (Autumn): 42–71.

Drinot, Paulo. 2003. Fighting for a closed shop: The 1931 Lima bakery workers' strike. *Journal of Latin American Studies* 35 (May): 249–78.

Dugas, John C. 2001. Drugs, lies, and audiotape. *Latin American Research Review* 36 (2): 157–74.

Dunkerley, James. 1992. Reassessing caudillismo in Bolivia, 1825–1879. In *Political suicide in Latin America*. London: Verso.

El Espectador. 1997. Colombia busca otro norte. July 7.

Ellner, Steve. 1980. *Los partidos políticos y su disputa por el control del movimiento sindical en Venezuela, 1936–1948*. Caracas, Venezuela: Universidad Católica Andrés Bello.

———. 1993. *Organized labor in Venezuela, 1958–1991*. Wilmington, DE: SR Books.

Gorriti, Gustavo. 1999. *The Shining Path: A history of the millenarian war in Peru*. Chapel Hill: University of North Carolina Press.

Gott, Richard. 2000. *In the shadow of the liberator*. London: Verso.

Guillermoprieto, Alma. 2001. The bitter education of Mario Vargas Llosa. In *Looking for history: Dispatches from Latin America*. New York: Pantheon.

Hirschmann, Albert. 1958. *The strategy of economic development*. New Haven, CT: Yale University Press.

Isaza, Eduardo Franco. 1994. *Las guerrillas del Llano*. Bogotá, Colombia: Planeta.

Karl, Terry Lynn. 1997. *The paradox of plenty: Oil booms and petro-states*. Berkeley and Los Angeles: University of California Press.

Knight, Alan. 2003. The domestic dynamics of the Mexican and Bolivian revolutions. In *Reclaiming revolution: Bolivia in comparative perspective*, ed. Merilee Grindle and Pilar Domínguez, 54–90. Cambridge MA: Rockefeller Center for Latin American Studies, Harvard University.

Kuczynski, Pedro-Pablo. 1977. *Peruvian democracy under economic stress: An account of the Belaúnde administration, 1963–1968*. Princeton, NJ: Princeton University Press.

Latin American Weekly Report. 1994. March 24.

LeGrand, Catharine. 1984. Labour acquisition and social conflict on the Colombian frontier. *Journal of Latin American Studies* 16 (May): 27–49.

López Maya, Margarita. 2003. The Venezuelan *caracazo* of 1989: Popular protest and institutional weakness. *Journal of Latin American Studies* 35 (February): 117–37.

Mallon, Florencia E. 1983. *The defense of community in Peru's central highlands: Peasant struggle and capitalist transformation, 1860–1940*. Princeton, NJ: Princeton University Press.

Manrique, Nelson. 1991. Gamonalismo, lanas y violencia en los Andes. In *Poder y violencia en los Andes*, comp. Henrique Urbano, 49–71. Cusco, Peru: Centro de Estudios Regionales Andinos Bartolomé de las Casas.

Mariátegui, José Carlos. 1971. The problem of land. In *Seven interpretive essays on Peruvian reality*. Austin: University of Texas Press.

McLean, Philip. 2002. Colombia: Failed, failing or just weak. *Washington Quarterly* 25 (Summer): 75–90.

New York Times. 1996. Clinton declares that Colombia has failed to curb drug trade. March 2.

Palacios, Marco. 1995. *Entre la legitimidad y la violencia: Colombia, 1875–1994*. Bogotá, Colombia: Editorial Norma.

Parker, David. 1998. *The idea of the middle class: White-collar workers and Peruvian society, 1900–1950*. University Park PA: Penn State University Press.

Restrepo, José Manuel. 1970. *Historia de la revolución de Colombia*. 6 vols. Medellín, Colombia: Bedout.

Rotberg, Robert I. 2002. Failed states in a world of terror. *Foreign Affairs* 3 (July–August): 12–24.

Sábato, Hilda. 2001. On political citizenship in nineteenth-century Latin America. *American Historical Review* 106 (October): 1290–314.

Sánchez, Gonzalo. 1983. *Bandoleros, gamonales, y campesinos: El caso de la violencia en Colombia*. Bogotá, Colombia: El Ancora.

———. 1991. *Guerra y política en la sociedad colombiana* Bogotá, Colombia: El Ancora.

———. 2001. Problems of violence, prospects for peace. In *Violence in Colombia: Waging war and negotiating peace*, ed. Charles Bergquist, Ricardo Peñaranda, and Gonzálo Sanchéz G., 1–37. Wilmington, DE: Scholarly Resources.

Skocpol, Theda. 1994. Explaining social revolutions: First-further thoughts. In *Social Revolutions in the Modern World*. New York: Cambridge University Press.

Stohl, Rachel. 2000. Protecting the failing state. *Weekly Defense Monitor* 4 (April 20): 21–34.

Tilly, Charles. 1990. *Coercion, capital, and European states, AD 990–1990*. Oxford, UK: Blackwell.

Trinkunas, Harold A. 2002. The crisis in Venezuelan civil-military relations. *Latin American Research Review* 37 (February): 70–85.

Urrutia, Miguel. 1969. *The development of the Colombian labor movement*. New Haven, CT: Yale University Press.

Villamizar, Darío. 1997. *Un adiós a la guerra*. Bogotá, Colombia: Planeta.

Wilson, Fiona. 2003. Reconfiguring the Indian: Land-labour relations in the post-colonial Andes. *Journal of Latin American Studies* 35 (May): 221–47.

3

A Transregional Security Cartography
of the Andes

ANN MASON AND ARLENE TICKNER

FOLLOWING THE SOUTHERN CONE DICTATORSHIPS AND
political convulsions in Central America during the 1980s, the Andean
region emerged as the flag bearer of Latin American crisis. Democratic
fragility, institutional weakness, poor articulation between state and society, social and economic exclusion, and unregulated forms of participation
are among the most critical problems besetting the five Andean countries
(Gutiérrez 2003; chapter 1). The ensuing combination of ungovernability
and social disintegration has made the northern part of South America the
epicenter of hemispheric instability at the start of the millennium.

These problems are common to all the states of the region, yet mani-
fest themselves uniquely in each national context. The notion of Andean
crisis is essentially an analytic device for conducting comparative country
studies according to a set of crosscutting categories and then aggregating
the results at the regional level. While it is true that many of the factors
that undermine the region operate at the level of state and society, other
dimensions of Andean turbulence are more transnational in nature,
encompassing the entire region. Security epitomizes this attribute. Often
neglected by comparative approaches, contemporary security processes

increasingly transcend territorial state units or link up national jurisdictions to craft multiple regional spaces.

While it is widely accepted that the Colombian conflict is the vortex of regional insecurity, we find this interpretation to be unsatisfactory both conceptually and empirically (Rabasa and Chalk 2001; Millett 2002). Such a reading reinforces the statist bias that characterizes both traditional security studies and comparative analyses, missing the complex, transborder, and intermestic (international and domestic) nature of security processes. Like other aspects of globalization, many of the security threats in the Andes, such as drugs and arms flows, are border blind, creating alternative spatial arrangements that are increasingly discontinuous with distinct, self-enclosed state units. Moreover, exclusive concentration on Colombia's high-profile crisis has acted to crowd out the consideration of other risks to the region's security that neither originate within, nor are confined to, a single national territory.

We propose a transregional framework for conceptualizing Andean security that takes into account the deterritorialized nature of those factors that most threaten to destabilize the region (Tickner and Mason 2003). Transregionalism comprises two elements: common problems shared by the area's states and societies and security processes that permeate a regional constellation and transcend the individual countries within it. In the Andean context, thinking beyond the state is a useful way to identify features and processes that may adhere to the entire region or, conversely, to subsets of the region and areas outside it that do not necessarily conform to political boundaries. Many of the most salient Andean security threats, for example, spill out into what are viewed as non-Andean spaces. Incorporating national-level sources of socioeconomic and political instability into a transregional analysis, however, is important to understand the complex linkages that exist between the internal dimension of crisis and regional security threats. Domestic instability is highly correlated with national and regional insecurities, which in turn exacerbate those same local problems. A transregional approach to security provides an important piece of the contemporary Andean puzzle by providing a framework for analyzing the interactions between the external and domestic faces of crisis.

Trans-Andean Security Logics

Political science's long-standing fixation on the state notwithstanding, global social and political geography is increasingly at odds with discrete, territorial units (Brenner 1999). A pluralist paradigm of world order (Clark 1999) in which the state coexists with a multiplicity of actors and processes appears to have effectively superseded the minimalist Westphalian model. Multilateral regimes, supranational structures, and world legal codes all suggest a shift toward global loci of political organization and authority. At the same time, transnational flows and processes slice through national spaces and connect a complex array of civil society actors, religious and ethnic associations, business and finance organizations, local government, and criminal structures.

An exclusively state-centered vision of world politics contradicts today's global realities in two important ways: it obviates dynamics that are found within these "multiple, overlapping and intersecting sociospatial networks" (Mann 1986, 1) and does not adequately consider the importance of nonstate actors, or nonstate units of analysis, to international relations (Keohane 2002). Our approach to security within the Andean region can be located at the intersection of these shortcomings. Not only is security illustrative of the borderless processes that are increasingly evident in world politics, but the security dynamic in the Andes has played itself out in such a way as to give shape to the region as an independent unit.

The Security Concept

Security has been virtually reconceptualized since the end of the Cold War.[1] There is little disagreement that the national security model that focused almost exclusively on protection of the state from external military threats is obsolete, having been replaced by a construct that better reflects global transformations in recent decades. First, security has been broadened to include multiple referents. The new security paradigm no longer privileges state security over the safety or welfare of nonstate actors, but rather acknowledges the validity of asking, "security for whom?" Not only states, but also individuals, societies, subnational actors, and transnational groups value security and experience threats to their security. Indeed, the human security model that places individual and community values and interests at the center of global order has emerged as one of the most vigorous alternatives to the conventional state-centered security framework (Gurtov 1999; McSweeney 1999; Terriff et al. 1999). In practice, employing multiple levels of security necessarily results in competing security interests and agendas.

The expansion of security values and threats to include a nonmilitary dimension is another key feature of the new security construct. Security is perceived positively, going beyond protection from threats to encompass the promotion of values equally important to quality of life, such as political, economic, environmental, and societal security (Buzan 1991; McSweeny 1999). The notion of democratic security that links security guarantees to the institutions related to the rule of law illustrates how new security principles transcend conventional categories (Mason 2003; Perina 2000). Democratic institutions designed to enhance participation, tolerance, and the common good all contribute to the creation of a secure society. Security analyses for any security referent, then, involve distinguishing among different types of insecurity and threats. Even states now adopt measures to respond to a much broader agenda of legitimate security threats that can include drugs, AIDS, and environmental degradation.

The post–Cold War security concept also softens the internal-external dichotomy that defined previous security studies. Domestic and international domains are enmeshed: security risks cannot be wholly contained at the local level; internal factors may become regional, transnational, or even global threats; and global processes may in turn cause insecurity for certain regions, states, or subnational groups. The effects of changes in the global economy, nuclear accidents, terrorism, contagious diseases, massive human rights violations, drug trafficking, and the military policies of individual countries are transnational and highly uneven, affecting various levels of security referents simultaneously. The provision of security has also been globalized, as the shift in responsibility for providing security from the domestic to the international level attests. Along with the blurring of the lines between internal and external security has also come new thinking on the role of the international community in protecting civilian populations and establishing order within state jurisdictions (Walter and Snyder 1999). As security conditions within sovereign states are increasingly considered part of transnational dynamics, and thus legitimate concerns of a broader global polity, governments have lost exclusive authority over internal problems (Falk 1999, 64–69; Mason 2005).

This expanded interpretation of security has produced a concept that is more meaningful but also more complex (Matthews 1989; Buzan 1991; Job 1992; Buzan, Waever, and de Wilde 1998; Klare and Chandrani 1998). If previous usages were too narrow, current conceptualizations of security risk being so broad as to lose analytical precision and utility (Morgan 1997). We adopt a middle-ground view of security in our Andean analysis that pushes back the boundaries of the traditional national security definition while seeking greater specificity than the all-inclusive human security or postmodern conceptualizations. The point of departure for our thinking on security is Morgan's physical-safety framework (1997, 22), which defines security as protection for both the state and society from violence, or the threat of violence, that is significant, organized, and deliberate. According to this approach, security threats refer to diverse forms of violence that result in loss of civilian life and that challenge state forces, including human rights violations, terrorism, the displacement of communities, the destruction of infrastructure, and the destabilization of state authority and public institutions.

Circumscribing what constitutes a threat attempts to address the dangers inherent in labeling too many things as security related. Nevertheless, we also argue that security dynamics in the global South warrant a somewhat more expansive lens for determining security issues. In peripheral contexts, more problems affect societal and state security, directly or indirectly, than in the developed world. While criminal behavior, political and institutional context, and socioeconomic background do not in and of themselves meet Morgan's definition of security threats, they are circumstances that commonly aggravate complex security situations and thus can reasonably be considered part of a security calculus. The Andean security matrix can best be understood as the result of systematic and destabilizing forms of violence against state and society that are frequently bound up with underlying political and socioeconomic conditions, all of which are mutually reinforcing. Thus justifiable concerns over adopting a broad security framework do not preclude its utility in nonconventional situations such as that of the Andean region.

The Andean Region

Current Andean security processes exhibit various features of this global security paradigm, strongly suggesting the appropriateness of adopting a regional unit of analysis.[2] Security interdependence, regional overlay, integration mechanisms, transnationalism, and the prevalence of nonstate actors are the defining characteristics of the security landscape in the Andes, making it increasingly problematic to conceptualize security exclusively at the national level. Furthermore, a country-by-country security analysis hinders the effective formulation of public policy toward problems that, by their very nature, are not confined to a single national context.

At the most rudimentary level, the Andean subsystem meets the definition of region by geographic contiguity. Although formal and informal interconnections have been irregular and uneven, there is a shared recognition both inside and outside the Andes that a distinct region exists. At the same time, Andean security interactions and relations are indicative of a regional security complex, in which regional clusters of security interdependence mediate conflict and competition (Buzan 1991). Not only do the region's states share many of the same security concerns (drug trafficking and illegal arms flows, increasing criminality, privatization of violence, and the U.S. regional antidrug posture), but understandings of national interests, security, and risks are also highly relational to those of the other Andean nations. Venezuela's and Ecuador's security agendas, for example, necessarily take into account Colombia's internal situation, and the Colombian drug problem is enmeshed with trafficking and laundering activities in neighboring countries.

The pattern of security relations among the Andean states is also deeply entangled with the U.S. posture toward the region. The Andean region is a security complex not only by virtue of local interdependence but also because such mutual dependencies are at least partially shaped by externalities such as shared threats and policies by outside actors that are common to the region. The strategic interests and role of great powers in particular can be "strong enough to suppress the normal operation of security dynamics among local states" (Buzan 1991, 198) within regional contexts. Indeed, a fundamental dimension of the current security dynamic in the Andes is the overlay of U.S. imperatives that has inhibited the articulation of local security concerns and responses. Washington's regional expression of its own national security interests has led to an externally imposed reading of the Andean security situation that has by and large been embraced by the region's governments.[3] The definition of drugs as a security threat, the correlative war on drugs, and more recently the incorporation of the Andes into Washington's global antiterrorist campaign have configured a regional security architecture built on U.S., not necessarily Andean, objectives. Thus, the U.S. strategic vision of the region, and policies such as the Andean Regional Initiative that make little distinction among the security particularities of its five states and societies, contribute to the idea that the region is an indivisible unit.

Structures of governance and integration constitute a third attribute of the Andean region suggestive of an aggregate composition. The blueprint of regional integration is, by any account, impressive, incorporating extensive supranational powers in the areas of foreign policy, security, economy, justice, human rights, and the environment. That integration to date has remained largely a formalism, limited principally to trade relations, should not diminish the importance of a regional governance project. The Comunidad Andina de Naciones (Andean Community of Nations) first and foremost signals the desire to cooperate and a recognition that by coordinating activities all states can realize mutual gains. So far the community is built on commercial interdependence, but, as the European Union and Mercosur suggest, shared material interests and the institutions they generate can be an important first step toward cooperation in other areas and an increasing density of social networks. The community's bid in the area of Andean security suggests such a movement toward a more inclusive regional governance project. The 2000 Carta Andina para la Paz y Seguridad (Andean Charter for Peace and Security) proposed a regional security scheme based on a shared commitment to negotiated solutions to the region's conflicts, prohibitions on the use of force, and international standards on human rights.

In spite of recent setbacks in economic integration, certain instrumental features of what Adler and Barnett (1998a, 50–53) refer to as a nascent security community may already be taking shape among the Andean nations. Even in the face of continuing territorial tensions and political discord in the region, such as those between Venezuela and Colombia, and Peru and Ecuador, governments generally cooperate to manage disputes and avoid war. Indeed, various explanations for the absence of international war in the region agree that the Andean nations share an interest in preserving their society of states and a strong normative commitment to accept international legal instruments of mediation, arbitration, and negotiation for conflict resolution (Kacowicz 1998; Hurrell 1998). But perhaps what is most striking about the sweeping proposal for regional structures is that it demonstrates the intention to construct a community and, although extremely rudimentary, a shared sense of identity.

A fourth set of factors that contributes to security's regional contour in the Andes is the prevalence of transnational processes and nonstate actors in security dynamics. Many of the most acute threats to Andean security are transborder in nature, epitomized by the flow of drugs and arms that crisscross the region irrespective of national boundaries. Transnational criminal organizations and extralegal networks that operate beyond the control of national governments manage these illicit activities both within the region and in conjunction with hemispheric and global criminal groups. Global tendencies have also given rise to the formation of transnational civil society networks related to security issues. Such nonstate actors, who range from individuals to indigenous groups to transnational corporations, are legitimate security referents who have specific agendas and policies and who experience risks to their well-being. At the same time, global nongovernmental organizations, international organizations, and even private security firms operationalize their concerns and programs within the Andean region, frequently in conjunction with local and regional civil society organizations, illustrating yet another way in which security processes are increasingly discontinuous with state units.

A Transregional Security Approach

Security imperatives in the Andes have two facets: problems that are shared across the region's states and societies and dynamics that traverse the region, irrespective of territorially defined borders. Common political, socioeconomic, and security difficulties typify most geographic regions and indeed are constitutive of them (Lake and Morgan 1997). The Andean subsystem is a case in point. Institutional weakness, problems of democratic governance, poverty, inequality, criminality, and political violence within each country are associated with the notion of a regional security and governability crisis.

However, shared problems are only one aspect of the region's security predicament. What most stands out about the current security climate is its intermestic and transborder nature. Regional security directly or indirectly involves processes that transcend individual states and indeed in some cases spill out of the region altogether. Security logics that diffuse the entire region constitute the defining characteristic of transregionalism. The most salient transregional security threats currently present in the Andean region are the effects of the enlargement of the Colombian conflict and illicit flows of drugs and arms, while U.S. policies toward the Andes constitute another security dynamic with a regional dimension.

Both types of security features are highly interdependent: shared problems are mutually reinforcing and nurture transregional processes. Regionwide dynamics themselves overlap and exacerbate each other, at the same time that they feed back into domestic developments. For example, the tendency toward institutional weakening and democratic deconsolidation has provided fertile ground for burgeoning levels of criminality and the formation of illicit transnational networks. These activities both depend on and deepen corruption at all levels of government, leading to further deterioration of public institutions and practices.

Shared National-Level Problems

Although the root causes and specific manifestations of crisis in the Andes may vary, each of the countries exhibits a series of similar social, political, and economic problems (Conaghan and Malloy 1995; Whitehead 2001; chapter 1).

Institutional Weakness

Weak institutions are one of the focal issues that challenge Bolivia, Colombia, Ecuador, Peru, and Venezuela. Relatively stable in comparison with the authoritarian tendencies that dominated Latin America during the 1970s and 1980s, all the democratic states of the Andean region have undergone distinct forms of institutional decline since the early 1990s. This deinstitutionalization has been accompanied by high levels of political volatility, social fragmentation, and multiple forms of violence. Despite the considerable intraregional diversity on this issue, state weakening and democratic deconsolidation have become pervasive throughout the region.

The Andean nations all receive low marks for their empirical attributes of statehood. Control over territory and populations; the provision of essential public goods such as services, security, and justice; sufficient coercive power to repel challenges to state authority and extract resources; and a national project capable of achieving a modicum of social cohesion are deficient. Basic functions of the state are poorly and sporadically performed. Stalled processes of modernization, the incomplete incorporation of social groups, and an underdeveloped idea of the state have resulted in legitimacy crises and social ruptures across the region. In all the Andean countries, vast areas of national territory are devoid of state presence and administration. Armed insurgencies, violent social movements, criminal organizations, and even common delinquency are beyond effective government control. To varying degrees they fail the basic Weberian test of maintaining a monopoly over the legitimate use of force within their national borders and providing security for their citizens.

State weakness is paralleled by a progressive deterioration in democratic institutions and practices. While Andean-style democracy has always been more procedural than substantive (chapter 1), democratic regimes in the region have further faltered during the past decade. The party system is in various stages of deconsolidation, thwarting representation and participation (Mainwaring and Scully 1995). From virtual collapse, as in Peru under Alberto Fujimori and in the Venezuelan Fifth Republic, to steady erosion in power relative to the explosion of smaller, independent parties in Colombia and Ecuador, political parties have "lost much of their ability to enroll, represent, and command large segments of the population" (chapter 1). The decline in party cohesion and credibility has been aggravated by a breakdown in traditional mechanisms of interest representation. Clientelism and patronage have been put under particular strain by economic crisis and public sector downsizing throughout the Andes, pushing the search for public goods into the private and illegal sectors. Party degeneration has also given rise to the personalization of Andean politics, as evidenced by the Fujimori, Álvaro Uribe, and Hugo Chávez phenomena, further contributing to the deinstitutionalization of democracy.

The Andean setting appears to be showing symptoms of democratic deconsolidation (Diamond 1997), in which there is little agreement regarding the rules and practices of democracy. Although relatively free and fair elections have achieved an impressive level of continuity, constitutional rule itself has been interrupted four times in the past five years, marring the region's reputation for having resilient democratic institutions in the face of domestic turmoil: in Ecuador in 1997 and 2000, in Peru in 2001, and in Venezuela in 2002. The deficient protection of civil liberties, horizontal and vertical legitimacy, and the party system, coupled with high levels of political and social violence, are indicative of illiberal (Collier and Levitsky 1997; Zakaria 1997, 24; Munck 2003, 8) or delegative democracies (O'Donnell 1999). Indeed, the notion of a democracy besieged by the steady erosion of the state, pervasive violence and criminality, noninstitutional competition, and public institutions unable to cope would seem to increasingly apply to the entire region (Bejarano and Pizarro 2001).

Poverty and Inequality

Of those regions of the world in which formal democracy is firmly established, Latin America is the most unequal (Munck 2003). Within the hemisphere, the Andean nations have a particularly bad record in terms of poverty and socioeconomic inequality. Although significant differences exist between Venezuela, Colombia, and Peru and Bolivia and Ecuador, the income levels in all five are consistently below the Latin American average (CEPAL 2001). High income and consumption inequalities are also prevalent in each country, as indicated by their respective Gini indexes: Bolivia 44.7, Colombia 57.1, Ecuador 43.7, Peru 46.2, and Venezuela 49.5

(United Nations Development Program 2003). More than half the population in Bolivia (61.2%), Colombia (54.9%), and Ecuador (60.2%) lives below the poverty line, while the numbers of poor persons in Peru (49%) and Venezuela (48.5%) are not far behind (CEPAL 2002).

Beginning with the debt crisis in the early 1980s, the Andean economies have undergone repetitive downturns associated with structural adjustment, the implementation of neoliberal reform, and the inability of the majority of the countries to effectively insert themselves into the global market (Smith and Korzeniewicz 1997; Sheahan 2001). This process has been extremely uneven. With the exception of Peru, all the countries in question experienced annual rates of growth below the Latin American average during the past decade. Downward shifts in the gross domestic product in the same period were also dramatic in Ecuador, Colombia, and Venezuela (World Bank 2000). More importantly, the overall results of structural reform in social and distributive terms have been dismal. The ensuing rise in unemployment, underemployment, and informal sector employment, combined with falling real wages, have created an alarming social situation throughout the subregion (Chalmers et al. 1997). One of the most immediate effects of poverty and inequality as measured by the Gini index has been the explosion of violent crime rates throughout the Andes (Fajnzylber, Lederman, and Loayzz 2002).

Deficient Governance

Poverty and inequality are highly correlated with inadequate structural power of the region's states or capacity to implement decisions and produce outcomes (Mann 1986). Indeed, poor government performance plagues the countries of the Andean region. The shift toward market economies and political reforms adopted throughout the 1980s and 1990s have so far failed to deliver the goods: economic liberalization has made no appreciable dent in the region's long-standing inequality, and institutional reforms have not achieved political and social inclusion. Decentralization agendas in Colombia, Bolivia, and Venezuela, in particular, seem to have only exacerbated state-society divisions (chapter 1). Public disaffection with governance projects that are not only highly corrupt but also unable to satisfy basic needs and to meet socioeconomic expectations has resulted in widespread protest against governments, soaring levels of criminality and violence, and a turning away from democracy. Thus multiple scenarios of legal and illegal resistance are played out repeatedly throughout the Andes and express a variety of demands ranging from improved wages, increased prices for agricultural goods, and access to public services, among others.

Corruption is highly correlated with poor performance of public institutions, low levels of competition, social inequality, and illegitimacy of governmental authority (Lambsdorff 1999; Munck 2003). In all of the countries of the Andean region, as well as in neighboring Panama and Brazil, corruption is widespread. Institutionalized bureaucratic fraud has become more egregious in recent years, however, with the scandalous cases of Carlos Andrés Pérez in Venezuela, Ernesto Samper in Colombia, and the Fujimori machine in Peru. The persistence of the institutionalized practice of particularism (O'Donnell 1996), the lack of horizontal and vertical accountability (O'Donnell 1999), the general deterioration of political institutions, state weakness, and the presence of transnational criminal networks (Williams 1998), most notably drug trafficking organizations, also account for this situation. The Andean countries rank among the most corrupt in Latin America and the world, according to the Transparency International Corruption Perceptions Index (2003). On a scale from zero (highly corrupt) to ten (highly clean), in 2002 Peru was classified with a 3.7 corruption index (placing it 62 out of 133 on the country rank, Brazil 3.9 (54 on the country ranking), Colombia 3.7 (59 rank), Panama 3.4 (67 rank), Venezuela 2.4 (104 rank), Ecuador 2.2 (114 rank), and Bolivia 2.3 (106 rank).

Transregional Security Dynamics

A second dimension of crisis in the Andes, and of the transregional model, consists of security processes that, while highly associated with internal instability, are more transnational than domestic in nature.

Enlargement of the Colombian Conflict

The intensification of nearly all facets of Colombia's security crisis and their displacement into adjacent countries illustrates the regional nature of what is normally assumed to be an exclusively Colombian problem. Guerrilla and paramilitary operations in frontier regions; diverse forms of interaction between Colombian armed groups and local officials and illegal counterparts in contiguous nations; the formation of criminal networks dedicated to contraband, kidnapping, and extortion that traverse the region; an upsurge in Colombian migration; and the effects of fumigation of illicit crops are the most notable examples of the transnational character of the conflict. Efforts to build collective strategies to address these issues at the Andean level have met with paltry results. Neighboring governments have taken the conventional view that Colombian "spillover" can be contained by militarizing national boundaries, obviating the embeddedness of many of Colombia's problems in complex regional dynamics.[4]

The unhampered movement of guerrillas and paramilitaries across all Colombia's international borders well illustrates the regionalization of the Colombian conflict. In Venezuela and Ecuador this situation is especially acute, given that large swaths of both countries' frontier zones coincide with areas in which intense armed confrontations take place. The existence of the Revolutionary Armed Forces of Colombia (FARC) camps has been documented in the northwestern Venezuelan provinces of Táchira and Zulia (Forero 2003; Guisti 2003). Northern Ecuador too has witnessed increased guerrilla and paramilitary presence in recent years, consisting primarily of training, supply, and recreational activities. In both cases, local police and military have established differing degrees of modus vivendi with Colombian illegal armed actors (International Crisis Group 2003). Crossfire with these groups, although documented in the case of Ecuador, is nevertheless rare, even though the number of troops stationed at Ecuador's border has increased dramatically over the past year.

The presence of Colombian insurgents in the Darien region of Panama is cause for alarm in that country, given the incapacity of the Panamanian National Guard to meet such a threat.[5] The lack of a military presence on both sides of the border, in combination with the area's harsh geography, has facilitated the extension of Colombia's armed conflict well into Panamanian territory. Violent confrontations between the FARC and the Autodefensas Unidas de Colombia (United Self-Defense Forces of Colombia) within Panama have become a regular occurrence, while armed groups commonly target both public officials and the civilian population in their battle for territorial control. In January 2003, four Panamanian civilians were killed by Colombian paramilitaries, forcing approximately six hundred individuals to temporarily abandon their villages (International Crisis Group 2003, 17).

Since the late 1990s, Brazil too has become more closely involved in the Colombian conflict. Brazil's traditional apathy toward Colombia has mutated into active participation on the part of the Luiz Inácio Lula da

Silva government in the search for a negotiated settlement to the armed conflict. A 1998 incident with the FARC is indicative of Brazil's current stakes in the Colombian crisis. Following a FARC attack on and consequent occupation of the town of Mitú, the Colombian military was forced to withdraw to a base within Brazilian territory. Some of the attacks to retake Mitú took place on Brazilian soil, highlighting the porous nature of the border separating these two countries in the Amazon.

To more effectively monitor the Amazonia Legal, which accounts for nearly 60 percent of Brazil's national territory, in 1997 the Brazilian government signed a five-year contract with U.S. Raytheon Systems to build the Amazon Vigilance System (Sivam).[6] Sivam consists of a sophisticated network of radars, satellites, and monitors originally designed to control deforestation, illegal gold mining, land disputes, and drug smuggling in the area. However, intensification of the Colombian crisis has meant that the military aspects of the system have acquired greater significance, given that since its full activation in 2002, Sivam is also being used to monitor the land and air movements of illegal Colombian actors.

Growing numbers of Colombian refugees provide an additional source of apprehension in Ecuador and Venezuela. Since 1985, 2,900,000 Colombian civilians have been displaced as a result of the armed conflict. In 2002 alone, 412,553 people were forced to leave their homes (Consultaría para los Derechos Humanos y el Desplazamiento 2003). Although early fears that the U.S.-backed Plan Colombia would cause massive displacement in neighboring countries have proven to be unfounded, between 2000 and 2002, approximately 50,000 Colombians sought refuge in Ecuador and Venezuela. Of these, 21,800 did so in 2002, suggesting that displacement into adjacent countries may be on the rise (Consultaría para los Derechos Humanos y el Desplazamiento 2003). Although failing to cross over into its neighbors' territory, an additional 47,375 displaced Colombians also settled in frontier areas during the same year.

The impact of the Colombian conflict in Peru and Bolivia has been minor in comparison to the experience of Brazil, Ecuador, Panama, and Venezuela. Although Peru shares a considerable border with Colombia in the Amazon, minimal spillover has occurred, primarily due to the difficult geographical terrain that separates the two countries. Peru and Bolivia's main concerns regarding Colombia remain drug related. Following sustained reductions since the mid-1990s in the acreage of illicit crops, both Peru and Bolivia experienced increases in 2002 (U.S. Department of State 2003). This problem is attributed to the balloon effect.[7] Given significant reductions in certain areas of southern Colombia targeted by the Colombian and U.S. governments for aerial fumigation, coca leaf production has merely migrated to other regions of Colombia and to neighboring countries (*Economist* 2003).

Transnational Criminal Flows and Networks

Criminal flows and networks constitute the second security problem that pervades the region. A major portion of the global cultivation, processing, and trafficking of cocaine (and to a lesser extent, heroin) are concentrated in the Andean countries. Colombia's borders with Brazil, Ecuador, Panama, Peru, and Venezuela operate as transit routes for the illegal passage of chemical precursors, cocaine and heroin, arms and munitions, and currency. Black markets in drugs and arms encourage corruption, the privatization of security, and the erosion of governmental authority (Serrano 2000). Although the arms trade has been fueled primarily by drug- and insurgent-related activities, it also furnishes weapons to common criminal organizations, creating extremely complex dynamics that enmesh a wide variety of transnational actors in highly interdependent, multidimensional relations. Transnational criminal networks are drawn to weak state or illegitimate governmental settings that provide favorable conditions for their illegal activities, given high levels of corruptibility as well as the incapacity to exercise traditional functions, such as the administration of security.

Arms transactions involving a wide array of state and nonstate actors are commonplace in the region. Although official figures are not available, arms, munitions, and explosives belonging to the armed forces of Ecuador and Venezuela have been confiscated periodically from illegal Colombian armed actors. In mid-2002, it was revealed that a year earlier the Autodefensas Unidas de Colombia had received a shipment of three thousand AK-47 rifles and 5 million bullets from Nicaragua. Nicaragua sold the weapons to a legal Israeli arms dealer stationed in Guatemala, who had allegedly signed a contract to sell them to Panama (Durán Pastrana 2003, 1–2). The now-infamous Peruvian-Jordanian arms scandal of 2000, in which national intelligence director Vladimiro Montesinos was found to be involved in arms sales to the FARC, vividly illustrates the linkages that illicit flows build between distinct legal and illegal actors (*El Tiempo* 2000, 1–11).

Arms for drugs exchanges also involve countless participants in complex barter arrangements that diffuse throughout the region and spill outside it. In the Colombian case, drug revenues constitute a significant source of income for guerrillas and paramilitaries (Rangel 2000). In the specific case of the FARC, in addition to suspected links with international terrorist organizations such as the Irish Republican Army, there is mounting evidence that links the guerrillas with the Russian mafia, which is actively involved in global arms, drugs, and money-laundering operations (Bagley 2003). One smuggling ring in use between 1999 and 2000 swapped large shipments of arms originating from the Russian black market for cocaine provided by the FARC for sale in Europe. In Jordan, used for refueling on both routes, corrupt governmental officials were bribed with cocaine. Brazilian drug lord Luiz Fernando Da Costa (alias Fernandinho), who was captured in Colombia in early 2001, was also discovered to have played an important intermediary role in these transactions (Bagley 2003, 124–26). Weapons left over from the contra war in Nicaragua are also smuggled regularly into Colombia through Panamanian territory and traded to the FARC in exchange for cocaine (Reuters 2000).

Brazil offers another example of how drug and arms flows and networks challenge conventional notions of the Andean region as a discrete unit. In addition to being a major cocaine distribution and transshipment area for drugs sent to Europe, the Brazilian Amazon, because of the virtual absence of the state, has become a haven for criminal activities. Brazil's role in the drug-traffic chain allowed for the emergence of drug gangs that virtually control the favelas of cities such as Rio de Janeiro and São Paulo (Leeds 1996; Bagley 2003). The transposing of drug- and arms-related transactions has allowed favela-based groups to increase both the scope of their operations and their relative power (Leeds 1996, 56). In addition to aggravating existing levels of violence in the favelas, drug-related corruption in Brazil has skyrocketed, while parallel power and security patterns have emerged in areas controlled by criminal organizations.

U.S. Role and Policies

The third regional security dynamic is related to what is commonly referred to as the war on drugs. Since the mid-1980s, when illicit narcotics were declared a threat to U.S. national security, the drug question has been central to relations with the Andean region. With the Cold War's end, the bulk of U.S. military assistance earmarked for Latin America shifted from anticommunism to counternarcotics programs, primarily in drug-producing countries such as Bolivia, Colombia, and Peru. Washington's antidrug policies consist of a repressive, prohibitionist orientation and military strategies that have changed little in the past few decades (Tickner, forthcoming).

As early as 1990, the United States began to develop and execute strategies at the level of the region, thereby helping to give shape to the Andes as a distinctive security unit. The first Bush administration Andeanized counternarcotics efforts in recognition of the dangers posed by illicit drugs in the subregion to both internal stability in these countries and U.S. security interests (Tokatlian 1995). The war on drugs was also expanded, primarily through direct interdiction in coca-producing areas and intensive U.S. and Andean military involvement in antidrug efforts (Bagley 1992; Washington Office on Latin America 1993). The most recent stage of U.S. counternarcotics endeavors, based in Colombia, has also broadened into an Andean strategy with regionwide consequences. In its 2002 counternarcotics budget, President George W. Bush jettisoned Plan Colombia in favor of the broader Andean Regional Initiative.[8] Washington's interest in assuaging the spillover of its Colombian strategy in neighboring countries has had the effect of drawing all of the region's states and societies into a regional drug war dynamic.

In practice, Washington's association of drugs with its own national security has meant that the ways the Andean countries have addressed the drug problem derive substantially from the U.S. approach. Coercive diplomatic strategies, among them the certification mechanism and the approval or withdrawal of economic and military support, have been central to Washington's success in assuring compliance with its policies. Efforts to multilateralize counternarcotics strategies in the Andes have been short lived and of limited impact (Pardo and Tickner 2000, 303–9). In 1990 and 1992, drug summits were held in Cartagena and San Antonio, Texas, respectively, to discuss cooperative strategies for confronting the illegal drug problem.[9] America's commitment to assist Bolivia, Colombia, Ecuador, and Peru in diversifying their exports materialized with the approval of the Andean Trade Preference Act in 1991. However, concrete, sustainable mechanisms for replacing Washington's unilateral approach to drugs never materialized.[10]

The construction of the drug issue as the primordial security risk in the region displaces other long-term objectives, including the strengthening of democratic institutions, the defense of human rights, the reduction of poverty, and the preservation of the environment. Andean acceptance of Washington's antidrug model has relegated the legitimate social, cultural, and economic aspects of drug cultivation to a secondary level of concern within the national drug-control strategy. Crop substitution and alternative development programs have been implemented throughout the region since the late 1970s. Nevertheless, viable, sustainable substitutes for coca cultivation have not been forthcoming (Thoumi 2002, 363–66), as recurrent social protests and the cyclical resumption of illegal crop cultivation in the coca-growing regions of Bolivia, Colombia, and Peru well indicate. Crop eradication, the backbone of the American drug strategy, has created a cyclical balloon effect among the Andean nations, by which illicit crops are simply ping-ponged between countries and distinct areas within them.[11]

In tandem with the drug war logic itself, increased U.S. military presence in Colombia and, to a lesser extent, Ecuador following the establishment of a forward operating location at the Manta air force base,[12] constitutes the basis for overlay (Buzan 1991, 198–208). Overlay consists of the suppression of local security patterns in the Andes and their replacement by U.S. imperatives. Notwithstanding the regional scope of its security agenda, Washington's counternarcotics strategies are based on bilateral bargaining on a country-by-country basis, encouraging zero-sum competition between the Andean nations. Instead of providing incentives to develop consensual, multilateral policies that reflect the interests (security and otherwise) of drug-producing countries, the war on drugs essentially pits each against the other in the bid for U.S. financial, military, and commercial support. The high levels of interdependence that underlie the drug issue as a common problem faced by the region as a whole have thus given way to complex forms of anomie that repress the identification of shared problems and interests and the consequent development of a regionwide response to Washington's Andean agenda.

Two additional factors accentuate the pertinence of the overlay concept for understanding Andean security dynamics. First, the global war on terrorism and the termination of the peace process with the FARC in Colombia in early 2002 have had profound effects on U.S. strategies in the region. Not only is the Colombian conflict viewed today as an instance of terrorist warfare, but neighboring countries have also come under pressure from both Bogotá and Washington to join their counterterrorist efforts in Colombia. To date, this particular facet of U.S. antiterrorist strategy in the region has been met with a tepid reception. Nevertheless, the potential insertion of Andean security arrangements into the war on terrorism reaffirms the impact of U.S. policy on regional security agendas and cooperation.

Second, the creation of a stable security environment in the Andes has become a priority for Washington. In addition to the growing strength of Hugo Chávez's regional Bolivarian aspirations and opposition to U.S. global diplomacy, oil resources in Venezuela, Colombia, and Ecuador are of increasing interest (Dunning and Wirpsa 2004; Washington Office on Latin America 2003). Security strategies in the wake of the September 11 attacks have included efforts to diversify U.S. oil imports away from the Middle East. Washington earmarked US$99 million in 2003 to train and equip two elite army battalions in Colombia to protect the Caño Limón–Coveñas pipeline, 44 percent of whose crude oil belongs to Occidental Petroleum. US$147 million has been requested in the 2004 foreign operations budget. Oil-rich portions of Ecuador and Venezuela also border the Colombian armed conflict. Together, counterterrorist activities and the pipeline protection program signal the expansion of the United States' military role in the region, with important repercussions for Andean security dynamics.

A New Andean Security Map

The accumulation and convergence of processes linking up distinct actors, problems, and spaces in relational and interdependent ways suggest the possibility of a new Andean security cartography. The conventional view of the Andean crisis, rooted in shared, but ultimately local political, institutional, and socioeconomic instability, is inadequate to capture the scope of regional turmoil. Andean security is an essential component of crisis, in that national-level problems are made more intransigent as they are exacerbated and even transformed by transregional security dynamics and the involvement of extranational nonstate actors. Not only is the Andean security question far more than the sum of five acute domestic situations, but it is also a highly fluid and changing scenario that is not necessarily synchronized with a static map of the region.

The principal security dynamics in the Andes contradict a standard geographical representation by involving a diverse array of state, substate, transnational, and global actors not normally considered to be Andean. The argument can be made, for example, that actors as unlikely as the U.S. military, Brazilian drug lords, and the Russian mafia are increasingly key players in the Andean security game. Indeed, that some of the most pressing security issues in the region not only involve non-Andean actors but also spill out into other non-Andean spaces underscores the disconnect between the Andean region in its traditional usage and our call for a transregional approach to the area's security problems.

Many of the specific security processes operating in the region suggest that there are intraregional orders that encompass distinct geographic spaces and actors. For instance, illicit drug activities span certain subregional territories but not others. The Colombian conflict has drawn in specific regional actors and areas, but cannot be said to affect the totality of what is commonly understood as the Andean region. U.S. overlay, for its part, is more prevalent in certain countries, and in certain issues, than others. In other words, the notion of the region itself is not a fixed one, but rather varies according to the security issue at stake as well as the primary actors involved.

A third and related reason for the disjuncture between what we see as the Andean transregional security dynamic and Andean geography is that the ways outside actors see and act with regard to the region is constitutive of it. What Washington or the European Union consider to be Andean, in combination with the policies that the two adopt toward the region, acts to change the meaning of what is a generally accepted regional unit. The Andean Regional Initiative, for example, which targets particular countries, issue areas, and strategies, serves to politically construct from without a counterdrug region that may vary according to U.S. drug war imperatives.

Certainly, the processes identified here are not all equally regional in scope. Some of the national-level characteristics are not shared uniformly by all countries, while some of the transregional processes fit certain spaces and actors better than others. In spite of these qualifications, our tentative conclusion is that a comprehensive representation of security dynamics in the Andean region does not mesh well with what is traditionally understood in geographic terms as the Andean region. Remapping the region according to its diverse security threats and processes would generate an alternative cartography of the Andes. Geographic imaging of sociopolitical processes constitutes a heuristic device not only for visualizing the transregional nature of insecurity but also for helping policy makers think regionally about solutions to problems for which nationally based strategies are destined to fall short.

Notes

1. Among the most important conceptual statements on the topic of post–Cold War security are Matthews (1989); Buzan (1991); Lipschutz (1995); Buzan, Waever, and de Wilde (1998); and Ayoob (1995).

2. A regional level of analysis is not new to international relations. Among the most prominent of these models are the region (Deutsch 1957; Nye 1971), the security com-

munity (Adler and Barnett 1998b), and the security complex (Buzan 1991; Morgan 1997).

3. To what extent U.S. imperatives have seeped down into the general Andean population is mixed, however. On the one hand, social actors involved in coca-growing activities in Bolivia and Peru have rejected the U.S.-imposed counternarcotics posture. Conversely, within Colombian society there is greater support for antidrug policies.

4. The spillover argument views the Colombian crisis as a regional contaminant, whereas our transregional approach places Colombian conflict-related insecurities within the broader context of transnational interactions. See Rabasa and Chalk (2001) and Millett (2002).

5. Following the U.S. invasion of Panama in 1989, the country's armed forces were dismantled. The 1999 withdrawal of U.S. troops from the Panama Canal Zone has inflated concerns related to Panama's ability to protect its national territory.

6. For extensive information on the origins, chronology, and operation of this surveillance system, see http://www.sivam.gov.br.

7. A similar effect was produced in Colombia in the mid-1990s as a result of successful manual eradication in both Bolivia and Peru.

8. Although Bolivia, Brazil, Ecuador, Peru, and Panama all receive varying levels of aid through this program, Colombia continues to be the primary recipient of U.S. counternarcotics assistance. See Center for International Policy (2002) for disaggregated amounts.

9. Bolivia, Colombia, Peru, and the United States participated in the first summit meeting; Ecuador, Mexico, and Venezuela joined them in San Antonio.

10. Efforts were in fact made to create a counternarcotics strategy at the hemispheric level. Specifically, the Plan of Action of the 1998 Summit of the Americas (Santiago, Chile) included a proposal to create a multilateral evaluation mechanism to be administered by the Inter-American Commission for the Control and Abuse of Drugs of the Organization of American States. Notwithstanding its ambitious nature, until now severe budgetary and human resource restraints with the commission, in conjunction with the Organization of American States' limited power vis-à-vis the United States, have acted to reduce the evaluation mechanism's scope and importance.

11. For the first time in nearly a decade, the U.S. Department of State (2003) reported reductions in the total acreage of coca cultivations in Bolivia, Colombia, and Peru for 2002. However, reductions in southern Colombia contrasted with slight increases in Peru and Bolivia, as well as the appearance of cultivations in different regions of Colombia.

12. In December 1999, Ecuador signed a ten-year agreement whereby the United States was granted use of the air force base to conduct counternarcotics air surveillance and reconnaissance missions. Three other forward-operating locations are located in Curacao, Aruba, and El Salvador.

Bibliography

Adler, Emanuel, and Michael Barnett. 1998a. A framework for the study of security communities. In *Security Communities*, ed. Emanuel Adler and Michael Barnett, 29–65. Cambridge: Cambridge University Press.
———, eds. 1998b. *Security Communities*. Cambridge: Cambridge University Press.

Ayoob, Mohammed. 1995. *The third world security predicament: State making, regional conflict and the international system.* Boulder, CO: Lynne Rienner.

Bagley, Bruce. 1992. Myths of militarization: Enlisting armed forces in the war on drugs. In *Drug policy in the Americas,* ed. Peter H. Smith, 129–50. Boulder, CO: Westview.

———. 2003. La globalización de la delincuencia organizada. *Foreign Affairs en Español* 3 (2): 110–36.

Bejarano, Ana Maria, and Eduardo Pizarro. 2001. The crisis of democracy in Colombia: From "restricted" democracy to "besieged" democracy. Paper presented at the Conference on Advances and Setbacks in the Third Wave of Democratization, Kellogg Institute for International Studies, University of Notre Dame, Notre Dame, Indiana, April 23–24.

Brenner, Neil. 1999. Beyond state-centrism? Space, territoriality, and geographical scale in globalization studies. *Theory and Society* 28:39–78.

Buzan, Barry. 1991. *People, states and fear: An agenda for international security in the post-cold war era.* Boulder, CO: Lynne Rienner.

Buzan, Barry, Ole Waever and Jaap de Wilde. 1998. *Security: A new framework for analysis.* Boulder, CO: Lynne Rienner.

Center for International Policy. 2002. U.S. military and police aid: The current outlook. http://www.ciponline.org.

CEPAL (Comisión Económica para América Latina y el Caribe). 2001. *Una década de luces y sombras. América Latina y el Caribe en los años noventa.* Bogotá, Colombia: Naciones Unidas-Cepal-Alfaomega.

———. 2002. *Panorama social de América Latina 2001–2002.* Santiago, Chile: Naciones Unidas-Cepal.

Chalmers, Douglas, Carlos Vilas, Katherine Hite, Scott Martin, Kerianne Piester, and Monique Segarra, eds. 1997. *The new politics of inequality in Latin America.* New York: Oxford University Press.

Clark, Ian. 1999. *Globalization and international relations theory.* Oxford: Oxford University Press.

Collier, David, and Steven Levitsky. 1997. Democracy with adjectives: Conceptual innovation in comparative research. *World Politics* 49 (3): 430–51.

Conaghan, Catherine, and James Malloy. 1995. *Unsettling statecraft: Democracy and neoliberalism in the Andes.* Pittsburgh, PA: University of Pittsburgh Press.

Consultoría para los Derechos Humanos y el Desplazamiento (Codhes). 2003. La otra guerra: destierro y redoblamiento. Informe sobre desplazamiento forzado, conflicto armado y derechos humanos en el 2002. *Boletín* 44, April 28.

Deustch, Karl. 1957. *Political community and the North Atlantic area.* Princeton, NJ: Princeton University Press.

Diamond, Larry. 1997. Is the third wave of democratization over? The imperative of consolidation. Working Paper 237, The Helen Kellogg Institute for International Studies, University of Notre Dame, March.

Dunning, Thad, and Leslie Wirpsa. 2004. Oil and the political economy of conflict in Colombia and beyond: A linkages approach. *Geopolitics* 9 (1): 81–108.

Durán Pastrana, Jorge Luis. 2002. Arsenal burló a 4 países. *El Tiempo,* April 25.

El Tiempo. 2000. Conexión peruana de las Farc. August 23.

Economist. 2003. The balloon goes up. http://www.economist.com. March 6.

Fajnzylber, Pablo, Daniel Lederman, and Norman Loayzz. 2002. Inequality and violent crime. *Journal of Law and Economics* 45 (1): 1–40.

Falk, Richard. 1999. *Predatory globalization: A critique*. London: Blackwell Publishers.

Forero, Alvaro. 2003 Colombia's long civil war spreads to Venezuela. *New York Times*, http://www.nytimes.com/2003/06/01/international/americas/01VENE.html. June 1.

Guisti, Roberto. 2003. Guerrilleros en zona militar. *El Tiempo*, May 17.

Gurtov, Mel. 1999. *Global politics in the human interest*. Boulder, CO: Lynne Rienner.

Gutiérrez, Francisco. 2003. Los tiempos de las involuciones democráticas. Crisis States Programme Working Paper 25. London: Destin–London School of Economics. http://www.crisisstates.com/Publications/wp25.htm.

Hurrell, Andrew. 1998. Security in Latin America. *International Affairs* 74 (3): 529–46.

International Crisis Group. 2003. Colombia and its neighbors: The tentacles of instability. Bogotá, Colombia: *Latin America* 3, April 8.

Job, Brian. 1992. The insecurity dilemma: National, regime, and state securities in the third world. In *The insecurity dilemma: National security of third world states*, ed. Brian Job, 11–35. Boulder, CO: Lynne Rienner.

Kacowicz, Arie. 1998. *Zones of peace in the third world: South America and West Africa in comparative perspective*. Albany: State University of New York.

Keohane, Robert. 2002. The globalization of informal violence, theories of world politics, and "the liberalism of fear." In *Understanding September 11*, ed. Craig Calhoun, Paul Price, and Ashley Timmer, 77–91. New York: New Press.

Klare, Michael, and Yogesh Chandrani, eds. 1998. *World security: Challenges for a new century*. New York: St. Martin's.

Lake, David A., and Patrick M. Morgan. 1997. Introduction. In *Regional orders: building security in a new world*, ed. David A. Lake and Patrick M. Morgan, 1–19. University Park: Pennsylvania State University Press.

Lambsdorff, Johan Graf. 1999. Corruption in empirical research—a review. Transparency International Working Paper, November.

Leeds, Elizabeth. 1996. Cocaine and parallel polities in the Brazilian urban periphery: Constraints on local-level development. *Latin American Research Review* 31 (3): 47–83.

Lipschutz, Ronnie D., ed. 1995. *On security*. New York: Columbia University Press.

Mainwaring, Scott, and Timothy Scully, eds. 1995. *Building democratic institutions: Party systems in Latin America*. Stanford, CA: Stanford University Press.

Mann, Michael. 1986. *The sources of social power: A history of power from the beginning to A.D. 1760*. Vol. 1. New York: Cambridge University Press.

Mason, Ann. 2003. Colombia's democratic security policy: Public order in the security tripod. *Security Dialogue* 34 (4): 391–409.

———. 2005. Constructing authority alternatives on the periphery: Vignettes from Colombia. *International Political Science Review* 26 (1): 37–54.

Matthews, Jessica. 1989. Redefining security. *Foreign Affairs* 68 (2): 162–77.

McSweeney, Bill. 1999. *Security, identity and interests: A sociology of international relations*. Cambridge: Cambridge University Press.

Millett, Richard. 2002. Colombia's conflicts: The spill-over effects of a wider war. *North-South Agenda*, North-South Center working papers series 57, September.

Morgan, Patrick M. 1997. Regional security complexes and regional orders. In *Regional orders: Building security in a new world*, ed. David Lake and Patrick Morgan, 20–42. University Park: Pennsylvania State University Press.

Munck, Gerardo. 2003. Gobernabilidad Democrática a Comienzos del Siglo XXI: Una Perspectiva Latinoamericana. In *La Crisis Colombiana: Más Que un Conflicto Armado y un Proceso de Paz*, ed. Ann Mason and Luis Javier Orjuela, 45–59. Bogotá, Colombia: Departamento de ciencia política–CESO–UNIANDES–Fundación Alejandro Angel Escobar.

Nye, Joseph S. 1971. Peace in parts: Integration and conflict in regional organization. Boston: Little, Brown.

O'Donnell, Guillermo. 1996. Otra institucionalización. *La Política. Revista de Estudios sobre el Estado y la Sociedad* 2: 5–27.

———. 1999. Horizontal accountability in new polyarchies. In *The self-restraining state: Power and accountability in new democracies*, ed. Andreas Schedler, Larry Diamond, and Marc F. Plattner, 29–51. Boulder, CO: Lynne Reinner.

Pardo, Diana, and Arlene B. Tickner. 2000. El problema del narcotráfico en el sistema interamericano. In *Sistema interamericano y democracia. Antecedentes históricos y tendencias futuras*, ed. Arlene B. Tickner, 291–309. Bogotá, Colombia: CEI-Ediciones Uniandes-OEA.

Perina, Ruben. 2000. El régimen democrático interamericano: el papel de la OEA. In *Sistema interamericano y democracia. Antecedentes históricos y tendencias futuras*, ed. Arlene B. Tickner, 311–76. Bogotá, Colombia: CEI-Ediciones Uniandes-OEA.

Rabasa, Angel, and Peter Chalk. 2001. *Colombian labyrinth: The synergy of drugs and insurgency and its implications for regional stability*. Santa Monica, CA: Rand.

Rangel, Alfredo. 2000. Parasites and predators: Guerrillas and the insurrection economy of Colombia. *Journal of International Affairs* 53 (2): 577–607.

Reuters. 2000. Panama arms trade a question of supply and demand. http://www.reuters.com.

Serrano, Mónica. 2000. Transnational crime in the Western Hemisphere. In *The future of inter-American relations*, ed. Jorge I. Domínguez, 87–110. New York: Routledge.

Sheahan, John. 2001. Growth and distribution in the Andes: Long-term strains and recurrent crises. Paper presented at the Social Science Research Council's workshop on the Crisis in the Andes, University of North Carolina at Chapel Hill, September 10–11.

Smith, William, and Roberto Korzeniewicz. 1997. Latin America and the second great transformation. In *Politics, social change and economic restructuring in Latin America*, ed. William Smith and Roberto Korzeniewicz, 1–20. Miami, FL: North-South Center.

Terriff, Terry, Stuart Croft, Lucy James, and Patrick M. Morgan. 1999. *Security studies today*. Cambridge, UK: Polity Press.

Thoumi, Francisco E. 2002. *El imperio de la droga. Narcotráfico, economía y sociedad en los Andes*. Bogotá, Colombia: IEPRI-Planeta.

Tickner, Arlene B. Forthcoming. U.S. foreign policy in Colombia: Bizarre side-effects of the "war on drugs." In *Democracy, human rights and peace in Colombia*, ed. Gustavo Gallón and Christopher Welna. Notre Dame: University of Notre Dame Press (Kellogg Series).

Tickner, Arlene, and Ann Mason. 2003. Mapping transregional structures in the Andean region. *Alternatives* 28 (3): 359–91.

Tokatlian, Juan Gabriel. 1995. *Drogas, dilemas y dogmas: Estados Unidos y la narcocriminalidad organizada en Colombia*. Bogotá, Colombia: CEI-Tercer Mundo.

Transparency International. 2003. Corruption Perceptions Index. http://www.transparency.org/cpi/2003/cpi2003.en.html.

United Nations Development Program. 2003. *UNDP human development report 2003*. http://www.undp.org/hdr2003.

U.S. Department of State. 2003. *International narcotics drug control strategy report 2002*. Washington, DC: GPO.

Walter, Barbara F., and Jack Snyder, eds. 1999. *Civil wars, insecurity, and intervention*. New York: Columbia University Press.

Washington Office on Latin America (WOLA). 1993. *¿Peligro inminente? Las fuerzas armadas de Estados Unidos y la guerra contra las drogas*. Washington, DC: WOLA.

———. 2003. Protecting the pipeline: The U.S. military mission expands. *Colombia Monitor*, May.

Whitehead, Laurence. 2001. Bolivia and the Viability of Democracy. *Journal of Democracy* 12 (2): 6–16.

Williams, Phil. 1998. Transnational criminal organizations and international security. In *World security: Challenges for a new century*, ed. Michael T. Klare and Yogesh Chandrani, 249–72. New York: St. Martin's.

World Bank. 2000. *World development report 2000/2001*. Washington, DC: World Bank.

Zakaria, Fareed. 1997. The rise of illiberal democracy. *Foreign Affairs* 76 (6): 22–43.

The Andean Economies

Questions of Poverty, Growth, and Equity

JOHN SHEAHAN

HE FIVE ANDEAN COUNTRIES CONSIDERED HERE SHARE
several structural characteristics that make it difficult to achieve anything resembling equitable patterns of development. That does not
make them radically different from the majority of Latin American countries, though they are on the high side of regional averages for poverty.
Between 1980 and 2000 income per capita fell for all of them except
Colombia. That put them all, even the previously higher-income
Venezuela, at levels of income below the average for Latin America. They
have in varying degrees been making some of the kinds of changes that
could open up a more promising future, especially in Bolivia, but have not
so far found effective ways to deal with their most serious problems.

High levels of chronic poverty, and the worsening effect of long-term
decreases in real income per capita, surely contributed a great deal to the
severity of social conflict and the sense of crisis in the Andean countries.
These strains were greatly aggravated in the 1980–2000 period, and on
through 2003, by adverse external factors that have at least temporarily

changed for the better. The more important question is whether or not the countries can change the underlying structural conditions that make them so dependent on external capital and the course of world markets for primary products. That is in part a matter of effective economic policy—no country is going to make real headway with the self-defeating economic policies of the past—but more fundamentally it requires a sustained effort to raise the economic and social mobility of the large shares of these populations that have been left out of opportunities for meaningful education, adequate health care, productive employment, and anything like equitable participation in national income.

Economic Performance

Levels of poverty and rates of growth keep changing in response to interactions between domestic and external forces. The decade of the 1980s was particularly difficult because world financial flows turned adverse after the Mexican debt crisis of 1982: the incidence of poverty increased for all the Andean countries in this decade. In the 1990s, up to 1997, capital inflows increased rapidly, economic growth resumed, and poverty fell. From 1997, capital flows headed down again in response to the financial crises in East Asia and Russia, and incomes fell in all the Andean countries except Bolivia.[1] If attention is focused on external causation, poverty in the Andes seems to float up and down on the waves made by world financial markets. That is a genuine part of the story, but only the surface part.

Whatever the outside world economy is doing, the incidence of poverty is consistently much higher in Bolivia and Ecuador than the average for the Andean group and in the group as a whole compared to the most successful Latin American countries. These persistent contrasts reflect both differences in productive capacity and differences in social concern. Effective social concern has been higher in Costa Rica and Uruguay than in the Andean countries, but not remarkably different in degree among them. For the group, the limits of productive capacity seem to be dominant. The hopeful side is that productive capacity can be increased: slowly through investment in human resources and capital equipment and sometimes more rapidly through improved management of the economy, more effective public institutions, or reduction of insecurity and social conflict. Productive capacity can also deteriorate badly when these underlying determinants change in harmful ways.

TABLE 4.1

ESTIMATES OF THE INCIDENCE OF POVERTY IN FIVE ANDEAN COUNTRIES
AND IN LATIN AMERICA AS A WHOLE, SELECTED YEARS

	Population below poverty line (%)		
	about 1990[a]	1997	1999
National measures			
Bolivia	—	—	60.6
Colombia	56.1	50.9	54.9
Peru (CEPAL)	—	47.6	48.6
Peru (PNUD)	55.3 (1991)	50.7	54.1 (2000)
Venezuela	40.0	48.1	49.4
Latin America and Caribbean region	48.3	43.5	43.8
Urban areas only			
Bolivia	53.1	52.3	48.7
Colombia	52.7	45.0	50.6
Ecuador	62.1	56.2	63.6
Peru	—	33.7	36.1
Venezuela	38.8	—	—
Latin America and Caribbean region	41.4	36.5	37.1

Sources: CEPAL (2002, 211–12); alternative estimates for Peru from PNUD-Peru (2002, 18).
Note: The CEPAL estimates are standardized to provide comparability among countries. The estimates for Peru by the PNUD (Peruvian office of the United Nations Development Program) provide added information on change in Peru but they are not comparable to the estimates for the other countries.
[a]Years in first column are 1989 for Bolivia, 1991 for Colombia and Peru.

Changes in the Incidence of Poverty

Nationwide estimates of changes in poverty during the 1990s, including rural as well as urban areas, are available for only three of the Andean countries. For the favorable period from 1990 to 1997, two of them, Colombia and Peru, achieved decreases parallel to that for Latin America as a whole (table 4.1). Bolivia and Ecuador, with measures limited to urban areas, also fit the regional pattern, with decreasing poverty between 1990 and 1997. Venezuela was the only case of increasing poverty during this period.

When capital flows turned down again after 1997, the incidence of poverty for Latin America increased, but only to a very slight degree, by 0.6 percentage points. For most of the Andean countries poverty worsened more seriously, especially in Colombia, in Peru as measured in table

4.1 by the PNUD (Peruvian office of the United Nations Development Program), and in Ecuador as estimated for urban areas. Bolivia was more successful: in contrast to the other Andean countries, and to Latin America as a whole, its urban poverty was reduced by 3.6 percentage points. Bolivia was doing something more positive than were the others. Still, when nationwide estimates of its poverty became available for 1999, it stood out with the highest incidence among the four Andean countries with national measures for that year.

Measures by the International Monetary Fund (IMF) of net external financing for developing countries in the Western Hemisphere show a decrease of two-thirds between 1998 and 2002 (IMF 2003, 220). Accordingly, this period was not favorable for reduction of poverty. Data available for Peru report an increase of 7 percentage points between 1997 and 2001 (Herrera 2002, 82). That more than wiped out the improvement from 1990 to 1997. Fortunately, the incidence of the much more severe level of extreme poverty did not worsen to anything like that of overall poverty. It increased too but only from 18.2 to 19.5 percent. That difference may have been due, at least in part, to active social programs directed specifically to geographical areas characterized by particularly high incidences of extreme poverty (Sheahan 2003, 20–24).

If the volatility of capital flows is ever to be moderated, the main part of the job needs to be done by the world financial centers and international institutions. Given the low likelihood under current conditions that

TABLE 4.2

LEVELS OF INCOME PER CAPITA IN 2000, ADJUSTED FOR PURCHASING POWER PARITY, AND PERCENTAGE CHANGES IN GDP PER CAPITA FROM 1980 TO 2000 IN FIVE ANDEAN COUNTRIES AND LATIN AMERICA AND THE CARIBBEAN REGION

	GNP per capita, 2000 (in dollars adjusted for purchasing power)	Change in GDP per capita, 1980–2000 (%)
Bolivia	2,424	−6
Colombia	6,248	+23
Ecuador	3,203	−8
Peru	4,799	−8
Venezuela	5,794	−17
Latin America and Caribbean region	7,273	+9

Source: Derived from World Bank (2002a).
Note: GDP, gross domestic product; GNP, gross national product.

they will do anything effective about it, the best hope for the Andean countries to hold down the damage would be to aim at reducing their own dependence on external capital. This is neither easy nor impossible.

Economic Growth and Retreat

Economic growth almost invariably decreases poverty, though the degree to which it does so varies greatly according to the particular structural conditions and economic policies of each country. The first problem for the Andean countries is that they have not had much growth in recent decades. Although in Latin America as a whole output per capita increased by 9 percent between 1980 and 2000, it fell by 6 to 8 percent in three of the Andean countries and by a brutal 17 percent in Venezuela (table 4.2). As of 1970 Venezuela had by far the highest income of the Andean countries, well above the Latin American average. But after decreasing for three decades it fell below the regional average and even below the level of Colombia.

Table 4.3 brings out the instability of growth rates for specified periods within these two decades. All these countries except Colombia suffered falling gross domestic product (GDP) per capita during the course of the 1980s, under the impact of the debt crisis. As world financial conditions improved again, up to 1997, all five countries managed to raise their output per capita. The Latin American growth rate recovered from its nega-

TABLE 4.3

GROWTH RATES OF GDP PER CAPITA FOR SELECTED PERIODS IN FIVE ANDEAN COUNTRIES, COSTA RICA, AND MEXICO, AND AVERAGES FOR LATIN AMERICA AND THE CARIBBEAN REGION

| | Average annual rates of growth (from data in 1995 U.S. dollars) | | | |
	1980–90	1990–97	1997–2000	1980–2000
Bolivia	-1.9	1.8	0.3	-0.3
Colombia	1.3	2.0	-2.1	1.0
Ecuador	-0.5	1.0	-3.5	-0.4
Peru	-2.9	3.4	-0.6	-0.4
Venezuela	-1.7	1.1	-2.9	-0.9
Costa Rica	-0.5	2.5	3.9	1.2
Mexico	-0.3	1.0	3.7	0.8
Latin America and Caribbean region	-0.8	2.2	0.4	0.4

Source: Derived from World Bank (2002).
Note: GDP, gross domestic product.

tive value in the 1980s to a positive 2.2 percent for 1990–1997. Peru, which had the worst deterioration of all in the 1980s, moved to a growth rate well above the regional average. But then, when world financial conditions worsened again from 1997, the Andean countries were set back much more seriously than Latin America as a whole: the wider region maintained a positive growth rate while income per capita fell in all of the Andean countries except Bolivia. That positive growth rate for the region for 1997–2000 was influenced particularly by the striking performances of Costa Rica and Mexico, included as contrasting examples in table 4.3.

Both capital flows and prices of primary product exports remained relatively weak from 2000 to 2003: for these years, Latin American GDP growth remained too low to keep up with the increase in population. But in 2004 an old-fashioned boom for exports of primary commodities took over, pulling up prices and revenue from commodity exports in response to strongly rising demand from China and the United States. GDP for Ecuador and Venezuela rose spectacularly, thanks mainly to their oil exports, and that of Peru almost as rapidly, especially through gains from copper and gold. For the whole period 2000–2004, cumulative GDP growth for all the Andean countries except Venezuela was distinctly higher than the average for Latin America (table 4.4).

The current boom may last some time, and should do some good, but at the same time it underscores the high degree of instability that these countries have to cope with.

TABLE 4.4

ESTIMATES OF THE GROWTH OF GDP IN FIVE ANDEAN COUNTRIES AND LATIN AMERICA
AND THE CARIBBEAN REGION

	Annual changes in GDP (%)				Cumulative total change (%)
	2001	2002	2003	2004	2000–2004
Bolivia	1.5	2.8	2.5	3.8	11.0
Colombia	1.5	1.9	4.0	4.0	11.9
Ecuador	5.1	3.4	2.7	6.6	19.0
Peru	0.2	4.9	3.8	5.1	14.7
Venezuela	3.4	-8.9	-7.6	17.3	2.1
Latin America and Caribbean region	0.2	-0.1	1.4	5.8	7.4

Source: Federal Reserve Bank of Atlanta (2005).
Note: Estimates for 2004 are subject to considerable revision (and earlier figures to possible revision as well).

On any list of fundamental weaknesses of the Andean countries, their excessive dependence on external markets for basic commodities and on foreign capital should rank high. It is true that their growth rates pick up well when capital inflows increase, even in the absence of a commodity boom, and that positive side could conceivably compensate for the setbacks when the inflows slow down or go into reverse. But for the 1980–2000 period the net result of swings in both directions was not favorable, at least as measured by any gains in per capita income. And even if the long-term balance were more favorable, these repeated setbacks would still intensify the social and political strains on these societies.

Should this kind of instability be considered a specifically Andean problem or a more general Latin American problem? In one sense it is clearly wider than an Andean problem: the growth rate for Latin America as a whole rose and fell in parallel to the changes in world financial markets. It is the severity of the consequences that differ for the Andean group. For Latin America, growth remained positive from 1997 to 2000 even while incomes were falling in all the Andean countries except Bolivia. Costa Rica and Mexico were responsible for much of that relative success outside of the Andean region: as shown in table 4.3, they both managed to raise their growth rates in the 1997–2000 period of sharply reduced capital flows.

Distribution of Income

For Latin America as a whole, poverty has been aggravated by the region's high level of inequality. An exceptionally thorough comparative study by Deininger and Squire (1996) for the World Bank reviewed every estimate they considered valid from the 1960s through the first half of the 1990s. Table 4.5 gives their averages for the Andean countries and for five developing regions, using two different indicators of inequality: Gini coefficients and the ratios of incomes between the highest quintile and the lowest quintile in each distribution.

By regions, Latin America stands out with the highest degree of inequality, on both of the two measures. Among the Andean countries, Colombia had the greatest inequality, as measured by both the Gini coefficient and the ratio of quintile incomes. It was the only Andean country for which either measure was above the Latin American average. These averages include the first half of the 1990s but do not give a picture of changes through the decade. A different set of estimates, by the Comisión Económica Para América Latina y el Caribe (CEPAL), gives measures for various early years and for 1999 (table 4.6).[2]

TABLE 4.5
ESTIMATES OF AVERAGE DEGREES OF INEQUALITY FOR OBSERVATIONS
FROM THE 1960S TO THE MID-1990S IN FIVE ANDEAN COUNTRIES
AND FIVE REGIONS OF DEVELOPING COUNTRIES

	Gini coefficients	Ratio of incomes, highest to lowest quintiles
Andean countries		
Bolivia	.42	9/1
Colombia	.52	14/1
Fcuador	.43	10/1
Peru	.48	9/1
Venezuela	.44	11/1
Developing regions		
Latin America and Caribbean	.50	16/1
Sub-Saharan Africa	.45	12/1
Middle East and North Africa	.41	7/1
East Asia and Pacific	.36	7/1
South Asia	.34	6/1

Source: Deininger and Squire (1996, 574–77).

The CEPAL estimates indicate that changes in the 1990s were modest, to the point of practically no change at all for the median. That fits one of the main messages of the World Bank studies: income distributions are in most countries highly persistent (Li, Squire, and Zou 1998). One of the authors' hypotheses about the reason is that higher inequality in the early stages of development gives the rich greater power to stave off pressures for redistribution. That sounds all too likely, but the emphasis on nearly unchangeable degrees of inequality may be overdone: several Latin American countries experienced worsening inequality in the early years following economic liberalization, and both Chile and Colombia have gone through decade-long trends of change (Berry 1997; Sheahan 1998, 30–35, 47–51).

The data in table 4.6 show that three Andean countries experienced some worsening of inequality, slightly so for Peru and Venezuela and more so for urban incomes in Ecuador. In contrast, urban inequality fell in Bolivia: the Gini coefficient decreased by 9 percent. Colombia also seems to show decreased inequality, but that could be misleading because the earliest year reported is 1994, which leaves out the period immediately following economic liberalization. Berry (1997) demonstrates some deterioration in that excluded period.

TABLE 4.6

ESTIMATED CHANGES IN GINI COEFFICIENTS OF INCOME CONCENTRATION
IN THE 1990S IN FIVE ANDEAN COUNTRIES, WITH MEDIANS FOR THE TWELVE
LATIN AMERICAN COUNTRIES THAT REPORT NATIONWIDE MEASURES

| | Gini coefficients of concentration | |
	1990 or nearest year given	1999
Bolivia Urban only	.54 (1989)	.50
National	—	.59
Colombia	.60 (1994)	.57
Ecuador Urban only	.46	.52
Peru (CEPAL)	.53 (1997)	.55
Peru (Alternative estimates[a])	.44 (1991)	.46 (2000)
Venezuela	.47	.50
Median for twelve Latin American countries	.555	.56

Sources: CEPAL (2002, 227–29), for all except alternative estimates for Peru.
Alternative estimates for Peru from Pascó-Font and Saavedra (2001, 217).
[a]Since the CEPAL estimates for Peru only go back to 1997, the alternative estimates are
given to bring out longer-term change. These alternative Gini coefficients are not
comparable to those for the other countries: the methods used give distinctly lower
measures than those of CEPAL.

Grounds for doubt about all comparisons of inequality argue against placing much weight on small differences. Inequality is far higher than it need or should be for all the Andean countries, but in this respect they do not differ greatly from the majority of the other countries of Latin America.

Education, Poverty, and Equity

Inequality in the distribution of income has many causes, some of them socially functional and others harmful, with a major element of just plain luck in between. Some high incomes reflect positive contributions to the society, when they are due to exceptional initiative, organizational capacity, and well-directed effort. Many low incomes may be due to obstacles that are on the contrary harmful to the society: blocked access to education, discrimination that limits economic and social mobility, poor health that could have been prevented or cured by better systems of public health, or insufficient opportunities for productive employment. All such factors operate everywhere, but a society's development is bound to be inequitable if the positive side is only a small part of the picture and the negative factors play important roles. For the Andean countries, as for most of Latin America, inequality of access to education has been particularly damaging for both equity and growth.

Education is no cure-all, but it is clearly one of the most essential conditions for effective participation in the process of economic change and modernization. At the national level, it plays a significant role in determining a country's ability to achieve technological change and compete in world markets. At the individual level, it can raise awareness of opportunity and capacity to acquire specialized skills and thereby to escape poverty: it is closely associated with differences in earnings and productivity. Inequality in access to education has been extreme in Latin America as a whole (with the notable exceptions of Costa Rica, Cuba, and Uruguay), and that inequality has been a major cause of the region's exceptionally high level of income concentration. People left out of education have little chance to escape poverty, even if national income is rising well.

Illiteracy is a strong indicator of being left out. In 1970, that meant 42 percent of the adults in Bolivia and a quarter of all the adults in Latin America (table 4.7). These proportions were too high to be consistent with either dynamic economies or moderation in degrees of inequality. But the Andean countries did a great deal to lessen inequity on this count in the course of the next three decades. Bolivia made the greatest improvement, reducing adult illiteracy from 42 to 14 percent. The other four all reached rates of adult literacy over 90 percent, above the Latin American average.

For secondary education, probably the level most directly relevant for abilities to participate effectively in more modern economies, Venezuela was the only Andean country to reach as high as a one-third net enrollment rate as of 1970. In the next three decades the others made much more rapid progress, three of them to enrollment ratios higher than Venezuela's and the fourth almost to its level. Again, Bolivia made the fastest improvement in the group, from below average in 1970 to the highest rate of all in 2001.

Beneath the measurable progress in terms of literacy and participation in schooling, the really tough problem has been the quality of education in public schools. Indicators of quality consistently show distinctly superior results in private schools: most of them are giving relatively good education to the children of upper-income families, but the great majority of children, those in the public schools, are not getting the quality of education that can do much to improve their life chances. Indicators of low

TABLE 4.7

IMPROVEMENTS IN LITERACY RATES AND SECONDARY SCHOOL ENROLLMENT IN
FIVE ANDEAN COUNTRIES AND LATIN AMERICA AND THE CARIBBEAN REGION

	Adult literacy rates (%)		Net secondary school enrollment (%)	
	1970	2001	1970	2001
Bolivia	58	86	24	68
Colombia	78	92	25	57
Ecuador	74	92	22	48
Peru	72	90	30	61
Venezuela	76	93	33	50
Latin America and Caribbean region	74	89	27	[50][a]

Sources: UNDP (2003, 270–73), for all 2001 estimates; World Bank (2002), for 1970 illiteracy rates; World Bank (1983, individual country pages and 159), for secondary school enrollment in 1970.
[a]No regional average is given in the source. The median is calculated for the seventeen Latin American countries for which data is given (not including Cuba or the English-speaking countries in the Caribbean). In 2001, inclusion of Cuba would raise the median: its net secondary enrollment ratio was 82, higher than any other Latin American country.

quality—grade repetition, drop-out rates, poor attendance of both children and teachers, low scores on international comparison tests, and low public spending per student—make clear that inequality of productive potential and of income are being steadily reinforced.[3]

Defects in the quality of public education go far beyond issues of financing, but serious improvement surely requires considerably higher, and more stable, public financing than in the past. Table 4.8 gives the ratios to GDP of public spending on education in three periods from the mid-1980s to 1998–2000. For Latin America, the median increased by nearly a third, to 4.2 percent, between the first and third periods. Bolivia did much better than that, more than doubling its ratio to 5.5 percent. In contrast, Peru allowed a small decrease and Ecuador's ratio fell by more than half.

It is not clear what the ideal target for public spending on education might be, though it surely should be high enough to achieve better-quality public education and more nearly complete enrollment rates for secondary school. Three countries with strong concerns for equity—Cuba, Norway, and Sweden—were grouped close to 8 percent in the 1990s. That may be out of reach for the Andean countries for some time, but Bolivia's 5.5 percent is a ratio that the Andean countries with distinctly higher incomes—Colombia, Peru, and Venezuela—should be able to exceed.

TABLE 4.8
PUBLIC EXPENDITURES ON EDUCATION IN FIVE ANDEAN COUNTRIES
AND LATIN AMERICA RELATIVE TO GDP

| | Public spending on education as a percentage of GDP | | |
	1985–1987	1995–1997	1998–2000
Bolivia	2.1	4.9	5.5
Colombia	2.6	4.1	—
Ecuador	3.5	3.5	1.6
Peru	3.6	2.9	3.3
Venezuela	5.0	5.2	—
Latin America (median for countries for which data are given in sources)	3.2	3.6	4.2

Sources: UNDP (2001, 170–72); UNDP (2003, 266–68).

The limiting factors for support of public education are essentially political: issues of the allocation of public spending and, crucially, the ability to maintain adequate levels of taxation. Chile and Costa Rica were among the most successful Latin American countries in the 1990s in combining strong social programs with sufficient taxation to avoid inflationary fiscal deficits. For both of them, tax revenue was 19 percent of GDP in 2000 (World Bank 2002). For the three Andean countries reported in this source for 2000—Bolivia, Peru, and Venezuela—the corresponding ratios were all either 13 or 14 percent. For Colombia in 1997 it was 11 percent. These levels of taxation are too low to provide noninflationary support for adequate social expenditures.

Structures of Production and Trade

Costa Rica and Mexico showed a striking ability to raise their growth rates in the difficult conditions of 1997–2000, when incomes fell in all the Andean countries except Bolivia. The contrast reflects several causes. On the most immediate level, the differences in growth trends were closely related to differences in the structures and growth of exports. Costa Rica and Mexico made much greater progress than the Andean countries in stimulating the growth of industrial exports. Their export success had an important weight in GDP growth: for Mexico exports reached nearly a third of GDP by 2000 and for Costa Rica almost half of GDP. Beyond the direct effect of exports as a stimulus to production, the gains in foreign exchange helped both countries stave off the adverse consequences of the downswing in world capital flows that did so much to choke off growth in the Andean countries.

The differences in export structures, in turn, reflect two complementary strands of economic strategy that favored Costa Rica and Mexico. One was the active use of direct government support for structural change toward industries with the capacity to develop exports: a strategy that was practically absent under the particular kinds of economic liberalization implemented in the Andean countries in the 1990s. The qualified versions of liberalization in Costa Rica and Mexico were more helpful than either the purer version of Peru or the erratic path of Venezuela. The second strand was the pattern of exchange rate changes in the 1990s: a pattern favorable for export diversification and growth in Costa Rica and Mexico but not, except for Bolivia, in the Andes.

Almost all Latin American countries began to make at least modest progress toward development of industrial exports in the 1960s and 1970s, as a joint by-product of slowly broadening access to education and skills, lessening emphasis on protection as the way to promote industrialization, and growing awareness of the gains being made by East Asian countries through export diversification. For the region, manufacturing exports as a share of total commodity exports grew from a mere 5 percent at the start of the 1960s to 20 percent by 1980. Colombia, the only one of the Andean countries that used exchange rate management to favor new exports in this period, was the only one that achieved a share of industrial exports as high as the regional average in 1980 (table 4.9).

Three of the Andean countries—Bolivia, Ecuador, and Venezuela— remained almost totally dependent on primary exports as late as 1980. Colombia and Peru were doing much better at diversification, with industrial export shares on a par with the Latin American average. The region as a whole strengthened its capacity for industrial exports through the 1980s and 1990s: their share was almost half of total exports by the year 2000. All of the Andean countries except Venezuela made some gains in the 1990s, but none came at all close to the regional average at the end of the decade.

The striking progress for the region was due to a combination of external and internal factors. On the external side, the demand for imports of manufactured goods by the region's main customer, the United States, grew extraordinarily fast through the 1990s.[4] China accounted for a much higher share of the corresponding export growth than the Latin American countries did, but the increase in imports by the United States was so large

TABLE 4.9
MANUFACTURING EXPORTS AS SHARES OF TOTAL COMMODITY
EXPORTS IN FIVE ANDEAN COUNTRIES AND TWO CONTRASTING
CASES AND AVERAGES FOR LATIN AMERICA

	Total commodity exports (%)		
	1980	*1990*	*2000*
Bolivia	2.9	4.7	28.9
Colombia	19.6	25.1	34.1
Ecuador	3.0	2.3	9.9
Peru	16.8	18.3	20.3
Venezuela	1.7	10.4	9.1
Costa Rica	28.3	26.8	65.6
Mexico	11.9	43.5	83.5
Latin America	19.6	34.0	48.5

Source: World Bank (2002).

that the Latin American countries had a great deal of room to increase their exports too. For Mexico, the North American Free Trade Agreement was an additional help.

On the domestic side in Latin America, progress in learning industrial skills, and in the business sector's connections to external markets, provided an improving background. In terms of economic strategy, the two most important factors were the spread of liberalization programs and the management of exchange rates. Degrees of liberalization differed notably, as indicated in table 4.10 by Inter-American Development Bank (IDB) measures of structural reform. The measures cover ratings in five categories of liberalization, with a theoretical index of 1.00 considered by the IDB as complete reform. As of 1995, Bolivia and Peru stood out with scores among the highest in Latin America (along with Argentina). The indexes for Colombia and Ecuador were much lower, slightly below the average for the region. Venezuela remained the holdout.

Trade liberalization considered separately should have favored both export growth and diversification. High protection for industry in general, without much concern for relative costs, helped keep industrial product prices higher than external levels and held down the profitability of exports relative to domestic sales. The reduction of trade barriers increased competitive pressures in domestic markets and favored greater efforts to move into export markets. Unfortunately, that positive stimulus was offset in some countries by two adverse changes. Governments that

TABLE 4.10

DIFFERENCES IN DEGREES OF STRUCTURAL REFORM AS MEASURED BY INDEX
OF THE INTERAMERICAN DEVELOPMENT BANK IN FIVE ANDEAN COUNTRIES
AND THE LATIN AMERICAN AVERAGE, 1985, 1990 AND 1995

Countries (ranked in order of index for 1995)	1985	1990	1995
Bolivia	.34	.55	.72
Peru	.23	.25	.71
Colombia	.44	.55	.59
Ecuador	.33	.36	.58
Venezuela	.30	.36	.46
Latin America and Caribbean region	.35	.48	.62

Source: IDB (1997, 96).
Note: Index value of 1.00 considered as complete reform.

carried liberalization to the extreme of abandoning export promotion activities left their exporters in a weaker position than might have been achieved with even mild forms of continuing promotion. Governments that allowed appreciation of their real exchange rates undercut earnings of their exporters and discouraged diversification. That was, unfortunately, the course of all the Andean countries except Bolivia.

Prior to liberalization, Colombia and Peru, in common with many other Latin American countries, promoted nontraditional exports with tax advantages and other forms of limited subsidies. Brazil and Mexico used much more active promotional measures through the 1970s and in the process began to become powerful industrial exporters. Selective promotion had considerable costs through the inevitable political dealing, inefficiencies, and just plain mistakes. But for Mexico, at least, its thorough and persistent support for particular industrial exports set the stage for strong export growth that carried on after direct subsidies were eliminated.

With its liberalization, Peru simply wiped out all forms of export subsidies and indirect support. The position of the government during the 1990s was expressed firmly by a member of the cabinet: the government had no intention of doing anything to favor industrialization or any other selective form of structural change; the structure of the economy would be determined by the market. If that resulted in reliance on fishing, mining, and tourism, that should be recognized as the most efficient structure possible.

Other governments, including those of Chile and Costa Rica, found it readily possible to combine liberalization with modest forms of help for nontraditional exporters. The means used in Costa Rica included tax advantages through export-processing zones, direct support for research and development activities, and government negotiations with foreign firms to bring in new investment in fields of advanced technology. The negotiations succeeded in bringing in direct investment on a large scale by Intel, which in turn stimulated a wave of domestic investment by firms in closely related activities. An international comparison of research and development efforts ranked Costa Rica second highest in Latin America, well above any of the Andean countries (Lall 2001, 1517). These qualifications to liberalization paid off well in the 1990s.

The second strand of policies that could have been favorable for escape from dependence on primary exports and from volatile flows of international capital, exchange rate management, remains highly sensitive both economically and politically. It is clearly possible to improve incentives for industrial exporters by raising real exchange rates (in essence, by raising the price of foreign exchange relative to domestic costs of production).[5] This can be done by devaluation—by raising the price of foreign exchange—provided that domestic prices are not allowed to rise to the same degree. The IMF frowns on the idea of using devaluation to strengthen a country's competitive position in export markets, and in practice the difficulties can be serious, but they are not insurmountable. Although devaluation is likely to raise domestic prices to some degree, monetary and fiscal restraint can do a good deal to hold down inflationary consequences. Industrial firms that are mainly producing for the domestic market in an economy with high protection may not be greatly concerned with the ups and downs of export incentives, but trade liberalization changes that context: it forces producers into active contact with external competitors and makes the exchange rate a powerful instrument to point incentives in desired directions.

In the late 1980s and early 1990s Bolivia provided a good example of what can be done. At the time it adopted liberalization, the exchange rate was initially frozen to help stop inflation, which it did. But three years later, with little revival of economic growth, the country began to use devaluation to promote exports. An econometric test of the results demonstrated that a 10 percent increase in the real price of foreign exchange promoted a 13 percent increase in industrial exports (Jenkins 1996). From then through the early 1990s Bolivia, alone among the Andean countries, pursued an active policy of devaluation in real terms, with the positive results shown in table 4.11.

In table 4.11, the five Andean countries and the two contrasting cases of Costa Rica and Mexico are ranked in order of their increases in real exchange rates between 1990 and the average for 1995–1997, with Costa Rica at the top and Colombia at the bottom. The close association between changes in real exchange rates and changes in export shares is evident, though in the absence of other relevant variables the simple correlation between them hardly constitutes any conclusive measure.[6] Only three of these countries raised their real exchange rates; they were by far the leaders for increases in manufacturing export shares. Bolivia was the only Andean country among the three and correspondingly the only one that did better than the regional increase for manufacturing export share.

The main reason that real exchange rates fell for most Latin American countries from 1990 to 1997 was the strength of the capital flows they received, keeping foreign exchange abundant. Mexico was a dramatic special case. It went through a period of high capital inflows up to late 1994, with a falling real exchange rate and rapidly rising debt, but by late 1994 it was no longer able to maintain debt service. That forced it into "the peso crisis" and its accompanying currency crash. Economic factors can outgun government intentions. The crisis set back the Mexican economy severely for a year but also raised the real exchange rate so steeply that exports soon led a strong recovery, with the trade and growth performances shown in tables 4.9 and 4.11.

While governments cannot just choose and maintain whatever ex-

TABLE 4.11

RELATIONSHIPS BETWEEN CHANGES IN REAL EXCHANGE RATES AND CHANGES IN SHARES OF MANUFACTURING EXPORTS IN FIVE ANDEAN COUNTRIES AND THE CONTRASTING CASES OF COSTA RICA AND MEXICO

Countries ranked in order of changes in real exchange rates	Change in real exchange rate, 1990, to average for 1995–1997 (%)	Change in percentage points of manufacturing export share, 1990–2000
Costa Rica	+9	+39
Bolivia	+6	+24
Mexico	+4	+40
Peru	-20	+2
Ecuador	-24	+8
Venezuela	-26	-1
Colombia	-31	+9
Latin America	—	+15

Sources: Real exchange rates derived from IDB (1999, 251); changes in export shares derived from World Bank (2002).

change rates they prefer, or at least not for long if their currencies are seriously overvalued, they can usually do a good deal to influence trends. The
conventional ways are through monetary policy, using interest rates to
alter incentives to hold or sell their currencies, and by directly buying or
selling foreign exchange. It is also possible at times to affect market expectations by declaring intentions that are at least plausible enough to be
taken seriously. The common mistake is to hang on to an overvalued
currency as long as possible, allowing the country's competitive position
to be progressively undermined, for fear of the consequences of corrective
devaluation.[7]

Management of exchange rates can often be, and in Latin America
always is, an intensely political matter (Wise and Roett 2000). It involves
conflicts of ideology, relationships among governments, and differential
advantages among economic sectors as well as particular firms. In general, governments of all political orientations dislike devaluation because
it makes them look bad: it is widely, usually correctly, taken as evidence
that they have failed to maintain stability. Devaluation has the ring of
defeat. And, of course, it can have a multitude of unpleasant consequences. It can seriously damage the financial sector if the latter has high
levels of external debt, aggravate inflation, weaken investor confidence,
reduce real wages, and at its worst force economy-wide contraction. On
the other side of the matter, to keep the domestic currency overvalued for
a long period can undercut all producers of tradable goods, set back the
industrial sector in particular, worsen unemployment, and increase
poverty.

Naturally, the issues look different to different governments, economic
sectors, and economists. The spirit of economic liberalization, aiming at
minimal discretionary intervention by governments, would seem to call
for either a totally hands-off policy to allow exchange rates to fluctuate
freely or the opposite extreme of full dollarization with no exchange rate
left to manage. Either approach means backing away from any systematic
effort to guide incentives in ways favorable for structural change. For the
Andean countries, that would probably mean that their economic performances would not change greatly from the past, at least for a long time
to come.

Differences among Countries

Common structural factors can help account for some of the strains of
the Andean economies but cannot explain such individual differences as

Venezuela's extraordinary nosedive from 1980 to 2003 or Colombia's fall from its superior performance in the 1970s to its unhappy record in the 1990s. The common strands must be understood in specific contexts, in which other factors may have more immediate importance.

Bolivia

Bolivia's social revolution of 1952 did not do much to reduce poverty, but it greatly reduced some of the country's worst kinds of inequity (Morales 2003; Gamarra 2003). It eliminated a dominant social class that had kept much of the rural population in conditions of serfdom and had provided even less access to education than was common in the rest of Latin America at the time. Universal suffrage replaced a political system that denied voting to women and to illiterates, in a country in which the majority of the population had been kept illiterate. Partial land reform and nationalization of the mining sector, the chief source of export earnings, must have reduced the degree of income concentration. But with little human or industrial capital to work with, successful transformation to a more dynamic economy with capacity for sustained growth would have been difficult even if the country had been blessed by coherent economic policies. For a long time, it was not (Morales 2003).

No government in the three decades following the revolution managed to establish any effective program for economic transformation. The country continued to be highly dependent on primary exports and external financing. The agricultural sector remained impoverished, and industry remained limited to the protected domestic market. Economic growth was only slightly slower than average for Latin America up to 1980, but then went into reverse. Still, despite the weakness of economic growth, Bolivia has in recent decades made greater progress in extending access to education than any of the other Andean countries (Klein 2003). The pitiful 42 percent rate of adult illiteracy in 1970, by far the highest of all the Andean countries, was reduced to 14 percent by 2001 (table 4.7). In line with that improvement, public financing of education as a percentage of GDP more than doubled from the mid-1980s to the mid-1990s, from below the median for Latin America to well above it (table 4.8). While the quality of public education remains low, a major reform law in 1994 introduced changes aimed more effectively at quality improvement, with a shift of emphasis toward bilingual education for the children of indigenous families (Contreras 2003).[8]

The economy went through a particularly painful period in the first half of the 1980s: inflation accelerated and GDP per capita fell in every year. In a context of near desperation, the presidential election of 1985 brought back into office one of the leaders of the 1952 revolution, Víctor Paz Estenssoro. Determined to break out of the country's impasse, he immediately reversed Bolivia's model of state-led development. His Nueva Política Económico started with a drastic stabilization program, followed by a strong version of economic liberalization (Grindle 2003). That provoked violent opposition but began to gain support when the rate of inflation fell from more than 11,000 percent to almost zero. GDP per capita stopped falling after 1985, though investment and growth remained very low in the next several years. In 1988, in the hope of stimulating faster growth, the government adopted a policy of devaluation that had significant positive effects (Jenkins 1996). The share of manufacturing products in total exports increased from 3 percent in 1990 to 29 percent by 2000 (table 4.9). That was by far the most impressive increase for any Andean country.

Bolivia's GDP per capita fell for the 1980s as a whole but then grew at a modest rate of 1.8 percent for 1990–1997, in the middle of the Andean group. It did better than the group in the difficult three years following: while GDP per capita fell in all the other countries, Bolivia was able to keep growing, though very slowly (table 4.3). Poverty in urban areas continued to decrease, in contrast to increases in all the other Andean countries (table 4.1). The distribution of income in urban areas also improved slightly (table 4.6). By such measures, liberalization of the economy seemed on balance helpful through the 1990s. Three successive coalition governments kept the strategy largely intact. That does not mean that it was popular. Persisting strains broke through in mass protests in 2003, provoking violent repressive measures. The president, a conservative closely associated with economic liberalization and with the U.S. policy prescription favoring eradication of coca production, resorted to military force that killed a large number of people demonstrating against these policies. That cost him practically all his remaining support and led to his hurried exit to safe haven in Florida. The new president did not, at least initially, introduce any significant change in the country's economic policies.

The violence in 2003 might be explained in part by renewed weakness of economic performance: growth of GDP per capita stopped again from 2000 through 2003. But other persistent issues were probably more important. One of the most intense conflicts centered on policies toward coca and cocaine. The political parties identified with the interests of the indigenous population gained strong support for legalization of coca production and cocaine exports, in direct opposition to the government's efforts to eradicate production. That battle was reinforced by a new controversy over projects approved by the government to export natural gas on a large scale. Both of these sharp divisions on specific questions soon became bound up with widespread opposition to globalization in general.

Each of these three conflicts has implications beyond the scope of this chapter, but together they constitute an important set of shared Andean interests. Coca is a traditional crop of strong emotional significance in the Andes, associated in the past primarily with small-scale family cultivation for coca leaves (not cocaine), to help relieve the strains of hard work at high altitudes. For many of the people of Bolivia, attempts to eradicate cultivation by force violate long-accepted customs. At the same time, the pull of strong demand for cocaine in the United States and other industrialized countries has made increased production of coca and cocaine a path for many rural families to escape poverty.[9] Defense of traditions combined with what is seen as arbitrary interference with a way to escape poverty—further poisoned by the conviction that the interference is dictated by U.S. rather than Bolivian interests—generated an explosive background that was too much for the government to handle.

Popular opposition to the projects for export of natural gas could be seen as inconsistent with the drive to remove restraints on growing coca intended for cocaine exports: objections to the gas exports stem in large measure from disgust with continued reliance on primary exports and failure to develop a competitive industrial sector, while insistence on freedom to produce coca and cocaine points instead toward increasing dependence on primary exports. Still, both positions share significant features: both are forms of protest against foreign influence in the structure of production and against economic policies that favor concentrated earnings of a few as opposed to directly increased earnings of the poor. It is possible that a more conciliatory government could negotiate an acceptable compromise on the natural gas, much more readily than on coca, by amending some of the exceptionally generous terms given to foreign investors for these projects, especially if it directed the added Bolivian revenue to support for job-creating industrial investment.

Finally, opposition to globalization is so strong because the majority of Bolivians have never gained significantly from the country's participation in international trade and finance. The fortunes made in the past from exports of tin and precious metals made no dent whatsoever in the deep poverty of most of the people. They are right to conclude that more direct action to promote a competitive industrial sector is essential for more dependable economic growth and for productive employment. But it is also true that the initial decade under economic liberalization, when monetary and fiscal restraint were used to stop inflation, along with exchange rate management to promote new industrial exports, was a significant step in exactly the direction needed. Participation in world markets can be either pointless for the poor or instead genuinely helpful, depending on how it is managed. It was managed distinctly better than in the past during that first decade, with some resultant reduction of poverty and inequality. But that promising orientation was then allowed to lapse as the government turned back to the old pattern of granting favors to foreign investors, aimed at promoting more natural resource exports, instead of strengthening incentives to move the economy toward rising production and exports of competitive industrial products.

Colombia

While Bolivia's economy improved somewhat in the first decade of economic liberalization, Colombia's did not. Three possible reasons might explain Colombia's weak economic performance in the 1990s, after a previous period of unusually effective economic management (Thorp 1991): (1) economic liberalization, (2) exchange rate management, and (3) worsening damage from the strains of the drug trade, political violence, and consequent weakening of the integrity of governmental institutions.

Economic liberalization would not seem to be an important explanatory factor. Liberalization in Colombia had almost none of the dramatic impact it had in Bolivia and Peru. In Peru the IDB index of structural reform tripled from .23 in 1985 to .71 by 1995, reflecting truly fundamental changes in its economic orientation; in Colombia, with a considerably more liberal economic regime in the first place, the index increased by only a third, from .44 to .59 (table 4.10). That does not mean that Colombia's reforms were insignificant, but they were hardly strong enough to account for the major reversal of economic performance.

Colombia had made significant change toward liberalization as far back as 1967. Protection remained but at relatively low levels, the government put new emphasis on fiscal and monetary balance, and it made an early move to promote export diversification through what was at the time a new exchange rate strategy. That strategy—the crawling peg—centered on almost daily devaluation in very small steps, too small to provoke any crisis but cumulatively sufficient to offset the negative effect of inflation on domestic costs. The price of foreign exchange was raised at rates roughly similar to the rate of inflation, providing a relatively stable real exchange rate. By keeping up the profitability of exports the government drew more and more of the industrial sector into exporting, with less reliance on protection (Urrutia 1981). The strategy worked well for more than a decade, for growth and employment as well as exports. It gave Colombia the highest ratio of manufactures to total exports of all the Andean countries (table 4.9). The country even began to reduce its high level of income inequality (Sheahan 1987, 271–96; Londoño de la Cuesta 1995).

No economic policy lacks problems. The strongly independent central bank—the Banco de la República—turned against use of the crawling peg in the 1990s, partly because it limited the scope for discretionary monetary policy but mostly because it impeded any all-out drive to stop inflation (Kamas 2001; Urrutia 2002). The new orientation emphasized higher interest rates and rejected intervention to manage the exchange rate. Under the new approach, the real exchange rate fell steeply (table 4.11). As a consequence, the competitiveness of Colombian industry and the economy as a whole were gravely weakened. The share of the manufacturing sector in GDP fell from 21 percent in 1990 to 14 percent by 2000 (World Bank 2002). GDP per capita fell from 1997 to 2000 and failed to recover in the three following years (tables 4.3 and 4.4).

The bad turn of the economy owed something to this unfortunate redirection of macroeconomic policy but probably more to deteriorating political conditions under the strains of worsening violence, insecurity, and weakening governmental institutions (Hartlyn and Dugas 1999; Moser 2000). The government seemed to lose any capacity to stop or punish political assassinations. Former members of the guerrilla organization M-19 who signed a peace agreement and returned to civilian life were hunted down and murdered in the hundreds. Paramilitary groups have wiped out whole villages, sometimes with tacit cooperation by the Colombian army, on the suspicion that they may have sympathized with guerrillas. Labor organizers and outspoken journalists are always at high risk: in 2003, ninety-four union activists were assassinated (Forero 2004; Gallón 1998; Pizarro 2000).

Drug violence may be less evident now than it was when the leading candidate for president, perceived as likely to take effective action against the drug rings, was murdered by a gang attack at a political rally. But the insidious side of corrupted institutions may have worsened. In the 1990s, political contributions of drug money reached high levels of government. For many years Colombians had reason for more confidence in the integrity of their governments than was common in Latin America. Between the role of drug money and the acquiescence in right-wing violence, the grounds for such confidence have been weakened.

Ecuador

Ecuador suffered the most striking fall in GDP per capita of all the Andean countries during the general downturn from 1997 to 2000. Much as for Venezuela, weakness in oil prices was a major factor, although that negative impact was aggravated by failure, in the first part of the decade, to prevent a costly fall in the real exchange rate. It would be difficult to prove that policy confusion was any worse in one country than in the other: both swung back and forth between tentative liberalization and returns to populism. Ecuador had five different presidents in the course of the 1990s and started the next decade with another, at that point a conservative. But nothing lasts forever. Within two years the strength of popular opposition to economic liberalization led to the election of a seemingly determined populist as president, only to have the circle turn again promptly as he found it necessary to accept IMF guidance in return for desperately needed financial help.

Any adequate explanation of Ecuador's crisis in the last years of the 1990s needs to include the familiar costs of excessive reliance on primary exports and unhelpful exchange rate management, but these are just two strands in a complex picture.[10] The most immediately pressing factor was the near collapse of the financial system. Heavy reliance on foreign borrowing by both the government and the private sector left them with unmanageable debt problems when it became impossible to keep up the overvaluation of the currency. That became impossible in 1998 when falling oil prices coincided with exceptionally tight conditions of external credit. As soon as the currency was allowed to move freely it plunged, as was only to be expected. That made the cost of debt service in terms of domestic currency—on debts denominated in dollars—shoot upward to a degree that paralyzed the financial system. It also accelerated the rate of inflation. Caught between fear of hyperinflation and a financial system no longer able to function, the government opted in January 2000 for a radical change that seemed to offer a way out: abandoning the battered sucre by adopting full official dollarization.

The main appeal of dollarization in this emergency context was that it offered a promise of stopping inflation. It eased inflationary expectations by providing credible reassurance that the currency would stop falling.

Further, in the context of relatively open trade, prices of goods that either were imported or competed with imports could no longer depart greatly from dollar prices in external markets. Of course, these and other possible gains also brought with them significant costs.[11]

A commonly recognized cost of dollarization is that it eliminates the possibility of using the exchange rate to strengthen export incentives and to shift demand away from imports when the country is hit by external shocks that drive down earnings. Absent this possible response, domestic deflation becomes practically inevitable. Incomes have to fall enough to bring imports down into consistency with lower export earnings. A classic thesis is that prices and wages should be driven down to restore competitive strength at a stable exchange rate. That looks like a costly prescription for modern economies that are "structurally incapable of undergoing significant deflation in this way" (Beckerman and Cortés 2002, 91). It implies a full-scale crisis, with at least as intense social conflict as correction of the exchange rate might cause, were there an exchange rate left to correct.

Beyond this familiar issue of macroeconomic management, a deeper problem is that dollarization implies rejection of any use of exchange rate management to promote industrialization and export diversification. It would have ruled out Colombia's gains of the 1970s, Chile's striking growth of exports and employment after revision of its economic strategy in 1983, and Costa Rica's exceptional success with promotion of industrial exports in the 1990s. For Ecuador, dollarization is likely to mean indefinite continuation of the dependence on primary product exports and foreign credit that have weighed it down through all its modern history.

Peru

Peru started toward a social revolution in the period 1968–1975, during the radical-reformist government of General Juan Velasco Alvarado, including a major land reform that displaced the prior ruling class (Sheahan 1999, 133–39; Wise 2003, 82–115). But poor macroeconomic management and far too much external borrowing forced a contraction that led to falling incomes and sharpening social conflict. Most of the changes introduced under Velasco, other than land reform, were soon reversed. The frustrations aggravated by that aborted effort at national transformation may well have contributed to the support that Shining Path was able to capture as it launched its murderous campaign of revolutionary violence in the 1980s.

The country's worst crisis came in the period from 1987 through 1991. That was the height of the violence coming from and directed against Shining Path, when the possibility that this destructive struggle would go on for many more years seemed all too real. It was also a period of economic breakdown, with incomes falling steeply, inflation rising over 7,000 percent, and pervasive deterioration of governmental institutions (Gonzales de Olarte and Samamé 1994; Wise 2003, 152–75).

Much as in Bolivia five years earlier, the depth of misery in Peru at the beginning of the 1990s created conditions that favored a drastic reorientation of economic strategy. The government of Alberto Fujimori repudiated any vestige of state-led development by a liberalization program that the IDB judged to be one of the strongest in Latin America, almost exactly matching the degree in Bolivia (table 4.10). Liberalization carried with it a determined drive to stop inflation, using fiscal and monetary restraint plus a decrease of the real exchange rate. That combination succeeded in slowing down inflation, but production and employment did not begin to recover until the Lima police captured the leader of Shining Path in September 1992. From that point, the combination of lessened violence with economic stabilization made Peru a great deal more attractive for foreign lenders and investors. The flow of capital toward Latin America that was rising swiftly at that time began to include Peru, helping greatly to support economic recovery.

With recovery, employment in the formal sector of the economy grew at a much more rapid rate than in the preceding decade, though still not fast enough to keep up with the growth of the labor force. Even through the years of good growth from 1994 to 1997 the overhang of labor without adequate opportunities for productive employment began to pull real wages down again. When the inflow of capital slowed down in 1997, growth stopped and poverty began to rise once more. Economic liberalization as implemented in Peru did not accomplish any structural transformation lessening the country's dependence on external capital (Gonzales de Olarte 1998; Sheahan 1999, 153–91).

Two first-class studies of the consequences of liberalization in Peru convey somewhat more positive evaluations, though each with important qualifications (Pascó-Font and Saavedra 2001; Wise 2003, 179–249). It makes a difference what factors are emphasized. In the study by Wise, much of the emphasis is on institutional change in the 1990s, especially the creation and strengthening of autonomous agencies focused on specific objectives. That is a vital part of the picture, which she conveys in careful detail. But it is notable that the institutions created or modernized by the Fujimori government were essentially limited to those that implement the decisions made by the executive branch, such as tax collection, tariff administration, and regulation of financial institutions. They did not include institutions needed to support democracy or to protect the society from abuses by the president. The government resolutely resisted decentralization, eliminated any shred of judicial independence, corrupted the electoral commission, and used a combination of threats and bribery to control television broadcasting. The administrative side of government was made more effective; the institutions vital for a democracy were devastated.

When evidence of pervasive corruption and political manipulation became glaringly public shortly after the elections of 2000, by the revelation of videotapes showing actual examples in the process of taking place, the president left abruptly for refuge in Japan. The interim government that took over for a year proved to be both reasonable and decisive, helping to undo a considerable part of the damage done by Fujimori. The economy responded fairly well in 2002–2003, at least in terms of renewed growth of GDP (table 4.4). The less fortunate side was that this growth was led once again by the mining sector, with its built-in volatility and its minimal help for employment. In its first two years, the government of Alejandro Toledo, which took office in 2001, did little to improve this orientation. Until more can be done to promote a competitive industrial sector, capable of growth through exporting, the chances of sustained growth and enduring reduction of poverty remain doubtful.

Venezuela

Venezuela has suffered the most drastic long-term economic decline of any of the Andean countries. GDP per capita fell 17 percent from 1980 to 2000, a period in which Latin American GDP per capita increased by 9 percent. Income per capita continued to fall through 2003, to a level almost one-fourth lower than in 2000. But then sharply higher prices and earnings for oil exports in 2004 generated a striking rise of 17 percent for GDP in 2004 (table 4.4).

Both poverty and inequality increased during the difficult 1990s: the incidence of poverty increased by 8 percentage points between 1990 and 1997, and the Gini coefficient of inequality increased as well (tables 4.1 and 4.6). Small wonder that the established political structure came under intense pressure and broke down.

Political and economic breakdowns aggravate each other. Salamanca

(1997) and Corrales (2000) bring the two sides together in somewhat different but complementary interpretations. For Salamanca, Venezuela went wrong in the 1960s when the dominant political parties settled on a system of distributing the revenue from the state-owned oil industry to promote rising standards of living that had little or no counterpart in growing productive capacity. The system gave them electoral support, and gave the country a considerable measure of social peace, as long as the demands placed on it stayed within the limits of oil revenue. But the demands constantly grew, the parties were unable to maintain adequate restraints, and the system began to break down in the early 1980s. Partial use of oil revenue to stimulate investment in other fields did not provide any help in complementing oil exports because the nonoil lines of production were oriented to the domestic market under high protection, not toward export competition. When oil revenue became inadequate, there was little else to rely on.[12]

Corrales concentrates more on the 1990s, with emphasis on lagging reform as the key problem. Partial modernization of institutions created inconsistencies and new strains in a context of many islands of resistance. On the economic side, up to the beginning of the Hugo Chávez government in 1999, an independent central bank was able and willing to exercise monetary restraint, but an unreformed ministry of finance was unable to limit fiscal deficits. Trade liberalization was not helpful, because successive governments failed to correct the overvalued currency. They experimented with a striking variety of methods of exchange rate management in the course of the 1990s, and allowed some depreciation in nominal terms, but not enough to offset inflation (Corrales 2000, 140–43). As shown in table 4.11, the real exchange rate fell greatly in the 1990s and Venezuela was the only Andean country for which the share of manufactures in total exports actually decreased.

The inability of the traditional political parties to find any solution set up conditions for a familiar reaction: strong public support for the demagogic savior. If Chávez had not arrived to take over, someone else would have. His version of populism is clearly popular with lower-income people, and apparently with the military, though also sufficiently threatening to frighten off investors. Unlike many others who have won election for their populist rhetoric but then turned conservative to gain the support of the international financial community, he has held on to the left-oriented path that so many Venezuelans welcome and so many others fear (López Maya and Lander 2004; Parenti 2005). That has included intensified political control of state-owned firms in oil and other fields, increased taxation of foreign oil companies, friendly cooperation with Fidel Castro, and a spectacular recent increase in spending on social programs.

The government had held down spending in its first years, under the constraint of relatively low income from oil. When oil revenue shot up in 2004, a high proportion of the gain was directed to increased spending on education, urban housing for the poor, productivity improvement in small-scale agriculture, and a host of projects that could—if implemented effectively—help reduce poverty and inequality. That "if" is a real question: similar programs in other countries have had very mixed results, with gains in some cases but fearful corruption and waste in others. The Chávez program has so far been welcomed by what seems to be a majority of Venezuelans, but its character and consequences have yet to be clarified. Naturally, it has been denounced by many Venezuelans, and outside critics too, as a case of diverting oil revenue toward welfare instead of investing it in projects to raise productive capacity. It is a choice of emphasis on consumption and welfare over physical investment, but in this case, unlike in most oil booms, on consumption and human investment by the poor.

Venezuela fully qualifies as a case of crisis in the political domain, continuously on the edge of explosion. Underlying that crisis, the economy has suffered a long-term process of deterioration. The oil boom of 2004–2005 has temporarily raised incomes but does not constitute any real solution. The country's Andean characteristics are certainly relevant, especially those of dependence on primary exports and foreign capital, widespread poverty, and high inequality. They have all contributed to intensifying political polarization.

A Possible Interpretation

Whether the Andean economies are perceived as sliding into dangerous kinds of crises or simply floating up and down with the currents of international capital flows and commodity prices or actually making some meaningful progress depends a great deal on the focus of the observer. The more that one concentrates on the separate woes of a particular country—on the details of actions and failures to act and on the choices of governments by its people (when they have a choice)—the more a sense of despair is likely to creep in. Comparisons with other countries can alleviate despair to some degree by lessening any sense that the Andean economies are exceptionally weak in some permanent way and by clarifying the nature of changes that could help them do better.

Compared with other Latin American countries on average, the Andean group looks somewhat worse in poverty and growth but not in inequality. For run-of-the-mill weaknesses such as fiscal irresponsibility, tax favors for the wealthy combined with starvation of social programs that could help the poor, and special advantages for corporations that made adequate political contributions, the Andean governments do not look at all bad compared with the present administration in the United States.

The role of external impacts on the Andean countries could be seen as consistent with the emphasis of dependency analysis. When external capital flows in strongly, the Andean economies come to life, output grows, and poverty falls. When the external flows slow down sharply, or go into reverse, so do the Andean economies. The net results of the swings in both directions for the decades of the 1980s and 1990s left four of them at lower levels of income per capita.

Although this type of externally caused instability is a crucial part of the picture, it is not something given to the Andean countries as an inescapable heritage. Their dependence on primary products for exports and on external capital could be changed, though not easily or rapidly. That change would require the development of capacity to produce some manufactures and modern services of international quality, in touch with external market preferences. Such capacity is much more likely to be created, and to be activated successfully, if it is supported by favorable incentives, by overall financial stability, and above all by wider distribution of investment in human resources to improve labor mobility and skills. That is asking for a lot of cohesive social effort to reshape the economic forces that have historically dominated performance. It is not asking the impossible.

The Andean countries have done much better in recent years at limiting excess demand that pulls producers toward domestic markets and generates heavy borrowing to cover domestic deficits. They have also done a great deal to extend access to education, if not much as yet to improve its quality. But the record on incentives for diversified export growth has remained more mixed: it was favorable for most countries in the 1980s but turned unfavorable for all except Bolivia in the 1990s. Policy failure in this respect contributed heavily to the severe breakdown in Ecuador and worsened the strains of both the economy and the political process in Colombia and Venezuela. Avoiding that particular failure helped Bolivia to make more progress toward export diversification than it has ever made before.

All of these countries are struggling uphill against the handicaps of past failures to provide adequate access to education and the continuing weakness in the quality of public education. These historical characteristics have left them with built-in inequity, in the sense that the majority of the population has been blocked from the possibility of competing on anything like equal terms in labor markets, acquiring skills, and being able to respond to opportunities. The same weaknesses help account for low productivity, low flexibility, and weak competitive positions of the modern sectors of these economies.

Some of these fundamental factors have been improving, even while others have driven both Colombia and Venezuela into deep crises. Wise brings out another possible line of improvement in her analysis of institutional change in Peru. She concludes that improvements of institutions have raised Peruvian capacity for effective performance to a degree that has left the other Andean countries far behind: Peru should now be seen as one of the more actively developing countries, no longer one of "an Andean bloc still struggling to implement market reforms" (2003, 222). That positive evaluation for Peru, on institutional issues not thoroughly considered here, is a valuable reminder of how many different ways there are to look at these questions. But it may be misleading in two respects. One is the dichotomy in Peru itself between the real improvements in agencies of governmental administration and the simultaneous degradation of institutions vital for democracy, meaning in particular those needed to restrain authoritarian presidents. The other is the suggestion that the key struggle is one of implementing more thorough market-oriented reforms.

I suggest instead that some aspects of economic liberalization have constituted helpful changes, most notably trade liberalization, but that market reform becomes an obstacle if it is pushed to the point of abandoning the use of promotional measures to achieve the structural changes these countries need. In the absence of coherent promotional policies, they may go on for many decades to come with degrees of inequity and dependence that continuously aggravate social conflict. In the presence of coherent promotional policies, if backed up by improvement in the distribution of investment in human resources, there is no reason that they could not accomplish something like the progress of Costa Rica and Mexico toward more competitive economies, of Chile in sustained economic growth and lower poverty, and of Costa Rica and Uruguay in social equity. The Andean countries will find their own paths, but they all need major structural changes to gain more stable and more equitable growth.

Notes

1. Between 1975 and 1982 the net annual flow of private capital to Latin America increased 3.7 times. It then went into reverse and as late as 1990 was barely above its rate in 1975. But from 1990 to 1997 it shot up again, to a peak nine times as high as in 1990 (World Bank 2002a). The wheel then turned down once more and remained down through 2002.

2. The CEPAL measures are in most cases higher than the averages from the World Bank study. That does not imply any general increase in inequality during the 1990s: the World Bank averages use estimates from many different sources, provided that they meet standards of acceptability, and are therefore not fully comparable to the CEPAL measures.

3. Barbara Hunt (2001) gives a gripping firsthand account of the stresses and strains of Peruvian primary education at the end of the 1990s and the uphill fight for improvement. Other helpful studies include Jiménez, Lockheed, and Paqueo (1991); Schiefelbein (1997); and Reimers (2000).

4. U.S. imports of industrial products shot up from $378 billion in 1990 to $971 billion in 2000 (derived from World Bank 2002).

5. The real exchange rate can be defined and measured in different ways, with the emphasis placed either on changes in the ratio of foreign to domestic prices (as in this discussion) or on changes in the ratio between prices of tradable goods and those of nontradable goods. An increase in either of these ratios implies improvement in the incentives to produce and sell exports. For a thorough analysis, see Edwards (1989).

6. A cross-section correlation extended to nineteen Latin American countries is significant at the 5 percent level (Sheahan 2003, 11).

7. This is a common mistake in Latin America, not everywhere. Both China and Japan, the world's most formidable export competitors in recent years, consistently strive to keep their currencies undervalued. They have succeeded so well that the U.S. government has applied strong pressure on both to allow their currencies to appreciate.

8. It may be misleading to cite Contreras for any positive view of progress in Bolivian education: his review of the subject is on the whole dismissive. But the change to bilingual education is seen as positive (simply far later than it should have been, in a system that never works well). He is certainly right that there is a long way yet to go.

9. James Painter (1994) provides a comprehensive analysis of coca production and processing in Bolivia. His chapter on costs and benefits (53–75) is particularly good. He estimates that coca accounted for close to one-fifth of the country's agricultural output in the early 1990s and that about 10 percent of the labor force is involved in the production of coca, paste, and cocaine (4, 41–50).

10. The studies in Beckerman and Solimano (2002), provide meticulous examinations of a multitude of problems underlying the economic crisis in Ecuador.

11. Key points of the far-ranging debates on the costs and benefits of dollarization, applied to Ecuador's context, are summarized neatly in Beckerman and Cortés (2000, 81–95). This is a helpful discussion but might be questioned for its tendency to give too little weight to the costs. For an enlightening and cheerfully unconventional review of the issues, in the form of a lively debate that does not insist on any conclusion, see Schuldt (1999).

12. Without questioning the severity of Venezuela's problems, consideration of the ways so many governments simply loot or waste the bulk of national earnings from oil exports makes the initial Venezuelan approach look appealing, at least for the first

decade after the establishment of democracy in 1958. In its social orientation and wide distribution of income it was truly exceptional. But the "natural resource curse" still undermined this promising start. A recent analysis of Nigerian experience concludes that "some natural resources—oil and minerals in particular—exert a negative and nonlinear impact on growth via their deleterious impact on institutional quality" (Sala-I-Martin and Subramanian 2003, 1).

Bibliography

Beckerman, Paul, and Hernán Cortés Douglas. 2002. Ecuador under dollarization: Opportunities and risks. In Beckerman and Solimano 2002, 81–126.

Beckerman, Paul, and Andrés Solimano, eds. 2002. *Crisis and dollarization in Ecuador: Stability, growth, and social equity.* Washington, DC: World Bank.

Berry, Albert, 1997. The income distribution threat in Latin America. *Latin American Research Review* 32 (2): 3–40.

CEPAL (Comisión Económica para América Latina y el Caribe). 2002. *Panorama social de América Latina, 2001–2002.* Santiago, Chile: Naciones Unidas.

Contreras, Manuel E. 2003. A comparative perspective on education reforms in Bolivia: 1950–2000. In Grindle and Domingo 2003, 259–86.

Corrales, Javier, 2000. Reform-lagging states and the question of devaluation: Venezuela's response to the exogenous shocks of 1997–98. In Wise and Roett 2000.

Deininger, Klaus, and Lyn Squire. 1996. A new data set measuring income inequality. *World Bank Research Review* 10 (3): 565–91.

Edwards, Sebastian, 1989. *Real exchange rates, devaluation and adjustment: Exchange rate policy in developing countries.* Cambridge, MA: MIT Press.

Federal Reserve Bank of Atlanta, Americas Center, 2005. Updated forecast: Forecast revisions. Second quarter 2005. http://www.frbatlanta.org.

Forero, Juan. 2004. Assassination Is an Issue in Trade Talks. *New York Times*, November 18.

Gallón, Gustavo. 1998. Interview. Newsletter of the Helen Kellogg Institute for International Studies, University of Notre Dame, no. 30: 12–18.

Gamarra, Eduardo. 2003. Political parties since 1964: The construction of Bolivia's multiparty system. In Grindle and Domingo 2003, 289–317.

Gonzales de Olarte, Efraín. 1998. *El neoliberalismo a la Péruana: Economía política del ajuste estructural, 1990–1997.* Lima, Peru: Instituto de Estudios Peruanos.

Gonzales de Olarte, Efraín, and Lilian Samamé. 1994. *El péndulo Peruano: Política Económica, gobernabilidad, y subdesarrollo, 1963–1990.* 2nd ed. Lima, Peru: Instituto de Estudios Peruanos.

Grindle, Merilee. 2003. Shadowing the past? Policy reform in Bolivia, 1985–2002. In *Proclaiming revolution: Bolivia in comparative perspective*, ed. Merilee Grindle and Pilar Domingo, 318–24. Cambridge, MA, and London: Institute of Latin American Studies, University of London, and David Rockefeller Center for Latin American Studies, Harvard University.

Hartlyn, Jonathan, and John Dugas. 1999. Colombia: The politics of violence and democratic transformation. In *Democracy in developing countries, Latin America*, 2nd ed., ed. Larry Diamond, Jonathan Hartlyn, Juan J. Linz, and Seymour Martin Lipset, 249–307. Boulder, CO: Lynne Rienner.

Herrera, Javier. 2002. *La Pobreza en el Perú 2001: Una visión Departamental*. Lima, Peru: Instituto Nacional de Estadística e Informática.

Hunt, Barbara. 2001. Peruvian primary education: Improvement still needed. Paper presented to the meeting of the Latin American Studies Association, Washington, DC, September.

IDB (Inter-American Development Bank). 1997. *Economic and social progress in Latin America, 1997 report*. Washington, DC: IDB.

———. 1999. *Economic and social progress in Latin America, 1998–1999 report*. Washington, DC: IDB.

IMF (International Monetary Fund). 2003. *World economic outlook* (April). Washington, DC: IMF.

Jenkins, Rhys. 1996. Trade liberalization and export performance in Bolivia. *Development and Change* 27 (4): 693–716.

Jiménez, Emmanuel, Marlaine Lockheed, and Vicente Paqueo. 1991. The relative efficiency of private and public schools in developing countries. *World Bank Research Observer* 6 (2): 205–18.

Kamas, Linda. 2001. Monetary and exchange rate policy in Colombia: Effects on the real exchange rate. *Journal of Development Studies* 38 (December): 38–2, 131–66.

Klein, Herbert S. 2003. Social change in Bolivia since 1952. In Grindle and Domingo 2003, 232–58.

Lall, Sanjaya. 2001. Competitiveness indices and developing countries. *World Development* 29:9, 1501–21.

Li, Hongyi, Lyn Squire, and Heng-fu Zou. 1998. Explaining international and intertemporal variation in income inequality. *Economic Journal* 108 (January): 26–43.

Londoño de la Cuesta, Juan Luis. 1995. *Distribución del ingreso y desarrollo económico: Colombia en el siglo XX*. Bogotá, Colombia: Tercer Mundo, 1995.

López Maya, Margarita, and Luis E. Lander. 2004. The Struggle for hegemony in Venezuela: Poverty, popular protest, and the future of democracy. In *Politics in the Andes: Identity, conflict, reform*, ed. Jo-Marie Burt and Philip Mauceri, 207–27. Pittsburgh, PA: University of Pittsburgh Press.

Morales, Juan Antonio. 2003. The national revolution and its legacy. In Grindle and Domingo 2003, 213–31.

Moser, Caroline. 2000. Violence in Colombia: Building sustainable peace and social capital. In *Colombia: Essays on conflict, peace, and development*, ed. Andrés Solimano, 9–77. Washington, DC: World Bank.

Painter, James. 1994. *Bolivia and coca: A study in dependency*. Boulder, CO: Lynne Rienner.

Parenti, Christian. 2005. Hugo Chavez and petro populism. *Nation* 280 (14): 15–23.

Pascó-Font, Alberto, and Jaime Saavedra. 2001. *Reformas estructurales y bienestar: Una mirada al Perú de los noventa*. Lima, Peru: GRADE.

Pizzaro, Eduardo. 2000. Interview. On the endangered list: Intellectuals in Colombia. Newsletter of the Helen Kellogg Institute for International Studies, University of Notre Dame, no. 35: 8–10.

PNUD-Perú (Programa de las Naciones Unidas para el Desarollo, Oficina del Perú). 2002. *Informe sobre Desarrollo Humano, Perú 2002*. Lima, Peru: PNUD.

Reimers, Fernando, ed. 2000. *Unequal schools, unequal chances*. Cambridge, MA: David Rockefeller Center for Latin American Studies at Harvard University.

Sala-I-Martin, Xavier, and Arvind Subramanian. 2003. Addressing the national resource curse: An illustration from Nigeria. National Bureau of Economic Research, Working Paper no. W9804.

Salamanca, Luis. 1997. *Crisis de la modernización y crisis de la democracia en Venezuela.* Caracas, Venezeula: Instituto Latinoamericano de Investigaciones Sociales (ILDES).

Schiefelbein, Ernesto. 1997. Financing education for democracy in Latin America. In *Latin American education: Comparative perspectives,* ed. Carlos Alberto Torres and Adriana Puiggrós, 31–64. Boulder, CO: Westview Press.

Schuldt, Jürgen. 1999. Dolarización oficial de la economía: Un debate en once actos. Lima, Peru: Universidad del Pacífico, Apuntes de Estudio 36.

Sheahan, John. 1987. *Patterns of development in Latin America: Poverty, repression and economic strategy.* Princeton, NJ: Princeton University Press.

———. 1998. Kinds and causes of inequality in Latin America. In *Beyond tradeoffs: Market reforms and equitable growth in Latin America,* ed. Nancy Birdsall, Carol Graham, and Richard Sabot, 29–61. Washington, DC: Inter-American Development Bank and Brookings Institution.

———. 1999. *Searching for a better society: The Peruvian economy from 1950.* University Park: Pennsylvania State University Press.

———. 2003. The persistence of poverty in Peru: Possible answers, their limits, and implications for Latin America. Washington, DC: USAID, Pro-Poor Economic Growth Research Studies.

Thorp, Rosemary. 1991. *Economic management and economic development in Peru and Colombia.* Pittsburgh, PA: University of Pittsburgh Press.

UNDP (United Nations Development Program). 2001 and 2003. *Human development report 2001 and 2003.* New York: Oxford University Press for the UNDP.

Urrutia, Miguel. 1981. Experience with the crawling peg in Colombia. In *Exchange rate rules,* ed. John Williamson, 207–20. New York: St. Martin's.

———. 2002. Una Visión Alternativa: La Política Monetaria y Cambiaria en la ÚltimaDécada. Bogotá, Colombia: Banco de la República, Borradores de Economía, No. 207.

Wise, Carol. 2003. *Reinventing the state: Economic strategy and institutional change in Peru.* Ann Arbor: University of Michigan Press.

Wise, Carol, and Riorden Roett, eds. 2000. *Exchange rate politics in Latin America.* Washington, DC: Brookings Institution.

World Bank. 1983. *World tables.* 3rd ed., vol. 2. Washington, DC: World Bank.

———. 2002. *World development indicators, 2002.* CD-ROM.

Technocrats, Citizens, and
Second-Generation Reforms

Colombia's Andean Malaise

ERIC HERSHBERG

A CORE CONTENTION OF THIS BOOK IS THAT THROUGHOUT the Andean region there is an exceptionally pronounced gap between public expectations of democracy and development and the capacity of the political-economic order to even remotely satisfy these expectations. We see this state of affairs, and the upheavals that it engenders, as rooted in factors that are both internal and external. Andean democracies operate with scant room for maneuver in an international economic environment in which conventional prescriptions for achieving growth decidedly favor forms of liberalization that populations believe—correctly or not—likely to generate negative consequences for their welfare. Because recent decades have witnessed an expansion of political space for domestic actors—particularly traditionally excluded groups—to voice their grievances, efforts to block enactment of orthodox economic measures are more successful today than they might have been at earlier points in the region's political history.

Policy makers in Andean democracies thus confront a dilemma that is difficult, if not impossible, to resolve. On the one hand, they must struggle to satisfy domestic elites and external interests that threaten to withhold investment, credit, or foreign assistance should orthodoxy be abandoned. On the other hand, they must mollify, isolate, or suppress domestic critics who mobilize incessantly to demand protection from the anticipated costs of economic restructuring called for by expert opinion at home and abroad. The result is a sort of paralysis that, while not unique to the Andes, is ubiquitous across all five countries in the region: reforms that policy makers consider essential to meet the challenges of globalization are not enacted at all, or are derailed at the implementation stage and thus never take hold. Yet, at the same time, currents of opposition that carry significant weight in civil society invariably lack the control over state power that would be needed to impose an alternative package of measures. Even when they gain a degree of access to the halls of government, as arguably has occurred in Venezuela under the government of Hugo Chávez or was promised by Colombia's 1991 constitution, the limited space afforded by the contemporary international environment or by established interests at home constrains opportunities for policy innovation.

The state-society disjuncture is revealed in especially stark fashion in the experience of Colombia, in the efforts of technocratic policy makers to enact so-called second-generation reforms amidst chronic fiscal constraints that, though comparatively recent in Colombia, are typical of the Andean region as a whole. Exclusionary policy-making processes and the ways officials endeavor to achieve fiscal stability while consolidating market-oriented policies are frequently in tension with democratic practices: so much so, indeed, that they become constitutive of the schisms that undermine governability throughout the Andes. The most carefully designed neoliberal policies fail once they move from the initial design phase to practical implementation. The current crisis is distinctive: Andean societies and polities are deeply fractured despite the genuine political and economic advances that are elucidated in chapters 4 and 6.

Second-Generation Reforms in an Apparently Propitious Context

The empirical focus of this chapter is on the fate of second-generation reforms that were pursued alongside political openings in Colombia beginning during the 1990s and particularly on the interactions between these two distinct but intertwined processes. The choice of cases reflects four key considerations.

First, Colombia's constitution of 1991 marked as ambitious an attempt as any in the Andes to transform the political realm in ways that would expand citizen participation and buttress the legitimacy of a traditionally exclusionary political system.[1] The 1991 constitution represented a watershed in Colombia's political history: it broke not only with the 1886 charter that it replaced de jure but also with the consociational logic of politics that had prevailed for the preceding three decades, even after arrangements for the two principal parties to share power formally had ended. By all accounts, that inherited framework was collapsing under the weight of a profound crisis of legitimacy by the close of the 1980s. Growing political violence, increasing lawlessness associated with drug trafficking, and the continuing presence of armed opposition in much of the countryside where the state had lost—or never really secured—its authority fueled public disillusion with established institutions that neither responded to mass demands nor delivered on the objectives of policy makers. The decision by the César Gaviria administration (1990–1994) to convene a constitutional assembly to rewrite the rules of the game enjoyed overwhelming public support, and was perceived in many quarters as a last-gasp effort to salvage state legitimacy in a context where the very viability of the Colombian state was increasingly coming into question (Posada Carbó 1998).

The 1991 constitution, in short, was a response by the state to an unsustainable political situation in which radical change was needed to open the possibility of stable governance. Struggles to fulfill the democratic aspirations of that new charter—or to constrain its putative excesses —would provide the leitmotiv for debates over economic and social sector policy throughout the ensuing decade.

Second, from the perspective of economic policy making, Colombia would appear to have been better positioned than any Andean country to make the difficult adjustment from the traditional model of inward-oriented accumulation to a new framework oriented toward the global economy and predicated on market-based criteria of resource allocation. Not only had Colombia's economy proven itself uniquely immune to the debt crisis that swept virtually all of Latin America throughout the 1980s, but it had never developed the degree of state centrism that characterized the development models of most countries in the region. Moreover, Colombia had begun the process of opening to external markets at a much earlier stage than its neighbors (Ocampo 2001), and once trade liberalization became a central part of the international consensus on economic policy, Colombia was among the earliest and most aggressive in introducing reforms (Edwards 2001).

Equally important, the country was endowed with an unusually cohesive, highly trained (primarily in the United States), and internationally respected cohort of economists who had long occupied key decision-making positions in the major policy-making institutions concerned with economic development (Thorp 1991; Estrada Alvarez 2004). Colombia's economic policy makers could cite a record of comparative success, most strikingly during the lost decade of the 1980s, during which growth remained steady and indicators of inequality actually declined (chapter 4). In this context, the opening to external markets, liberalization of trade and capital flows, and greater participation of foreign capital in domestic activities were achieved with comparatively little open dispute.[2] Although other Andean countries could draw on some degree of such expertise (Morales 2003; Conaghan and Malloy 1994), Colombia stood out for the extent to which technocratic experts had enjoyed uninterrupted latitude across government ministries and in autonomous agencies such as the powerful Central Bank, the Banco de la República. When the Gaviria administration came to power, the president could draw on an especially ambitious set of economic reform proposals put forth by the Club Suizo. This small group of "technopols," named for the Swiss restaurant in which they met regularly, provided a brain trust of sorts for the administration's efforts to transform the economy in ways that would facilitate its incorporation into global markets (Edwards 2001; Estrada Alvarez 2004). Significantly, however, although there was a clear societal consensus that the polity was in crisis, Gaviria's effort to bring about wholesale change in the economy did not take place in a context in which the populace perceived the economy to be failing.

Finally, the 1990s witnessed repeated efforts to implement a cluster of policy changes in Colombia that fell within the category of second-generation reforms (Birdsall and de la Torre 2001; Edwards 2001; Stallings and Peres 2000) and to do so amidst increasingly severe fiscal constraints and heightened pressure from mobilized constituencies. Second-generation reforms go beyond the dismantling of a putatively exhausted, state-centric model of economic and social development and seek to effect a far more ambitious agenda for refashioning the institutions that help to configure relations between state and society. For policy makers in Colombia, as elsewhere in the Andes and indeed throughout Latin America, the thinking has been that once first-generation reforms achieve (or restore) macroeconomic balance and establish the framework for an outwardly oriented development strategy, additional measures are needed in order for domestic institutions to adequately reflect the market-based logic that underlies the new accumulation model. In effect, second-generation

reforms entail a more thoroughgoing restructuring of state-society relations, encompassing the dismantling of inherited mechanisms for financing and delivering an array of public goods, ranging from education to
health care to retirement pensions.

The distinction between first- and second-generation reforms is crucial. First-generation reforms that open economies to outside forces have
been more or less fully achieved throughout Latin America, albeit with
varying degrees of consistency and following uneven levels of resistance.
Yet second-generation reforms have frequently been frustrated where
democratic political arrangements have been present. This has proven to
be the case even in contexts such as Colombia, where the tradition of powerful technocratic leadership and the comparatively limited weight of
populism would appear to have created especially propitious conditions
for such measures.[3]

In Colombia, as elsewhere in the region, mass opposition to first-
generation reforms was not entirely absent and was often shared by fragments of the elite worried about losing rent-seeking opportunities (e.g.,
tariff protection) on which they had relied for their prosperity. Yet a combination of external pressures, cohesiveness of policy experts, and the
promise of compensatory measures was sufficient to ensure that a substantial degree of trade liberalization, privatization, and capital mobility
became standard practice throughout most of Latin America and certainly
in Colombia. These policies, not coincidentally, tended not to place
greater burdens on public finances. Indeed, particularly where privatization was widespread, first-generation reforms frequently offered temporary influxes of revenue for cash-strapped states. By contrast, the second
generation of reforms needed to fully transcend the old model for linking
state and society—to permanently constrain expenditures in keeping with
the vision put forth by advocates of the Washington Consensus—has not
been implemented where democratic politics have remained vibrant, as
has been the case across much of the Andes from the 1990s to the present.

Most importantly, it is in the frustration of second-generation
reforms—more than in perhaps any other policy-making arena—that the
neglect of societal incorporation in the Andes becomes clearly evident.
Policy packages designed to introduce greater market discipline in such
domains as health care and retirement pensions, to rationalize the tax system, or to transfer to lower levels of government responsibility for social
services and education require cooperation and coordination among
multiple actors who have direct stakes in the sectors being reformed.
Absent at least tacit consent of these stakeholders, including public sector

employees and the managers of institutions through which these services are supplied, even the most modest reform effort is likely to prove highly conflictive and to be frustrated at the implementation stage.

In Colombia, this truism became all the more relevant in that the trend toward decentralization—which accelerated with the 1991 constitution and was further defined by a series of laws enacted during the Gaviria administration—transferred key social service responsibilities to subnational levels of government without fully removing the centralized state and without establishing autonomous mechanisms for financing local expenditures. Largely as a result, ambitious efforts to reform these services not only engendered resistance from stakeholders but also created unprecedented pressure on public finances. How best to enact second-generation reforms while maintaining fiscal balance thus became the core challenge facing economic policy makers throughout the second half of the 1990s and beyond.

Strikingly, the commitment of Colombia's technopols to second-generation reforms was matched by their inability to implement them consistently.[4] In one case after another, carefully designed policies were derailed amidst resistance from workers in the affected sectors, congressional opposition, and widespread public protest. Contentiousness over second-generation reforms cannot be explained away as the product of a singularly extreme crisis that gripped Colombia during these years, for in many respects the economically stable 1980s were no less dire a period than the ensuing decade in the overall functioning of national affairs: had this not been the case, the 1991 constitution would never have been seen as so urgent. Rather, to understand the impediments to reforms during the 1990s requires analysis of how policy challenges were defined by their advocates and how approaches to policy making that might have worked in the past provoked unforeseen tensions in the changed political environment of that decade.

Financing the Decentralized State

Tax reforms were once a rarity in Colombia, as governments relied on income from tariffs and a variety of user fees for the resources needed to conduct the activities of a minimalist state. From 1991 onward, by contrast, each administration has tinkered with the tax code in a never-ending effort to raise additional revenues. These efforts, in turn, have been needed largely because of the increasing pressure on state resources brought about by transfers to subnational levels of government and by

steadily expanding spending on both internal security and social programs. Government spending as a percentage of gross domestic product
(GDP) nearly doubled during the last decade of the twentieth century,
and while higher expenditures were a predictable consequence of the
social provisions put forth in the 1991 constitution, little thought was
given early on to the potential difficulties this would impose on the public balance sheet. On the one hand, Colombia's history suggested the real
possibility that commitments extended on paper would not be fulfilled in
practice. On the other hand, even if these expenditures were to come
about, it was plausible that sufficient resources could be generated: economic growth had been steady for decades, and the tax burden was low,
even by the unexacting standards of contemporary Latin America.

At least two trends complicated this vision in practice. The first concerned expenditures. Contrary to initial expectations, spending at the
level of the central government did not decline in tandem with the transfer of additional funds and responsibilities to subnational entities. Not
only was there excessive duplication of functions across different levels of
government, but the formula used to determine transfers from the central
government to subnational units lacked flexibility. The flow of money to
regions and municipalities increased steadily despite the failure to
achieve expected rates of economic growth.[5] Complicating matters further, institutional impediments emanating from application of key features of the 1991 constitution—such as the Constitutional Court's October
2000 decision to overturn a measure that limited public sector wage
hikes—further impeded efforts to diminish pressures on state resources.[6]
The cost of education, health care, and pensions soared throughout the
decade, as successive governments were unable to contain spending in
policy domains in which pressures of pent-up demand were exacerbated
by institutional weaknesses and political conflict.

Second, economic expansion in fact did not continue as anticipated
when the constitution was being debated. Average annual growth rates
from 1990 to 1997 were a meager 2 percent, and the period between 1997
and 2000 witnessed average declines of 2.1 percent per year (chapter 4).
As a result, after an initial period of easy revenue hikes, the task of raising funds for a more expensive state became more difficult, and fiscal
gaps widened in tandem with economic stagnation. Once again, the situation was especially bleak between 1997 and 2000, when public sector
deficits averaged roughly 4 percent of GDP.

That the Colombian system has faced chronic pressure to increase revenue is evident in the fact that eight full-fledged tax reforms were enacted

during the two decades beginning in 1982. Consistent with the logic of Colombia's opening to the international economy, a decreasing portion of state revenue could be raised by trade-related taxes. Instead, levies on income and value-added taxes (generally on consumption) would have to pick up the lion's share of this burden. The cumulative effect of all these reforms has been a decline in tax evasion, particularly with regard to the corporate income tax, for which evasion rates fell from 25 percent in 1988 to roughly half that a decade later.[7] Yet the decline in evasion rates resulted in part because successive reforms narrowed the tax base considerably: fewer and fewer citizens are responsible for transferring a growing portion of GDP to state coffers.

The share of GDP represented by taxes has indeed increased, though estimates vary on the magnitude of change. Whereas chapter 4 draws on World Bank data to conclude that tax revenues accounted for 11 percent of GDP during 2000, Kalmanovitz (2001) calculates the figure at 14 percent, in contrast to 11 percent of GDP in 1987–1990. These figures compare to 7.6 and 9.2 percent, respectively, during the first and second halves of the 1980s (Steiner and Soto 1999, 22). Regardless of the precise number, there is general agreement that by the end of the 1990s Colombia had caught up with the Latin American norm for tax revenues as a percentage of GDP. Nonetheless, the figure remains far below Organisation for Economic Co-operation and Development rates, somewhat below Asian standards, and substantially inferior to what would be needed to balance public finances or to fulfill the social aspirations of the 1991 constitution. Colombia arguably could afford to devote a considerable portion of its resources to building an efficient state and providing quality public services. While current rates of taxation may be typical of Latin American countries, social scientists are widely agreed that the profound inequalities that plague the region, and the weakness of states throughout Latin America, are consequences of inadequate levels of taxation (Cheibub 1998; Huber 2001).

Ultimately, the incremental hikes in revenue achieved through successive tax reforms have been insufficient to prevent growing deficits, since total government spending increased from around 12 percent of GDP during 1987–1990 to nearly 20 percent by the turn of the century. Clearly, then, the immediate cause of fiscal crisis has been a rapid growth of government spending that has not been matched by corresponding revenue increases.

The relative ease with which tax reforms are introduced in Colombia likely reflects the degree to which politically powerful sectors are confident of their ability to remain insulated from their potentially adverse effects. Because the tax base is so narrow, and the tax code affords ample opportunities for influential groups to gain exemptions, achieving modest reforms in fiscal policy is far less complicated than might be expected, particularly given how elusive reform has proven to be in other policy domains. Yet the contrast is hardly surprising given the degree to which reforms are limited to domains in which groups that historically have enjoyed de facto veto powers in the complex universe of Colombian politics are not called upon to make sacrifices. One implication is that while the ability of the Colombian state to raise additional revenues in recent years may help to redress fiscal imbalances, it may not contribute to the quest to build confidence in the transparency or equity of state policies and thus may fail to strengthen regime legitimacy.

No consideration of Colombia's fiscal circumstances would be complete without specific mention of fiscal decentralization, an ongoing process that began with a 1983 reform and was accelerated by the 1991 constitution and subsequent enabling legislation. Transfers from the national treasury to the periphery are only one aspect relevant to gauging the fiscal impact of decentralization: regional capacities to raise revenues are equally important (Steiner and Soto 1999, 126). Herein lies one of the major drawbacks of the decentralization process pursued in Colombia: while responsibilities accruing to subnational regions and the portion of central state revenues channeled through them have both grown rapidly, those regions have lacked capacity to generate substantial resources of their own through subnational mechanisms of taxation.

Complicating matters further, fiscal laziness has been encouraged by a perception that subnational deficits will be compensated by the central authorities to avoid situations of default (Hershberg 2001). Moreover, land holdings, perhaps the most obvious source of potential tax revenues for local and departmental governments, remain largely exempt from taxation, a situation that is arguably scandalous in a country marked by the dramatic indices of inequality (and rural asset polarization) that plague Colombia. One reason for this deficiency, aside from the reluctance of authorities to demand cooperation from local economic elites, is the woeful state of land registries throughout most of the country. This is combined with the technical and resource weakness of public administration, which lacks reliable mechanisms for assessing the value of assets for tax purposes.

It is widely argued that Colombia's experience with fiscal decentralization has been complicated by weak institutional capacity, inadequate human resources, and the reluctance of the central government to grant autonomy to subnational units, which has saddled them with unfunded mandates (Hershberg 2001). It is further argued that critically needed reforms have not been possible, in part because electoral rules induce members of Congress to serve narrow interests and because the fragmentation of political parties has rendered ambitious legislation all but unattainable (see chapter 9). All of these phenomena are important, and all need to be overcome if the increasingly decentralized Colombian state is to make better use of its resources. But that cannot occur merely through the introduction of coherent policies that reflect international best practice. Rather, the central obstacles to successful policy implementation in Colombia remain the absence of stakeholder backing for rational reforms undertaken by a leadership that enjoys legitimacy and confidence. The prospects for building such legitimacy and confidence hinge on the capacity of the Colombian state to strengthen its presence in society and to project itself as an agent that attenuates rather than exacerbates conflicts, as a source of empowerment rather than exclusion. The political decentralization envisioned in the 1991 constitution constituted an ambitious step in this direction and merits continued support, despite the fiscal inefficiencies that have accompanied its development.

Transforming the Health Sector

In Colombia, as elsewhere in Latin America, implementation of social sector reforms encompassing health, education, and pensions was a central objective of technocrats committed to forging what Edwards (2001, 23) has labeled a new national project, in which a broad coalition of interests would come to accept market-oriented principles for linking state and society in domains that had previously been exempt from logics of competition. Policy makers recognized that in each of these arenas powerful pressures from entrenched interests would resist efforts to replace the state-centric arrangements that had evolved during the previous decades with a more market-driven alternative. Yet they understood their preferences to reflect technical rather than political considerations (Teivanen 2003), and they calculated that public opinion would be largely indifferent toward reforms and could be won over to the cause by increased quality of services and compensatory measures aimed at minimizing costs of transition (Edwards 2001, 37). The experience of efforts to enact these second-generation reforms makes clear, however, that this confidence of the technopols was remarkably misplaced: not only did public opinion side with the opposition to the proposed changes, but significant blocs of politicians defected from the proreform coalition soon after their introduction during the second half of the Gaviria administration. The struggle over health sector reform is illustrative of the general pattern.

Prior to the 1990s, each institutional segment of the health sector in Colombia—the Ministry of Health, the social security institutes, and the private sector—performed each of the myriad functions of a health care system,[8] and the population was stratified by social group, with different groups served by different segments of the system (Frenk, Londoño, and Knaul 1997, 11). Formal sector employees and their relatives were covered by one or another of several social security institutes. Significant portions of the urban middle and upper classes were not covered by social security and met their health needs through the private sector, with financing coming principally from out-of-pocket payments. Finally, both the rural and urban poor relied on the Ministry of Health for medical services, since their lack of formal employment excluded them from social security.

This configuration, which was common in Latin American countries prior to structural adjustment, has multiple weaknesses, including duplication of resources, vast differences in the quality of care offered across the various segments of the system, and high costs to consumers, since in practice a large proportion of social security beneficiaries pay for care provided by the private sector or the Ministry of Health despite already having paid into the social security system (Frenk, Londoño, and Knaul 1997, 11). Recognition of these problems generated consensus in decision-making circles in Bogotá and in Washington on the need to transform the health sector and on several key objectives of reform. Inadequate coverage was undeniable: in 1992 only 20 percent of the population was covered by social security, even though affiliation was supposedly compulsory, and about 80 percent of workers affiliated with the system did not receive family coverage. In addition to segmented access to health care, prohibitive costs for the very poor and unacceptable levels of inefficiency were all to be addressed by reform (Ministerio de Salud 1998).

The model of regulated competition or structured pluralism established with the December 1993 passage of Law 100 aimed to address these shortcomings and to fulfill the aspirations of the 1991 constitution, which envisioned a new, financially stable social security system characterized by universality, solidarity, and efficiency. Universal and compulsory health insurance would supply a package of basic services, while newly created insurance administrators and health care providers, which could be either public or private, would compete to attract clients. Basic coverage would be provided both to participants in the contributory system, whose formal sector employment generated revenues through payroll taxes, and to those who lacked such income and thus formed part of the subsidized system created by the new legislation (Londoño, Jaramillo, and Uribe 2001, 25). A portion of the cost for the subsidized system would be borne by participants in the contributory system (or at least a portion of them, since some negotiated exemptions from the very outset), with the remainder provided by the state. Initially, the package of health coverage that providers were obliged to offer encompassed basic services, with public hospitals continuing to provide services not covered in the basic package. Funding levels for the public hospitals would no longer be determined by the supply of services they offered but rather by a formula based on levels of consumer demand, and the expectation was that this would gradually curtail costs as private providers would increasingly fill needs previously met through the state system.

At the outset it seemed that the resources to fund reform would be adequate, but resistance from key players in the existing public health system combined with erratic shifts in policy, particularly during the first two years of implementation, to create unforeseen inefficiencies and shortfalls in revenues (Fedesarrollo 1998). Between 1993 and 1996, public resources dedicated to health care grew at a rate of 21 percent per year, accounting for 2.4 percent of GDP by the end of the period. From 1995 to 1998, the combined effects of Law 60 (governing decentralization) and Law 100 had tripled the level of resources available for public health and the subsidized regime. Despite this expansion, coverage remained unsatisfactory, duplication of functions was rampant, and the quality of care remained uneven. The explanation for these problems lies in the gap between policy design and policy implementation.

The travails of health sector reform in Colombia are ultimately a saga of political failure. The Gaviria government introduced the reforms toward the end of its term in office, and there was never any assurance that its enthusiasm for change would be shared by the ensuing administration. Indeed, the following years witnessed repeated shifts in sentiment within the health ministry, which changed course on reform following the wishes of each new minister of health—of which there were three during the first twenty months of the Ernesto Samper administration (González-Rossetti and Ramírez 2000, 52). The first minister, Alonso Gómez, attempted a counterreform and introduced a series of measures that delayed implementation and reinforced the position of reform opponents, such as public hospitals, health workers unions, and, in some cases, subnational authorities. Augusto Galán, appointed minister of health in

February 1996, promoted legislation to recover the initial spirit of the Gaviria adminstration's reform, but was stymied by congressional factions opposed to the more market-oriented framework. Finally, María Teresa Forero de Sade, Samper's third minister of health, proceeded to advance reform after two years of delay (González-Rossetti and Ramírez 2000, 53–55), but by then key elements of the reform package had been watered down beyond possibility of repair. Funding to public hospitals, for example, continued to be allocated based on supply rather than demand, and efforts to reduce both the number and the wages of public employees had been blockcd by legislative and judicial decisions.

The reforms enacted under the Gaviria administration assumed autonomy of policy makers from entrenched interest groups, yet the officials who came to power with Samper were committed to work with those very groups. Thus policy design was divorced from implementation. To be sure, the ministerial team responsible for crafting reform had contemplated various strategies to institutionalize its work. One strategy involved enactment of legislation such as Law 100 and corresponding regulatory provisions, another was to change the personnel as well as the structure of the health ministry, and yet another was to lobby the ministry's employees. Advocates of reform endeavored as well to convince their successors of the benefits of the proposed system and reinforced this effort with the promise of loans from the World Bank and the Inter-American Development Bank. Yet the reality was that the new system lacked support not only from the new administration but also from the broader society, and its opponents were ready to act as soon as Gaviria's team left office. In hindsight, theirs was a *fracaso anunciado*, or, in English, a failure foretold.

In many respects structured pluralism offered an appealing alternative to the segmented system of health care delivery that in Colombia as elsewhere in Latin America has failed to provide adequate care for citizens. Yet to implement policies successfully requires more than a compelling blueprint and commitments from well-trained technocrats determined to design ideal systems without regard for the existing context. As noted by Grindle and Thomas (1990) and by the policy analysis literature more generally, even the wisest of policies is destined to fail if its architects do not take into account the complexities of implementation. Rare indeed is the case where technocrats can launch an entirely new structure, untainted by the context of preexisting institutions, competing interests, and suboptimal technical and administrative capacities inherited from the past. This was all the more true in the post-1991 environment, when dissenting voices had unprecedented—and legitimate—opportunities to mobilize and to be heard. In this regard, the story of health care reform in Colombia offers a textbook case of how a reform that makes sense abstractly becomes distorted in practice. There was a striking failure to incorporate critical interests and institutions in the process of design, as well as during the process of implementation. The staying power of inherited practices was seriously underestimated, as were the implications of introducing radical reforms in an environment of unprecedented opening to democratic participation.

By the end of the 1990s practically the sole point on which competing factions could agree was that health sector reform had been a dismal failure. Whereas the opposition to reform attributed the situation to misguided attempts to impose market-driven arrangements in a sector that was concerned with the provision of fundamental public goods, advocates of the second-generation reforms placed the blame squarely on the shoulders of rent-seeking actors and the congressional factions that advocated on their behalf and that successfully blocked implementation of crucial elements of the policy package introduced in 1993.

Causal Stories and Policy Bias in the Aftermath of the 1991 Constitution

In keeping with the spirit of the 1991 constitution, spending on social programs rose steadily during the 1990s, with most of the increase channeled through the departments and municipalities whose expanded mandate focused primarily on provision of health and education services. Initially, these investments made significant inroads on redressing the country's persistent social deficit: poverty rates declined, school enrollments and retention rates rose, and growing portions of the population fell under the scope of traditionally limited schemes for medical care and retirement pensions. State revenues failed to keep pace with these advances, however, generating growing fiscal gaps that turned into a veritable crisis toward the end of the decade, when Colombia faced soaring interest rates and capital outflows in the wake of the financial crises in East Asia, Russia, and Brazil (Kalmanovitz 2001, 290).

By the end of the 1990s, as the deficit reached 5 percent of a declining GDP, experts wavered as to whether the economic crisis confronting the besieged administration of Andrés Pastrana represented the worst in the country's history or merely the most serious since the Great Depression. A growing number of analysts leaned toward the former assessment. Indeed, the most comprehensive study of institutional performance in

Colombia in recent years opens with the observation that by the end of the decade the country's economy was "on the brink of collapse" (Alesina 2000, 1). To understand how this came about and to account for the frustrations experienced by policy makers, it is useful to emphasize the particular ways in which the need for second-generation reforms was articulated and opposition to them was portrayed.

As Stone has argued compellingly (1989), causal stories are crucial to formulating explanations for societal ills and thus for elaborating proposals for how best to overcome those problems through policy solutions. Causal stories consist of a narrative in which a problem is defined, blame for its origins and persistence is attributed to a particular phenomenon or actor, and plausible mechanisms are put forth for effecting change in the particular phenomenon or actor. Absent a causal story, there is no space for policy interventions to have an impact on outcomes. Of course, there is seldom only one story that could be told about any given circumstance, yet for policy makers to acknowledge such complexity is problematic: it highlights the multiplicity of factors that must change in order for policy interventions to succeed and may raise explicitly the role of powerful interests in sustaining adverse conditions. It is typically easier, then, for the policy maker to identify a single actor or group of actors as the source of problems and thus as the target of policies directed to effect change. Ideally, moreover, the choice of targets will be groups with apparently relatively little power to resist demands for change and with limited capacity to compel others to change along with them. Stated differently, the causal stories that motivate policy choices tend all too frequently to focus attention on the sins of the weak and to overlook those of the powerful (Edelman 1988).

This image of the relationship between power and blame for societal troubles is rendered more concrete in the case of debates surrounding particularly contentious second-generation reforms in Colombia. Policy makers and mainstream analysts coincided in emphasizing the negative role played by unions, particularly those of teachers and health workers and other public employees who jealously guarded costly wage and pension packages and insisted on preserving rigid work rules that were deemed to be constraints on efficiency. Citing Weisner (1997), for example, Edwards (2001) identifies Gaviria's inability to move ahead with second-generation reforms as a product of opposition from public sector unions that remained an "untamed monster." Elaborating on this point, and filling in the causal story, Edwards attributes provisions of the 1991 constitution to reserve local resources for health and education to the rent-seeking abilities of public sector workers rather than to public demand for greater attention to those domains.

Accounts such as these devote far less attention to analogous privileges of less vulnerable interests, such as military and elected officials, whose benefits packages were equally exceptional and often far more lucrative. Similarly, amidst the litany of complaints about tax evasion by the minority of Colombians from whom the state secures revenue, little is said about the need for reforms to broaden the reach of the tax system, to encompass owners of vast swaths of underutilized land, for example. The point here is not that the causal stories that emphasize one source of blame for policy failure as opposed to another are incorrect—they may be substantially accurate—but rather that they are consistently partial, and predictably so. Highly instructive in this regard was the Pastrana administration's decision to augment already bloated military pensions as compensation for the military's acquiescence to government negotiations with guerrilla groups. This move was directly at odds with the agreement signed with the International Monetary Fund and in striking contrast to the austerity demands aimed at public sector workers and organized labor. For Colombians and outsiders alike, these sorts of contradictions suggested that the political order remained captured, unable to impose costly adjustments on the wealthy, the political elite, or entrenched interests such as the military and all too inclined to place the blame for the country's problems on small-scale rent seekers, on the war, and on external factors.

Yet especially in a war-torn country in which a new constitution had been enacted in an effort to broaden regime legitimacy, the implications of such partial narratives are worth pondering with care. Responsible recommendations for dealing with the problems of governance in Colombia and other Andean countries cannot overlook the need to forge dynamics of cooperation that are required not only for success in isolated policy domains but, more generally, for the urgently needed process of national reequilibration (Garay 1999). Thus, proposals that on paper, in a sociopolitical vacuum, might appear to make sense hold the potential to effect immeasurable harm if applied in a volatile context such as that gripping Colombia during the 1990s. Stated differently, the temptation to apply purely economic criteria to policy domains that are fundamentally political in nature has the potential both to undermine support for democracy and to result in policy failure (Teivanen 2002). Specialists called in during moments of crisis may succeed in convincing power holders of the need for reform, but as one sympathetic observer has acknowledged, "At the implementation phase the technopols usually find out that the realities of politics conflict with the simple world of economics" (Edwards 2001, 16).

Policy Design and Implementation in Contested Terrain

There is a striking tension in the literature on policy reform, which analysis of Andean travails can help to clarify. On the one hand, there is the conventional—and not inaccurate—claim that policies succeed best when they result from participation by the broadest array of potential stakeholders (Tendler 1997). On the other hand, there is the understanding that to succeed in introducing far-reaching reforms, policy makers must insulate themselves from societal pressures, particularly from those sectors that could derail their initiatives (Tendler 1997; Grindle 2000; Nelson 1989). Drawing on the experience of Mexico, Centeno points out (1997, chap. 2) that technocratic elites are likely to succeed in imposing a solution reflective of a single, consensus view where they enjoy autonomy, control over the state apparatus, and unity with elites. But where any of these factors are absent, the task of isolating critics opposed to reform surpasses the ability of technocratic elites to ensure implementation of their agendas.[9] Similarly, the most compelling analysis to date of policy-making processes in the Andes demonstrates beyond any inkling of doubt that first-generation reforms carried out during the 1980s succeeded precisely where popular participation was nil (Conaghan and Malloy 1994). Whereas the inclusionary line argues for transparency, that emphasizing state autonomy (or separation) from societal pressures suggests a need to hold deliberations close to the vest, to line up one's ducks, as it were, in order to be prepared to successfully overcome the inevitable resistance of entrenched interests with a stake in the existing (presumably suboptimal) state of affairs.

Both accounts, of course, contain a good deal of validity. The question is how best to find a workable balance in contexts where pressures for participation are real and legitimate and where in any event political constraints have the potential to derail the best laid of technocratic blueprints. With the opening to greater political participation, gone are the days when technocrats can launch an entirely new structure, untainted by the context of preexisting institutions, competing interests, and suboptimal technical and administrative capacities inherited from the past. The experience of health sector reform in Colombia offers a textbook case of how measures that make sense abstractly become distorted in practice. There was a striking failure to incorporate critical interests and institutions in the process of policy design, as well as during the phase of implementation, and the power of inherited practices was seriously underestimated.

Assessing Effective Public Policies in a Colombian Context

Accumulated experiences in Latin America—if not from the eastern bloc at the beginning of the past decade and East Asia at its conclusion—suggest that in matters economic one size cannot be forced to fit all. Rhetorically, this is accepted widely nowadays, yet in practice it is not clear that the lesson has been assimilated.[10] Few observers would dispute the notion that public policies are more likely to be implemented and sustainable if they enjoy support and legitimacy from key stakeholders. Nor is there doubt that policies are apt to be more effective if they pursue objectives that are shared by broad segments of interested publics. To be successful, policies must also reflect the capabilities—encompassing expertise, resources, and authority—of the institutions and individuals charged with their implementation and with ongoing monitoring. Those capabilities are more likely to be translated into effective performance in environments characterized by predictable, transparent, and efficient procedures for reaching decisions and for adjudicating differences of interpretation or interests (through formal legal mechanisms or other broadly accepted means). Mechanisms for midcourse corrections, for adaptation, and for accountability are also conducive to maintaining the stakeholder support that is needed for success. Taken together, these criteria amount to saying that where there is effective governance, policies are more likely to be implemented successfully and to enjoy widespread legitimacy.

Given these criteria, it is hardly surprising that many observers of the policy process in Colombia and of the impact of state policies in that country emphasize that there exists a profound crisis of governance. The country's experience with second-generation reforms during the 1990s was one in which key policy initiatives were advanced without the benefit of legitimacy from the full range of crucial stakeholders, many of whom were in a position to block full-scale implementation. Whereas effective policies require institutions with the capacity to enforce their decisions, this has often been lacking, whether because of flawed institutions or because of impediments erected by crucial players in the system. As a result, decisions were frequently made, or remade, on the basis of criteria and processes that bore little resemblance to constitutionally sanctioned mechanisms for managing public affairs in a putatively democratic order.

Yet the problems of governance in Colombia during the 1990s and across the Andes today are not merely a consequence of poor policy design or of institutional weaknesses that specifically concern particular policy domains. Rather, they reflect deeper societal crises, with multiple yet intertwined roots, ramifications, and symptoms that affect the economy and polity alike. Accounts of the recent travails of Colombian society typically focus on the startling levels of violence, the multiplicity of armed actors competing with the state for control over territory and resources, and the particular role played by narcotics trafficking and the U.S.-sponsored war on drugs. Each of these factors is significant for understanding the present phase of crisis, as is the incapacity of a chronically weak state to combat them. But it is important to embed analysis of outward symptoms of breakdown in an understanding of far deeper crises of the society and polity. The role of policy paralysis with regard to second-generation reforms may well have the unanticipated consequence of further eroding legitimacy.

For many observers the political system appears ineffective—and it is—yet we cannot overlook the degree to which it also functions as a mechanism for drawing the loyalty of competing fragments of the society who otherwise share little in common. Peculiar features of the post-1991 system—such as Constitutional Court decisions that strike many observers both outside and inside the country as economically indefensible—may be among the last remaining sources of regime legitimacy in public opinion (interview with A. Mockus, 2001). As one Bogotá-based analyst put it, what to some look like privileges to others constitute legitimate conquests of social struggle (interview with A. Vargas, 2001). Imposition of either interpretation, rather than negotiation and compromise, invites further division in a society that cannot afford that luxury.

Seen in this light, the overarching objective of public policy at this critical juncture of Colombia's history, as elsewhere in the Andes, must be to strengthen spaces for dialogue, cooperation, and tolerance of differences (Garay 1999). Rhetoric by proponents of the government's reforms that labels legislative advocates for the teachers' union as fronts for the guerrillas is not credible and can be construed as ominously threatening (*El Tiempo* 2001).[11] It is partly for this reason that public opinion is so strongly supportive of public sector workers and so skeptical of governing elites and technocrats who plead, hardly without reason, for the need to enact painful reform.

Indeed, as Uprimny Yepes (2001) argues, this exclusionary mode of doing politics may not be unrelated to the predilection of political actors in Colombia to resort to violence. Rather than being a simple reflection of poverty, social fragmentation, or the drug trade, violence emerges from the inability of working people to develop powerful collective organizations able to transfer social demands into the political arena. The challenge facing would-be reformers is to identify strategies for achieving fiscally sound, efficient, and equitable policies without replicating styles of policy making that have helped to bring Colombia to the brink of disaster. Only then can Colombia satisfy the aspirations of a citizenry that, as stated succinctly by Hommes (2000), longs for a country that is livable.

Notes

1. Arguably, Bolivia's experiment with *participación popular* matched Colombia's reforms in ambition, but as Conaghan and Malloy show compellingly (1994, chap. 7), they were decidedly top-down in origin, and they followed rather than coincided with dramatic reorientation of economic organization. (For further reflections on the Bolivian case, see Crabtree and Whitehead 2001; Grindle and Domingo 2003.) Venezuela during the Chavez administration has also undertaken remarkable steps to link traditionally excluded sectors of the population to decision making in various domains, but this has been part and parcel of the Bolivarian project discussed in chapter 10 by Miriam Kornblith, who notes its dubious relationship to democratic practices.

2. As elsewhere in Latin America, privatization was a first-generation reform that provoked considerable conflict in Colombia, even though state-owned enterprises were far less ubiquitous than the regional norm. Both the Gaviria administration's efforts to privatize telecommunications at the beginning of the 1990s and the Pastrana government's efforts a decade later to sell off assets in such sectors as utilities and banking became a source of acute conflict that undermined public support.

3. Chile is a lone exception to this regional pattern (Stallings and Peres 2000), although many of the reforms occurred prior to democratization. In the Andes partial exceptions are found in Bolivia and Peru, but again this occurred during the most exclusionary moments of the governments of Victor Paz Estenssoro and Alberto Fujimori, respectively (Conaghan and Malloy 1994; Conaghan 2001; Wise 2003).

4. Arguably, government advocacy of reform was more consistently evident under the administrations of César Gaviria (1990–1994), Andrés Pastrana (1998–2002) and Alvaro Uribe (2002–present) than during the Ernesto Samper years (1994–1998). Mainstream analysts portray the latter as excessively vulnerable to pressures from special interests, thereby exacerbating the country's fiscal woes (e.g., Hommes 2000; Edwards 2001).

5. While a highly contested 2001 reform paved the way toward slowing this dynamic, the fiscal impact of this correction will not be felt directly for several years.

6. Meanwhile, the country's spiraling civil war placed further pressure on the public coffers, as spending on security, including control of drug trafficking, diverted resources that might have gone elsewhere.

7. For individuals, the corresponding evasion rates were 37 percent in 1989, 52 percent in 1991, and slightly below 25 percent by 1995 (Steiner and Soto 1999, 17). Though still too high, these figures reflect substantial progress over a relatively brief period. Of

course, as Steiner and Soto note (67–68), these data fail to take into account evasion based on illegal income, which is known not to have been trivial in Colombia.

8. These include modulation, financing, articulation, and delivery of services (Frenk, Londoño, and Knaul 1997).

9. "Those democratic regimes that are best able to cope with the political traumas of economic adjustment are those in which power is heavily concentrated, in which interest groups have been institutionalized, or in which private and public elites cooperate; that is, those states in which polyarchical arrangements have previously institutionalized the management and exclusion . . . of particular social voices" (Centeno 1997, 30). In a similar vein, Edwards (2001, 20) argues that technopols are most likely to enjoy broad influence during moments of crisis but that their weight diminishes once the agenda moves to the phase of policy implementation.

10. See Giugale, Lafourcade, and Luff (2003) for a particularly extensive example assessing challenges facing the Uribe administration and its successors.

11. Similar criticism can be leveled against President Uribe's contention in early 2003 that human rights nongovernmental organizations were directly or indirectly benefiting Colombia's guerrilla movements.

Bibliography

Alesina, Alberto, ed. 2005. *Reformas institucionales en Colombia*. Bogotá, Colombia: Alfaomega.

Birdsall, Nancy, and de la Torre, Augusto. 2001. *Washington contentious: Economic policies for social equity in Latin America*. Washington, DC: Carnegie Endowment for International Peace Press.

Centeno, Miguel. 1997. *Democracy within reason: Technocratic revolution in Mexico*. 2nd ed. University Park: Pennsylvania State University Press.

Cheibub, Jose. 2001. Political regimes and the extractive capacity of governments. *World Politics* 50 (3): 349–76.

Conaghan, Catherine. 2001. Making and unmaking authoritarian Peru: Re-election, resistance and regime transition. Miami, FL: *North-South Center Papers* 47 (May).

Conaghan, Catherine, and James Malloy. 1994. *Unsettling statecraft: Democracy and neoliberalism in the Central Andes*. Pittsburgh, PA: University of Pittsburgh Press.

Crabtree, John, and Laurence Whitehead, eds. 2001. *Towards democratic viability: The Bolivian experience*. London: MacMillan.

Edelman, Murray. 1988. *Constructing the political spectacle*. Chicago: University of Chicago Press.

Edwards, Sebastian. 2001. *The economics and politics of transition to an open market economy: Colombia*. Paris: OECD.

El Tiempo. 2001. June 18.

Estrada Alvarez, Jairo. 2004. *Construcción del modelo neoliberal en Colombia 1970–2004*. Bogotá, Colombia: Ediciones Aurora.

Fedesarrollo. 2000. *Coyuntura Económica*. Bogotá, Colombia: Fedesarrollo.

Frenk, Julio, José Luis Londoño, and Felicia Knaul. 1997. The transformation of health systems in Latin America. Paper presented at the Latin American Studies Association meeting, Guadalajara, Mexico.

Garay S., Luis Jorge. 1999. *Globalización y crisis: Hegemonía o corresponabilidad?* Bogotá, Colombia: TM Editores/Colciencias.

Giugale, Marcelo, Olivier Lafourcade, and Connie Luff, eds. 2003. *Colombia: The economic foundation of peace*. Washington, DC: World Bank.

González-Rossetti, Alejandra, and Patricia Ramírez. 2000. *Enhancing the political feasibility of health reform: The Colombia case*. Monograph, Harvard School of Public Health, Harvard University. June.

Grindle, Merilee, and Pilar Domingo, eds. 2003. *Proclaiming revolution: Bolivia in comparative perspective*. Cambridge, MA, and London: Institute of Latin American Studies, University of London.

Grindle, Merilee. 2000. *Audacious reforms: Institutional invention and democracy in Latin America*. Baltimore: Johns Hopkins University Press.

Grindle, Merilee, and John Thomas. 1990. *Public choices and policy change*. Baltimore: Johns Hopkins University Press.

Hershberg, Eric. 2001. Governance in Colombia: Rethinking priorities. Unpublished manuscript.

Hommes, Rudolf. 2000. ¿Como vamos a hacer para que el pais sea vivible? In *Crisis: antecedentes, incertidumbres y salidas*, ed. Marcela Giraldo Samper, 137–52. Bogotá, Colombia: Ediciones Aurora.

Huber, Evelyne. 2001. *Models of capitalism and Latin American development*. University Park: Pennsylvania State University Press.

Kalmanovitz, Salomon. 2001. *Las instituciones y el desarrollo económico en Colombia*. Bogotá, Colombia: Editorial Norma

Londoño, Beatriz, Iván Jaramillo, and Juan Pablo Uribe. 2001. *Descentralización y reforma en los servicios de salud: el caso colombiano*. Washington, DC: Latin America and the Caribbean Regional Office, World Bank.

Ministerio de Salud 1998. *Informe de Actividades 1997–1998 al Honorable Congreso de la República*. Bogotá, Colombia.

Morales, Juan Antonio. 2003. The national revolution and its legacy. In *Proclaiming revolution: Bolivia in comparative perspective*, ed. Merilee Grindle and Pilar Domingo, 213–31. Cambridge, MA: David Rockefeller Center for Latin American Studies and Institute of Latin American Studies.

Nelson, Joan. 1989. *Fragile coalitions: The politics of economic adjustment*. New Brunswick, NJ: Transaction Books.

Ocampo, José Antonio. 2001. *Un futuro para Colombia*. Bogotá, Colombia: Alfaomega.

Posada Carbó, Eduardo, ed. 1998. *Colombia: The politics of reforming the state*. London and New York: Macmillan and St. Martin's.

Stallings, Barbara, and Wilson Peres. 2000. *Growth, employment and equity: The impact of the economic reforms in Latin America and the Caribbean*. Washington, DC: Brookings Institution.

Steiner, Roberto, and Carolina Soto. 1999. *Cinco ensayos sobre tributación en Colombia*. Cuadernos Fedesarrollo 6. Bogotá, Colombia: Fedesarrollo and Tercer Mundo Editores.

Stone, Deborah. 1989. Causal stories and the formation of policy agendas. *Political Science Quarterly* 104 (1): 281–300.

Teivanen, Teivo. 2002. *Enter economism, exit politics: Experts, economic policy and the damage to democracy*. London: Verso.

Tendler, Judith. 1997. *Good government in the tropics*. Baltimore: Johns Hopkins University Press.

Thorp, Rosemary. 1991. *Economic management and economic development in Peru and Colombia*. London: MacMillan.

Uprimny Yepes, Rodrigo. 2001. Violence, power and collective action: A comparison of Bolivia and Colombia. In *Violence in Colombia 1990–2000: Waging war and negotiating peace*, ed. Charles Bergquist, Ricardo Peñaranda, Gonzálo Sánchez, 39–52. Wilmington, DE: Scholarly Resources Books.

Weisner, Eduardo. 1997. Transaction cost economics and public sector rent-seeking in developing countries: Towards a theory of government failure, second conference on evaluation and development. Washington, DC: World Bank.

Wise, Carol. 2003. *Reinventing the state: Economic strategy and institutional change in Peru*. Ann Arbor: University of Michigan Press.

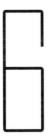

Turning Crisis into Opportunity
Achievements of Excluded Groups in the Andes

DONNA LEE VAN COTT

THE INTENSITY AND DEPTH OF ETHNIC AND RACIAL CLEAVAGES distinguish the Andean region from others in Latin America. Outside of Guatemala, the central Andean countries have the highest proportion of unassimilated, culturally distinct indigenous communities. Outside of Brazil and the Caribbean, Colombia and Venezuela contain the proportionally highest population of African descent (see table 6.1). In the Andes these identities often coincide with geographic regions, deepening the barriers among social groups. Regional identities may mask ethnic and racial identities that are not expressed because such identities are considered incompatible with national myths of *mestizaje* (racial mixing).[1] The persistence of distinct nonnational identities coincides with ingrained patterns of political, economic, and social discrimination and impedes national integration.[2]

A serious crisis of representation exists in the Andes. Political elites have excluded particular population groups from autonomous representation and participation (see chapter 1). Voters and collective social actors

TABLE 6.1
INDIGENOUS AND AFRO-LATIN AMERICAN POPULATIONS IN THE ANDES

	Bolivia	Colombia	Ecuador	Peru	Venezuela
Indigenous (%)	62.05	2.7	24.85	38.39	1.48
African descent (%)	.04	26	10	5	10

Sources: 2001 Bolivian census, 1993 Colombian indigenous census, Deruyttere (1997, 1), Inter-American Dialogue (2003, 1). The latter two sources are likely to undercount ethnic minorities.

are disconnected from political institutions, especially political parties, which are failing to aggregate pressing societal needs and to represent politically salient collective identities.[3] This problem spans Latin America, but it is pronounced in the Andean region, where it has caused a decline in public support for parties. According to a 1998 survey of seventeen Latin American countries by the widely cited survey Latinobarómetro, only 21 percent of the public reported "much" or "some" confidence in parties, with 76 percent reporting "little" or "none." The Andean countries fall in the bottom half in public support.[4] The crisis of representation is exacerbated by an economic context in which all choices are painful, policy implementation may provoke mob violence, and decision making is increasingly removed from citizens and even political parties.

Yet, within this context of crisis and despair, subordinate ethnic groups and women made striking gains in political representation, with the most successful group being indigenous peoples. By the 1980s indigenous peoples in all five countries, albeit to a lesser extent in Peru, had formed modern social movement organizations. In the 1990s they secured the region's most progressive constitutional regimes of special rights, which they used to achieve unprecedented levels of representation in formal politics. Today they govern dozens of municipalities throughout the Andes and regional governments in Colombia, Ecuador, and Venezuela, and they are powerful national forces in Bolivia and Ecuador.

Increasing Representation as Social Movements

In the 1960s and 1970s indigenous people formed social movement organizations in all five countries to provide an alternative to the exclusionary patterns of representation offered by white- and mestizo-led political parties and civil society organizations, such as organized labor. These organizations incorporated Indians but failed to combat their internal racism and refused to share decision-making power or to embrace ethnic and cultural demands. In the central Andes, Indians mobilized separately and for different reasons in the highlands and lowlands before forming unified national organizations and movements. Highland Indians promoted an agenda of agrarian rights and cultural autonomy in the 1960s and 1970s in densely populated regions where demographic growth had reduced the amount of land available to each indigenous family. During those decades indigenous communities and organizations pulled away from political parties, unions, and churches that held them in a subordinate position and refused to recognize the cultural basis of their struggle.

At the same time, in the lowlands, more isolated indigenous communities united to combat intrusions by extractive enterprises, ranchers, and colonists. By the 1980s, geographically extensive, independent indigenous social movement organizations had formed in all five countries. After the quincentenary in 1992, many international donors made funding of indigenous organizations a priority, and those in Bolivia, Ecuador, and Peru gained regular access to these resources.[5] Successful indigenous mobilizations in Bolivia and Ecuador shattered the vision propagated by national elites of docile, backward Indians, whose cultures were destined to disappear into the larger, culturally integrated homogeneous national society. The visible exclusion of so large a sector of the population constituted convincing evidence of the exclusionary nature of the political model and the national myths that underpin it.

In Ecuador, the Communist Party assisted indigenous leaders who organized highland indigenous peasants as rural workers into the Federación Ecuatoriana de Indios in 1944. Progressive Ecuadorean governments that followed tried to counter the influence of communists among highland Indians by offering agrarian reform. After the 1964 Agrarian Reform Law, Indians organized to demand or protect communal land rights, autonomy over natural resources, and access to agricultural assistance programs. The Catholic Church also sought to reduce the influence of the Communist Party by promoting independent indigenous movements. It sponsored the conference of local highland organizations that formed the highland confederation ECUARUNARI (Ecuador Runacunapac Riccharimui, Quichua for the Awakening of Indigenous Ecuadoreans) in 1972.

ECUARUNARI established strong local federations for virtually every distinct highland cultural group. In the central highlands, it has had to compete with a network of evangelical indigenous organizations. The

Missionary Evangelical Union began promoting Protestantism in the highland province of Chimborazo in the 1960s. Its first generation of pastors became the founding leaders of provincial-level Associations of Evangelical Churches (Lucero 2002, 82). These were grouped into a national Ecuadorean Federation of Evangelical Indians, known by its Spanish acronym, FEINE, in 1980. Although FEINE claims a national presence, its greatest influence is in four central highland departments. It originally tried to stay out of politics and to promote mainly confessional activities. However, in the past ten years FEINE has become more involved in politics to counter the popularity of the Confederation of Indigenous Nationalities of Ecuador (CONAIE).

In the Amazon, Shuar indigenous communities organized in the 1960s to defend their territory, culture, and language from incursions by the state, evangelical religious organizations, colonists, and private companies. The discovery of oil in the Amazon in the 1970s and the influx of highland colonists after the new Agrarian Reform Law passed led other Amazonian indigenous groups to organize. Their new ethnic-based federations formed the Confederation of Indigenous Nationalities of the Ecuadorean Amazon (CONFENIAE) in 1979. CONFENIAE, ECUARUNARI, and a weaker coastal indigenous organization formed a national confederation in 1979. This was converted into a more formally structured organization in 1986: CONAIE. By the late 1990s CONAIE represented 80 percent of the country's indigenous population (PRODEPINE 1998).[6] CONAIE led major indigenous mobilizations in 1990 and 1994 that secured substantive rights, including collective land titling and the redrafting of the proposed agrarian reform law (Selverston 2001). In 1998 CONAIE led a popular movement that ousted President Abdalá Bucaram and forced the convocation of a National Constituent Assembly.

Since 2000 CONAIE-led mobilizations have focused on blocking neoliberal reform laws and have gained considerable support from nonindigenous poor and struggling middle sectors. However, CONAIE and the Ecuadorean indigenous movement more generally have lost strength since participating briefly in the Lucio Gutiérrez government in 2003, an experience that exacerbated intense personal, philosophical, and regional divisions within the movement. As a result of the weakening of the indigenous movement and its component organizations—due partly to the decision of some to continue working with the government while others worked to oppose it—the indigenous movement was a relatively minor player in the massive demonstrations that led to Gutiérrez's ouster in April 2005.

In Bolivia, Indians are organized into distinct highland and lowland movements that unite at times to pursue common goals. The Unified Union Confederation of Bolivian Peasant Workers (CSUTCB), established in 1979, has affiliates throughout the country but is strongest in the highlands. Recently it has been challenged by fierce internal divisions and by the emergence of a movement to reconstruct ancient ethnic forms of transcommunity organization (*ayllus*).[7] In the lowlands, most indigenous communities are linked to the Confederation of Indigenous Peoples of Bolivia (CIDOB), established in 1982. After 1997, however, the organization began to lose credibility with a sector of the lowland movement because of its close ties to the government. In 2002, its most vibrant member organization, the Coordinator of Ethnic Peoples of Santa Cruz, left CIDOB, and it has superseded the parent organization in mobilizing power (interview with Carlos Romero, La Paz, June 23, 2002; Rodríguez P., 2002).

Both CSUTCB and CIDOB led major nationwide mobilizations in the 1990s. CSUTCB has had few policy successes. The coca growers' movement dominated the organization from the late 1980s until 1998. The growers' resistance to the state's eradication efforts has earned them a great deal of popular support but has done little to change the policy. In 1998, a radical leader of the Aymara indigenous group, Felipe Quispe, took advantage of a split within CSUTCB leadership to be voted secretary general. Since that time he has led a series of disruptive and often violent roadblocks to pressure the government to provide more economic support to poor highland farmers. Few of the promises made have been fulfilled.

CIDOB has been more successful by adopting a more conciliatory attitude toward the state, which has secured the organization access to policy spheres and resources. That began after a highly successful march from the Beni to La Paz in 1990, which had a profound effect on the nation's political elite. But CIDOB's more pragmatic approach has divided the movement. For example, CIDOB, CSUTCB, and the Syndical Confederation of Bolivian Colonists organized a march in late 1996 to oppose the government's proposed agrarian reform law. CIDOB made a deal with the government that fulfilled most of its demands. CSUTCB held out for more and ultimately was disappointed. The experience embittered relations between the two organizations. A second major joint effort did not occur until 2002, when CIDOB and the ascendant ayllu movement, organized under the Council of Ayllus and Markas of Qullasuyo, led a nationwide march demanding constitutional reform.

Bolivia's indigenous organizations enjoyed a resurgence in October 2003, when the two most prominent indigenous leaders—Quispe, secretary general of CSUTCB, and Evo Morales, leader of the coca growers—led their constituents in a nationwide mobilization that toppled President Gonzalo Sánchez de Lozada and shelved a proposed deal to sell natural gas to the United States and Mexico. Quispe and Morales, who represent two new indigenous political parties in the national Congress, effectively placed issues of concern to the indigenous majority on the national agenda. As this book went to press in the summer of 2005, Morales and Quispe were among the leaders of an indigenous-peasant uprising demanding the nationalization of Bolivian oil and gas and the immediate convocation of a constituent assembly.

In Peru, indigenous organizations were slower to form at the regional and national levels than in Ecuador and Bolivia. This lag is attributable to the dominance of Marxist and Maoist ideologies in the majority-indigenous highlands; the negative connotations attached to indigenous ethnicity there; the partial success of land reform in the 1970s; a legal system that traditionally has treated highland and lowland Indians separately, making joint action more difficult; the policy of the Shining Path during the 1980s and early 1990s to assassinate rival leaders of subaltern groups; the policy of the Alberto Fujimori government to label as terrorist any oppositional political activity; and heavy migration to the cities during the 1980s and 1990s, which removed Indians from areas that were traditional indigenous territories (De la Cadena 2000; Fernández Fontenoy 2000; Mallón 1998, 97–98; Rénique 1991; interviews in Lima with Rodrigo Montoya, July 17, 2002, and Richard Chase Smith, July 16, 2002). Since the recuperation and defense of indigenous territories is the centerpiece of indigenous mobilization in neighboring countries, the dislocation of much of Peru's indigenous population deprives the Peruvian movement of a powerful organizing theme.

Nevertheless, it is incorrect to say that ethnic cleavages have not yet been politicized in Peru or that there is no ethnic political movement. The rise of presidents Fujimori and Alejandro Toledo is intimately linked with the desire of the majority of Peruvians to overthrow the light-skinned, Europhile elite that traditionally has dominated Peruvian politics. Although it is weaker than indigenous movements in neighboring countries, a coherent national indigenous movement emerged in the 1990s. It has been hampered by organizational disunity in both the highland and lowland regions.

In the lowlands, the Interethnic Association of the Peruvian Amazon

(AIDESEP) and the Confederation of Amazonian Nationalities of Peru compete for prominence. The first was created by ethnic federations in 1979; the latter was formed after several groups left AIDESEP in 1987. Similarly, in the highlands, two confederations vie for dominance. The Peasant Confederation of Peru was created in 1947, when leftist parties controlled the peasant movement. The Revolutionary Government of the Armed Forces created the National Agrarian Confederation in 1971 as a less radical alternative, but it became independent in 1980. A national organization to unite both regions, the Permanent Conference of the Indigenous Peoples (COPPIP), was created in 1997. A group of leaders from Peru's two most dynamic indigenous organizations—AIDESEP and a new highland organization, the National Coordinator of Communities Affected by Mining[8]—left and formed their own COPPIP, substituting the word conference for coordinator.

The new COPPIP has adopted a more independent, confrontational stance toward the government, while the original group works more cooperatively with government institutions. The Peruvian movement has made few substantive policy gains, but it has secured direct relations with the Peruvian state through the establishment of a variety of ad hoc working groups. Since the strategic defeat of the Shining Path and the ouster of President Fujimori, the Peruvian indigenous movement has become more active and has earned more attention from the Peruvian state and international donors.

Despite the minuscule size of the indigenous population, indigenous organizations in Colombia and Venezuela have mobilized thousands of constituents for dramatic political actions that resulted in the satisfaction of many of their symbolic and substantive rights claims. These movements have been less divided by region than in the central Andes. In Colombia, most indigenous communities are affiliated with the National Indigenous Organization of Colombia (ONIC), which was formed in 1982. The main instigator for the creation of ONIC was the departmental organization Regional Indigenous Council of Cauca, which formed a decade earlier. A less classist, more ethnicist organization, Indigenous Authorities of Colombia, emerged in Cauca in 1977. Today ONIC has regional affiliates representing twelve departments, as well as dozens of lower-level ethnic federations and zonal organizations. In Venezuela, the Indian Council of Venezuela, formed in 1989, represents the majority of indigenous peoples, apart from those affiliated with traditional political parties. Its sixty affiliates represent thirty distinct peoples. The most important state-level affiliates represent Amazonas, Bolívar, and Zulia.

The problem of national identity in the Andes is framed in chapter 1 as a crisis of domination. Indigenous movements in all five countries represent a broad sector of society that questions the legitimacy of the claim to rule of an economically privileged and politically overrepresented minority. These movements have been part of an effort to expose and destroy the myth of a homogeneous, elite-defined national culture and the manipulation of that myth to exclude the majority from political participation. As Chilean anthropologist José Bengoa argues, "In proposing a multiethnic and multicultural society, the indigenous not only have questioned their own situation of poverty and marginality, but also have questioned the relations of domination of Latin American society based in racial discrimination, in ethnic intolerance, and in the domination of one culture over others. Indians have questioned the bases of the Latin American Republican State, constructed over the idea of 'one single people, one single Nation, one single State'" (Bengoa 2000, 27, my translation).

The way indigenous movements challenge the legitimacy of elite domination differs somewhat between the northern and central Andes. In Colombia and Venezuela, where their numbers are minuscule, Indians "perform" their identities as an important symbol of the historical exclusion of many Colombians and Venezuelans, particularly the poor, from participation in relatively closed two-party–dominant formal political systems and the clientelist networks the dominant parties have imposed.[9] The creation of special rights for indigenous communities is part of a larger effort to demonstrate the state's adherence to international standards of human rights, to tolerate multiple forms of diversity, and to make government structures more accessible, flexible, and responsive, particularly at the municipal level.

In the central Andes, where indigenous peoples are a more substantial sector of the population, their exclusion takes on more practical meanings. The political exclusion of indigenous peoples in Bolivia, Ecuador, and Peru is not merely a symbolic problem, since it affects such a large part of the population. The central Andean political systems were constructed in the nineteenth and early twentieth centuries for the purpose of dominating the indigenous majority and preventing them from entering formal politics, except as the submissive vassals of elites and after undergoing cultural assimilation. The incorporation of proportionally significant, culturally distinct indigenous populations in the central Andes may require not just the opening of existing political institutions but also their alteration to accommodate indigenous political values and customs. Indigenous organizations' claims for such alterations have received little support from the general public, at least when aimed at national political institutions. Indigenous organizations are more successful when they can frame their agenda as an alternative to neoliberal reforms and offer their leaders as an alternative to the corrupt, unresponsive political elite.

For a variety of reasons beyond the scope of this chapter, few Latin Americans of African descent organize politically around ethnic or racial identities (Serbin 1991). In the Andes, blackness is expressed mainly as a socioeconomic category, since skin color is a strong determinant of poverty and political exclusion. In most countries blacks are made invisible by dominant discourses of racial harmony that deny the discrimination they suffer, their underrepresentation in public office, and their higher levels of poverty. They are ignored by academics, nongovernmental organizations (NGOs), and international donors, which have been key supporters of less numerous indigenous populations (Halpern and Twine 2000). Where black populations are large—in Colombia and Venezuela—blackness usually is not politicized. Few people self-identify as black, apart from some local cultural movements, because of the stigma attached to blackness, and no national black political movements have emerged (Wade 1993; Wright 1990).

In the central Andes, where black populations are small, all three governments treat them as an indigenous people, and their concerns are addressed within ministries and government commissions addressing indigenous rights, where they are always outnumbered by indigenous representatives. In Bolivia, the tiny black population brought to work in the mines during the colonial era has assimilated into the Aymara group. In Peru, small, urban-based black organizations have little political presence but are included in the Toledo administration's National Commission for Andean, Amazonian and Afro-Peruvian Peoples. They often work with the main indigenous organizations.[10] In both countries incipient black movements have benefited from emulating and joining the activities of more coherent indigenous movements, essentially adopting the discourse of indigeneity and the rights of peoples to self-determination (Halpern and Twine 2000; Van Cott 2000).

There have been some signs of greater political activity among blacks in Colombia and Ecuador, where significant concentrations span the Pacific coast. A tiny, educated elite inspired by the U.S. black power movement and the Haitian ideology of negritude[11] dominates urban black politics. These movements have not grown appreciably since the 1970s. In rural areas, however, activity increased in the 1980s. Many rural blacks are settled in geographically remote communities established by runaway slaves in the sixteenth and seventeenth centuries. A weak movement in favor of the cultural and territorial rights of isolated, riverine black communities in the Pacific coast region emerged in Colombia and Ecuador in the late 1980s. Like their indigenous neighbors, they mobilized for territorial rights based on historic claims as peoples dating back hundreds of years. Geographic isolation enabled them to develop and maintain distinct cultures derived from their African ancestry. In both countries they emulate the successful discourses and strategies of the indigenous movement.

Afro-Colombians were too weak to gain representation in the 1991 National Constituent Assembly. Instead, indigenous assembly delegates advanced Afro-Colombian rights claims. As a result, Afro-Colombian territorial and cultural rights were codified, and some groups have used these as a basis to form new organizations and to make territorial, educational, and resource rights claims (Van Cott 2000; Wade 1993).[12] The political awakening of Colombian blacks, and the government attention they received, inspired Afro-Ecuadorean communities to intensify their efforts. Just as Afro-Colombians formed multiethnic coalitions with Emberá Indians in Chocó, Afro-Ecuadoreans in Esmeraldas united with the Chachi (Halpern and Twine 2000). After 1995, when Afro-Colombian constitutional rights were being implemented, Ecuador's rural black organizations became more assertive. Some worked within the National Federation of Peasant, Indigenous and Black Organizations. Afro-Ecuadoreans concentrated on the coast formed the Process of Black Communities and the National Confederation of Afro-Ecuadoreans (interview with Pablo de la Torre, July 28, 1999).

Improved Representation through Institutional Reform

In the 1990s the Andean countries undertook constitutional reforms to modernize inefficient state bureaucracies and to restore the legitimacy of failing democratic regimes. These were responses to public demands for greater participation and representation, as well as efforts by the political elite to increase the legitimacy and governability of state institutions that had become deadlocked, inefficient, and riddled with corruption. All incorporated extensive judicial reforms influenced by European constitutions, international law, and multilateral institutions, particularly the Inter-American Development Bank (Jarquín and Carrillo 1998, 152–153; Landa and Faúndez 1996). The strengthening of judicial systems facilitated the adoption and (partial) enforcement of international standards of human rights for disadvantaged groups. In addition to new constitutional rights, in the 1990s ethnic minorities and women gained a champion within the state bureaucracy to defend them. Defensorías del pueblo (human rights ombudsmen) were established in Colombia in 1992, Peru in 1996, Ecuador in 1997, Bolivia in 1998, Venezuela in 1999. These have paid special attention to the rights of women and indigenous peoples.

Indigenous Rights

Within the context of a search for national political renovation, indigenous movements in all five countries presented proposals to define a

TABLE 6.2
ETHNIC CONSTITUTIONAL RIGHTS IN THE ANDES

	Columbia 1991	Bolivia 1994	Ecuador 1998	Peru 1993	Venezuela 1999
Rhetorical recognition	"The State recognizes and protects the ethnic and cultural diversity of the Colombian Nation" (Art. 7)	"Bolivia free, independent, sovereign, multiethnic and pluricultural ..." (Art. 1)	"Ecuador is a ... pluricultural and multiethnic state." (Art. 1)	"The State recognizes and protects the ethnic and cultural plurality of the Nation" (Art. 2)	"To establish a democratic ... multiethnic and pluricultural society ..." (preamble)
Customary law[a]	Yes	Yes	Yes	Yes	Yes
Collective property	Yes	Yes	Yes	Yes[b]	Yes
Indigenous languages official	In indigenous territories	No	In indigenous territories	In indigenous territories	For Indians
Bilingual education	Yes	Yes	Yes	No	Yes
Reserved seats in government	Yes, Senate	No	No	No	Yes, all levels
Black rights	Limited territorial and self-government rights	Legally equivalent to indigenous peoples	Comparable to indigenous rights to the extent applicable	No	No
Autonomy regime	Yes, resguardos comparable to municipalities	No	Awaits implementing legislation	Indigenous municipalities, per statute	Indigenous municipalities^

[a]In most cases, indigenous customary law is limited by the constitution. In Peru, customary law is limited only by international human rights standards; in Venezuela, by the constitution, as well as "the law and public order."
[b]The 1993 constitution allowed for the sale and mortgaging of indigenous communal lands.

more culturally inclusive national identity. They stimulated an important debate on the nature of citizenship and the failure of traditional elites' homogenizing national project. All five countries in the 1990s adopted constitutional language recognizing the ethnic and cultural diversity of the nation. Bolivia, Ecuador, and Venezuela went the furthest by specifically recognizing the "pluricultural and multiethnic" nature of their societies (see table 6.2). The debate on national identity introduced new themes into mainstream politics and provided a legal basis for future, more substantive, cultural rights claims.

In Colombia (1991), Ecuador (1998), and Venezuela (1999) indigenous activists participated as voting members in constituent assemblies. In Ecuador, Indians gained seven representatives to the constituent assembly through the new CONAIE-based political party Pachakutik Plurinational Unity Movement–New Country, known as Pachakutik. In Colombia, the public elected two indigenous delegates, and one was appointed to represent a demobilized indigenous guerrilla group (Quintín Lame). In Venezuela, indigenous peoples selected representatives for three reserved seats, and two additional indigenous delegates were elected in competition with non-Indians in regional districts. In all three countries indigenous delegates participated actively in the debate on the nature of citizenship, helping to define it in more participatory terms, for example, by advocating the legalization of more direct forms of democracy. They joined center-left blocs that removed institutional barriers to political participation. Effective participation in constitutional reform processes provided to indigenous movements an experience of direct, successful engagement with the state and political elite, as well as a sense of their ability to mobilize supporters. Indigenous assembly delegates forged alliances with a broad spectrum of sympathetic allies, while the intense and disproportionate media attention they received made them national figures (Van Cott 2000, 2003).

In Bolivia and Peru, indigenous activists and organizations had less access to the constitutional reform process. In Bolivia, the lowland organization CIDOB and some more conciliatory sectors of the highland peasant movement met frequently with officials in the Sánchez de Lozada government, which oversaw constitutional reforms between 1994 and 1997. They secured recognition as distinct peoples, as well as important substantive rights concerning collective ownership of land, exercise of customary law, participation (without a vote) in local government decision-making processes, and bilingual education. However, the inability of

indigenous representatives to bargain as equals with other assembly delegates—no constituent assembly was convened—led to a less satisfactory
set of rights than in the three countries where Indians were direct participants. As a result, between 2000 and 2003 Bolivian indigenous organizations mobilized in favor of a constituent assembly in which they would
have equitable representation. After weeks of pressure from indigenous
organizations, in October 2003 President Sánchez de Lozada promised to
put the convocation of a constituent assembly at the top of the political
agenda; after his ouster, his successor, Carlos Mesa, promised to fulfill this
promise. As this book went to press, that assembly was expected to be
elected in June 2006.

In Peru, indigenous organizations were too weak to elect delegates to
the 1993 Constituent Congress. President Fujimori, who opposed indigenous rights, dominated that body and rejected their claims. The result was
a serious setback for Peruvian Indians. Since taking office in 2001, President Toledo has stimulated a participatory process of constitutional
reform, but indigenous organizations have seen their proposals ignored,
and most do not appear in the 2003 version of the proposed constitution.
A lack of political consensus more generally has impeded progress on the
entire constitutional project (personal communication from Martín Tanaka, April 29, 2005).

The present regimes of indigenous rights are presented in table 6.2.
Those secured through constituent assemblies in which indigenous delegates participated contain a set of rights that constitute a regional model
of multicultural constitutionalism (Van Cott 2000, chap. 9). These include
(1) the rhetorical recognition of their status as distinct peoples that make
up part of the nation; (2) the recognition of indigenous legal systems as
legitimate and binding; (3) the protection of collective lands from sale,
dismemberment, or confiscation; (4) the right to bilingual education; and
(5) the official recognition of indigenous languages. This model reflects
the commitment thirteen Latin American countries made when they
signed International Labour Organization Convention 169 (1989) on the
rights of indigenous and tribal peoples. All five Andean countries signed
the convention, and the Bolivian, Colombian, and Ecuadorean constitutions largely fulfill this international commitment. Bolivia falls short of
the model because it fails to give official status to indigenous languages.
The 1993 Peruvian constitution is even less satisfactory: it removed the
official status that the Quechua language had enjoyed in the previous
charter, while weakening collective land rights by allowing indigenous

lands to be dismembered and sold. It also failed to guarantee bilingual education.

Some of the new Andean constitutions guarantee the representation of Indians in public office and provide space for the exercise of political autonomy at the subnational level. The latter is particularly important because the demand for an autonomous geographic space wherein indigenous peoples can govern themselves using their own laws, authorities, and forms of organization is the overarching, articulating demand of indigenous peoples' movements throughout the world. Such geographic spaces, anchored in collectively owned, inalienable territories, provide the material basis for the protection and development of indigenous cultures.

Colombian Indians are guaranteed two seats in the 102-seat Senate. Venezuelan Indians are guaranteed three seats in the National Assembly, plus a seat on state-level assemblies and municipal councils in districts where they have a significant presence. In both cases, only Indians can run in these districts, but anyone can vote in them, which creates a risk that Indians representing independent organizations may lose to those sponsored by political parties. In Peru, an indigenous quota of 15 percent was instituted for party lists for regional elections in 2002 as part of Toledo's Regional Elections Law (Article 12). The quota only applied to the Amazon, and there was no mandate as to the placement of indigenous candidates on the lists. In Bolivia in 2004, in response to pressure from indigenous groups during the October 2003 uprising that toppled the president, the Bolivian Congress passed a constitutional reform that gave indigenous peoples the right to participate in municipal and national elections as indigenous organizations without having to fulfill the more onerous registration requirements that political parties face (Van Cott 2005).

All Andean constitutions or laws, except Bolivia's, provide for the creation of indigenous municipalities, where indigenous peoples can govern themselves according to their customs and exercise their customary law (the issue was pending in Bolivia in 2005). In Colombia, indigenous *resguardos* (reserves governed by indigenous authorities) covering one-quarter of the national territory enjoy the same status as autonomous municipalities elsewhere in the country, as well as special rights and resources as resguardos. The 1991 constitution envisions joining these to create extensive Indigenous Territorial Entities. Similarly, in Ecuador, the 1998 constitution provides for geographically extensive Indigenous Territorial Circumscriptions, but political turmoil and a lack of consensus within the indigenous movement have delayed implementing legislation. In Bolivia, indigenous districts within municipalities have no autonomous rights. The current draft Law of Constitutional Reform would allow the creation of indigenous municipalities.

Afro-Descendent Rights

Colombia and Ecuador incorporated special rights for black communities into their constitutional reforms. In both cases, indigenous movement allies secured rights for rural, culturally distinct black communities that are similar to but less extensive than those secured for indigenous cultures and territories.[13] The process of negotiation between black activists and the state over this legislation enabled incipient black rights movements in both countries to grow. For example, by 1997 there were more than eighty Afro-Colombian organizations in Colombia, most of them formed after the 1991 constitutional reform. The most important effect of constitutional recognition was the public legitimation of black identity and culture, which encouraged more Colombians to self-identify as black (Grueso 1995, 5–6; Grueso, Rosero, and Escobar 1998; Van Cott 2000, 97–98; Wade 1993, 182, 356–58). Similarly, Afro-Ecuadoreans have mobilized to influence the implementing legislation for their new constitutional rights, forming several important organizations after 1998 (interview with Pablo de la Torre, July 1999).

The 1991 Colombian constitution allowed for the creation of two reserved seats in the lower chamber of Congress for representatives of black communities, as that term is ambiguously used in the constitution and Law 70 of 1993. This ambiguity reflects a tension between the vision of constitution makers, the state, and political elites that these rights apply to the minority of Afro-Colombians who live in rural, riverine communities on the Pacific Coast and practice aspects of African cultures and the vision of some black activists that the term be more broadly defined to include all Afro-Colombians. The seats were instituted for the 1994 elections, but the Constitutional Court subsequently struck them down on technical grounds. Black politicians lacked the support to reinstate them until 2001, when a seat in the lower chamber for indigenous communities also was reinstated (interview with Piedad Córdoba, Bogotá, 1997; Cunin 2003).[14] However, as Cunin argues, the two winning candidates did nothing to facilitate the representation of poor, rural blacks: they had no political experience or ties to black political organizations. Both were urban-based athletes who attracted votes based on their athletic prowess and paid lip service to the idea of black political rights. In fact, the strongest candidate opposed affirmative action for blacks, ethno-education, and the idea of categorizing Colombians ethnically, since "we are all mestizos" (90). Although all Colombians are eligible to vote in the district, only 2 percent chose to do so, a slight decline from the 1994 results, despite a decade of consciousness raising by the state and black organizations. As Cunin concludes, not only did the 2002 elections reinforce stereotypes about blacks and shut out black politicians, "The election of María Isabel Urrutia and Welington Ortiz, under the criteria of sports success and absent any type of political commitment or competence, appears clearly as a political failure for the ethnic social movement, incapable of appropriating for itself the electoral space reserved in its name" (78, my translation).

Even where ethnic rights proposals have survived opposition from elites (particularly rural elites) in constituent assemblies and congresses, they often must overcome intense elite resistance to their implementation. In Colombia, legislators representing rural elites have prevented the passage of statutory laws required to establish the extensive mandated territorial circumscriptions for more than ten years. In Bolivia, the Hugo Banzer–Jorge Quiroga administration, which received considerable support from lowland ranchers, stalled the distribution of land in the eastern lowlands decreed by the Sánchez de Lozada administration. Indians have repeatedly sought protection of their rights from the courts and human rights ombudsmen in Bolivia, Colombia, Peru, and Venezuela and against the violence of elites toward combative indigenous communities and leaders, particularly in rural areas. Blacks in Colombia have several times sought court action to broaden the narrow interpretation of their new constitutional rights that elites have tended to impose.[15]

Women's Rights

Women's movements also secured a variety of rights in the new constitutions. The most important political advance was the adoption of quota laws requiring parties to include female candidates in their legislative lists. Argentina was the first to institute quotas in 1991, with great success. This model inspired other elite women to press for quotas, particularly after a process of networking and strategizing leading up to the 1995 UN Conference on Women in Beijing. According to Htun, the women's movement "gained visibility and legitimacy" during that process (1998, 7–8).[16] After Beijing, all Andean countries except Colombia instituted legislative quotas, as did six other Latin American countries. Colombia instituted a 30 percent quota for senior executive positions in 2000.

As a subregion, the Andean countries lead the Americas in women's political representation (see table 6.3). In 2000, Andean legislatures were approximately 14.4 percent female, while in the five Southern Cone countries, the average was 11.8 percent—despite the fact that this subregion includes the outlier Argentina, whose legislature is 27 percent female. Mexico and Central America average 11.3 percent (based on unicameral or lower-chamber data from Htun 2001, 7). With respect to cabinet appointments, there is a clear divide between the northern and central Andes, which may reflect the larger pool of educated, professional women in those countries.[17] Women average one-fifth of cabinet positions in Colombia and Venezuela, but only 4.7 percent in the central Andes (8). Most cabinet positions have been in lower-status ministries, but there are notable exceptions. Colombia has had several female ministers of foreign relations. Ecuador gained its first female foreign relations minister, indige-

TABLE 6.3
WOMEN'S PROGRESS IN ATTAINING POLITICAL OFFICE IN THE ANDES

	1980 (%)	1990 (%)	2000 (%)	2003 (%)	Quota law? Size/date instituted/ placement mandate? (%)
Bolivia					
Ministers	—	0 ('93)	0	—	—
Chamber of Deputies	1	9	12	18.5	30, 1997, yes
Senate	8	4	4	14.8	25, 1997, no
Mayors	—	—	6	—	
Ecuador					
Ministers	—	8	7	—	—
Congress	0	7	15	16	20, 1997, no
Mayors	0	4	3	—	—
Peru					
Ministers	—	13 (1988)	7	—	—
Congress	7	6 (1988)	20	17.5	25, 1997, no raised to 30 in 2002
Mayors	—	6 (1993)	2	—	—
Colombia					
Ministers	—	7	19		30, 2000, n.a.
Chamber of Deputies	5	9	12	12.0	—
Senate	1	1	13	8.8	—
Governors	—	—	3	—	—
Mayors	—	6	6	—	—
Venezuela					
Ministers	0	13	21	—	—
Congress	5	10	9.7	9.7	30, 1998, no
Governors	—	0 (1989)	9	—	—
Mayors	—	9 (1989)	4	—	—

Sources: Htun (2001, 8), Inter-American Dialogue (2001, 12–15), Inter-Parliamentary Union (n.d.).

nous activist Nina Pacari, in 2003. In Colombia and Venezuela, women have parleyed visible executive positions into serious presidential campaigns.

The presence of women in legislatures and top executive positions has enabled multipartisan female coalitions to pass legislation of great importance to women, particularly in the areas of domestic violence, gender discrimination, and women's health (Htun 2001, 8). Legislative coalitions are most effective when they can partner with coherent women's movements (Htun 1998, 6). For example, Peru's Movimiento Manuela Ramos "accompanies women elected to Congress and lobbies for bills promoting women's rights" (Htun 2001, 9). Women's organizations also are dynamic and organized in Venezuela and Colombia, but less so in Bolivia and Ecuador.[18]

Improved Representation through Political Parties

While women and Afro-Latin Americans improved their representation in formal politics in the 1990s through participation in existing parties, indigenous peoples in all five countries formed their own parties. Only in Bolivia, where tiny Katarista[19] parties won a few seats in legislatures during the 1980s, were indigenous parties formed prior to the 1990s. Onerous ballot-access requirements and loyalty to better-financed clientelist and leftist parties prevented these early electoral vehicles from surviving. In addition, they lacked a firm base in social movement organizations, which provided free labor, campaign resources, and loyalty to fledgling parties in the 1990s.[20]

In the mid-1990s (earlier in Colombia), indigenous peoples' movements shifted from a strategy consisting entirely of extrainstitutional social movement activity to a dual strategy combining social mobilization with autonomous electoral participation. While continuing to press for policy change through massive social mobilizations, the most consolidated indigenous organizations in all five countries formed their own electoral vehicles and won autonomous representation for the first time. Two types of institutional reforms helped them. Decentralization was the most important.[21] It enabled new, weak parties to compete at a level that is less expensive than national contests and in areas where indigenous peoples are concentrated and their organizations are strong. Moreover, decentralization provided a structural framework for the exercise of indigenous movements' key articulating demand—the right to autonomous self-government.

The second important institutional reform was the lowering of party registration barriers, which occurred in Bolivia, Colombia, Ecuador, and Venezuela. The 1991 Colombian constitution allows social movements to compete in elections without registering as political parties. The 1998 Venezuelan constitution allows indigenous organizations to run without forming a party. In Ecuador, in 1994 the ban on electoral alliances was repealed and individuals and social organizations were allowed to participate in elections in any province where they could register 1.5 percent of voters. Parties are no longer required to register members in ten provinces, three of which must be the country's most populous provinces. Since the country's most populous provinces are on the coast, where the indigenous population is small, this helps indigenous peoples (Birnir 2000, 10). In Bolivia, indigenous organizations were first allowed to compete as such in municipal elections in December 2004.

Indigenous peoples' parties also have been aided by dealignment and fragmentation within party systems, which opens the political system to new entrants. In fact, the formation of viable indigenous parties in the 1990s is an indicator not only of the maturity and consolidation of indigenous movements but also of the weakness and instability of Andean party systems. Indigenous parties are most successful where the founding indigenous organization is unified and well rooted in a dense, geographically extensive network of affiliates. They thrive in national politics when they lead a coalition of leftists and anti-neoliberals that transcends the appeal of ethnocultural demands and where established, experienced, and militant indigenous movement organizations spawn parties that absorb the remnants of an electorally defeated Left, as well as unattached intellectuals and less dynamic social movements. Through their interaction with nonindigenous popular and middle-class sectors, such parties articulate a discourse that weds the indigenous drive for self-determination to the Left's goal of blocking and reversing neoliberal economic policies (Van Cott 2005).

The most successful of the new indigenous peoples' parties was formed in Ecuador. Pachakutik formed in 1995 immediately after improvements in ballot access were instituted and following a successful CONAIE-led mobilization to defeat President Sixto Durán Ballén's neoliberal reform proposal. This experience demonstrated to CONAIE leaders the mobilizing power of and popular support for the indigenous movement and helped to convince them that an electoral vehicle might be successful (Sánchez López and Freidenberg 1998, 72). In Pachakutik's first elections in 1996, it won eight seats in the eighty-two-seat national Congress and became the fourth largest bloc in a fragmented Congress. In

2002 Pachakutik formed an electoral alliance with the Partido Sociedad Patriótica (PSP), the party of Lucio Gutiérrez, a former military officer who had joined CONAIE president Antonio Vargas in a brief coup attempt in January 2000. The PSP-Pachakutik alliance won the presidential elections, netting Pachakutik leadership of the cabinet ministries of foreign relations and agriculture. Pachakutik won five congressional seats on its own, six with the PSP, and three more in alliance with other parties.[22] The alliance could not withstand the tension between the indigenous party and the increasingly neoliberal policies of Gutiérrez. The president ejected Pachakutik from the government in August 2003, as Pachakutik leaders were considering a voluntary exit.

In Bolivia, the impetus to form an indigenous electoral vehicle emerged from within the coca growers' movement, although the possibility had been discussed within CSUTCB since 1992. The movement competed in Bolivia's first-ever municipal elections in 1995 through the Assembly for the Sovereignty of the Peoples (ASP). The ASP elected ten mayors, forty-nine municipal councilors, and eleven departmental *consejeros* (counselors). In 1997 it won four uninominal seats in the Chamber of Deputies. In 1998 personal conflicts split the party. The rump ASP, led by Alejo Véliz, won twenty-eight council seats and five mayoral positions in the 1999 municipal elections, all in Cochabamba, a total of 1.12 percent of seats nationwide.[23] The populist, Cochabamba-based party New Republican Force successfully courted Véliz and other peasant leaders by offering privileged candidate positions. In fact, an expected increase in the success of indigenous movement–sponsored parties, after two years of intensive popular mobilization, led all major parties to court indigenous candidates before the 2002 elections (interviews in La Paz with Marcial Humerez Yapachura, June 25, 2002, and Jorge Lema, June 20, 2002; *Los Tiempos* 2002).

After the 1998 split, coca growers leader Evo Morales formed a new party, the Political Instrument for the Sovereignty of the Peoples (IPSP). Using the valid registration of the Movement toward Socialism (MAS), in the 1999 elections the IPSP elected seventy-nine municipal councilors in seven of the country's nine departments. The party's status as a national political force improved dramatically between 2000 and 2002, as Morales became a national symbol of rejection of the economic and political status quo. Meanwhile, the populist party Conscience of the Fatherland, which had drawn most of its votes from the indigenous highlands, collapsed. As a result, in 2002 the MAS won 20.94 percent of the national vote, which netted eight senators and twenty-seven deputies. The party finished second in the presidential contest, less than 2 percentage points behind the winner. A second new indigenous party, Pachakutik Indigenous Movement (MIP), formed by CSUTCB general secretary Felipe Quispe in 2000, also competed in 2002. The MIP won 6.09 percent in 2002, earning six deputies. Political analysts were quick to observe that the indigenous parties combined won 27 percent of the vote, more than the winning National Revolutionary Movement. Their success literally changed the face of Bolivian politics. In addition to the forty-one seats they obtained, at least ten additional indigenous legislators entered Congress in 2002 with other parties.[24] The MAS was in first place in the 2005 presidential and congressional races as this book went to press.

Forming their own parties has been a lower priority for Peru's indigenous organizations. Some encourage members to run with existing parties that have the potential to win. The Peasant Confederation of Peru has made formal alliances with parties. It supported Toledo's presidential bids in 1999 and 2001, and several of its leaders ran on his Perú Posible ticket. The National Agrarian Confederation encourages affiliates to focus on local elections and to avoid involvement in national politics that might split the movement. Inspired by the success of indigenous parties in Bolivia and Ecuador, in July 2002 some peasant leaders expressed the desire to form their own vehicle for the next national contests (interviews with Wilder Sánchez, Lima, July 12, 2002, and Nestor Guevara, Cuzco, July 23, 2002).

The Amazon organization AIDESEP launched a new party, the Indigenous Movement of the Peruvian Amazon (MIAP), at a 1996 national congress (MIAP 2001, 1). According to AIDESEP leader Wrays Perez, MIAP and its affiliated lists elected thirteen indigenous mayors in various Amazonian provinces in the 1998 municipal elections (interview, Lima, July 11, 2002).[25] In 2002, MIAP was only able to register the party in one province; elsewhere it formed alliances with registered parties, particularly with Perú Posible. According to León (2002, 24), Amazonian Indians won seven mayoral contests—all of them through alliances between MIAP and registered parties. MIAP has been unable to collect fifty thousand signatures to register the party for elections above the municipal level. Leaders are hoping to do so by the 2006 elections and to expand the party to include Afro-Peruvian and Andean Indians (interview with Wrays Perez). Another barrier to electoral success has been fraud, which has prevented some winning MIAP candidates from taking office (interview in Lima with Jorge Agurto, July 11, 2002; Defensoría del Pueblo 2000, 11–13).

In Colombia, several indigenous parties have emerged. The most successful is Indigenous Social Alliance (ASI), which first competed in 1991 in local and national elections. The Regional Indigenous Council of Cauca, in alliance with the demobilized Quintín Lame guerrillas and other popular organizations, created ASI to compete in the first post–constituent assembly elections. ASI elected one senator in open competition with nonindigenous candidates and parties in 1991, and in 1994 elected eight mayors, eighty-four municipal councilors, and three departmental deputies. In coalition with another party, it elected Afro-Colombian leader Zulia Mena to the lower chamber of Congress in the reserved black district. In 2000 ASI joined with Indigenous Authorities of Colombia to elect the first indigenous governor of Cauca, and ASI elected eleven mayors in four departments, 146 municipal councilors in twenty departments, and eight departmental deputies in five departments (Registraduria de Colombia n.d.).

Thus, despite the small size of the indigenous population and its lack of resources, ASI has had astounding success. In a study of the performance of forty-eight nontraditional parties following the 1991 constitutional reform, García Sánchez found ASI to be among only five that had gained power in more than 2 percent of the country's eleven hundred municipalities between 1988 and 2000. It was one of only eight parties that had been reelected (2001, 7). A key reason for this success is ASI's ability to reach out to nonindigenous sectors, particularly in Cauca, which is only 15 percent indigenous.

In Venezuela, indigenous parties have been successful in Amazonas state, where the population is approximately 49 percent indigenous. The Regional Organization of Indigenous Peoples of Amazonas created the United Multiethnic People of Amazonas (PUAMA) in 1997 to further its fight for indigenous rights in the Amazonas state constitution. PUAMA won a seat in the state assembly in 1998 and a seat in the constituent assembly in 1999. In 2000, in alliance with the leftist Fatherland for All, PUAMA elected an indigenous governor of Amazonas, a representative to the National Assembly, a deputy in the state's legislative assembly, and ten municipal councilors.

In addition to the challenges all new parties face, indigenous parties must combat efforts by political elites to disqualify them from running and to usurp their victories. On several occasions the Peruvian human rights ombudsman has had to intervene when Amazonian elites stole victories from tiny indigenous parties. In Bolivia, elites have conspired to have indigenous mayors removed from office, often by tricking them into signing documents that they cannot read or falsifying municipal ledgers to incriminate them. In Bolivia indigenous parties have had their registration denied, often on suspicious grounds, and at the behest of traditional parties. Conversely, the questionable registration of Felipe Quispe's party was allowed to stand in order to split the indigenous vote (Van Cott 2005). In Venezuela, the state governor opposed the indigenous party PUAMA's registration and delayed its publication in the *Gazeta Oficial*. Traditional politicians accused the party of being "subversives and revolutionary guerrillas" who are manipulated by the Catholic Church (Pérez 1999, 9). In Colombia, numerous indigenous public officials have been threatened and even assassinated, usually by guerrillas or paramilitaries who accuse indigenous officials of supporting both armed groups' opponents or usurping their territorial authority.

Upon entering national office, indigenous parties have fought against corruption and clientelist practices, fulfilling their promise to provide a more honest, more accountable political model. In the Ecuadorean Congress, although some indigenous legislators have been jailed for corruption, Pachakutik has crusaded against corruption and expelled party members linked to it. It also has refused to participate in the distribution of patronage. As former Pachakutik deputy Luis Macas recalls, "We refused to agree with any other party or the government on the distribution of *prebendas* [patronage], for example, which we oppose. . . . We have always tried to avoid these activities and to denounce them when they occur" (interview, July 28, 1999, my translation).

In Bolivia, the MAS has distinguished itself by its ethical behavior. In late 2002 it championed a failed proposal to lower congressional salaries, and it returned approximately US$580,000 of public election funds it received to the National Electoral Court, just over half the total amount received, which it had not used. In June 2003 MAS and MIP representatives were among fifty opposition legislators who went on a hunger strike to demand that the government end congressional holidays one month early so that the Congress could address serious social issues and that the government stop dragging its feet on legislation affecting land rights and help for farmers. After forty-two of the legislators gave up the strike, seven legislators, most of them indigenous, continued, demanding that a poor community be allowed to establish a university (CNN 2003).

Indigenous parties have put themes on the agenda that had not previously found a place in mainstream political discourse, such as the value of cultural diversity, the problem of racism, and the need for nonpartisan means of representation and participation for civil society groups. Their popularity has forced traditional parties to include these themes in their own agendas. Even when they fail to secure legislative and policy changes, as is common, indigenous parties provide a national platform to challenge the political status quo and the ideologies, symbols, and values on which it is based. They serve as voices for all of the disenfranchised and disaffected, offering a critique of the state and regime that otherwise might not be represented in national politics.

At the local level, particularly in Ecuador, some indigenous municipalities have instituted more participatory, intercultural forms of decision making that incorporate indigenous consensus-building processes while reaching out to all ethnic groups, urban and rural (MUPP 1999; León 2002; *Latin American Andean Group Report* 2001). These experiments are helping to construct citizenship from the ground up and to restore the legitimacy of public authority, at least at the local level. It remains to be seen whether they can be adapted to the intermediate level of government (state/ department/province), where indigenous parties gained office in Colombia, Ecuador, and Venezuela. It also is uncertain whether they can be disseminated to nonindigenous municipalities, which attract far less international development aid, or even sustained in indigenous municipalities after that aid inevitably dries up.

Explaining Achievements of Marginalized Groups

What explains these improvements in the representation of marginalized groups at a time when systems of representation are considered to be in crisis and most civil society actors must struggle for voice and influence? First, they are taking advantage of institutional reforms that lowered barriers to participation in formal politics and created space for new forms of participation. Second, declining support for traditional political parties and increased party system fragmentation opened space in party systems for new entrants, particularly on the left of the political spectrum. Indigenous movements have been more successful than other popular, anti-neoliberal movements partly because they have the advantage of drawing on global indigenous rights networks. Powerful international actors such as the World Bank, the Inter-American Development Bank, the European Union, sympathetic governments, and NGOs often pressure weak, aid-dependent Andean executives to accede to indigenous demands (Brysk 2000). These demands are increasingly viewed as legitimate by political elites who are sensitive to changes in international human rights standards and discourses and who seek to be viewed as abiding by them. Multilateral organizations, under pressure from transnational indigenous rights networks, particularly in the United

States and Europe, have altered their lending and development policies in ways that require states to protect indigenous cultures and consult with their representatives. Policies with respect to other disadvantaged groups are relatively less developed.

Domestic and international economic forces also help explain the emergence and success of indigenous movements. But it is simplistic to suggest that their success is attributable directly to these forces. First of all, while the middle and working classes were incorporated into the power structures of society incompletely, indigenous peoples were barely incorporated at all. Living in extreme poverty, their lands were confiscated or encroached on, and their labor was coerced. The benefits received through clientelism and populism were meager relative to those received by the urban poor and wealthier rural peasants. The neoliberal economic reforms of the 1980s provoked a collective political response not because they dramatically increased indigenous poverty but rather because they threatened to reduce indigenous autonomy. Privatization of land, and encroachments by agribusiness, ranching, and extractive industries threatened to dismember the material basis of their cultures and their status as self-governing peoples. Neoliberal reforms also were important because they reduced the ranks of unions and peasant movements and decimated the electoral Left in most Andean countries. After a decade of economic decline, clientelist and populist parties were less able in the 1990s to deliver material benefits to the expanding poor majority.

Thus, voters seeking an alternative to the pain of structural adjustment and the corruption of the political elite had few options. Indigenous peoples not only articulated an anti-neoliberal, antiglobalization alternative, they visibly and explicitly challenged the homogenizing national project of the light-skinned minority and its subservience to foreign economic and political powers. This is seen most clearly in Bolivia, where coca growers' leader and presidential candidate Evo Morales gained the support of middle-class voters by running against the U.S. embassy while dismissing his opponents as self-serving, anti-Bolivian embassy stooges. He refused to debate the other candidates, arguing that only the U.S. ambassador was worth engaging. Ironically, non-Indians seeking a more authentic and defiant national identity increasingly embrace the counternationalisms of indigenous movements. Indigenous peoples persuasively claim more authentic forms of authority than are held by the state or political elites. They symbolize a new era of political inclusion and legitimacy.[26]

It is wrong, however, to attribute the emergence and growth of indigenous political movements mainly to economic forces (e.g., Brysk and Wise 1997; Yashar 1998, 32–33). Although indigenous peoples mobilize to defend class interests, most abandoned classist organizations and parties in the 1980s because their central concern is the expression and recognition of their status as distinct peoples. Moreover, economic changes since the mid-1970s have generated a variety of social changes that benefited marginalized groups. Women and ethnic minorities gained better access to education and the paid, formal labor market, resulting in larger pools of educated professionals from which the current generation of feminist, indigenous, and black leaders emerged. Their successes have changed public opinion about the political capacity of women and minorities (Htun 1998, 3). The greater availability of technology has enabled marginalized groups to interact with each other and to disseminate their messages over vast geographic spaces for a fraction of the cost required in previous decades. Neoliberal economic reforms have fostered increasing hemispheric economic integration, which, in turn, has fostered the drive for greater social, scientific, and political cooperation in the Americas. Commitments made at Summits of the Americas in Miami, Santiago, and Quebec have led to advances in government attention to feminist and indigenous rights demands (Htun 2001).

Finally, the spread of minority rights and feminist movements demonstrates a strong diffusion effect within Latin America that is particularly intense within the Andes. Contacts among indigenous organizations in the Americas are more intensive within the Andean subregion, because of geographic proximity; historical, linguistic, and cultural ties among indigenous groups that transcend national borders; and the policies of NGOs and multilateral organizations that sponsor indigenous movement activities. The two main NGOs sponsoring indigenous movements in South America, Oxfam America and Denmark's Ibis, work exclusively in the central Andean countries, where they sponsor exchanges that strengthen national and transnational movements and contribute to the relatively greater resource base of central Andean movements. During constitutional reforms, Andean governments and indigenous organizations met with experts and participants in constitutional reform from Andean countries that had already undergone reforms. This diffusion effect is the main reason that the Andean constitutions (except Peru's) are the most advanced with respect to indigenous rights. There is also an intra-Andean diffusion effect in the formation of indigenous political parties: the success of parties in Colombia and Ecuador inspired indigenous organizations in the other three countries to give electoral politics a try, notwithstanding their less favorable institutional and political environments.

Indigenous peoples' achievements demonstrate that marginalized groups can convert crises of representation into opportunities for representation as established patterns of interest intermediation break down. Thus the contemporary crisis of representation may be a necessary condition for the creation of radically new forms of political representation and participation that can replace institutions that were created to monopolize power and to exclude darker-skinned groups. If new forms of political action are not mediated by existing institutions, we should not be overly concerned, provided that they are governed by democratic norms and that they give rise to new institutions that channel popular demands and construct inclusive spaces for public policy formation. Indigenous movements have been at the forefront of constructing democratic, participatory spaces, particularly in Ecuador, where some indigenous-run municipalities hold regular popular assemblies and where indigenous legislators have inspired other parties to incorporate civil society representatives into policy-making processes. Thus in some contexts indigenous peoples not only have improved their own level of representation, they have improved the quality of democracy for all citizens.

These participatory spaces, and the public sphere in which they are embedded, are more likely to descend into violence and chaos where fiscal pressures prevent elites from acceding to redistributive demands or where elites resort to repression to contain them. This is a particular danger where democratic institutions are weak, as they are in the central Andes. It is also the case that not all of the ethnically oppressed groups discussed here adhere to democratic values, such as tolerance of difference, a commitment to nonviolence, and an inclination to pursue consensus rather than coercion.

These inauspicious conditions converged in Bolivia during 2005. After months of tense negotiations and threats by lowland elites and highland indigenous organizations, beginning in mid-May and extending into June, tens of thousands of primarily indigenous Bolivians, frustrated by the failure of either the president or Congress to convoke a promised constituent assembly or to respond to several other urgent national issues, paralyzed transportation and commerce. Indigenous protesters and their supporters seized the sidewalks and streets of the capital for several weeks, leaving residents to protect themselves against the vandalism and violence of a minority of the protesters as police tried to protect key government buildings from occupation or destruction. As white youths in the lowland city of Santa Cruz attacked indigenous protesters and shouted racist slogans, indigenous protesters menaced and assaulted white pedestrians, tearing off their neckties.

Evo Morales and other popular indigenous and leftist leaders convened massive public assemblies that were billed as democratic spaces of discussion. In practice, dissenting voices were silenced and these spaces were used solely to build and to demonstrate mass support for the demands of a small group of charismatic leaders. The escalating political crisis in Bolivia demonstrates the futility of excluded groups' gaining access to formal democratic institutions when such institutions are unable to function and when deeply embedded racism and the resentment engendered by centuries of oppression and humiliation provide incentives to political leaders to avoid compromise and maintain extremist positions.

Notes

1. For example, in the Atlantic Coast of Colombia Afro-Colombians self-identify as *costeños*.

2. By nonnational, I mean an identity that does not coincide with the dominant identity projected by national elites as identical with the state.

3. A large literature examines the region's low levels of political party system institutionalization and high level of institutional deadlock, the recent collapse of party systems in Peru and Venezuela, and the fragmentation of party systems in Bolivia and Ecuador. See, for example, Dietz and Myers (2001), Levitsky and Cameron (2001), Mainwaring and Scully (1995), Roberts (2002), Romero (1994), Rospigliosi (1995), Tanaka (1998), and Whitehead (2001).

4. Of the seventeen countries surveyed, Venezuela, Ecuador, Argentina, Panama, Nicaragua, Peru, Colombia, and Bolivia, in that order, elicited the most "no confidence" responses (Alcántara and Freidenberg 2001, table 4).

5. Two nongovernmental organizations give priority to the funding of indigenous peoples' movements in Bolivia, Ecuador, and Peru: the Danish group Ibis and Boston-based Oxfam America. The Inter-American Foundation, the World Bank, and the Indigenous Peoples' Fund also fund indigenous organizations, particularly in these three countries (telephone interview with Martin Scurrah, May 14, 2003; e-mail from Pilar Martínez, April 29, 2003).

6. Another important national indigenous organization is the National Federation of Peasant, Indigenous and Black Organizations, formed originally as the National Federation of Peasant Organizations in 1968.

7. An ayllu is a preconquest form of indigenous organization common to the central Andean highlands consisting of discontinuous community lands in distinct ecological zones that facilitate a variety of productive activities.

8. The new organization was created in 1999 to unite communities hurt by mining activities and has quickly become the most mobilized, unified highland indigenous organization. In 2002 it had thirteen regional affiliates in sixteen departments, representing 1,135 communities, and had ties to indigenous organizations in Bolivia and Ecuador.

9. See Jackson (2002, 85) on the performance of indigenous identity.

10. For example, the Black Association for Human Rights joined four indigenous organizations in demanding the creation of a permanent mechanism to enable indigenous peoples to participate in policy decisions and a Fund for the Development of Indigenous Peoples and Afro-Peruvians (*Servindi* 2003).

11. *Negritude* promotes the positive features of blackness and critiques ideologies of racial improvement through *mestizaje* (race mixture) and *blanqueamiento* (whitening; Halpern and Twine 2000).

12. In Venezuela, no black organizations lobbied for political rights during the 1999 national constituent assembly, apart from a small women's organization working within the women's rights lobby (interviews in Caracas with Luis Gomez Calcano, May 15, 2000, and María Pilar García, May 16, 2000).

13. In Colombia, these rights were implemented through statutory legislation in 1993 (Law 70). In Ecuador, they await legislative action (Van Cott 2000, 276–77).

14. Colombians living abroad and political minorities also gained reserved seats in Law 649 of 2001. See Cunin (2003) for an excellent discussion of the impact of this law.

15. For example, the Constitutional Court agreed with black activists that the city of Santa Marta must extend to them the protection of the constitution, even though they are not organized according to the narrow definition of black community in the constitution (interview with Constitutional Court magistrate Eduardo Cifuentes Muñoz, March 17, 1997).

16. Quotas only significantly improve women's representation if parties are required to place women in electable positions on a closed list, rather than at the bottom or letting voters express a preference. They are more effective if their implementation is clearly delineated and mandatory and district magnitudes are large (Htun and Jones 2002, 32). These conditions rarely exist.

17. In Bolivia and Ecuador, parties have had difficulty filling their quotas with willing, qualified female candidates.

18. My opinion is based on the effectiveness of women's organizations involved in constitutional reform during the 1990s. According to Htun, women organized successfully in Venezuela to influence the 1982 civil code reform and in Peru in the mid-1990s to influence domestic violence legislation (1998, 6).

19. They are named after the eighteenth-century Indian rebel Tupaj Katari. This section on indigenous parties is based on Van Cott (2005).

20. The most successful one was the Movimiento Revolucionario Tupaj Katari de Liberación, which formed in 1985. In 1993, Víctor Hugo Cárdenas was elected vice president on a joint ticket with the National Revolutionary Movement. The party declined thereafter and did not compete in 2002, when it would have had to pay fines because of its poor showing in 1999.

21. In Peru, municipal decentralization occurred in 1981. The Toledo administration in 2002 passed a new Law of Regionalization, which reestablished the regional governments that Fujimori dismantled in 1993. In Ecuador, municipal decentralization followed the democratic transition in 1983. In Colombia, municipal decentralization began in 1988 and was extended to departments in 1991. In Bolivia, the 1994 Law of Popular Participation achieved municipal decentralization. In Venezuela, direct elections for mayors and governors began in 1989.

22. FEINE formed Amauta Jatari in the mid-1990s to challenge Pachakutik. It finished last in 2002 with less than 1 percent of votes.

23. Figures are according to Alejo Véliz (interview in La Paz, July 17, 2001). The National Electoral Council lists twenty-two seats won by the ASP, which borrowed the registration of the Bolivian Communist Party for these elections.

24. This estimate is based on Rivero (2003, 21) and *La Razón* 2002.

25. AIDESEP documents and interviews with militants indicate that between

twelve and fourteen indigenous mayors held office as of July 2002, but not all of these ran with MIAP. Many ran with Perú Posible or We Are Peru; others formed local indigenous parties for the 1998 municipal elections (Defensoria del Pueblo 2000, 11–13).

26. Colombian president César Gaviria and Venezuelan president Hugo Chávez made this claim during their country's constituent assembly.

Bibliography

Alcántara Sáez, Manuel, and Flavia Freidenberg. 2001. Los partidos políticos en América Latina. *América Latina Hoy* 27 (April): 17–35.

Bengoa, José. 2000. *La emergencia indígena en América Latina*. Santiago, Chile: Fondo de Cultura Económica.

Birnir, Johanna Kristin. 2000. The effect of institutional exclusion on stabilization of party systems in Bolivia, Ecuador and Peru. Paper presented at the 22nd International Congress of the Latin American Studies Association, Miami, FL, March 16–18.

Brysk, Alison. 2000. *From tribal village to global village: Indian rights and international relations in Latin America*. Stanford, CA: Stanford University Press.

Brysk, Alison, and Carol Wise. 1997. Liberalization and ethnic conflict in Latin America. *Studies in Comparative International Development* 31 (Fall): 76–104.

CNN. 2003. Bolivia calls emergency session of Congress amid hunger strike. http://www.cnn.com. June 2.

Cunin, Elisabeth. 2003. La política étnica entre alteridad y estereotipo. Reflexiones sobre las elecciones de marzo de 2002 en Colombia. *Análisis Político* 48 (January–April): 77–93.

Defensoria del Pueblo. 2000. *Situationes de afectación a los derechos políticos de los pobladores de las Comunidades Nativas*. Serie Informes Defensoriales, no. 34. Lima, Peru.

De la Cadena, Marisol. 2000. *Indigenous mestizos: The politics of race and culture in Cuzco, Peru, 1919–1991*. Durham, NC: Duke University.

Deruyttere, Anne. 1997. *Indigenous peoples and sustainable development: The role of the Inter-American Development Bank*. Washington, DC: Inter-American Development Bank.

Dietz, Henry, and David Myers. 2001. The process of party system collapse: Peru and Venezuela compared. Paper presented at the 2001 Congress of the Latin American Studies Association, Washington, DC.

Fernández Fontenoy, Carlos. 2000. Sistema político, indigenismo y movimiento campesino en el Perú. In *Los movimientos sociales en las democracias andinas*, ed. Julie Massal and Marcelo Bonilla, 193–211. Quito, Ecuador: FLACSO, IFEA.

García Sánchez, Miguel. 2001. La Democracia Colombiana: Entre las reformas institucionales y la guerra. Una aproximación al desempeño de las terceras fuerzas en las alcaldías municipales, 1988–2000. Paper prepared for presentation at the 2001 Congress of the Latin American Studies Association, Washington, DC, September 6–8.

Grueso, Libia. 1995. Cultura política y biodiversidad en el proceso de comunidades negras del pacífico colombiano. Paper prepared for presentation at the 21st Congress of the Latin American Studies Association, Washington, DC.

Grueso, Libia, Carlos Rosero, and Arturo Escobar. 1998. The process of community organizing in the southern Pacific Coast Region of Colombia. In *Cultures of politics/politics of cultures: Revisioning Latin American social movements*, ed. Sonia Alvarez, Evelina Dagriho, and Arturo Escobar, 196–219. Boulder, CO: Westview.

Halpern, Adam, and France Winddance Twine. 2000. Antiracist activism in Ecuador: Black-Indian community alliances. *Race and Class* 42 (October–December): 19–31.

Htun, Mala. 1998. Women's political participation, representation and leadership in Latin America. Issue Brief. Washington, DC: Inter-American Dialogue.

———. 2001. Advancing women's rights in the Americas: Achievements and challenges. Issue Brief. Washington, DC: Inter-American Dialogue.

Htun, Mala, and Mark Jones. 2002. Engendering the right to participate in decision-making: Electoral quotas and women's leadership in Latin America. In *Gender and the politics of rights and democracy in Latin America*, ed. Nikki Craske and Maxine Molyneux, 32–56. London: Palgrave.

Inter-American Dialogue. 2001. *Women and power in Latin America: A report card*. Washington, DC: Inter-American Dialogue.

———. 2003. *Race report*. Washington, DC: Inter-American Dialogue.

Inter-Parliamentary Union. n.d. www.ipu.org/wmn-e/classif.htm.

Jackson, Jean E. 2002. Contested discourses of authority in Colombian national indigenous politics: The 1996 summer takeovers. In *Indigenous movements, self-representation, and the state in Latin America*, ed. Kay B. Warren and Jean E. Jackson, 81–122. Austin: University of Texas Press.

Jarquín, Edmundo, and Fernando Carrillo, eds. 1998. *Justice delayed: Judicial reform in Latin America*. Washington, DC: Inter-American Development Bank.

Landa, César, and Julio Faúndez, eds. 1996. *Contemporary constitutional challenges*. Lima, Peru: Pontificia Universidad Católica del Perú.

La Razón. 2002. Algunas características del próximo parlamento. June 7. http://www.la-razon.com.

Latin American Andean group report. 2001. The rise of Auki Tituaña. *Latin American Andean Group Report*, April 3.

León, Jorge. 2002. *La política y los indígenas en América Latina: La redefinición de las relaciones entre el Estado y los pueblos indígenas*. Oxfam America and Ford Foundation.

Levitsky, Steven, and Maxwell Cameron. 2001. Democracy without parties? Political parties and regime collapse in Fujimori's Peru. Paper prepared for presentation at the Congress of the Latin American Studies Association, Washington, DC, September 6–8.

Los Tiempos. 2002. Campesinos las nuevas 'vedetes' electorales, April 4. http://www.lostiempos.com

Lucero, José Antonio. 2002. *Arts of unification: Political representation and indigenous movements in Bolivia and Ecuador*. PhD dissertation, Department of Politics, Princeton University.

Mainwaring, Scott, and Timothy Scully. 1995. *Building democratic institutions: Party systems in Latin America*. Stanford, CA: Stanford University Press.

Mallon, Florencia E. 1998. Chronicle of a path foretold? Velasco's revolution, Vanguardia Revolucionaria, and "Shining Omens" in the indigenous communities of Andahuaylas. In *Shining and other paths: War and society in Peru, 1980-1995* ed. Steve J. Stern, 84–117. Durham, NC: Duke University Press.

MIAP. 2001. El MIAP y su aporte a la construcción de un nuevo Perú. Satipo, Peru. Mimeo.

MUPP. 1999. Desafíos de los municipios innovadores: Pachakutik. *Revista de debate político* 1 (July): 66–67.

Pérez, Benjamin. 1999. Participación en movimiento Politico Indigena Pueblo Unido Multiétnico de Amazonas (PUAMA). La Inglesia en Amazona 85 (September): 8–9.

PRODEPINE. 1998. *Censo nacional de organizaciones indígenas y negras e indice de fortalecimiento institucional.* Quito, Ecuador: PRODEPINE.

Registraduria de Colombia. n.d. http://www.registraduria.gov.co.

Rénique, José Luis. 1991. *Los sueños de la sierra: Cusco en el siglo XX.* Lima, Peru: CEPES.

Rivero, Wigberto. 2003. Indígenas y campesinos en las elecciones: El poder de la Bolivia Emergente. http://www.developmentgateway.org.

Roberts, Kenneth M. 2002. Party-society linkages and democratic representation in Latin America. *Canadian Journal of Latin American and Caribbean Studies* 27 (53): 9–34.

Rodríguez P., Alfredo. 2002. Se profundiza división entre indígenas. *El Deber* (Santa Cruz), October 29. http://www.eldeber.com.bo.

Rospigliosi, Fernando. 1995. La amenaza de la 'Fujimorización' gobernabilidad y democracia en condiciones adversas: Perú y los países andinos. In *Partidos y clase política en América Latina en los 90,* ed. Carina Perelli, Sonia Picado S., and Daniel Zovatto, 311–33. San José, Costa Rica: IIDH.

Sánchez López, Francisco, and Flavia Freidenberg. 1998. El proceso de incorporación política de los sectores indígenas en el Ecuador: Pachakutik, un caso de estudio. *América Latina Hoy* 19:65–79.

Selverston, Melina. 2001. *Ethnopolitics in Ecuador: Indigenous rights and the strengthening of democracy.* Miami, FL: North-South Center Press.

Serbin, Andrés. 1991. Por qué no existe el Poder Negro en América Latina? *Nueva Sociedad* 111 (January–February): 148–157.

Servindi. 2003. Proponen sistema institucional para Pueblos Indígenas y Comunidades. *Servindi* 24 (June): 5–6.

Tanaka, Martín. 1998. *Los espejismos de la democracia: El colapso del sistema de partidos en el Peru, 1980–1995, en perspectiva comparada.* Lima, Peru: Instituto de Estudios Peruanos.

Van Cott, Donna Lee. 2000. *The friendly liquidation of the past: The politics of diversity in Latin America.* Pittsburgh, PA: University of Pittsburgh Press.

———. 2003. Andean indigenous movements and constitutional transformation: Venezuela in comparative perspective. *Latin American Perspectives* 30 (1): 49–70.

———. 2005. *From movements to parties in Latin America: The evolution of ethnic politics.* New York: Cambridge University Press.

Wade, Peter. 1993. *Blackness and race mixture: The dynamics of racial identity in Colombia.* Baltimore: Johns Hopkins University Press.

Whitehead, Laurence. 2001. High anxiety in the Andes: Bolivia and the viability of democracy. *Journal of Democracy* 12 (2): 6–16.

Wright, Winthrop R. 1990. *Café con leche: Race, class, and national image in Venezuela.* Austin: University of Texas Press.

Yashar, Deborah J. 1998. Contesting citizenship: Indigenous movements and democracy in Latin America. *Comparative Politics* 31 (1): 23–42.

7

Ethnic Politics and Political Instability in the Andes

DEBORAH J. YASHAR

NDIGENOUS MOVEMENTS AND MOBILIZATIONS HAVE BECOME a significant part of the contemporary Latin American political landscape. This marks a historic and consequential change for a region where ethnic cleavages were once widely characterized as comparatively weak. Indeed, by the end of the twentieth century, indigenous movements had emerged throughout North, Central, and South America—shaping political debates (e.g., about constitutions, decentralization, representation, and political parties), demanding economic reforms on a wide range of issues (e.g., land reform, privatization, dollarization, and drug policy) and even mobilizing cross-class coalitions that took part in pushing elected presidents from office. Nowhere has this sea change of indigenous organizing and claim making been more apparent than in Ecuador and Bolivia, where indigenous movements have proven to be the strongest and most consequential in Latin America.

This chapter focuses on indigenous mobilization in the Andes, with a particular emphasis on the cases of Ecuador and Bolivia. It does so with three goals in mind. First, and most substantively, it explains the emergence of indigenous movements in both countries by featuring three explanatory factors: changing citizenship regimes, transcommunity networks, and political associational space. Different types of citizenship regimes (and the consequences that they had on local autonomy) first diffused and then activated different ethnic cleavages.[1] These earlier citizenship regimes unintentionally enabled indigenous communities to carve out spaces of local autonomy, with limited interference from the state in matters of local governance. Subsequent citizenship regimes, however, threatened the autonomy that had been secured and, consequently, politicized ethnic cleavages.[2] The first indigenous communities successfully mobilized to defend their autonomy, however, only where they could draw on existing transcommunity networks and political associational space.

Second, and more briefly, this chapter highlights how indigenous movements have become the central social movement actors on the contemporary national stage. While Bolivian and Ecuadorean indigenous movements have demonstrated a remarkable and growing ability to mobilize indigenous, interethnic, and cross-class constituencies, more traditional class-based union and peasant movements have experienced a decline. In other words, there is a crisis of sorts for Andean social movements, save those that are indigenous. Even the once-radical and much-discussed Bolivian miners are a distant memory in many Bolivian social movement circles. In both Ecuador and Bolivia, traditional labor movements have taken a backseat to indigenous movements, even when it comes to traditional areas of protest—such as privatization, cost of living, and fiscal policy. Indeed, indigenous movements have spearheaded protests against all forms of neoliberalism in both countries.

Finally, this chapter addresses the argument that the rise of indigenous movements has proven detrimental to democratic stability in the region. It is true that Bolivian and Ecuadorean indigenous movements have increasingly come to demand and put into practice a more populist (or plebiscitary) form of democratic accountability. Rather than depend on political institutions (i.e., elections and courts) to hold elected officials accountable, they have increasingly assumed a role as mass arbiter in cases where elected presidents have announced or implemented unpopular economic policies. Indigenous movements have led mass protests and organized opposition that have resulted in the toppling of five presidents: Abdalá Bucaram, Jamil Mahuad, and Lucio Gutiérrez in Ecuador and Gonzalo Sánchez de Lozada and Carlos Mesa in Bolivia; in an unprecedented political move, indigenous movements in Ecuador formed part of a coup coalition that forced Mahuad from office. Indigenous movements have therefore increasingly rejected more traditional forms of representative democracy and presumed alternative methods of implementing democratic accountability. This section argues, however, that political instability is tied not to indigenous mobilization per se but to a set of prior structural conditions that severely constrain and weaken the fragile democracies currently in place.

In short, this chapter provides a fulcrum for analyzing the ebb and flow of social movements and their implications for democracy. As such, it probes the central themes of the volume in light of concerns about ethnic politics, incorporation, and democratic participation.

Emergence of Indigenous Movements

By the end of the twentieth century, indigenous movements had emerged throughout Latin America.[3] Ethnic cleavages were once weak in Latin America despite dramatically high levels of social and economic inequality. The rise in indigenous mobilization throughout the region and in the Andes in particular can be explained by analyzing three factors: citizenship regimes, transcommunity networks, and political associational space. To demonstrate the causal impact of these three factors, I compare Ecuador, Bolivia, and Peru, three cases with the largest indigenous populations in South America.[4] Indigenous movements emerged in the first two cases but not the third.

Corporatist Citizenship Regimes and Local Autonomy

The politicization of ethnic cleavages and the motive for organizing resulted from the shift in citizenship regimes and the challenge to local autonomy that ensued. Latin America essentially experienced an arc of citizenship regimes that moved from corporatist citizenship regimes toward neoliberal ones. While corporatist citizenship regimes advanced civil and social rights (and at times political rights) alongside class-based forms of interest intermediation, neoliberal citizenship regimes advanced civil and political rights alongside pluralist forms of interest intermediation. Corporatist and neoliberal citizenship regimes had foundational projects for state and society that were consequential. However, they were unevenly institutionalized. From the top looking down, these projects restructured society in radical ways. From the bottom looking up, however, these new projects of state formation and interest intermediation have been contested at many steps along the way. The formal goals and the unintended consequences of these two citizenship regimes help to explain both why ethnic cleavages were once weak and why they subsequently became politicized.

Corporatist patterns of organizing and interest intermediation figured heavily in the national populist projects of the mid-twentieth century, in both democratic and authoritarian regimes. As the working class and peasantry started to mobilize for resources, inclusion, and justice, political parties and the state sought to capture political support and to control the masses with the creation of new modes of interest intermediation and social rights. Corporatism did not necessarily grant free and universal suffrage. But it did create and promote labor and peasant associations that to varying degrees structured, and often monopolized, official representation; received state subsidies; and were controlled by the state. A new type of state-society relations, therefore, was adopted that (1) institutionalized a new mode of class-based interest intermediation and (2) extended social rights through the extension of social policies designed to provide a modicum of social welfare (including education, health, credit, subsidies, and the like).[5] In other words, at midcentury, Latin American countries started to institutionalize corporatist citizenship regimes.

Less commonly explored, or even questioned, are the ways indigenous peoples were affected by the corporatist project. Yet corporatist citizenship regimes unwittingly institutionalized autonomous spaces for indigenous peoples. Relatively unmonitored local spaces were created where indigenous people could sustain their local indigenous identities and forms of governance. So too they gained institutional mechanisms to access the state and its resources. Many indigenous communities survived and grew beyond the de facto reach of the state.

The new modes of interest intermediation and the new social programs fundamentally changed the terms of state-Indian relations. Labor laws freed indigenous peoples from slave labor, debt peonage, and other forms of repressive labor control. Accordingly, these laws provided Indians with a degree of freedom previously denied them. The laws recognized indigenous peoples as candidates for citizenship rather than objects of local control. Land reforms, alongside other social programs, moreover, granted indigenous communities land titles and social services and, in the process, provided them with a basis for securing a basic standard of living (i.e., social rights) and the geographic space to secure cultural practices and political autonomy. Peasant federations, as the primary mode of interest intermediation, provided Indians with institutional avenues for accessing and interacting with the state.

Land reforms in Bolivia (1953), Ecuador (1964 and 1973), and Peru (1968), for example, weakened landed elites' control of the countryside, redistributed land, and provided incentives for Indians to register as peasant communities (McClintock 1981, 61; Eckstein 1983). This registration reorganized the countryside along state-regulated corporatist lines, with many peasant communities joining peasant federations in hopes of gaining access to land and the state. These corporatist reforms brought with them the creation and expansion of social services in the areas of agricultural support, infrastructure, education, and health. Access to land and these services was often gained through corporatist associations.

The corporatist citizenship regime recognized Indians' freedom from elite control, recategorized Indians as peasants, and granted them rights and access previously denied them. The state and union organizations imposed a peasant identity on Indians as the ticket for political incorporation and access to resources. With the distribution of land, extension of agricultural credits, and provision of agricultural subsidies, peasants developed a new relationship with the state, which subordinated them into official channels in exchange for clientelist rewards. While the actual implementation of these reforms was quite uneven within and across countries, they generated political ties with those rural sectors that had gained (or hoped to gain) access to land and the state (Grindle 1986, 113–15, 137, 158).[6]

The registration of peasant communities and the growth of peasant federations in particular fostered the fiction that the state had turned Indians into peasants and stripped indigenous ethnicity of its salience. Official political discourse promoted assimilation into mestizo culture and extended resources to rural citizens insofar as they identified and organized as peasants. Until recently, studies of corporatism highlighted the strong reach of these corporatist institutions and their capacity to control and remake these social sectors. Latin American corporatist states presumably centralized state-society relations. Yet this enterprise was compromised by the absence of a rationalized bureaucracy, the failure to establish authority, and a lack of monopoly on the legitimate use of force. This is nowhere more apparent than from the vantage point of the countryside. Hence, despite official statements and institutions of corporatist control, large areas of the country operated beyond the reach of the state. Authoritarian enclaves were dominated by patronage and clientelist networks. Caudillos and landlords at times deployed their own paramilitary forces, created their own political rules, displayed greater allegiance to subnational politics than to national politics, and deployed state institutions for their benefit.

The weak reach of the state had implications for both those areas that were targeted by corporatist citizenship regimes (the Andean highlands) and those that were not (the Amazon). Studies of the Amazon have long noted the failure of states to govern the Amazon—leaving large swaths of territory and significant numbers of Indians beyond the political and military control of the state. States did not actively seek to harness the Amazon region until the latter part of the twentieth century. Prior to that they had mapped out boundaries that de facto included Indians as members, though not necessarily citizens, of the given state (Ruiz 1993, Santos Granero 1996, Smith 1996). With this de facto policy of disregard, Indians did not gain access to state resources, but they did maintain substantial, if not complete, political autonomy from the state—leaving indigenous authorities and practices to govern social, political, economic, and cultural relations therein.

While colonization schemes beginning in the 1960s (which in some places coincided with land reforms) posed a threat in some places, these schemes hardly changed the circumstances for most indigenous communities in the Amazon, which remained beyond the reach of the colonists or which resettled in areas not yet claimed by them. In short, while corporatist citizenship regimes granted access to the state and social rights, the uneven reach of the state undermined the centralizing program and allowed for local authorities—indigenous and otherwise—to act autonomously (to one degree or another).

The uneven reach of the state also had an impact on the capacity of Latin American countries to incorporate those areas most affected by the corporatist citizenship regimes. In the agricultural highlands of Bolivia, Peru, and Ecuador, the state could not assert the pervasive control that the overwhelming majority of studies of corporatism have tended to assume.[7] To the contrary, indigenous communities managed to carve out a degree of local autonomy that remained beyond the reach of the corporatist institutions themselves. Indeed, because of labor laws, land reform, and credit programs (fundamental components of the corporatist citizenship regimes in the countryside), Indians secured the spaces in which they could institutionalize indigenous community practices at the local level.[8]

In more ways than one, the distribution of inviolable communal lands to registered peasant communities provided Indians with the physical space not only for farming (understood as a social right) but also for securing governance by traditional indigenous authorities and the public expression of cultural ties. In this way the legal registration of communities and granting of community-based property created a legally defined, state-sanctioned geographic area that allowed for the growth and maintenance of politically autonomous local enclaves, indigenous culture, and political practices. Land reforms (which extended social rights in the countryside) masked the maintenance of indigenous autonomy and in some cases even engendered the (re)emergence of indigenous leaders, the (re)constitution of communities, and the expression of (evolving) indigenous identities at the community levels.

In Bolivia, the national revolutionary governments of the 1950s and the subsequent military governments between 1964 and 1974, for example, incorporated Indians into the state as peasants. They depended on alliances and pacts with peasant federations, which were expected both to deliver votes to the government and to control the local communities. Contrary to the hopes of politicians and military officers, Bolivia witnessed the maintenance of *ayllus* (kinship groups governed by a set of local-level indigenous authorities) in several regions in the Bolivian Andean countryside (Rivera Cusicanqiu and Equipo THOA 1992, Ticona, Rojas, and Albó 1995, Ströbele-Gregor 1996). In Ecuador the 1937 community law and later the 1964 and 1973 land reforms defined indigenous men and women as peasants and gave them access to the state insofar as they represented themselves as peasant communities or unions. Greater state penetration, land reforms, and freedom of movement often increased indigenous peasant independence from local landlords and, moreover, enabled indigenous communities to strengthen and (re)construct local public spaces for community authority structures and customary law (Guerrero 1993). Indeed, the number of registered peasant communities skyrocketed in the 1960s and 1970s (Zamosc 1995).

Short-lived state efforts to incorporate indigenous people as national peasants also occurred in Peru (1968–1975) during the populist government of General Juan Velasco Alvarado. Through the 1970 Statute on Peasant Communities, the creation of the peasant confederation Confederación Nacional Agraria (National Agrarian Confederation), and the formation of the multiclass corporatist organization Sistema Nacional de Apoyo a la Movilización Nacional (National Support System for Mobilization), the populist military government of Velasco sought to redefine Indians as peasants and to reorganize the heretofore indigenous communities along class-based lines.[9] Hence, as in Ecuador and Bolivia, Velasco set out to reframe Indians as peasants, to institutionalize their ties to the land and their ties to the state, and to organize them in state-sanctioned and regulated organizations. As in Ecuador and Bolivia, efforts to regulate these communities and restructure their internal organization were only partially successful. As Gonzales de Olarte (1994, 186–88) explicates, even following the land reform, these communities continued to maintain traditional systems of authority to govern intracommunity relations. While the state imposed new forms of governance, these often became shells for prior systems of authority to govern.

Corporatist citizenship regimes, therefore, created a dynamic dualism, with identities shifting according to the locale. Before the state, Indians assumed identities as peasants—thereby gaining access to social services and goods (in other words, social rights). Within the community, peasants assumed their identities as Indians—thereby securing local cultural enclaves. Location therefore mattered for the expression of identity. Where the state incompletely penetrated local communities (nowhere more evident than in the Amazon), Indians sustained and asserted varying degrees of political autonomy by retaining authority systems and customs.[10] If states did not respect indigenous jurisdiction in these communities, indigenous communities often did.

Shifting Citizenship Regimes and Challenging Local Autonomy

This particular balance in state-society relations, however, would not survive the century. Military and economic elites did not necessarily accept the rising power of class (including peasant) federations, and economic constraints made it difficult for states to sustain social programs that had extended the host of social programs associated with the corporatist citizenship regimes. Moreover, states increasingly responded to economic pressures to open up markets that had protected or ignored indigenous lands. As elites started to erode corporatist citizenship regimes and to try to gain command of national territories, they politicized ethnic cleavages by challenging the two types of autonomy that had developed: (1) among the peasantized and corporatized areas of the Andes and (2) within the Amazon.

The erosion of corporatist citizenship in the Andes culminated with the replacement of corporatist citizenship regimes with neoliberal citizenship regimes in the 1980s and 1990s. By the end of the twentieth century, citizenship regimes had changed radically as neoliberal ideas came to define the rights of citizens and the predominant mode of interest intermediation. With the third wave of democracy and the economic crises of the 1980s and 1990s in particular, politicians throughout the region started to advocate individual autonomy and responsibility, a program based on granting individual political and civil rights (but not necessarily social rights), the emasculation of corporatist organizations, and the promotion of free markets in land and labor. The last of these amplified the challenge to local autonomy that had begun in earlier periods and provided the language that movements would use to challenge neoliberalism and to articulate a postliberal challenge.

Eroding Corporatist Citizenship Regimes and Politicizing Ethnic Cleavages in the Andes

One wave of ethnic politicization occurred in the very Andean areas that had been explicitly targeted by the corporatist citizenship regimes. In these areas—which had been formally granted labor freedoms, social rights in the form of land and social services, and peasant-based representation—Indians eventually confronted the erosion of corporatist citizenship regimes and a corresponding challenge to local autonomy. In some cases this was a slow process (as in Ecuador and Bolivia); in others it was a sudden reversal (as in Peru). But in all cases, it eventually resulted in the political project and economic imperative associated with the neoliberal citizenship regimes of the 1980s and 1990s.

In Ecuador and Bolivia the weakening of rural peasant programs was a slow and steady process. In Ecuador, this happened shortly after the military government had introduced land reforms in the 1960s and 1970s. In Bolivia, the military governments of the 1960s sought to reassert control over the peasantry in the Military-Peasant Pact, which essentially imposed leaders on peasant federations and imposed stabilization packages during the 1970s. In each of these cases, there was a steady erosion of corporatist citizenship regimes—which resulted in the steady weakening of state-sanctioned peasant federations, the slowing down of land reform commitments, and increasing efforts by the state to control local politics.

Neoliberal citizenship regimes were implemented in Ecuador and Bolivia in the 1980s and 1990s and delivered the final coup de grace against corporatist citizenship regimes in general and local autonomy in particular. While neoliberal citizenship regimes did not cause indigenous mobilization in the first place, in the following ways they catalyzed additional mobilization in the second place (and shaped the political agendas that emerged). Stabilization and structural adjustment measures resulted in reduced ministerial budgets for ministries of agriculture, social services, and economic programs, including protection of peasant lands, access to credit, and agricultural subsidies. Real wages in the agricultural sector steadily declined from the 1980s and by 1992 had declined by 30 percent in Latin America as a whole (Wilkie, Contreras, and Komisaruk 1995, Conaghan and Malloy 1994, Urioste Fernández de Córdova 1994, Lustig 1995, de Janvry et al. 1994, Morley 1995). By the mid-1990s, land reforms proposals were made to privatize land markets in Ecuador (1994) and Bolivia (1996) in ways designed to make previously inalienable lands open for sale. In short, indigenous communities definitively lost their interlocutors with the state, land security, and social resources. Under these circumstances, the ability to maintain local autonomy and secure a stable relationship with the state seemed increasingly remote.

In Peru (in contrast to Ecuador and Bolivia), the overthrow of corporatist citizenship regimes did not occur slowly but took place suddenly in 1975. In post-1975 Peru, the military repressed peasant unions, weakened and even reversed land reform distribution, and weakened social programs that had granted social rights to this sector. In other words, they reversed the corporatist citizenship regimes that had incorporated Indians into the polity and promised to support indigenous communities as economically viable entities. With the turn to civilian rule in the 1980s and 1990s (an uneven and torturous process), the Peruvian state neither recognized social rights from earlier periods nor supported the formation of corporatist peasant federations. To the contrary, the state enacted reforms that further cut state-run social programs—except for targeted safety net programs—and delimited the spaces for class-based organizing. Neoliberal reforms, in particular in Peru, further inserted instability into the countryside as poverty and inequality rates soared in the 1980s and 1990s. Local autonomy was challenged not only by the reversal of state reforms in the 1950s and 1970s but also by a subsequent civil war that ravaged the countryside through the 1980s and part of the 1990s.

Both the slow (Ecuador and Bolivia) and sudden (Peru) reversal of corporatist citizenship regimes have had significant consequences—not least for indigenous peoples. Class-based federations have lost political and social leverage throughout the region, and consequently Indians have lost their formal ties and access to the state.[11] Most dramatically for Indians, states have slowed down (in some cases reversed) land reforms, privatized land markets, liberalized agricultural prices, eliminated agricultural subsidies, and diminished credit programs (Conaghan and Malloy 1994, Urioste Fernández de Córdova 1992, de Janvry et al. 1994, Morley 1995). The reforms threaten a communal land base that the state had once made inviolable. In other words, they have threatened the social rights that had been extended with the earlier corporatist citizenship regimes.

In all three cases, the weakening of corporatist modes of interest intermediation and the dismantling of rural programs (including land reforms, credit programs, and the like) have further increased uncertainty about property regimes among peasants in the Andes. Liberalizing states have made it clear that they will not maintain (Ecuador and Bolivia) or reestablish (Peru) special forms of property rights, credit, and subsidies for peasants. Consequently, the contemporary period challenges poor people's access to the state and its resources. In all five countries, status as a peasant now provides limited political purchase as peasant programs are dismantled and peasant organizations weakened. Rural organizing and protest respond to this material uncertainty, as peasants fear indebtedness, declining incomes, and the loss of land. The indigenous character of the contemporary movements, however, extends beyond material concerns for land as a productive resource. The potential loss of land also affects the viability and autonomy of local indigenous political institutions that had operated in and assumed a relatively well-defined and stable geographic space.

In this context of reduced spaces for local autonomy and access to the state, ethnic cleavages have been politicized and indigenous movements —particularly those that mobilize in the countryside—have protested the restrictions that state reforms have placed on the inalienable community rights and de facto local autonomy that they had secured during the earliest days of the corporatist citizenship regimes. Indigenous movements have come to demand that the state officially recognize indigenous communities (*Ojarasca* 1995, Díaz-Polanco n.d., Mattiace 1997). In Bolivia, indigenous activists since the end of the 1990s have worked to recognize, reconstitute, and register ayllus that have dotted the Andean countryside;[12] through the Ley Inra (Law of the National Institute for Agrarian Reform), this has become possible and more prevalent.[13] In Ecuador, this public discussion became particularly salient in the discussions prior to and during the 1997 constituent assembly (Andolina 1997).

Promoting Development and Politicizing Ethnic Cleavages in the Amazon

A second type of indigenous movement developed in areas that had fallen beyond the scope of corporatist citizenship regimes. In the Amazon the state has historically been weak, with limited impact on policy, social services, infrastructure, government access, or institution building. Corporatist citizenship regimes did not find significant institutional expression in the Amazon. While the state expanded in the three decades after World War II in the Andes, the Amazon remained relatively marginalized from contemporary politics, the market, and the state's role in each.

Colonization programs and development agencies in the 1960s, however, altered this relationship between the state and the Amazon. Ecuador passed colonization laws in 1964 and 1977, Bolivia passed a colonization law in 1966, and Peru passed an indigenous community and agrarian development law for the Amazon in 1969. These laws and associated programs set out to increase state regulation of the area, to title these vast lands (in part as a means to relieve land pressures in the Andes), and to generate new growth opportunities. Accordingly, colonization by both small and large landholders increased, particularly from the 1960s on. Many Andean peasants (who came to be known as *colonos*) moved from the tighter land market in the Andes to the Amazon, where land seemed more abundant and fertile. Domestic entrepreneurs interested in large landholdings for cattle grazing and logging set up shop in the Ecuadorean, Bolivian, and Peruvian Amazon, particularly following additional legislation that made it easier to exploit natural resources, such as Bolivia's Forestry Law, Fauna and Wildlife Law, and Mineral Law and Peru's Agrarian Promotion and Development Law. As a whole, the ensuing patterns of colonization led to significant waves of internal migration and titling that pushed indigenous communities off lands that they used (i.e., for hunting, fishing, gathering, etc.) and to which they did not have title or "proof of use" (since they did not necessarily cultivate and farm these lands).

In turn, indigenous communities in Bolivia and Ecuador, in particular, started to mobilize against national migrants and economic entrepreneurs (particularly the latter), as they were moving in on what was seen as indigenous territory and therefore were challenging the communities' material, political, and social autonomy. The Shuar of Ecuador and the Izoceños-Guaraníes of Bolivia were among the first to mobilize to defend their local autonomy from this encroachment; they became models for other Amazonian peoples in their country. Indeed, the first, most prevalent, and widespread indigenous organizing in the Amazon has been against these domestic actors and companies that moved into the Amazon.

If Amazonian indigenous protest has most clearly been against domestic actors, so too it emerged quite clearly against international companies that moved into the Amazon; nowhere has this been more apparent and visible than in Ecuador. With the 1967 discovery of large oil reserves in the Ecuadorean Amazon and the 1982 changes to the Hydrocarbon Law (which once again opened up areas for exploration) foreign oil companies started to return to the Ecuadorean Amazon (Kimmerling 1993, 13, 19, 21). Unlike the earlier round of colonization, oil exploration did not require title to vast tracts of land, per se. Oil companies had a primary interest in subsoil rights and infrastructure (roads, pipelines, etc.); consequently, their claims were apparently more targeted and less intrusive than the vast agricultural colonization efforts that had occurred previously. The state, indeed, was selling/renting public subsoil rights to the oil companies. "According to Ecuadorean law, all petroleum reserves are state property, regardless of who owns topsoil rights" (Kimmerling 1996, 35, my translation). The state, however, rarely regulated the oil companies to ensure that they lived up to environmental and civil code regulations (Kimmerling 1996, 13–143).

The oil companies' actions would also have a detrimental environmental impact on the surrounding forests, rivers, lands, and, therefore, people (Kimmerling 1993). As the environmental consequences became apparent, indigenous communities were increasingly politicized—seeking to defend their communities and to secure better relationships with the state. Organizations also emerged among the Cofán and Siona-Secoya in Napo and among the Quichua, Achuar, and Shiwiar in Pastaza. The U.S. Agency for International Development has reported on the linkage between highway building by oil companies and the increased colonization of these areas. By the early 1990s, an estimated five hundred kilometers of highways and roads had been built, which facilitated colonization of some 1 million hectares of tropical forests (Kimmerling 1993, 56). The issue of oil companies continues to mobilize and divide indigenous communities in Ecuador (Forero 2003).

State-sanctioned development plans sparked significant waves of agricultural colonization, cattle grazing, logging, and oil exploration, all of which resulted in nonindigenous claims to lands that had previously been used by indigenous communities. These developments (both national and international) posed a clear threat to indigenous material and political autonomy and survival. Indigenous organizations emerged to combat what was seen as predatory and environmentally destructive land grabbing. To do so, they used legal measures affiliated with the land reform and other state statutes to form rural organizations and to gain legal title to the land. These Amazonian movements assumed particular visibility in the 1980s and 1990s when states accelerated programs to promote more open land markets in the Amazon. Not only were regionwide Amazonian movements created in both Bolivia and Ecuador, but Amazonian movements in each country organized marches to the national capital in Ecuador

(1992) and Bolivia (1990)—marches that captured the imagination of the national press and sparked significant debate about indigenous rights.

Throughout Latin America (including Peru), therefore, the contemporary period has challenged the space for indigenous local autonomy secured during the prior corporatist citizenship regimes. In Mesoamerica and the Andes, the state has supported the dismantling of corporatist forms of representation, agricultural subsidies, and protection of communally and individually held lands. In the Amazon, the state has increased its presence and promoted colonization by Andean nationals and foreign companies. In both cases, the state's challenge to land tenure and use has threatened material livelihoods and indigenous forms of autonomous local governance—both of which had depended on more stable property relations. In this context, indigenous movements are asserting the right to new administrative spheres with a certain degree of political autonomy at the local level. This is not just a call for more land, although that is certainly a core component of the demands. It is also a demand that the state recognize and respect autonomous indigenous political jurisdiction and authority over the communities that inhabit that geographic space.

These movements gained momentum in the context of neoliberal citizenship regimes. They were not caused by them, but they were spurred on by them. For as Smith wrote, in the years prior to neoliberal hegemony, "The issues of land and ethnic identity coalesced the ethnic federations. In each case, a particular group felt its collective land base and identity threatened by both state policies of colonization and integration and by the expanding capitalist market economy. Virtually every ethnic federation began as a meeting of headmen or representatives of different settlements of a particular ethnic group who were looking for common strategies to defend the land and their nationality" (1985, 17).

Smith was insightful and prescient. For while he was talking about the Amazon in 1985, his observations have rung true throughout Latin America as a whole.

Networks and Capacity

Challenges to local autonomy provided a motive for organizing along ethnic lines. However, these movements only took form where indigenous activists confronted (and in some cases were able to build) organizational capacity. Networks provided this organizational capacity. They fostered the communication and cooperation that was essential for transcending geographic dispersion, language barriers, and cultural unfamiliarity (and in some cases hostility). Networks provided the forum for future indigenous leaders to meet, share common experiences, develop a common language, identify common problems, and articulate common goals. In turn, indigenous people developed ethnic identities that referred not only to their local Indian communities but also to a more transcommunity indigenous identification. This indigenous identity was a product more than a cause of the first-generation networks that were in place. It did not necessarily include a close national identification with all indigenous communities. Indeed, Andean and Amazonian indigenous movements in Ecuador and Bolivia (and even Peru) formed separately and did not necessarily or easily translate those regional ties into national ones. Significantly different historical experiences had resulted in very different cultural norms, understandings of autonomy and land, and styles of negotiation. Without networks, it was impossible to bridge these divides.

Networks, therefore, constitute a second part of the explanation of indigenous movement formation in Latin America, insofar as they provided the organizational capacity necessary to build indigenous movements.[14] I take networks to refer to the repeated exchanges and resulting relationships that are constructed among individuals or social units by formal and informal institutions. Networks can take many forms. The one distinguishing feature that proved essential for indigenous movement formation was geography. Only where transcommunity networks were in place could and did indigenous communities possess the organizational capacity to forge broad indigenous movements. The existence of these networks more than their organizational features (vertical or horizontal; coercive or cooperative; social, political, economic, cultural, or religious; etc.) proved key to explaining where indigenous leaders possessed the organizational capacity to build indigenous movements.[15]

The state, unions, churches, and nongovernmental organizations provided many of these networks. Each forged rural organizations that bridged local communities. Indigenous activists in Bolivia and Ecuador often emerged within these organizations and then harnessed them to forge new ethnic-based movements and agendas. In notable cases, these networks were shaped by or supported transnational forces, as with international development agencies (such as Oxfam, the Ford Foundation, and several Scandinavian organizations), transnational advocacy networks (Cultural Survival and Rainforest Action Network), and the Catholic Church (Brysk 2000). In the lion's share of cases, however, domestic networks provided the foundation for scaling up and building indigenous movements.

In Peru, by contrast, these networks were severely weakened both by the authoritarian crackdown in 1975 and the civil war that raged in the 1980s during Peru's "democratic opening."[16] Not only did the state militarize the countryside, thereby weakening existing networks between rural communities, but Shining Path also aggressively set out to destroy whatever alternative networks or organizational infrastructure remained —notoriously killing well-respected activists who were working independently from the guerrilla organization.[17]

Given the relative weakness of these networks in Peru, no comparable movement organizing could or did take place (Yashar 2005). In the absence of these kinds of networks, it has been difficult to construct an indigenous identity and organization that transcends its more localized referent. And while the church was active in Peru, it never managed to sustain transcommunity ties—in large part because of the repression that ensued in the countryside.

States, unions, churches, and, more recently, nongovernmental organizations (particularly in Bolivia) have provided networks that enabled indigenous communities to transcend localized identities and to identify commonly trusted leaders. In some cases these networks were internationally inspired and supported; in many they were not. In all cases, however, these networks built literacy skills and cross-community social capital that enabled indigenous leaders to move between communities, build support, and develop frames that resonated within and across communities. In turn, indigenous leaders gained access to information and resources that enabled them to communicate with the state. When confronted with changing rural-state relations that threatened property relations and local autonomy, these networks provided the organizational bases for coordinating significant indigenous mobilizing from the 1970s to the 1990s.

Political Associational Space

Movements could only emerge if a third factor, political associational space, was also in place. The need for associational space is painfully obvious (particularly for scholars of social movements)[18] but often overlooked in discussions of ethnic politics, as it is all too common to assume that ethnic cleavages naturally translate into political organizations and protest. Political associational space (in conjunction with changing citizenship regimes and transcommunity networks), however, proved crucial to the emergence and growth of indigenous movements.[19]

Political associational space refers to the de facto existence of freedom of association and expression. It is not reducible to regime type; it is not equal to democracy. To the contrary, political associational space can exist (to varying degrees) in different political contexts, including where states are virtually or largely absent (as in the Amazon), in democratic regimes where states protect civil rights in practice and not merely in theory, and in transitional regimes where authorities initiate a process of political liberalization that includes a decline in repression and a corresponding increased respect for civil rights.[20] The common denominator in these three contexts is that the state does not trample on the capacity to associate and to speak out.

Political associational space has mattered in both its de facto and de jure forms. In the Amazon, where the state has historically been weak (in some places relatively absent), a generalized associational space existed independent of changes in the national political regime. For even if national governments deployed repression in other areas, this rarely affected the Amazon in a direct way. Associational space existed de facto and was relatively constant in the Amazonian regions.[21] Amazonian indigenous communities had the political opportunity to organize transcommunity movements (although they often confronted local forms of oppression from landlords and churches) absent state regulation, control, and repression. Indigenous activists (confronted with challenges to local autonomy and drawing on social networks) capitalized on the de facto existence of freedom of expression and organization (both a consequences of low levels of state penetration and corresponding low levels of state repression) to organize.

In the Andean region, where the state incorporated and penetrated the highlands to a greater degree than that found in the lowland areas of the Amazon, political associational space has been more variable. It fluctuated in tandem with periods of national political closure and political liberalization. During periods of political closure and militarization, states restricted freedom of association in these regions and therefore closed off opportunities for legal organizing among communities. This type of closure occurred in Bolivia in the 1970s and in Peru from the mid-1970s through the 1990s (with a brief opening at the end of the 1970s and early 1980s). During these periods of political closure, indigenous organizing did not emerge or simply dissipated. Indeed, Jenaro Flores, a prominent indigenous leader who cofounded Bolivia's Andean indigenous movement, commented that political closure preempted incipient efforts to organize indigenous movements and weakened those that had started organizing during earlier and more open times (interviews in La Paz, 1995 and 1997). Where, however, political liberalization legally and practically resulted in the freedom to organize, there was greater opportunity to mobilize along indigenous lines. Political liberalization refers here to the extension of an associational space that legally and practically entails freedoms of association and expression.

In the Andean regions, a strong correlation exists between indigenous organizing and the extension of political associational space. National political associational space was extended the furthest in Bolivia (late 1970s and early 1908s) and Ecuador (late 1970s), and the two strongest movements are found in these two countries. During research trips I made in 1995, 1996, and 1997, indigenous leaders generally stated that political liberalization had created a more propitious environment for organizing. Indeed, the establishment and growth of indigenous movements largely coincides with or follows increased respect for civil liberties.

It is in this context of political associational space that national indigenous movements emerged in Bolivia and Ecuador. In each case, movements built on preexisting dense social networks that allowed for both the construction of transcommunity ties and the creation of panethnic movements. Where these networks did not exist, it was close to impossible to organize beyond the local community level, particularly where there was nonexistent or limited associational space.

Where, however, widespread repression continued and freedom of association was foreclosed, as in Peru, political closure preempted indigenous movement formation. The violent civil war closed off avenues for freedom of organization and expression, with the declaration of states of emergency that affected significant parts of the territory.[22] Moreover, it destroyed existing organizations and obstructed the formation of transcommunity networks that proved so important elsewhere, with the partial exception of the *rondas campesinas* (peasant nightwatch patrols), which in the south ultimately aided in the militarization of the countryside. In this context, sustained regional and national indigenous organizing was elusive—with some notable exceptions in the Amazon and Puno—not least because of the serious constraints on political associational space (Yashar 2005, chap. 6).[23]

Shifting citizenship regimes challenged local autonomy and politicized ethnic cleavages. Social networks provided the capacity to organize beyond local communities and to scale up efforts into regional and national indigenous organizations. Political associational space provided the necessary political opportunity for doing so. For these reasons, the existence and interplay among these three causal factors best explain the contemporary and uneven emergence of Latin America's indigenous movements.

Indigenous Movements Assume a Leadership Role in Civil Society

Indigenous movements in Ecuador and Bolivia have become the primary political actors in civil society. Indeed, in Ecuador, the Confederation of Indigenous Nationalities of Ecuador (CONAIE), with its constitutive confederations, Ecuador Runacunapac Riccharimui (ECUARUNARI; Awakening of the Ecuadorean Indian) in the Andes and the Confederación de Nacionalidades Indígenas de la Amazonía Ecuatoriana (CONFENAIE; Confederation of Indigenous Nationalities of the Amazon) in the Amazon, alongside other indigenous movements, has taken on a leadership role—first in promoting a new set of ethnic demands and second in mobilizing and speaking out on behalf of popular sectors more broadly. CONAIE has taken a leadership role in promoting and implementing bicultural education (Selverston 1997), rejecting the 1994 land reform (Pacari 1996), and defining the 1997 constituent assembly agenda (Andolina 1997). With their ability to mobilize massive numbers in various indigenous marches and demonstrations throughout the 1990s and their presumed ability to shape how people would vote, CONAIE indigenous activists achieved a political power that no one could have imagined just a decade before. Most dramatically of all, CONAIE came to play a key role in mobilizing multiclass forces against then-president Jamil Mahuad (2000) and Lucio Gutiérrez (2005), a maneuver that ultimately forced both presidents from office. Moreover, leaders from CONAIE have forged a political movement that has successfully fielded political candidates at all levels of government.

In Bolivia as well, two important regional federations—the Confederación Sindical Unica de Trabajadores Campesinos de Bolivia (CSUTCB; Bolivian Unitary Syndical Confederation of Peasant Workers) of the Andes and the Confederación Indígena del Oriente Boliviano (CIDOB; Confederation of Indigenous Peoples of Bolivia) in the Amazon—have taken on a leadership role to organize massive marches, press for land reform, and protest privatization policies. Most notably, the mobilizations that have occurred against the privatization of water (2000) and then gas (2003) companies solidified the role of Bolivia's indigenous movement as the vanguard voice for both ethnic and popular-based agendas. So too the indigenous movement has diversified, with a notable and increasingly powerful branch mobilizing to defend the right to coca production—arguing that the chewing of the coca leaf is an integral part of indigenous cultural practices. Ultimately, as in Ecuador, Bolivia's indigenous movements helped forge multiclass mobilizations against Presidents Sánchez de Lozada (2003) and Mesa (2005), both of whom left office before completing their terms.

Today, indigenous politicians in both Ecuador and Bolivia are present throughout government, in both elected and designated posts. Víctor Hugo Cárdenas was vice president in Bolivia from 1992 to 1997, and Evo Morales was nearly elected president in 2002. Numerous indigenous legislators were elected to office in both countries, as well as numerous local councilors.

As indigenous people have gained strength as social movements and political actors, their agendas have received a greater hearing. Indigenous movements have articulated a postliberal challenge—demanding that states recognize indigenous communities as a necessary precondition for protecting individual rights and institutionalizing collective rights (including local autonomy, national representation, and legal pluralism). Several Latin American countries have started to recognize multiethnic and plurinational diversity in their countries—not only in an international forum, by signing International Labour Organization Convention 169, but also in their national constitutions (including, but not limited to Bolivia, Ecuador, Colombia, and Venezuela). So too there have been increasing entry points to the democratic polity via decentralization policies, in particular in Bolivia, Ecuador, Colombia, and most recently Peru, among other places.

Remarkably, some states have also recognized (although not fully implemented) some degree of territorial autonomy—Ecuador, Bolivia, and even Mexico (although the Ejército Zapatista de Liberación Nacional [EZLN; Zapatista Army of National Liberation] is far from satisfied with the content of the autonomy recognized by the Mexican state). Others, as in Guatemala, Brazil, and Bolivia, have set up land institutions to address the morass of incomplete/contradictory land titling and land reform, although these institutions have not been able to fulfill their mandates, at least not yet. Bicultural education is part of the policy debate, with the most notable advances in Ecuador and Guatemala. And organized indigenous participation in political parties and political office has also increased, in the ways noted in chapter 6.

The meteoric rise of these movements has occurred against a startling backdrop. Confidence in Latin American democracies (including the Andean cases) is devastatingly low, as consistently highlighted in recent Latinobarómetro surveys (see Lagos 2003). Other social movements have declined in prominence, most notably Bolivia's once-powerful and militant labor movement. And strikingly, political parties are in disarray. While Ecuador's political parties have always been weak by any measure, Bolivia's and Peru's once-powerful political parties also have lost their power to mobilize, sustain allegiance, and deliver/defend a programmatic position. In other words, indigenous movements are emerging in a vacuum. Consequently, they are playing a much-needed role in speaking out on behalf of the multitudes of unrepresented indigenous peoples and in shaping political agendas, but they do not have the institutional support to push their agendas forward. In the absence of a viable and meaningful party system and a state capable of implementing and upholding laws, indigenous people are seriously constrained in what they can do—even if they win elections or are appointed to political office.

Indigenous activists have played a key role in toppling democratically elected presidents, but it is reasonable to ask if they are really the cause or simply the reflection of a much deeper problem that underlies the political instability in the region.

Mirror Not Motor of Political Instability

Indigenous movements have been at the forefront of protests that resulted in the resignations of Ecuadorean presidents Mahuad (2000) and Gutiérrez (2005) and Bolivian presidents Sánchez de Lozada (2003) and Mesa (2005). While it is clear that indigenous movements played a key role in opposing these presidents, it is misleading to argue that these indigenous movements are the cause of political instability in both countries.

First, the crises in both countries are part of a much broader crisis that affects the entire Andean region; presidents were forced from elected office three times in Ecuador (Bucaram in 1997, Mahuad in 2000, and Gutiérrez in 2005), twice in Bolivia (Sánchez de Lozada in 2003 and Mesa in 2005), and once in Peru (Alberto Fujimori in 2000) and Venezuela (Hugo Chávez in 2002, although he was reinstated shortly thereafter). Moreover, Argentina (not an Andean country), also experienced its bout of presidential instability in 2001–2002, when Fernando de la Rúa was forced from office in December 2001, followed by a quick succession of interim presidents who resigned before Eduardo Duhalde was constitutionally appointed in January 2002. Indigenous movements were not present in each case (not in Argentina, Peru, or Venezuela, at least not in any meaningful sense). Moreover, in all cases (including in Argentina) the opposition was multisectoral—including the middle classes alongside other popular sectors.

Powerful established social actors often appear to have played a decisive role in the overthrow of existing governments. For example, it was the Ecuadorean legislature that ruled in 1997 that Bucaram could not rule by reason of mental incapacity; CONAIE joined forces with members of the military and Supreme Court to topple Mahuad; 2005 mobilizations against Ecuadorean president Gutiérrez were consequential in no small part because he alienated legislators when dismissing Supreme Court judges and when bargaining to allow former president Bucaram back into the country. In Bolivia, moreover, multiclass actors joined forces with indigenous organizations to topple Bolivian presidents Sánchez de Lozada and Mesa, not least because of concerns that included international control of natural resources and the calling of a constituent assembly and because of a lack of support in the legislature. President Fujimori of Peru was forced to flee to avoid corruption charges that were going to be investigated by government agencies. And Venezuelan president Chávez was toppled by a multiclass coalition that included the oil sector and organized workers, among others. When looking at this broader universe, it is striking that indigenous people are not always the primary or key opposition actors—even in Ecuador and Bolivia. The comparative lesson here is that political instability is logically the result of some other underlying factors that can explain the broader universe of cases.

Not all indigenous mobilizations necessarily have led to the downfall of governments. We therefore need more research into the underlying causes of political instability in the region. Clearly, problems of poverty, inequality, and weak states provide a foundation for this instability, but as constants, they cannot explain the contemporary changes. Candidates for further exploration reasonably include (but are not limited to)

• Increasingly inchoate/weak party systems. Party systems in the Andes are considered inchoate by Mainwaring and Scully (1995). Bolivia has witnessed the decline of the Movimiento Nacionalista Revolucionaria (MNR; National Revolutionary Movement), Ación Democrática Nacional (ADN; National Democratic Action), and Movimiento de la Izquierda Revolucionaria (MIR; Left Revolutionary Movement), while Ecuador's parties have always been ephemeral, with politicians regularly switching partisan affiliations. So too, once-stable party systems in Peru and Venezuela have been seriously weakened. In this context, there are no institutionalized and reliable channels for society to participate, seek representation, and hold government responsible. This context does not bode well for trust in government.

• Declining levels of trust. By all accounts, trust levels in democracy and political institutions are remarkably low. Following the 2000 coup in Ecuador, Lucero (2001) reported that there was higher support/trust for the military, church, and CONAIE than for political institutions. Moreover, Latinobarómetro's 2001 surveys revealed 60 percent confidence in the armed forces compared to 9 percent for the Congress. Again, these indicators demonstrate the fragility of any contemporary elected government in the region.

• Rising cachet of the military? States in the Andes are weak by most standards. Certainly in Bolivia and Ecuador, they remain wracked by clientelist and inefficacious institutions that generally have lacked a monopoly on the use of force. In this context, it is striking that the military has become among the more trusted forces in society. We have very little understanding of the role of the military in the region. The military once played a populist role in Bolivia, Ecuador, and Peru. It has at times been portrayed as an ally of the people in Ecuador—with indigenous movements initially joining forces in 2000 with Colonel Gutiérrez in 2000 to topple President Mahuad and then initially supporting Gutiérrez when he successfully ran for president in 2003. Similarly, we do not quite understand the role played by the military in Bolivia—even less so now following General/President Hugo Banzer's death. Yet the military helped overthrow at least one of these governments and, at the very least, did not effectively defend the others.

This list is not exhaustive but is representative of the factors that form part and parcel of the underlying crisis in the region. These contemporary changes play out against long-standing structural issues that include underlying poverty and inequality, weak states, and poor economic performance. Viewed together, these combined factors appear to be better candidates to explain the widespread political instability in the region than are indigenous movements, whose presence and impact have been more varied. Indigenous activism is not the cause of political instability but is a reflection of it.

It is in this context that we should understand the current round of indigenous mobilizations as a form of plebiscitary politics (as noted by Coppedge 2003) or accountability politics. Indigenous movements have taken on the role of protesting against presidents perceived as selling away national patrimony without concern for indigenous peoples in par-

ticular and national citizens in general. Where parties are weak, the rule
of law is uneven, clientelism reigns supreme, and there is little trust that
existing institutions will hold politicians accountable. Moreover, there is a
shortened time horizon, with little faith that the next election will provide
the basis for correcting decisions and indiscretions made in the current
period. In Ecuador and Bolivia (as well as Argentina), these popular
plebiscites have happened not in the voting booth but through street
mobilizations and occupations. These demonstrations are, in other words,
an example of the rising distrust in existing political institutions and elected officials. We therefore are seeing a new form of accountability politics—one where activists leverage their mobilizing capacity to shape
policy and to make elected officials more accountable. Viewed from this
vantage point, indigenous mobilizations are a mirror and not a motor of
political instability.

Concluding with Fragile Democracies

The last two decades of the twentieth century are a cautionary tale for
the Andes—weaving optimistic trends with uncertain ones. New democratic regimes have advanced political rights and witnessed the emergence of an unprecedented set of indigenous movements that have
reshaped political debate about identity, autonomy, and community. Over
time, they have come to speak not only for the large indigenous populations in both Ecuador and Bolivia but also for the broader popular movements of which they are now first among equals. These are unprecedented developments that have resulted in changes that were unfath-
omable just a few decades ago, with new constitutions recognizing multiethnic and pluricultural populations, legislation recognizing territorial
autonomy, bicultural education programs, and popular mobilizations
undermining some privatization efforts. Insofar as indigenous people
have emerged as an active and important part of civil society, and insofar
as they have pushed for a more inclusive society, significant advances
have indeed taken place.

However, significant challenges remain. While noteworthy macroin-
stitutional changes have ushered in a categorically democratic Andes, the
quality and stability of the democracies in place are uneven at best. These
democracies face seemingly insurmountable problems of weak state
capacity, clientelism, corruption, weak party systems, high levels of
inequality and poverty, and declining levels of trust. These political conditions are obstacles to democratic inclusion and representation that have

often worked against the inclusion of indigenous people and the stability of the system itself. These are some of the many challenges that indigenous peoples face as they seek to institutionalize their role as central players in fragile democracies.

Notes

1. I borrow the phrase citizenship regime from Jenson and Phillip (1996). They use the term to refer to the varying bundles of rights and responsibilities that citizenship can confer. I amend the concept partially to refer to a bundle that includes three dimensions: (1) who can be a member of the polity, (2) what rights (à la T. H. Marshall 1963) do they have as citizens, and (3) what modes of interest intermediation are used (i.e., plural versus corporatist). Contemporary Latin American states have not explicitly extended/restricted these rights along ethnoracial lines (although literacy restrictions did effectively serve this function, historically speaking). However, the content of citizenship rights has shifted over time, with striking consequences for Latin American indigenous people.

2. This argument about changing citizenship regimes agrees with the arguments in chapter 1 insofar as this comparative historical approach privileges the fundamental importance of different and changing modes of political incorporation.

3. This section draws on Yashar (1988, 1999, and 2005).

4. Yashar (2005) includes the universe of Latin American countries with indigenous populations over 10 percent: Ecuador, Bolivia, Peru, Guatemala, and Mexico. Among these five cases, Peru still stands out as having relatively weak or nonexistent indigenous movements, in contrast to the other four cases.

5. For classic perspectives on Latin American corporatism, see Malloy (1977). For a seminal comparative analysis of Latin American corporatism, see Collier and Collier (1991).

6. Even after the Bolivian, Ecuadorean, and Peruvian states reformulated rural development policy to the advantage of agricultural elites, the states kept the older legislation on the books and maintained institutional ties with the peasantry—fostering the rural poor's dependence on the state for (piecemeal) access to land, credit, and services.

7. Rubin (1997), for example, highlights how corporatism in Mexico was much more porous than commonly portrayed and that alternative spaces for organizing were therefore present for social movement formation and political contestation.

8. In Weber's classic study of nation building (1976), he illuminates how the French state turned peasants into Frenchman. I suggest here that Latin American efforts to turn Indians into peasants in fact created the space in which they could defend and develop a local indigenous identity.

9. The following discussion of the 1970 statute draws from Bourque and Palmer (1975, 189–90, 204–5), McClintock (1981, 36–37), Remy 1994, 115), and Seligmann (1995, 60–62).

10. Corporatist citizenship regimes barely penetrated the Amazon. Amazonian Indians rarely formed part of peasant federations and states did not have the resources to control them. Consequently, Amazonian Indians had even more autonomy than did Andean and Mesoamerican Indians.

11. Several states did have national indigenous institutes. However, these rarely if ever served as interlocutors between Indians and the state.

12. Ayllus often claim sovereignty over discontinuous land bases. This geographical spread poses a challenge to Western ideas of state formation, which generally assume that continuous areas coincide with a single political administration.

13. I conducted several interviews with each of the following people between May and August 1997: Constantino Lima, Aymaran nationalist activist since the 1970s; Carlos Mamani, María Eugenia Choque Quispe, and Ramón Conde, researcher-activists at Taller de Historia Oral Andina (THOA; Andean Oral History Workshop); and Ricardo Calla, former director of Taller de Apoyo y Pueblos Indígenas (TAYPI; Workshop to Support Ayllus and Indigenous Peoples). See also Molina and Arias (1996).

14. See, for example, Granovetter (1995); Tarrow (1994); McAdam, McCarthy, and Zald (1996); McAdam (1982 and 1988); Putnam (1993); and Varshney (2002). I thank Arang Keshavarzian for his insight into networks.

15. These other organizational features of networks do not explain movement emergence, although they probably do provide insight into the types of movements that did emerge. Further work is needed to explain why some networks lead to unified movements in a given area and why others lead to competitive ones. Podolny and Page (1998, 73) also note that more work is needed to explain why and how networks generate trust.

16. See McClintock (1989), Palmer 1992, Degregori (1997, 1998), Hinajosa (1998), Mallon (1998), del Pino (1998), Manrique (1998), Starn (1998), Burt (1997), and Basombrío (1998).

17. Shining Path emerged as an all-consuming kind of military organization. As described in chapter 8, it did not tolerate alternative forms of organization and set out to destroy independent associations, organizations, and networks. In this context, existing organizations were snuffed out and leaders were often silenced. Hence, Shining Path essentially destroyed potential frameworks for legal organizing along ethnic lines, destroying the communication links for sharing of experiences, for the rise in alternative leaders, and for the maintenance of organizations working on related issues. These guerrilla movements are often portrayed as indigenous movements that have launched a violent war to defend indigenous ways. Indeed, Shining Path set out to recruit among indigenous men and women—particularly from those who had migrated to the urban areas and particularly among those who had attended the University in Ayacucho. However, Shining Path and Movimiento Revolucionario Tupak Amaru (MRTA; Tupak Amaru Revolutionary Movement) did not promote ethnic claim making per se. Scholars of Shining Path have noted that the movement set out to undermine indigenous communal systems—often leading to resistance in the highland communities where these ethnic authority and governing systems were strongest (Degregori 1998; del Pino 1998).

18. The social movement literature has long argued that political opportunity structures shape the prospects for movement emergence. McAdam (1996, 27) outlines four dimensions that constitute political opportunity structures: the degree of political opening, elite alignments, presence of elite allies, and the state's capacity and propensity to use repression. In the case of Latin America's indigenous movements, elite alignments and access to elite allies do not uniformly play a role in movement formation—even if they do affect policy success. I emphasize here the first and fourth dimensions identified by McAdam.

19. Where political associational space has been closed off, innovative activists have been known to create it (see, for example, Navarro 1998; Tarrow 1998; Keck and Sikkink 1998; Tilly 2002). They have used nonpolitical forums to engage in political activities, or they have built alliances with domestic elites and international activists to overcome political obstacles. This exceptional heroism on the part of some activists is incontrovertible. However, the examples are noteworthy precisely because they have been the exception. In general, closed political associational spaces have worked against movement building, particularly in indigenous rural areas where activists could not organize, speak out, and mobilize without incurring repression against them and their communities.

20. See Davenport (n.d.) for a description of indicators of political violence versus political restrictions.

21. Again, Peru is a partial exception in this regard.

22. With the civil war, the military reasserted its power in the countryside and within governing political institutions. In contrast to the military populism of 1968–1975, the 1980s military started to conduct a war against its own population, targeting the guerilla forces but affecting the countryside as a whole.

For example, with the intensification of the civil war in the early 1980s, President Fernando Belaúnde declared states of emergency in various provinces (Mauceri 1997, 34; Roberts and Peceny 1997, 195–97). Mauceri reports, "By the late 1980s, nearly 60 percent of the country's territory was under a state of emergency" (1997, 34). By July 1991, states of emergency still affected more than 50 percent of the population and 40 percent of the national territory (Roberts and Peceny 1997, 198). During this period, several forces (including the military, insurgencies, drug traffickers, death squads, and civilian paramilitary patrols/rondas campesinas) committed civil and human rights violations (Roberts and Peceny 1997, 192)

23. With the dissipation of the civil war in the early 1990s, political associational space remained tenuous. The government of Alberto Fujimori implemented a 1992 *autogolpe* (self-coup) that shut down civilian courts and representative institutions and undermined constitutional rights and protections (Roberts and Peceny 1997, 202). Moreover, presses were closed, political parties were weakened, and civil liberties were often trampled. Roberts and Peceny (1997) conclude that the military acted with increased power and impunity. Hence, while political violence fell from 1992 to 1993, the number of provinces under a state of emergency increased form fifty-two to sixty-six. "At the end of 1994, nearly half the population continued to live in emergency zones" (Roberts and Peceny 1997, 203). Since the mid-1990s, these numbers have decreased significantly (particularly during the Valentín Paniagua interim administration). In this context, there is now greater political associational space for organizing (when compared with the 1980s), but the horizon for organizing remains uncertain.

Bibliography

Andolina, Robert James. 1997. Colonial legacies and plurinational imaginaries: indigenous movement politics in Ecuador and Bolivia. PhD diss., University of Minnesota.

Basombrío Iglesias, Carlos. 1998. Sendero Luminoso and human rights: A perverse logic that captured the country. In Stern 1998, 425–46.

Bourque, Susan C., and David Scott Palmer. 1975. Transforming the rural sector: Government policy and peasant response. In *The Peruvian experiment: Continuity and change under military rule*, ed. Abraham F. Lowenthal, 179–219. Princeton, NJ: Princeton University Press.

Brysk, Alison. 2000. *From tribal village to global village: Indian rights and international relations in Latin America*. Stanford, CA: Stanford University Press.

Burt, Jo-Marie. 1997. Political violence and the grassroots in Lima, Peru. In *The new politics of inequality in Latin America: Rethinking participation*, ed. Douglas A. Chalmers, Carlos M. Vilas, Katherine Roberts Hite, Scott Martin, Kerianne Piester, and Monique Segarra. New York: Oxford University Press.

Cameron, Maxwell A., and Philip Mauceri, eds. 1997. *The Peruvian labyrinth: Politics, society, economy*. University Park: Pennsylvania State University Press.

Collier, Ruth Berins, and David Collier. 1991. *Shaping the political arena: Critical junctures, the labor movement, and regime dynamics*. Princeton, NJ: Princeton University Press.

Conaghan, Catherine M., and James M. Malloy. 1994. *Unsettling statecraft: Democracy and neoliberalism in the central Andes*. Pittsburgh, PA: University of Pittsburgh Press.

Coppedge, Michael. 2003. Venezuela: Popular sovereignty versus liberal democracy. In *Constructing democratic governance*, 2nd ed., ed. Jorge I. Domínguez and Michael Shifter, 165–92. Baltimore: Johns Hopkins University Press.

Davenport, Christian. n.d. Human rights and the promise of democratic pacification. Unpublished manuscript, University of Maryland.

Degregori, Carlos Iván. 1997. After the fall of Abimael Guzmán: The limits of Sendero Luminoso. In Cameron and Mauceri 1997, 179–91.

———. 1998. Harvesting storms: Peasant *rondas* and the defeat of Sendero Luminoso in Ayachucho. In Stern 1998, 128–52.

Del Pino, Ponciano. 1998. Family, culture, and "revolution": Everyday life with Sendero Luminoso. In Stern 1998, 158–92.

Díaz-Polanco, Héctor. n.d. La rebelión de los más pequeños: Los Zapatistas y la Autonomía. Unpublished manuscript.

Eckstein, Susan. 1983. Transformation of a "revolution from below"—Bolivia and international capital. *Comparative Studies in Society and History* 25 (1): 105–35.

Forero, Juan. 2003. Seeking balance: Growth vs. culture in Amazon. *New York Times*, December 10.

Gonzales de Olarte, Efraín. 1994. *En las fronteras del mercado: Economía política del campesinado en el Perú*. Lima: Instituto de Estudios Peruanos.

Granovetter, Mark. 1995. *Getting a job: A study of contacts and careers*. 2nd ed. Chicago: Chicago University Press.

Grindle, Merilee L. 1986. *State and countryside: Development policy and agrarian politics in Latin America*. Baltimore: Johns Hopkins University Press.

Guerrero, Andrés. 1993. De sujetos indios a ciudadanos-étnicos: De la manifestación de 1961 al levantamiento de 1990. In *Democracia, etnicidad y violencia política en los países andinos*, ed. Alberto Adrianzén, Jean Michel Blanquer, Ricardo Calla, Carlos Iván Degregori, Pierre Gilhodes, Andrés Guerrero, Patrick Husson, et al., 83–101. Lima, Peru: Instituto de Estudios Peruanos and Instituto Francés de Estudios Andinos.

Gurr, Ted Robert, with Barbara Harff, Monty G. Marshall, and James R. Scarritt. 1993. *Minorities at risk: A global view of ethnopolitical conflicts*. Washington, DC: United States Institute of Peace Press.

Hinajosa, Iván. 1998. On poor relations and the nouveau riche: Shining Path and the radical Peruvian left. In Stern 1998, 60–83.

de Janvry, Alain, Alison Graham, Elisabeth Sadoulet, Ramon Espinal, and Walter Spurier. 1994. *The political feasibility of adjustment in Ecuador and Venezuela.* Paris: OECD.

Jenson, Jane, and Susan D. Phillips. 1996. Regime shift: New citizenship practices in Canada. *International Journal of Canadian Studies* 14 (Fall): 111–36.

Kay, Cristóbal. 1982. Achievements and contradictions of the Peruvian agrarian reform. *Journal of Development Studies* 18 (2): 141–70.

Keck, Margaret E., and Katheryn Sikkink. 1998. *Activists beyond borders: Advocacy networks in international politics.* Ithaca, NY: Cornell University Press.

Kimmerling, Judith, with Federación de Comunas Unión de Nativos de la Amazonía Ecuatoriana (FCUNAE). 1993. *Crudo amazónico.* Quito, Ecuador: Ediciones Abya-Yala.

———. 1996. *El derecho del tambor: Derechos humanos y ambientales en los campos petroleros de la amazonía ecuatoriana.* Quito, Ecuador: Ediciones Abya-Yala.

Lagos, Maria L. 2003. A road with no return? *Journal of Democracy* 14 (2): 163–73.

Lucero, José Antonio. 2001. High anxiety in the Andes: Crisis and contention in Ecuador. *Journal of Democracy* 12 (2): 59–73.

Lustig, Nora. 1995. *Coping with austerity: Poverty and inequality in Latin America.* Washington, DC: Brookings Institution.

Mainwaring, Scott, and Timothy R. Scully. 1995. Introduction: Party systems in Latin America. In *Building democratic institutions: Party systems in Latin America*, ed. Scott Mainwaring and Timothy R. Scully, 1–34. Stanford, CA: Stanford University Press.

Mallon, Florencia. 1998. Chronicle of a path foretold? Velasco's revolution, Vanguardia Revolucionaria, and "shining omens" in the indigenous communities of Andahuaylas. In Stern 1998, 84–117.

Malloy, James M., ed. 1977. *Authoritarianism and corporatism in Latin America.* Pittsburgh, PA: University of Pittsburgh Press.

Manrique, Nelson. 1998. The war for the central Sierra. In Stern 1998, 193–223.

Marshall, T. H. 1963. *Class, citizenship, and social development.* Garden City, NY: Doubleday.

Mattiace, Shannan. 1997. ¡Zapata vive! The Ezln, Indian politics and the autonomy movement in Mexico. Ethnicity, identity, and citizenship in the wake of the Zapatista rebellion, special issue, ed. George A. Collier and Lynn Stephen. *Journal of Latin American Anthropology* 3 (1): 32–71.

Mauceri, Philip. 1997. The transitions to "democracy" and the failures of institution building. In Cameron and Mauceri 1997, 13–36.

McAdam, Doug. 1982. *Political process and the development of black insurgency, 1930–1970.* Chicago: Chicago University Press.

———. 1988. *Freedom Summer.* New York: Oxford University Press.

McAdam, Doug, John D. McCarthy, and Mayer N. Zald, eds. 1996. *Comparative perspectives on social movements: Political opportunities, mobilizing structures, and cultural framings.* Cambridge: Cambridge University Press.

McAdam, Doug, Sidney Tarrow, and Charles Tilly. 2001. *Dynamics of contention.* New York: Cambridge University Press.

McClintock, Cynthia. 1981. *Peasant cooperatives and political change in Peru.* Princeton, NJ: Princeton University Press.

———. 1989. Peru's Sendeo Luminoso rebellion: Origins and trajectories. In *Power and protest: Latin American social movements*, ed. Susan Eckstein, 61–101. Berkeley: University of California Press.

Molina, Sergio, and Iván Arias. 1996. *De la nación clandestina a la participación popular*. La Paz, Bolivia: Centro de Documentación e Información, CEDOIN.

Morley, Samuel A. 1995. *Poverty and inequality in Latin America: The impact of adjustment and recovery in the 1980s*. Baltimore and London: Johns Hopkins University Press.

Navarro, Maryssa. 1998. The personal is political: Las Madres de Plaza de Mayo. In *Power and popular protest: Latin American social movements*, ed. Susan Eckstein, 241–58. Berkeley: University of California Press.

Ojarasca. 1995. 45 (August–November).

Pacari, Nina. 1996. Ecuador taking on the neoliberal agenda. *NACLA Report on the Americas* 29 (5): 23–30.

Palmer, David Scott, ed. 1992. *The Shining Path of Peru*. New York: St. Martin's Press.

Podolny, Joel M., and Karen L. Page. 1988. Network forms of organization. *Annual Review of Sociology* 24:57–76.

Putnam, Robert D. 1993. *Making democracy work: Civic traditions in modern Italy*. Princeton, NJ: Princeton University Press.

Remy, María Isabel. 1994. The indigenous population and the construction of democracy in Peru. In *Indigenous peoples and democracy in Latin America*, ed. Donna Lee Van Cott, 107–30. New York: St. Martin's Press and Inter-American Dialogue.

Rivera Cusicanqui, Silvia, and Equipo THOA. 1992. *Ayllus y proyectos de desarrollo en el norte de Potosí*. La Paz, Bolivia: Ediciones Aruwiyiri.

Roberts, Kenneth, and Mark Peceny. 1997. Human rights and United States Policy toward Peru. 1997. In Cameron and Mauceri 1997, 192–222.

Rubin, Jeffrey W. 1997. *Decentering the regime: Ethnicity, radicalism, and democracy in Juchitán, Mexico*. Durham, NC: Duke University Press.

Ruiz, Lucy, ed. 1993. *Amazonía: Escenarios y conflictos*. Quito, Ecuador: CEDIME and Ediciones Abya-Yala.

Santos Granero, Fernando, ed. 1996. *Globalización y cambio en la amazonía indígena*. Quito, Ecuador: FLACSO and Ediciones Abya-Yala.

Seligmann, Linda J. 1995. *Between reform and revolution: Political struggles in the Peruvian Andes, 1969–1991*. Stanford University Press.

Selverston Melina. 1997. The politics of identity reconstruction: Indians and demoracy in Ecuador. In *The new politics of inequality in Latin America: Rethinking participation and representation*, ed. Douglas A. Chalmers, Carlos M. Vilas, Katherine Roberts Hite, Scott Martin, Kerianne Piester, and Monique Segarra, 170–91. New York: Oxford University Press.

Smith, Richard Chase. 1985. A search for unity within diversity: Peasant unions, ethnic federations, and Indianist movements in the Andean republics. In *Native peoples and economic development*, ed. Theodore MacDonald, 5–38. Cambridge, MA: Cultural Survival.

———. 1996. La política de la diversidad COICA y las federaciones étnicas de la Amazonía. In *Pueblos indios, soberanía y globalismo*, ed. Stefano Varese, 81–126. Quito, Ecuador: Ediciones Abya-Yala.

Starn, Orin 1998. Villagers at arms: War and counterrevolution in the central-south Andes. In Stern 1998, 224–57.

Stern, Steve J., ed. 1998. *Shining and other paths: War and society in Peru, 1980–1995*. Durham, NC: Duke University Press.

Ströbele Gregor, Juliana. 1996. Culture and political practice of the Aymara and Quechua in Bolivia: Autonomous forms of modernity in the Andes. *Latin American Perspectives* 23 (2): 72–90.

Tarrow, Sidney. 1998. *Power in movement: Social movements, collective action and politics.* New York: Cambridge University Press.

Ticona A., Esteban, Gonzalo Rojas O., and Xavier Albó C. 1995. *Votos y wiphalas: Campesinos y pueblos orginarios en democracia.* La Paz: Fundación Milenio and CIPCA.

Tilly, Charles. 2002. Repression, mobilization, and explanation. Unpublished manuscript, Columbia University.

Urioste Fernández de Córdova, Miguel. 1992. *Fortalecer las comunidades: Una utopía subversiva, democrática . . . y posible.* La Paz, Bolivia: AIPE/PROCOM/TIERRA.

Varshney, Ashutosh. 2002. *Ethnic conflict and civic life: Hindus and Muslims in India.* New Haven, CT: Yale University Press.

Weber, Eugen. 1976. *Peasants into Frenchmen: The modernization of rural France, 1870–1914.* Stanford, CA: Stanford University Press.

Wilkie, James W., Carlos Alberto Contreras, and Katherine Komisaruk, eds. 1995. *Statistical abstract of Latin America.* Vol. 31. Los Angeles: UCLA Latin American Center Publications, University of California.

Yashar, Deborah J. 1998. Contesting citizenship: Indigenous movements and democracy in Latin America. *Comparative Politics* 31 (1): 23–42.

———. 1999. Democracy, indigenous movements, and the postliberal challenge in Latin America. *World Politics* 52 (October): 76–104.

———. 2005. *Contesting citizenship in Latin America: The rise of indigenous movement and the postliberal.* Cambridge: Cambridge University Press.

———. Forthcoming. Indigenous politics in the Andes: Changing patterns of recognition, reform, and representation. In *The crisis of democratic representation in the Andes,* ed. Scott Mainwaring, Ana Maria Bejarano, and Eduardo Pizarro Stanford, CA: Stanford University Press.

Zamosc, Leon. 1995. *Estadística de las áreas de predominio étnico de la sierra ecuatoriana: Población rural, indicadores cantonales y organizaciones de base.* Quito, Ecuador: Ediciones Abya-Yala.

Contesting the Terrain of Politics
State-Society Relations in Urban Peru, 1950–2000

JO-MARIE BURT

THE EXPLOSIVE INTERNAL CONFLICT IN COLOMBIA AND the decision of the U.S. government to commit significant resources to aiding that country's government under the guise of the war on drugs has raised the profile of the Andean region in both scholarly and journalistic analyses. In Peru, the collapse in late 2000 of a mafia-like predatory state run by Alberto Fujimori and his shadowy advisor, Vladimiro Montesinos, revealed how electoral processes and the formal separation of powers may conceal authoritarian power relations and massive corruption. Massive social uprisings resulting in the peaceful but unconstitutional overthrow of elected presidents in Ecuador and Bolivia in the past few years have heightened awareness of the disconnect between political elites and the societies in whose interests they claim to govern. In Venezuela, the attempted overthrow of former paratrooper-turned-president Hugo Chávez and his increasing concentration of power amidst concerted efforts by the opposition to bring about a recall election have also raised concerns about political polarization and the future of democracy in that country.

Much of the writing on Andean affairs frames these national-level crises as crises of governability, emphasizing the weakness of democratic institutions plagued increasingly by guerrilla insurgencies, drug-trafficking networks, charismatic authoritarian leaders, and such mobilized social actors as the indigenous movements in Ecuador and Bolivia. The study of institutions is an important and valid endeavor, and indeed, institutionalist scholarship has made significant contributions to our knowledge of political preferences and behaviors. Such research has also increased our grasp of how specific institutions might be reengineered to reflect, promote, and even shape democratic values and practices. However, the emphasis on the state that is inherent in institutionalist approaches may unwittingly obscure the sociopolitical nature of the struggles that are shaping the Andean region's politics. The state is not a fixed entity; rather, as Migdal has suggested, the state is a field of power that is "constructed and reconstructed, invented and reinvented, through its interaction as a whole and of its parts with others" (2001, 23).

In many parts of the third world, state authority is fragmented and contentious (Migdal 2001; Tilly 2003). In particular, the monopoly of (legitimate) violence over a defined territory, which is assumed to be a defining element of a modern state, as defined by Weber (1958), is often contested, challenged, and subject to negotiation, as is evident in many of parts of the Andes today. Contenders promoting alternative sets of rules and norms (such as armed guerrilla movements) compete with the central state for hegemony and control in local and regional contexts or seek to bypass it altogether (as with drug-smuggling networks); elsewhere, organized social movements fundamentally challenge the established order and demand basic reconfigurations of state power, economic privilege, and social citizenship. As Lechner (1998) has suggested, while institutions matter, it is because they are also contextual and contested that in some places they reveal little about the actual workings of politics and power. This is particularly the case in the Andean region, most notably in the central Andes, where democratic institutions have always been weak and underdeveloped, and the locus of power is often found outside the margins of institutional politics.[1]

In this sense, the social and political struggles currently under way in the Andes might appropriately be conceived as processes of contention over the nature, scope, and reach of the state; its relationship to society and the economy; and the nature and scope of citizenship. Rather than assume the legitimacy of the state and frame analysis of the political process in terms of governability, such an approach takes as its point of

departure the notion that the legitimacy of the state is open for contestation both discursively (Habermas 1987) and through what Anderson
(1967) once called "demonstrations of power." As theorists of citizenship
have noted, it has historically been through long, drawn-out processes of
contestation and negotiation with states that social groups have demanded and (sometimes) achieved more expansive and inclusive definitions of
citizenship and more democratic mechanisms of governance and accountability (Tilly 1996, 2003).

It is in this context that institutionalist analyses focused on procedural aspects of democracy may overlook a significant problem that only
recently is being addressed theoretically in the democratization literature:
the uneven reach of the state throughout the national territory and the
implications of this for state-society relations, state organization and legitimacy, and democracy itself (O'Donnell 1993; Tilly 2003). Stateness is
often presumed, when in fact the notion of the state as an entity that exer-
cises control and administers policy throughout the national territory is
often more image than reality (Migdal 2001).[2] Social scientists are thus
tasked with analyzing the image of stateness portrayed by state elites and
the reality of stateness on the ground, as well as the ways state policies
and societal responses strengthen or undermine stateness. Analyses of
state-society relations that are historically grounded and that examine
these relationships in a multiplicity of arenas are a more useful way of
examining politics and power in the Andean region in particular and in
developing societies in general.

These relationships are most fruitfully examined as a political process,
following the model developed by social movement theorists such as
McAdam, Tarrow, and Tilly (2001), which views politics as an ongoing
arena of contestation, accommodation, and negotiation. While starting
and ending points may differ, these scholars have argued, the mechanisms and processes that shape outcomes are often similar, pointing to a
useful way for social scientists to better understand social change in a
complex and dynamic manner rather than in the single-shot, static
approaches that tend to prevail in the social sciences. The state and elite
politics are neither given priority nor isolated but rather are analyzed in
relationship to the societies they seek to govern and dominate, while the
focus also extends to the ways societies shape, limit, and resist state policies and practices. This is not just a plea to move beyond the state-centric
literature, which has tended to exaggerate the extent of hegemony and to
miss the nature of contestation and resistance at local and regional levels
(Rubin 1997; Migdal 2001). Nor is it a call, to paraphrase Oxhorn (1995,

1988), "to bring society back in." Rather, building on the insights of other scholars promoting a relational perspective on state and society, it proposes that examining these relationships as a political process will provide insights about the nature of contestation over the forms and scope of state and citizenship and will help illuminate the mechanisms and processes that shape political outcomes. Such an approach enables us to better understand the conflicts and apparent stalemates characterizing state-society relations in Peru and in the Andean region more broadly.[3]

State-Society Relations in Urban Peru

Peru has been transformed in the past fifty years from a predominantly rural society to an overwhelmingly urban one. In the 1940s, 70 percent of Peruvians lived in rural areas; today 75 percent live in urban areas, and one-third of the population lives in the capital city, Lima. Two-thirds of Limeños, moreover, live in the squatter settlements that ring the capital city and since their emergence in the 1940s have been the object of efforts on the part of state elites to incorporate, co-opt, and repress the "unruly" urban poor. Close examination of state policies geared toward these ends and the societal responses they have elicited at different junctures generates an anthropology of state-society relations in the context of the dramatic demographic and social changes Peru—like other developing societies—has experienced over the last half century.

The focus on urban politics also reveals the ways in which social mobilization—understood as the demographic movement inherent in rural-to-urban migration and urbanization, as well as the more explicitly political mobilization that emerged as collective identities were transformed in ways that contributed to the constitution of new societal actors—influenced the state and state policies as well as the nature of state-society relations, which in turn altered the nature and shape of social action and organization.

Villa El Salvador is a squatter settlement that emerged in the early 1970s and has since become one of Peru's largest cities, with a population of more than 380,000. From its origins as an experiment in corporatist forms of interest mediation under the reformist military regime of General Juan Velasco Alvarado (1968–1975), Villa El Salvador was transformed into a showcase of the Marxist Left and its model of participatory democracy and social justice. This shift occurred at least in part as a result of state policies that helped constitute new actors who soon began to resist corporatist state policies and practices. Indeed, Villa became a symbol of social mobilization against economic austerity policies and state repression embodied in the second-phase military government of Francisco Morales Bermúdez (1975–1980) and the new democratic government of Fernando Belaúnde (1980–1985).

By the end of the 1980s, however, the Left's experiment had collapsed, revealing the inner contradictions within the Left itself, as well as the external pressures that undermined it. Those pressures included the challenges of state populism, exemplified by the government of Alan García (1985–1990), and the violence of Shining Path, which targeted Villa El Salvador with special vehemence because its model of peaceful social change within the democratic system represented a fundamental challenge to Shining Path's proposal of violent revolution. The subsequent rise of independent politicians in Villa, which was accompanied by a dramatic rise in corruption, highlights the shift that occurred under the regime of Alberto Fujimori (1990–2000), as state-society relations were restructured along neoliberal and authoritarian lines. Villa El Salvador and its changing relationship with the state reflect in telling ways the multidimensional and ongoing conflict in Peruvian society over the nature and scope of state organization, state penetration into society, societal accommodation and resistance, and alternative modes of mediation—both democratic and authoritarian in nature—between state and society.

Squatters, Oligarchs, and Generals

The historically exclusionary nature of the Peruvian state has been extensively analyzed.[4] It is sufficient here to note that an alliance between rural landowners, known as *gamonales*; the commercial and financial elites of the coast; and foreign capital, which extracted raw materials for the international market, maintained a tightly controlled system that restricted citizenship and resorted to repression and traditional forms of clientelism to contain and delimit challenges to its rule (Cotler 1978). The mass-based, antioligarchic political parties that emerged in the 1930s—the populist American Popular Revolutionary Alliance (APRA) and the Communist Party—were substantially weakened by repression and, particularly in the case of the Communists, by factional and ideological splits. Neither party, despite a lower-class orientation, was able to challenge the deeply entrenched forms of clientelism that dominated state-society relations, and oligarchic rule endured in Peru well into the 1960s (Stokes 1995). The middle-class parties that emerged in the 1950s, Popular Action (AP), under the leadership of Fernando Belaúnde, and the Christian

Democratic Party, were similarly unable to culminate their efforts to reform the oligarchic state.

It was not until the military intervention of 1968 that the power of the oligarchic state was broken with the implementation of a broad reformist program under the leadership of General Velasco. The Velasco regime sought to expand the power of the Peruvian state to regulate foreign capital and promote industrial development even as it sought to develop a more encompassing notion of Peruvianness and of citizenship. Strengthening state capacity and broadening its reach throughout the national territory were seen as key to developing Peru's economy, while overcoming the historic racism and structures of exclusion were seen as necessary to broaden state legitimacy and authority. Both efforts—state making and nation building—were viewed by the Peruvian military as necessary to undercut potential revolutionary projects, an alternative to the repressive solutions to popular mobilization being carried out by the bureaucratic-authoritarian regimes of the Southern Cone during the 1960s and 1970s.

Migration as Social Movement

The uneven process of capitalist modernization that was unfolding in Peru was one element that severely undermined the agricultural sector and by the 1940s prompted a massive influx of rural peasants into the cities, seeking better living conditions. In 1940, Lima had slightly more than 500,000 inhabitants; by 1961, that number had nearly quadrupled to 1,846,000.[5] This explosive growth rate meant an increased demand for housing. Initially, new migrants were absorbed into existing poor districts in downtown Lima, which became known as *tugurios*, or inner city slums. As these areas became overpopulated, city dwellers began organizing land invasions that began to spill over the traditional demarcations of Lima into the deserts to the city's north and south, far from any locus of economic activity. City slum dwellers led massive and organized land invasions, primarily on state-owned land, which became known as *barriadas*; invasions of privately owned land were usually violently repressed, and state elites were usually more lenient toward squatters who invaded vacant or unused state-owned lots. In some cases, state elites even sponsored land invasions in clientelist fashion, offering squatters protection and promising them land titles in exchange for political support.[6] Because they lacked land titles and faced the constant threat of eviction, urban squatters were highly vulnerable to such dependent and paternalist state policies.

In sum, the oligarchic state sought to incorporate barriada dwellers into the polity not as citizens but rather as clients—when they were not violently repressed when invasions were considered to have overstepped the boundaries permitted by the state and economic elites (Collier 1976). This dynamic mirrored state-society relations in more general terms during the period of the oligarchic state: clientelism when possible, repression when clientelism failed (Cotler 1978). State elites were careful to protect property rights but lacked the autonomy to forge an urban development plan to adequately address the demographic shifts created by massive migration to the cities.

This laissez-faire approach to urban policy allowed the Peruvian state to channel popular discontent for housing while limiting its own responsibilities in forging an urban housing and development policy. The state, in other words, while forced to react to the social movement represented by urban squatters, responded in a way that minimized its cost and maximized its benefit. This would change with Velasco, less by design than because continued social movement from below—in the form of a massive land invasion on the outskirts of Lima—compelled the state to change its policy toward the urban poor.

Velasco's Experiment in Social Inclusion

The military regime led by General Velasco marked the culmination of the crisis of the oligarchic state that had dominated Peru since the nineteenth century and the failure of various reformist movements to institute change in the structures of economic and political power. In the context of a deeply divided bourgeoisie, state elites acquired greater autonomy to carry out reforms that increased the power of the state itself, its ability to restructure the Peruvian economy, and its relationship with the international economy (Quijano 1971). Unlike other military regimes in Latin America at the time, which sought to remove radical challenges to the status quo by violently repressing working- and lower-class movements, Velasco's experiment was based on notions of social inclusion, in an effort to undercut more radical options and to extend and deepen the legitimacy of the Peruvian state. It endeavored to create new mechanisms of representation based on a direct relationship between the state and society as organized in specific functional groups (peasants, industrial workers, squatters).[7]

In effect, the government used distributive policies as a means of incorporating lower-class groups into new state-chartered associational groups, effectively extending citizenship not through political rights but through social and economic rights. It sought to do so through a program that was neither capitalist nor communist but a vaguely defined third way based on the notion of social property as practiced in socialist countries such as Yugoslavia and Cuba. Velasco's experiment was the most ambitious state-building and nation-building project in modern Peruvian history (McClintock and Lowenthal 1983; Stepan 1978).

The Velasco regime's corporatist efforts primarily focused on the rural sector (through its agrarian reform law and recognition of indigenous culture and language) and the urban industrial sector (creating worker-run factories, extending social benefits to industrial workers, etc.). As for the urban poor, it expressly rejected the reigning laissez-faire policy toward land invasions, but it was slow to devise a workable urban policy to deal with the continued rural-to-urban migration and the doubling of family units in Lima's tugurios and shantytowns. In the meantime, it prohibited unauthorized land invasions and repressed them where they occurred (Driant 1991; Dietz 1980).

Social movement from below, however, forced the regime to rethink its urban policy. On April 28, 1971, a group of some two hundred families from the inner city district of La Victoria, encouraged by the Velasco regime's stated commitment to the poor, invaded a small piece of state-owned land in Pamplona Alta, an existing barriada in southern Lima. Within days, some nine thousand families had joined the invasion, which had spilled over onto privately owned land and threatened to create a serious problem for the Velasco regime.[8] The long-held fear of Limeño elites—that the poor, Indian, and cholo[9] masses would descend upon them and take over the city—seemed to be coming true.

Several days after the initial invasion, a police contingent appeared and tried to dislodge the squatters. The squatters resisted, and one of them was killed in the ensuing melee. The news spread quickly, prompting an angry response from the squatters, who took two policemen as hostages. Local members of the Catholic Church steeped in the doctrine of liberation theology defended the squatters, and members of the church hierarchy, including the Bishop of Lima, Juan Carlos Landázuri, became involved in negotiations with the government to avoid further bloodshed. The initial repressive response was reportedly the work of anti-regime sectors of the military, evidence of the growing tensions within the armed forces over Velasco's experiment and the social mobilization it was engendering. To counter this sector—and because he realized that creating a new urban settlement could bolster his corporatist project—Velasco announced a plan to relocate the squatters to an extensive terrain of seventy-eight hundred acres of barren desert located eighteen miles south of Lima. This gave birth to the Velasco regime's urban showcase settlement, Villa El Salvador.[10]

Villa El Salvador exemplified the corporatist model of state-society relations implemented by the Velasco regime. The regime's architects believed that such a model would more effectively link state and society, giving the state the legitimacy and authority it lacked and creating a more stable and viable polity that would not be susceptible to radical challengers. State planners in the National System to Support Social Mobilization, an agency created to oversee the organization of the population into functional and territorial units, began to direct the organization of the new settlement and tightly controlled decisions affecting its development. Concrete benefits (land titles, service provision) were delivered to create more enduring links between the urban poor and the state, while state-chartered associations would create a direct tie between local elected leaders and the state bureaucracy. Block-level representatives elected a ten-member executive council to govern the Self-Managed Urban Community of Villa El Salvador (CUAVES), which would mediate the settlement's relationship with the state. Elections were held at the block level only, effectively weakening broader political activism and facilitating the state's ability to create vertical linkages with society (Stepan 1978, 173–74). The weak nature of preexisting organization in squatter settlements such as Villa made implementation of such top-down forms of organization relatively easy, particularly compared with other sectors (such as the sugar workers along the coast), where a history of more independent organization made the state's task much more difficult (Stepan 1978).

Yet despite heavy state presence and control, resistance to the regime's corporatist model was germinating, and spaces for autonomous political activity were being carved out in barriadas such as Villa El Salvador.[11] Perhaps most important was the presence of a group of secondary school teachers steeped in classist politics who opposed the regime's corporatist program, which they viewed as an effort by the state to co-opt the popular sectors.[12] This group successfully leveraged state funds to create the Centro de Comunicación Popular (Center for Popular Communication), which became an important space for the classist leadership in Villa. While their opposition was not frontal (which would probably have been suicidal in the context of a military regime), they sought to build a more radical grassroots movement by influencing a new generation of community leaders (CELADEC 1983); indeed, many of the left-wing leaders who rose to positions of authority in Villa El Salvador in the 1980s came from this cohort.

This classist nucleus (like others elsewhere in shantytowns, factory shop floors, and peasant unions throughout Peru) was linked to the new Left parties that flourished in the late 1970s and helped lead massive social protests against the so-called second phase of the military regime. Thus, a small nucleus of societal resistance within Villa El Salvador not only challenged Velasco's corporatist model but also sought to recast state-society relations along more radical lines. In addition, there is evidence that several local leaders grew increasingly resentful of the top-down policy-making style employed by state managers and felt a growing desire to exercise greater autonomy in local decision making, creating a reserve of resistance that could be tapped as the corporatist experiment began to falter (Zapata 1996). This was evident in other sectors as well, such as in the trade unions, where resistance to the corporatist mechanisms of control was stronger from the start, growing in intensity particularly after the economic crisis of 1974.

As in other arenas, then, the state's efforts to organize the urban poor had the dual, unintended effect of politicizing shantytown dwellers and providing them with the resources to organize. Of particular importance was the way the state helped create a local identity of neighbors (vecinos) in the community of Villa El Salvador (Tovar 1986), which a new generation of activists would promote as a way of mobilizing people against the more conservative regime that succeeded Velasco's. Equally important, the crucial start-up costs for organization had been borne by the state when it helped create CUAVES, which proved to be an important model of local-level organization in Villa and which helped acquaint an entire generation of pobladores (barriada residents) with the tools of social activism, from petitioning the state to holding an assembly to organizing a protest march.

The state thus played a key role in what social movement theorists call actor constitution (McAdam, Tarrow, and Tilly 2001): state policies helped foster a local identity among the inhabitants of Villa El Salvador while also providing crucial resources to facilitate mobilization, thus contributing to the constitution of new actors in society. While societal resistance to Velasco's efforts to create state-controlled organizations in barriadas such as Villa El Salvador was minimal at the outset, the very tools of identity and resource mobilization afforded to the pobladores of Villa by the state made more autonomous forms of organization, and hence societal resistance to the regime's corporatist structures, a possibility.[13]

Ironically, what ignited this resistance was the retreat of the state from the social contract developed under the Velasco regime: the withdrawal of state support from CUAVES and from the settlement as a whole sparked popular disillusionment and outrage, which was fueled by the regime's repressive response to social mobilization. When coupled with policies that were perceived as harmful to popular economies, this led to societal polarization and a growing rejection of the phase-two military regime. This growing discontent was exploited by the classist activists within Villa who sought to orient social mobilization toward more radical forms of action. The myriad forms of resistance to the state that were brewing in settlements such as Villa El Salvador became the basis for contesting state action and inaction, particularly after the fall of Velasco in 1975.

The Armed Retreat of the State and Societal Radicalization

The special status afforded to Villa El Salvador in particular, and to squatter settlements more generally, vanished after Velasco was removed in 1975 in a bloodless palace coup. The new military government, led by General Morales Bermúdez, was concerned about the growing politicization of the military and was wary of the growing social mobilization unleashed by Velasco's reforms. A new ruling coalition was developing, in which more conservative sectors of the armed forces joined forces with commercial and financial elites who were hostile to Velasco's reforms (such as progressive labor legislation and land reform) and who sought to check the growing power of the state and create more amicable relations with foreign capital. In this second phase of the military government, pro-Velasco officers were ousted, reforms were scuttled, and economic orthodoxy was implemented. The Velasco regime's reliance on foreign loans to subsidize its reformist program had left the country severely indebted, prompting the International Monetary Fund to condition future loans on orthodox economic reforms and revealing the structural constraints to economic policy imposed by international actors (Mauceri 1996).

The austerity measures implemented by Morales Bermúdez—which included the elimination of subsidies on basic food items, the freezing of wages, and reductions in state spending—fueled growing popular unrest. The language of rights and social justice so widely used during the Velasco period emboldened popular sectors in the cities and countryside to demand what they considered rightfully theirs. Most of the instruments of state corporatism were dismantled or gutted, leaving the regime with few mechanisms but co-optation—which was ineffective given the newfound autonomy of social movements—and repression. This process can be characterized as the armed retreat of the state: the state sought to disengage itself from an interventionist and developmentalist role in society and the economy and used repressive measures to deal with social protest of its retreat, which in turn had serious consequences for social organization and mobilization.[14]

On the one hand, the retreat of the state meant that organizations such as CUAVES won the organizational and political autonomy many leaders were demanding. The opening of political space created new opportunities for other groups, particularly the Marxist Left. In Villa, for example, the pro-Velasco leadership of CUAVES was ousted in elections by Patria Roja (Red Fatherland), marking a shift in Villa's relationship with the state from one of collaboration to confrontation.[15] This was best symbolized by the massive protest march organized by CUAVES in collaboration with the teachers' union and local PTAs in April 1976, in which an estimated thirty thousand people marched to downtown Lima demanding that the state provide teachers, schools, and other basic services.

However, the retreat of the state also meant economic debacle for organizations such as CUAVES. The withdrawal of state funding led to the collapse of the experiments in social property being administered by CUAVES and cut to the heart of CUAVES itself. The Communal Bank, for example, which had been enthusiastically supported by the population, collapsed after the state withdrew its funding, and most families lost their entire savings.[16] The debacle of this and other community enterprises severely eroded popular confidence in CUAVES and its leadership. Left-wing groups that had championed the new-found autonomy of social movements and organizations such as CUAVES failed to appreciate the social fragmentation that this engendered. They also overlooked the extent to which social protests, while confrontational and couched in anti-statist rhetoric, were largely defensive struggles against a retreating state and declining living standards. Social movements rejected the state's effort to co-opt and repress their organizations, as well as the retreat of the state from its role as architect of social and economic development. Civil society, which had acquired new tools of organization and mobilization largely thanks to state policies, was rejecting the armed retreat of the state and demanding a broad notion of citizenship that went well beyond political freedoms to include social and economic rights.[17]

The imperative of economic austerity made dealing with rising social demands through traditional forms of clientelism and co-optation impossible. Instead the regime turned increasingly to repression, suspending constitutional guarantees and declaring a curfew in mid-1976. Trade union and popular leaders were arrested or forced to go into hiding, but this did not dampen social mobilization: indeed, two massive general strikes in 1977 and 1978 are widely seen as contributing to the military's decision to announce a timetable for elections and a return to democratic rule. Growing social mobilization may not have forced the regime from power per se, but it exacerbated existing institutional tensions within the armed forces concerning both their role in government and the growing militancy of an increasingly organized civil society. Sectors of the economic elite seeking a return to a civilian-led process that would ensure that their interests were represented coincided with this institutionalist sector of the military.[18]

Nevertheless, the military regime's call for elections created a new political dynamic, channeling popular discontent toward institutionalized mechanisms of participation and conflict resolution. The process of social mobilization that occurred under the Velasco regime was like a genie that could not be simply put back into its bottle. As social movements from trade unions to the barriada movements developed increasing autonomy vis-à-vis the state, they began to mobilize in more sustained and confrontational actions. Many saw in this more autonomous, confrontational attitude on the part of CUAVES and other social organizations the seeds of an independent, progressive social movement, particularly given the way the Marxist Left was able to enter into the spaces left vacant by the retreating state. However, while social mobilization was helpful in obtaining some local benefits for the community, over time it would become evident that the armed retreat of the state effectively shifted the terms of state-society relations so that social mobilization would be less capable of extracting concrete benefits and services from a disappearing state. This is crucial to understanding the decline in social mobilization in the 1980s, although other factors—the devastating economic crisis and political violence—would also contribute to the ebbing of social mobilization even as the country was liberalizing politically.

Transition to Democracy and the Rise of Local Politics

There were widespread popular expectations that the transition to democratic government in 1980 would translate into better living conditions for poor Peruvians and create a new model of state-society relations. However, the government of Fernando Belaúnde pursued broadly similar policies to those of the second-phase military regime. His government continued to implement orthodox economic policies that undermined popular living standards, and the state continued its retreat from a developmentalist role in society and the economy. In addition, repression and, increasingly in the context of electoral politics, co-optation and clientelism, remained the principal means of dealing with a mobilized civil society. While the Belaúnde government pursued a decentralization policy, its efforts to undermine local organization in municipalities controlled by rival political parties revealed the way the central state would continue to circumscribe local politics and dampen the democratizing potential of decentralization.

Under the military regime, municipal authorities were appointed by the central government and were thus perceived as representatives of the state rather than of societal interests. In an effort to make local government more responsive, the Belaúnde government reinstated the direct vote for municipal authorities. But in a sequence of events that would be repeated elsewhere in the Andes during the ensuing decade, even as local governments were granted administrative autonomy, they remained dependent on the central state for resources. This effectively undermined their ability to devise solutions to local problems, placing enormous stress on municipal governments as demand making shifted from the central state to local and regional governments in the context of decentralization. Despite the promise of decentralization to mobilize participation around specific needs rather than control over the central state apparatus, the contours of what Chalmers (1977) terms the politicized state remained essentially intact and continued to shape the behavior of political parties at the national and local level.

That municipal governments often lacked the power or resources to resolve problems was evident in the case of Villa El Salvador, where local needs were not being addressed either by the central or the local government. Laws designed to disarticulate existing urban social movements by forcing them to reorganize in juntas controlled by the municipal governments evoked fierce resistance on the part of social movements such as CUAVES.[19] Continued incursions by the state into arenas deemed the responsibility of local actors—such as the use of communal land—created further conflict between Villa and the central state, reflecting the tension between the Belaúnde government's promise of decentralization and the reality of continued manipulation from the center. A broad coalition of social and political actors began demanding autonomy, and in 1983 Congress established Villa El Salvador as an independent municipal district.[20]

The legal repression of existing organizations, the use of state resources through programs such as Popular Cooperation to develop clientelist networks in poor urban and rural areas of the country, and efforts to assert state control in local communities such as Villa El Salvador were designed to weaken the opposition while bolstering AP's popular support base. However, the resistance of an active and mobilized civil society both to top-down attempts to disarticulate them and to neoliberal austerity measures led to a situation of impasse by the mid-1980s. Efforts on the part of economic and state elites to reduce the role of the state and impose neoliberalism were met by broad societal resistance. Broad parallels can be drawn here to the situation elsewhere in the Andes, where mobilized civil societies effectively blocked neoliberal reform.

In the case of Peru, the failed populist revival led by APRA's Alan García, the collapse of the left-wing experiment in local government after the division of the United Left (IU) in 1989, the ravages of hyperinflation, and the clearing effect created by the political violence that swept the nation in the late 1980s would effectively destroy the capacity of civil society to continue to mobilize against the retreat of the state. Thus, when the Fujimori government aggressively pursued a policy of state retreat, it was met with relatively little opposition. This was particularly ironic given that Fujimori came to power largely thanks to backing by APRA and the Left, only to abandon his anti-neoliberalism platform days after assuming the presidency.[21]

The Left between Reform and Revolution

The Left became an important electoral force in Peruvian politics almost despite itself. The diverse left-wing parties mobilizing against the Morales Bermúdez government in the late 1970s had revolution, not transition to democracy, in mind when they cheered on and helped organize the massive social mobilizations that rocked the military regime between 1977 and 1979. The call for elections for a Constituent Assembly to draft a new constitution in 1978 left them with little choice but to participate, however, and they did surprisingly well, winning one-third of the vote for the Constituent Assembly. The Left's poor showing in the 1980 presidential and congressional elections was attributed to a lack of unity, leading to the creation of IU for the November 1980 municipal elections (Nieto 1983). IU did surprisingly well, and in 1983 its president, Alfonso Barrantes, was elected mayor of Lima, and it won nineteen of the capital's forty-one municipal districts. IU had come to represent nearly a third of the electorate, making it a significant political force at the local and national levels.

IU proposed to use its power in local government to develop a model of participatory democracy that was an alternative to more traditional clientelist and corporatist modes of social and political organization. The two constituent elements of the Left's vision were active participation in local self-government and cogovernment between local government and popular organizations.[22] Participation was seen as a key pillar of democratic governance, and local government was perhaps the space most suited for building new modes of popular participation and decision making in government (Comisión de Plan de Gobierno de la Izquiera Unida 1983). The Left thus sought to transform the state and state-society relations by building a grassroots, participatory democracy, an alternative to the formal, electoral democracy at the national level. It also emphasized social justice and an expanded notion of citizenship that included not only formal political rights but also economic and social rights.

Villa El Salvador was perhaps the most important urban site of IU's project, and Michel Azcueta, who had led the campaign to establish Villa as a municipal government and was elected to two successive terms as mayor (1984–1986, 1987–1989), was one of the foremost advocates of the emerging Gramscian approach to politics within IU. His administration sought to revive the neighborhood-level organizations that were the grassroots constituency of CUAVES, and he used the power of city government to empower existing organizations such as the Popular Women's Federation (FEPOMUVES) and to create new ones, including a market cooperative, the agricultural zone development committee, an association of small industrialists, and the Youth Federation. This was intended to strengthen community-level organizations while also building partisan support for IU. For example, when Azcueta granted administrative control to FEPOMUVES over a new municipal program providing a glass of milk daily to children and pregnant women in low-income districts of the capital, he helped turn FEPOMUVES into an organization with districtwide reach and influence among women's organizations while also building popular support for his administration and for IU projects more broadly.

Some have argued that such policies of fostering grassroots participation and devolving power to social organizations is evidence of the role that the Left came to play as a link between state and society during the 1980s (Schönwalder 2002). Others have suggested that because it occurred primarily outside of legal channels, the Left's devolution of power to social organizations represented an abdication of the state's role (Mauceri 1996). While both interpretations make valid points, they do not account for the way the Left's use of local state power constituted civil society even as it sought to obtain partisan benefits for its political project or for the ways this process reproduced tensions and conflicts within social movements, within IU coalition, and between the Left and other external actors in specific local contexts.

Social organizations would become the battleground for the different member parties within IU for power and status within the electoral coalition, and new conflicts would emerge over leadership, power, and control over resources at the local level. Tensions and conflicts between radical and moderate sectors within IU soon would explode, and this jockeying for hegemony within social organizations in districts such as Villa El Salvador effectively contributed to the fragmentation of urban social movements at a time when they were already under increasing pressure from new forms of state clientelism under APRA, from the looming economic crisis, and from growing political violence (Burt 1997). These conflicts and tensions are at the heart of the eventual collapse of the Left's project and of IU itself by the end of the decade.

The Populist Revival

The triumph of Alan García in the 1985 presidential elections gave a great deal of impetus to APRA's organizational efforts in popular districts such as Villa and represented a key challenge to IU's project. García was widely popular, winning an absolute majority in all of Lima's popular districts, including Villa (Tuesta 1989). García sought to resurrect populist notions of the state as the central organizer of political and social life. He organized tripartite negotiations between the state, capital, and labor; promised state support for the urban and rural poor through a plethora of social programs; and vowed to limit foreign debt payments to free up cash for local development initiatives.

APRA, like AP before it, sought to use its power as governing party to direct state resources toward patronage networks that would bolster its popular support, particularly in areas where IU—its chief rival for votes among the popular sectors—was the dominant force. A temporary employment program, the Temporary Income Assistance Program (PAIT), effectively drew people away from collective forms of organization by offering them cash benefits, while the Direct Assistance Program avoided funding existing communal soup kitchens, many of which had links to left-leaning nongovernmental organizations and church organizations, and instead funded the creation of new soup kitchens that could be more easily tied to APRA's political project (Graham 1992). In popular districts such as Villa El Salvador, this added another layer of competition among grassroots organizations and further fragmented civil society. The municipal government of Lima, which APRA won control of in the 1986 elections, became one more instrument at the disposal of the central government to undermine IU-controlled municipal governments such as Villa. For example, the Lima municipality cut sanitation services to Villa, and public works programs financed by a municipal agency also ceased (Tuesta 1989).

Two years of economic growth and exuberant state spending fueled García's popularity, but by mid-1987, the heterodox model was faltering, effectively undermining the regime's ability to sustain these clientelist networks.[23] The fiscal crisis of the state, marked by severe hyperinflation in 1987–1989, led to the collapse of García's populist program and a de facto return to a state in retreat.[24] Without resources, state programs dried up, traditional services were severely compromised amidst plummeting budgets for health and education, and popular confidence in the state and its ability to structure daily life—from relations in the marketplace to basic issues of citizen security—disappeared.

Some authors have emphasized the nature of the APRA party to explain this economic and political debacle. The use of state resources for clientelist purposes most certainly alienated social groups who were not direct beneficiaries of party politics and thus contributed to the widening gap between state and society and to the polarization that undermined democratic government (Graham 1992, 199). However, the 1980 transition to democracy did not alter the basic contours of the politicized state (Mauceri 1997). In such a state, access to state power is widely seen as an opportunity for private gain, bureaucratic posts are a function of party or personal loyalty rather than professional merit, and the state is not seen as acting and does not act on behalf of universal interests but rather out of segmented loyalties and political motives.[25] APRA, like AP before it, was operating in the context of such a system, though it is probably also true that APRA's hegemonic aspirations led it to widely adopt clientelist modes of linking state and society. When the state's capability of sustaining these clientelist networks faltered, support for the García administration plummeted and undermined popular confidence in democratic governance and in the state itself.

The political and economic debacle, coupled with repeated corruption scandals, severely undermined the state's capacity to perform basic administrative functions and weakened its institutional, administrative, and coercive presence in society. The state's growing incapacity to ensure public order, exacerbated by the expansion of guerrilla violence and drug trafficking, added to the erosion of popular confidence in public authority and in the political parties whose leaders seemed incapable of responding to the country's mounting and multiple crises.

The Left was not immune from this process. Once considered a dominant contender in the 1990 presidential elections, IU faced increasing internal divisions that led to its division in 1989 and its eventual eclipse as a significant political force. State policies under APRA contributed to this process, highlighting the ways in which state clientelism can undermine alternative political projects. The Left also found itself uncomfortably positioned between APRA's reformism and Shining Path's call to violent revolution, which further exacerbated the differences between the moderate and radical factions within IU. For moderates within the coalition, who rejected Shining Path's extreme violence, the only answer was a resolute defense of democratic institutions in the face of economic debacle and expanding guerrilla violence. For radicals, this amounted to a betrayal of the Left's ideals, and the government's use of repression against Shining Path reinforced their notion of the state as an instrument of class domination and bolstered their belief that revolutionary violence was necessary to producing social change. In the 1990 election, a divided Left won less than 12 percent of the vote combined, and it lost its relevance as a national-level actor.

The Maoist Challenge

The collapse of traditional structures of mediation—and particularly of APRA and IU, which together garnered nearly 75 percent of the vote throughout much of the 1980s—created a political vacuum that new actors quickly sought to fill. Political independents—such as Fujimori—emerged to contest elections and, to the surprise of many observers at the time, were successful (Degregori and Grompone 1991; Panfichi 1997). At the local level, however, Shining Path, which was seeking to extend its presence in urban areas to prepare for the next stage in its revolutionary war, also ably exploited this situation.[26] In barriadas such as Villa El Salvador, Shining Path built local networks of support by championing local causes, imposing strict codes of moral behavior and swift punishment of transgressions, and exploiting existing conflicts to its advantage.[27] Shining Path was less interested in resolving local problems than in taking up the demands of the local population to win sympathy and then radicalizing popular struggles vis-à-vis the local and central state to exacerbate the contradictions of the "bureaucratic capitalist state" (Guzman 1989, 220). Radicalizing popular struggles in the face of an inert state would also demonstrate, according to Shining Path's logic, the futility of peaceful forms of organization as championed by the United Left, which Shining Path considered to be revisionist and a brake on its popular revolution.

Villa El Salvador was of particular importance to Shining Path precisely because of the alternative model of state-society relations that IU was attempting to construct there. Shining Path had begun organizing in the district in the early 1980s, trying to win recruits and gaining intimate knowledge of the political and social terrain of the district. In the late 1980s, *El Diario*, Shining Path's weekly newspaper, began publishing vociferous critiques of local leaders, including former mayor Michel Azcueta, current mayor Johny Rodríguez, and Rodríguez's vice mayor and former president of FEPOMUVES, the women's federation, María Elena Moyano, each of whom had spearheaded local efforts to resist Shining Path's advance in the district.

A series of attacks made it evident by the early 1990s that Shining Path was making a stand in Villa, seeking to decapitate the IU leadership, take over the district's key organizations, and extend its presence at the grassroots.[28] Local authorities, political leaders, and community activists Shining Path deemed an obstacle to its revolutionary project became the object of physical attack and systematic intimidation. In this lethal mix of politics and terror, and in the context of the division of the Left, a deepening economic crisis, and state retreat, Shining Path advanced steadily in Villa El Salvador. By the early 1990s it had infiltrated many of the district's key organizations; placed allies in leadership positions in organizations such as CUAVES, the Autonomous Authority of the Industrial Park, and FEPOMUVES; and created a climate of fear that inhibited opposition and further weakened local forms of organization.

The Peruvian state failed to provide a local context of security for citizens and local authorities, contributing to this sensation of fear. The state's counterinsurgency strategy, which sought to establish an alliance between the armed forces, popular leaders, and local authorities already under threat by Shining Path made the situation more complicated and difficult for local leaders. For example, some moderates within IU had sought to build bridges with local police forces to defend the district from Shining Path. Such efforts collapsed after Fujimori closed Congress and suspended the constitution in the 1992 *autogolpe* (self-coup) and implemented a more aggressive counterinsurgency strategy. Moreover, Shining Path and state violence and intimidation reduced public space and made social organization and action virtually impossible. Shining Path's brutal 1992 murder of María Elena Moyano, who had publicly resisted Shining Path's inroads into Villa even as she criticized the military's counterinsurgency strategy, brought this point home to many activists. The murder of Moyano symbolized Shining Path's extreme authoritarianism and willingness to use violence to eliminate its rivals in IU, but it also underscored the extreme dispersion of the Left and its paralysis in the face of the dramatic challenge Shining Path represented to its political project as well as to the physical integrity of its members (Burt 1997). It also revealed the state's incapacity—or perhaps its unwillingness—to protect governing authorities and citizens such as Moyano who also questioned the state.[29]

The Authoritarian Solution

Less than two months after Moyano's murder, President Fujimori closed Congress, suspended the constitution, and announced the reorganization of the judiciary, with the institutional support of the armed forces. The April 5, 1992, autogolpe, as it was called, marked a rupture in the organization of state power—though it could also be considered the logical, if more extreme, extension of the trend toward the increasing militarization of the state that started in the early 1980s with the creation of emergency zones in areas of conflict that were effectively controlled by the armed forces to the detriment of civilian authorities. Antiterrorist legislation that was put in place after the autogolpe allowed the state to cast a wide net and incarcerate anyone suspected of terrorist affiliations or sympathies (Human Rights Watch 1995, 1997). Hundreds of local activists, some who were involved in Shining Path's networks and many who were not, were imprisoned, held for long periods without trial, and convicted without due process. This further contributed to the sensation of fear and demobilization.

While some scholars viewed Fujimori's agreement to call Constituent Assembly elections in November 1992—after significant international pressure—and the approval of a new constitution in 1993 as a sign of Peru's transition to democracy, others questioned the democratic credentials of the regime, given its systematic centralization of power in the hands of the executive, its willingness to eviscerate democratic checks and balances when they got in the way, and its persistent authoritarian practices (Burt 1998a, 2004; McClintock 1999; Conaghan 1999). The autogolpe destroyed the tentative efforts being made by local-level activists such as those in Villa El Salvador to build bridges with the state to check Shining

Path's advance in the district. While some championed the autogolpe as a necessary move to restore order and eliminate subversion, others worried that a dangerous political vacuum was opening up that could be exploited by Shining Path.

The political situation shifted radically in September 1992 when Shining Path's top leader, Abimael Guzmán, was arrested along with other top leaders of the organization. These arrests, along with the later publication of Guzmán's letters requesting peace talks with the Fujimori government, signaled the strategic defeat of the insurgency. This would translate by 1994 into significantly reduced levels of violence and some return to normalcy in daily life. The state's ability to reassert its authority in this context (aided by Peru's reinsertion into the international economy, which meant renewed and much needed international loans to revive the economy) was a political boon for the Fujimori government. But the regime's long-term authoritarian project became evident when instead of using this opportunity to rebuild democratic institutions, the government intensified its antipolitics discourse to keep any alternative form of organization from materializing, sought to further centralize its power, and used its triumph in the war against subversion as a way of justifying its authoritarian practices (Burt 1998b; CVR 2003).[30]

The antipolitics discourse filtered to the grassroots. In Villa El Salvador, for example, the Left, once dominant in the district, lost control of the municipal government in 1993 to a political unknown, Jorge Vásquez, from the independent Obras movement. Local forms of mediation lost their autonomous character and increasingly became defined by brokerage and clientelist politics controlled from the center. This was exacerbated by regime policies that sought to curtail the fiscal and administrative autonomy of municipal governments and that centralized most social spending into the hands of the Ministry of the Presidency by 1993–1994. Local initiatives dried up or were bypassed by this new and well-financed state apparatus, thus redefining the nature of state-society relations in Villa El Salvador and elsewhere in Peru. It was now the central state, through powerful new agencies (funded primarily by international loans and from sales of state-run enterprises), such as the Fund for Social Compensation and Development (FONCODES) and the National Food Assistance Program (PRONAA), that distributed scarce resources and reset the rules of the game.[31] This was not another populist revival, however; social programs were devised as a means of facilitating an overall retreat of the state.[32]

As democratic forms of accountability were eviscerated in a context of a severely weakened civil and political society, corruption flourished in local governments during this period, and Villa was no exception. Vásquez was arrested during his first year as mayor on charges of malfeasance, corruption, and abuse of authority, and his successor fled to avoid similar charges a year later. Subsequent regimes, including that of Martín Pumar, a former IU activist and disciple of Azcueta who governed between 1998 and 2002, were also marred by charges of corruption and malfeasance. But most importantly, local government was no longer considered a significant political space by residents of the district itself.

State-run clientelism was back with a vengeance and with it the tactics that undermined horizontal linkages among social groups by reinforcing control at the center and the utter dependency of social groups on the beneficence of state elites. This was particularly damaging given that it was occurring not in a relatively open, pluralist context—as had been the case with the Belaúnde and García governments[33]—but in the context of a highly personalist regime that engaged in authoritarian practices designed to keep civil and political society demobilized and disorganized.

In this context, the growing dependence on government handouts made it increasingly difficult for local organizations to avoid some form of co-optation by the government.[34] Thus even autonomous organizations such as the *comedores populares*, or communal soup kitchens, had little choice but to become enmeshed in the regime's new clientelist networks (Blondet 1999). In Villa, for example, some leaders of the Women's Federation developed close ties with congressional leaders from the official party, Change 90/New Majority, to secure government support for development projects. Leaders of formerly autonomous comedores say they felt compelled to acquiesce to government officials' demands to send their members to progovernment rallies and demonstrations of support for the regime (including a luncheon celebration of President Fujimori's birthday in the government palace) to ensure the continued flow of government support. They also noted their reluctance to voice any criticism of state policies.[35] State-society relations were now mediated only by the president himself, revealing the extremely personalist and even autocratic nature of the regime.

Coupled with this resurgence of state clientelism were tactics designed to keep organized politics permanently on the defensive. The regime's antipolitics and antiparty rhetoric has been widely discussed (Roberts 1995; Panfichi 1997; Tanaka 1998; Degregori 2000), but most analysts view this as a consequence and not a cause of the destruction of organized politics in Peru. While it is true that Fujimori and the broader rise of independents were a result of the growing disillusionment with traditional political parties, it is also true that once in power, and particularly after the 1992 autogolpe, Fujimori continued to rally tirelessly against the old political class to keep the political opposition off balance and unable to articulate any kind of organized response to Fujimori's growing centralization of power and his alliance with the Peruvian armed forces.

This interpretation is further bolstered by the similarities between Fujimori's antipolitics discourse and the core tenets of national security doctrine, in which parties and politicians are portrayed as favoring partisan politics over the good of the nation, which only the armed forces can ensure and protect; elimination of political parties is viewed as a positive and desirable goal.[36] Given the evidence that the autogolpe was inspired by a plan designed by leaders within the armed forces to remove civilian leadership, create a military-led government, and rule for a period of twenty to thirty years to restore economic and political stability (Rospigliosi 1996; CVR 2003), these parallels are more than circumstantial.

The Fujimori regime's antipolitics discourse was accompanied by fear mongering, another tactic used by the regime to keep its opponents in political and civil society off balance and demobilized. From the use of the military in countrywide sweeps of rural and urban communities to clean up areas of terrorists to massive civic action campaigns designed to win the hearts and minds of the urban and rural poor to the continued use of excessively draconian antiterrorist legislation as a disciplinary tool well after the Shining Path threat was contained to the hyping up of the continued terrorist threat to justify its heavy-handed measures, the regime used fear to keep civil and political society on the defensive (Burt 2002; CVR 2003).

At the grassroots level, regime supporters also replicated this discourse of fear to intimidate and keep dissidents in line. Interviews with grassroots organization leaders in Villa El Salvador and elsewhere revealed that proregime activists often accused those critical of the regime and its policies of being terrorists, creating a chilling effect on the opposition's ability to vocalize discontent or to publicly organize. At a time when those accused of terrorism faced sentences of twenty years to life in prison, the rights of due process were systematically denied by antiterrorist legislation and by questionable judicial practices (including the use of hooded secret military courts), and hundreds if not thousands of people innocent of any crime were imprisoned and condemned to long prison sentences, accusations of this kind were a powerful demobilizing tool.[37]

Finally, the neoliberal economic model put in place during the Fujimori decade contributed to the continued atomization of society. Privatization of formerly state-run utilities such as electricity meant that the previous methods of obtaining basic services—mobilizing social protests and petitioning the state to expand services—had become moot. The massive deregulation of private enterprise and liberalization policies allowed for an explosion of small businesses, but these operated in extremely haphazard way, evincing a survival instinct and *sálvase quien pueda* (every man/ woman for him-/herself) mentality that some analysts began to call the *cultura combi*, in reference to the extremely chaotic, ruthless, and sometimes homicidal way in which *combis*, privately owned taxi-vans, drove in a rush to compete for passengers and to make as many runs per day as possible. In such a context, individual strategies of survival reigned supreme and collective strategies seemed outmoded and ineffective.

Thus, in Peru the armed retreat of the state took place in a context in which society was atomized, demobilized, unconnected to the political sphere, and hence unable to articulate opposition or any viable alternative political project. Two factors account for this. First, as several authors have noted, Fujimori astutely harnessed the antipolitics sentiment that grew in the wake of the economic and political debacle of the 1980s in support of his neoliberal economic model, creating a base of political support that allowed him to implement difficult austerity measures without suffering serious political setbacks until the end of the 1990s (Roberts 1995; Stokes 1999b; Carrión 1999). Second and equally important, the economic crisis and political violence of the 1980s had produced a clearing effect, weakening and demobilizing those social forces—particularly labor and the legal Left—that might have opposed neoliberal economic policies in other circumstances. The state-society stalemate evident in the 1980s had been broken. APRA was on the run, the Left had collapsed, and civil society was demobilized. The radical insurgency of Shining Path, which represented another political project altogether, had also been defeated. In this context, the resurgent Right, represented by Fujimori and his authoritarian coalition, was able to set the agenda and impose one of the most far-reaching neoliberal economic programs in Latin America (Mauceri 1995). By recasting the terms of state-society relations on an individualist basis, the advocates of neoliberalism were challenging not only state corporatism but also the very notion of social and economic rights.[38] This was the intellectual justification for the retreat of the state.

Despite the collapse of the Fujimori regime in 2000 and its replacement first by a consensus government of transition and then by the elected Alejandro Toledo administration, neoliberalism continues to reign supreme.[39] This remained true as late as 2005, despite massive social mobilizations in Lima and provincial cities such as Arequipa, where widespread protests in 2002 against the privatization of utilities testified to societal rejection of the basic contours of neoliberalism and its model of state-society relations. It is telling that the resurgence of APRA under Alan García—who came close to defeating Toledo in the 2001 elections—is at least partly due to his anti-neoliberal discourse and his championing of a more activist state, particularly for reducing poverty and inequality.

The revival of social mobilization since Peru's transition to democracy in 2000–2001 has alarmed many observers, who see it as a sign of the ungovernability that characterizes the Andean region today. There are clearly problems of creating and sustaining workable democratic institutions, just as there are serious problems of political leadership (as suggested by Toledo's anemic approval ratings, which hovered at around 8 percent during 2004 and failed to break into double digits well into 2005). It might also be suggested that Peru is witnessing the return of the social actor, but in a dramatically different context than in previous decades. The state-centric model of representation no longer exists, but political society has also failed to develop enduring mechanisms of representation between state and society.

Today a variety of political movements and parties, some new and some not so new, occupy public space but remain weakly articulated with civil society. A wide range of social actors have reemerged (trade unions, state employees, peasant federations, university students) or come into existence (regional fronts, coca growers) that challenge different aspects of neoliberal policies but without articulating a coherent alternative model.[40] Nor have they been able to build alliances and coalitions among themselves to strengthen their collective bargaining power. In effect, Peru today can be characterized by widespread social mobilization but without the constitution of a political subject capable of articulating these diverse societal demands into the political arena. Thus the scenario is distinct from the late 1970s and 1980s, when widespread social mobilization was accompanied by the constitution of political actors, such as the parties of IU, who sought to articulate social demands into the public realm.

Missing from this scenario is the urban barriada movement, which was such an important social movement actor in the 1970s and 1980s. Urban social movements such as those found in Villa El Salvador were severely challenged by the economic crisis and the guerrilla and state violence of the 1980s, as well as by the implosion of key allies in political soci-

ety, particularly APRA and IU. Under the Fujimori regime, the reassertion
of state-led clientelism, the effects of neoliberal economic policy, and the
manipulation of fear further disarticulated urban social movements, to
the point that today they are not a significant actor in the current phase of
contentious politics.

Unlike the generation of young people active in these movements in
the 1970s and 1980s, young people in Villa today are focused on finding
jobs that will help them contribute to their household incomes, often
shared between three or even four generations to make ends meet. Many
older activists, still reeling from the effects of violence and state repression
and in some cases wrongful imprisonment, avoid the public sphere altogether (Burt 2002). "Some condemned us as terrorists; others as traitors,"
laments a former CUAVES leader. "The leader-activist has taken refuge in
silence."[41] While the key organizations of the district, such as CUAVES
and FEPOMUVES, continue to exist, many observers note that they lack
any real social or political significance. Violence of a different sort has
also taken hold in the district (as in the rest of Lima), with an explosion
of youth gangs, petty crime, and violent assaults.[42] Indeed, after trash
collection, crime is seen as the most pressing problem facing the district
(Abad 2003).

The return to democratic politics has led municipal governments like
that of Villa to focus on providing more efficient public services, such as
trash collection, citizen security, and educational services, and this has
fueled greater citizen participation vis-à-vis local government. Projects
such as the Participatory Budget, which was pioneered in Villa El Salvador and has since been adopted nationwide, have also helped reestablish linkages between citizens and local government by involving them
in decision making about municipal budget priorities, though the broader decentralization process of which this is an integral part has stalled
(Llona and Soria 2004). But the kind of social movement activism of previous decades is largely absent in urban popular districts such as Villa El
Salvador. This is partly a reflection of the disarray of social forces but also
an indication of the decentering of the state that has occurred under
neoliberalism.

The explosion of social protests in Lima and in provinces throughout
the country suggests that a new arena of contestation is opening up over
the nature of the neoliberal model itself. Thus, those most involved in
social protest of state action and inaction are those actors who are able to
generate and sustain local social or political identities and who feel that
their interests are being threatened by neoliberal economic and social

policies. This is a process that has been evident in neighboring Ecuador and Bolivia over the past decade or so, as shown by the emergence of social movements with strongly rooted social identities (such as the indigenous movement in Ecuador) or political identities (such as the *cocalero* [coca growers] movement in Bolivia) and their vanguard role in challenging the neoliberal model of state-society relations.

Contesting State Power and Citizenship

State-centered approaches are limited in their ability to help us understand the complex dynamics of contention occurring in the Andean nations today. Rather than relying on static images of the state as suffering crises of governability or as weak or failing, my analysis conceives the state as an arena of conflict and contestation. Examining state-society relations in Peru as a political process illuminates the ways in which ruling coalitions and societal groups favoring different visions of the state and state-society relations are constituted, dissolved, and restructured in different historical periods and in the context of societal action and resistance. Peru has been marked by a deep conflict over the contours and scope of the state and citizenship since the demise of the oligarchic state in the 1960s that has involved domestic actors, including economic and technocratic elites (including the armed forces), and political parties and movements; organized groups in civil society (labor unions, urban social movements, peasant federations, university students); and international actors (international financial organizations, foreign capital, etc.). None of these actors obtained sufficient organizational and mobilizational strength to impose their vision on the other groups, nor were they able to build enduring coalitions with like-minded groups to implement their programs (at least in the medium term), which helps account for the high level of political conflict, violence, and polarization in the 1970s and 1980s.

Thus, this period marks a process of intense contestation over the way the state should be conceived and organized: in the mold of state corporatism, as proposed by the Velasco regime; in a classic liberal sense of a limited constitutional state, as put forward by the Center-Right in the early 1980s; in the classic populist mold represented by APRA under Alan García; as some version of democratic socialism, as championed by the legal Left; as some form of agrarian communism, as envisioned by Shining Path and its popular revolutionary war; and finally, as the night watchman state of neoliberalism, as championed by key sectors of the financial and commercial elite and technocratic elites, and ultimately implemented under the Fujimori regime.

In effect, the Peruvian state was being contested not only by a violent guerrilla movement, but by different political and social groups whose mobilizational capacity ebbed and flowed over time. At the same time, the margin of autonomy enjoyed by state elites to define the nature and scope of the state and its relationship with society varied as well, increasing when political and civil society was fragmented and demobilized or repressed (as during the start of the Velasco period, and during most of the Fujimori regime) and decreasing when civil society was able to develop more autonomous forms of organization (as at the end of the Velasco period and into the early to mid-1980s).

By the 1990s, the neoliberal view of the state prevailed with the formation of specific alliances among the armed forces and other technocratic elites, domestic business elites, and transnational capital that favored this view of the state and were willing to dispense with democratic legalities to implement it. Advocates of this model considered the interventionist state developed under Velasco and championed as the solution to underdevelopment and poverty by García to be the source of social conflict. The radical restructuring and privatization of the state and state-society relations were seen by new liberals as key to both reviving the process of capital accumulation and depoliticizing social struggles by removing the state as the main actor directing economic and social development.

The dramatic reordering effect that violence and hyperinflation had on Peruvian politics and society facilitated this process, producing a clearing effect that in essence broke the stalemate that characterized state-society relations in the 1970s and especially the 1980s. The key actors contesting the state and proposing alternative models of the state were, if not eliminated entirely, reduced significantly in political strength and capacity: APRA was reduced to a mere shadow of its former self (although its organizational structure remained intact, which was crucial to its resurgence in 2001 with the return of García to Peru after a decade of self-imposed exile); IU, paralyzed between APRA's reformism and Shining Path's revolution and mired in its own internal contradictions, imploded; and after the arrest of Shining Path's top leadership, Guzmán himself recognized the organization's defeat and the ascendancy of a newly reassertive state under Fujimori and the armed forces.

The Center-Right, meanwhile, subordinated its constitutionalist project to Fujimori's neoliberal authoritarianism also in part because of the reordering effect of violence, which led elite groups as well as sectors of the middle and lower classes to willingly accept an implicit trade-off between democracy and order. The popularity of the 1992 autogolpe, which registered 70–80 percent approval ratings and reflected the way the political violence and economic chaos of the 1980s undermined the population's faith in democracy as a system capable of regulating conflict and resolving social tensions and led many to accept an authoritarian solution to reimpose order and reassert the power of the state to regulate social conflict. Finally, while it is true that societal contestation played an important role in the ultimate demise of the Fujimori regime and the restoration of democracy, to date such actors have proven insufficiently strong or unified to produce major changes in the neoliberal vision of state and society that continues to dominate Peruvian politics.

The aim of this analysis is not to produce grand theorizing but rather to help discern the mechanisms and processes producing political outcomes. By examining the way specific ruling coalitions emerged, the vision of the state and state-society relations they embraced and the nature of the policies implemented, the way state action and inaction shaped societal formations, and the response on the part of societal groups to these policies, we can uncover some of the processes and mechanisms that produced intense political conflict over the past several decades in Peru over the nature and scope of the state and citizenship. While the specific outcome of the Peruvian case may be distinct from that in other countries, which seems likely given the nature of the Shining Path guerrilla movement, broadly similar processes and mechanisms are evident in other Andean nations, particularly given the similar structural positions these nations occupy in the international division of labor, the international hegemony of neoliberal economics, and the weakness of both state capacities and societal organization.

Notes

I thank the editors of this volume for their insightful comments and corrections and Francisco Gutiérrez, César Espejo, and an anonymous reviewer for their comments on an earlier version of this chapter. I am also grateful to the participants in the Social Science Research Council Andes Workshop in Quito, Ecuador, in October 2001, especially Eric Hershberg and Carlos Iván Degregori, whose observations helped refine the analytical framework developed here. Any shortcomings remain my sole responsibility.

1. A stronger case could be made for an institutionalist framework in the Northern Andes (Colombia and Venezuela), given the durability of democratic institutions and political parties, but the recent processes of decay of these institutions—both mediating institutions such as political parties and state institutions—and power dynamics

outside these frameworks (as in Colombia's internal conflict) also suggest the limitations of such a framework.

2. In their work on the relationship between the state and democratization, for example, Linz and Stepan (1996) do not view stateness as a problem in Latin America.

3. North (2004) examines the ways oligarchic elites in Ecuador have used the state to block political and economic reforms to benefit the poor and indigenous majority, which in turn have fueled highly contentious oppositional politics in Ecuador.

4. See, for example, Cotler (1978), Flores Galindo and Burga (1981), and Flores Galindo (1988).

5. Today, some 8 million people live in the capital.

6. In some instances, private sector elites sponsored land invasions to extend the urban frontier and create development opportunities that they could exploit for economic gain.

7. In effect, Velasco sought to impose a type of state corporatism. On the distinction between state and societal corporatism, see Schmitter (1974). On the corporatist nature of the Velasco regime, see Stepan (1978).

8. The presence of the international press corps, which was in Lima for an Inter-American Development Bank meeting, also played a role in the regime's decision-making process.

9. In Peru's categories of racial-ethnic hierarchy, *cholo* refers to urbanized people of indigenous descent.

10. This extraordinary history has been widely documented. See, for example, CELADEC (1983) and Zapata (1996). Blondet (1991) analyzes the women's movement in Villa.

11. The emergence of these spaces was overlooked by traditional state-centered analyses. Stepan (1978) briefly mentions ways the urban poor bypassed the corporatist state structures created by Velasco but focuses on events that occurred largely after Velasco's ouster, when such structures were being dismantled in any case. Detecting the kinds of semiclandestine, class-based resistance noted here is inevitably complicated in the context of a military regime, yet this underscores the utility of in-depth ethnographic fieldwork for revealing how social actors engage in various forms of negotiation, accommodation, and resistance to state structures (Scott 1985).

12. On the emergence of classism in the Peruvian labor movement, see Parodi (1986), Rospigliosi (1988), and Balbi (1989). For a discussion of how classist ideologies translated into the barriadas, see Stokes (1995).

13. Stokes (1995) analyzes the role of the state, as well as other actors, such as the liberation theology church, in the emergence of autonomous social movements in urban and rural Peru.

14. I borrow the concept of the armed retreat of the state from Gill (2000), an incisive analysis of the neoliberal restructuring of the state and state-society relations in urban Bolivia in the 1990s.

15. In early 1976, the pro-Velasco leadership of CUAVES was ousted by the Marxist Left during the second convention of CUAVES with the election of Odilón Mucha Orihuela of Patria Roja as general secretary.

16. See Zapata (1996). Tuesta (1989) argues that mismanagement and petty corruption also contributed to the failure of these community enterprises, a conclusion supported by numerous interviews I conducted.

17. Franco (1998) offers an insightful analysis of popular notions of democracy in Latin America that incorporate social and economic rights, in contradistinction to traditional views of liberal democracy that focus principally on civil and political rights.

18. On the transition to democracy in 1980, see Cotler (1986), Lynch (1992), and Mauceri (1997).

19. For example, legislation, including the Organic Law of Municipalities and the Statute of Neighborhood Juntas, denied legal recognition of existing organizations such as CUAVES (Tuesta 1989).

20. Some CUAVES leaders opposed this, fearing that it would afford the central state further opportunity to destroy community organizations in Villa.

21. Stokes (1999b) analyzes the implications of such departures from campaign promises for representation and democratic accountability.

22. For an analysis of the Left's politics and its demise, see Calderón and Valdeveallano (1991) and Roberts (1998). Schönwalder (2002) analyzes the IU's politics and performance in metropolitan Lima and in the popular district of El Agustino.

23. For an analysis of the factors contributing to the collapse of García's program, see Pastor and Wise (1992). On the García regime, see Reyna (2000) and Graham (1992).

24. This was widely celebrated by an emboldened group of neoliberal technocrats who saw the spontaneous dismantling of the state as a positive development. See, for example, Webb (1991). Their analysis did not take into account the parallel process of privatization of violence and the expansion of Shining Path.

25. The García regime also faced enormous international constraints, as actors such as the U.S. government and the international financial institutions were largely hostile to such heterodox experiments and sought the implementation of strict free market policies (Mauceri 1996).

26. Structural conditions were also important, including the dramatic expansion of the barriada population from 1.5 million in 1981 to an estimated 3.5 million in the early 1990s. In Villa El Salvador, the population grew from 168,000 in 1984 to 260,000 in 1993—a 5 percent annual growth rate (CUAVES/CIDIAG 1984; INEI 1993).

27. This has long been a strategy used by Shining Path in both rural and urban contexts. See, for example, Manrique (1989), Isbell (1992), Berg (1992), and Smith (1992).

28. This corresponded to Shining Path's declaration in May 1991 that it had achieved strategic equilibrium with the armed forces, the intermediate stage of its plan to overthrow the Peruvian state. For an analysis of Shining Path's advance and societal resistance to it in Villa El Salvador, see Burt (1998a).

29. The Peruvian Truth and Reconciliation Commission (CVR 2003) suggests that in some cases, including those of Huaycán and Villa El Salvador, the state may have deliberately sought to recruit local leaders such as Moyano and Pascuala Rosada of Huaycán to confront Shining Path and to lend legitimacy to the state's cause, placing them in harm's way without providing adequate protection.

30. For an analysis of why and how an authoritarian outcome to the conflicts and crises of the 1980s was more likely, see Burt (2004).

31. See Schady (2000) for an excellent analysis of the Fujimori government's political use of FONCODES resources.

32. There is abundant literature analyzing the neopopulist character of the Fujimori regime (Roberts 1995; Weyland 1996). My view parallels the analysis presented in Stokes (1999a), which suggests that Fujimori's social policies were not a revival of pop-

ulism but rather a palliative that made the imposition of neoliberal restructuring more feasible.

33. An important exception is the areas ruled directly by the military because of political violence.

34. For example, more than 50 percent of the population had become dependent on government food programs by the late 1990s. See APRODEH/CEDAL (2000).

35. These observations are based on interviews with comedor leaders carried out in Villa El Salvador in field visits in 1998, 1999, and 2000.

36. For an analysis of the doctrine of national security, see Crahan (1982) and Weiss Fagen (1992).

37. See Human Rights Watch (1993, 1995) for an analysis of the antiterrorist legislation.

38. For an insightful analysis into citizenship regimes and the shift from corporatism to neoliberalism, see Yashar (1999).

39. See Conaghan (2001) and Balbi and Palmer (2001) for analyses of the collapse of the Fujimori regime and the challenges facing the new civilian government.

40. See Pizarro, Trelles, and Toche (2004) for a cogent analysis of these diverse movements.

41. Interview in Villa El Salvador, December 2002.

42. There are an estimated five hundred youth gangs operating in Lima, involving some ten thousand young people. The municipal government of Villa El Salvador estimates that about one thousand youths are involved in gang activity in the district (Agencia de Información Solidaria 2004).

Bibliography

Abad, Dante. 2003. Este es Villa. http://venus.unive.it/sattin/estaesvilla.htm#7.9.

Agencia de Información Solidaria. 2004. Juventud sin rumbo. August 1. http://www
.lainsignia.org/2004/agosto/soc_002.htm.

Anderson, Charles. 1967. *Politics and economic change in Latin America.* Princeton, NJ: Princeton University Press.

APRODEH/CEDAL. 2000. *Informe Anual: Perú diez años de pobreza y autoritarismo.* Lima, Peru: APRODEH/CEDAL.

Balbi, Carmen Rosa. 1989. *Identidad clasista en el sindicalismo.* Lima, Peru: DESCO.

Balbi, Carmen Rosa, and David Scott Palmer. 2001. "Reinventing" democracy in Peru. *Current History* 100 (643): 65–72.

Berg, Ronald. 1992. Peasant responses to Shining Path in Andahuaylas. In Palmer 1992, 83–104.

Blondet, Cecilia. 1991. *Las mujeres y el poder: Una historia de Villa El Salvador.* Lima, Peru: Instituto de Estudios Peruanos.

———. 1999. *Las mujeres y la política en la década de Fujimori.* Lima, Peru: Instituto de Estudios Peruanos.

Burt, Jo-Marie. 1997. Political violence and the grassroots in Lima, Peru. In Chalmers 1997, 281–309.

———. 1998a. Shining Path and the "Decisive Battle" for Lima's barriadas: The case of Villa El Salvador. In *Shining and other paths: War and society in Peru, 1980–1995,* ed. Steve Stern, 267–306. Durham, NC: Duke University Press.

———. 1998b. Unsettled accounts: Militarization and memory in postwar Peru. *NACLA Report on the Americas* 32 (2): 35–41.

———. 2002. Quien habla es terrorista: Fear and loathing in Fujimori's Peru. Paper presented at the Fujimori Legacy and Its Impact on Public Policy in Latin America conference, Dante B. Fascell North-South Center, University of Miami, and University of Delaware Department of Political Science and International Relations, Washington, DC, March 14.

———. 2004. State-making against democracy: The case of Fujimori's Peru. In *Politics in the Andes: Identity, conflict, reform*, ed. Jo-Marie Burt and Philip Mauceri, 247–68. Pittsburgh, PA: University of Pittsburgh Press.

Calderón, Julio, and Rocío Valdeveallano. 1991. *Izquierda y democracia entre la utopía y la realidad: Tres municipios en Lima.* Lima, Peru: Instituto de Desarrollo Urbano (CENCA).

Carrión, Julio. 1999. La popularidad de Fujimori en tiempos ordinarios, 1993–1997. In Tuesta 1999, 231–46.

CELADEC. 1983. *Villa El Salvador: Del arenal a distrito municipal.* Lima, Peru: CELADEC.

Chalmers, Douglas. 1977. The politicized state in Latin America. In *Authoritarianism and corporatism in Latin America*, ed. James M. Malloy, 47–87. Pittsburgh, PA: University of Pittsburgh Press.

Chalmers, Douglas A., Carlos M. Vila, Katherine Roberts Hite, Scott Martin, Kerianne Piester, and Monique Segarra, eds. 1997. *The new politics of inequality in Latin America: Rethinking participation and representation.* New York: Oxford University Press.

Collier, David. 1976. *Squatters and oligarchs: Authoritarian rule and policy change in Peru.* Baltimore: Johns Hopkins University Press.

Comisión de Plan de Gobierno de la Izquierda Unida. 1983. *Plan de Gobierno de la Izquierda Unida.* Lima, Peru. Comisión de Plan de Gobierno de la Izquierda Unida.

Conaghan, Catherine. 1999. Entre las amenazas y la complicidad: El estado y la prensa en el Perú de Fujimori. In Tuesta, 247–72.

———. 2001. *Making and unmaking authoritarian Peru: Re-election, resistance and regime transition.* North-South Agenda Papers no. 47, May.

Cotler, Julio. 1978. *Clases, Estado y Nación en el Perú.* Lima, Peru: Instituto de Estudios Peruanos.

———. 1986. Military interventions and "transfer of power to civilians" in Peru. In *Transitions from authoritarian rule: Latin America*, ed. Guillermo O'Donnell, Philippe C. Schmitter, and Laurence Whitehead, 148–72. Baltimore: Johns Hopkins University Press.

Crahan, Margaret, ed. 1982. *Human rights and basic needs in the Americas.* Washington, DC: Georgetown University Press.

CUAVES/CIDIAG. 1984. *Un Pueblo, Una Realidad: Villa El Salvador: Resultados del II Censo organizado por la CUAVES el 8 de abril de 1984.* Lima, Peru: CUAVES/CIDIAG.

CVR (Comisión de la Verdad y Reconciliación del Perú). 2003. *Informe Final.* Lima, Peru: CVR.

Degregori, Carlos Iván. 2000. *Década de la antipolítica: Auge y huida de Alberto Fujimori y Vladimiro Montesinos.* Lima, Peru: Instituto de Estudios Peruanos.

Degregori, Carlos Iván, and Romeo Grompone. 1991. *Elecciones 1990: Demonios y redentores en el nuevo Perú.* Lima, Peru: Instituto de Estudios Peruanos.

Dietz, Henry. 1980. *Poverty and problem-solving under military rule: The urban poor in Lima, Peru.* Austin: University of Texas Press.

Driant, Jean-Claude. 1991. *Las Barriadas de Lima: Historia e Interpretación*. Lima, Peru: IFEA/DESCO.

Flores Galindo, Alberto. 1988. *Buscando un Inca*. 3rd ed. Lima, Peru: Editorial Horizonte.

Flores Galindo, Alberto, and Manuel Burga. 1981. *Apogeo y crisis de la república aristocrática*. Lima, Peru: Ediciones Rikchay Peru.

Franco, Carlos. 1998. *Acerca del modo de pensar la democracia en América Latina*. Lima, Peru: Fundación Friedrich Ebert.

Gill, Lesley. 2000. *Teetering on the rim: Global restructuring, daily life, and the armed retreat of the state*. New York: Columbia University Press.

Graham, Carol. 1992. *Peru's APRA: Parties, politics, and the elusive quest for democracy*. Boulder, CO: Lynne Rienner.

Guzmán, Abimael. 1989. Desarrollar la guerra popular sirviendo a la revolución mundial. Originally published in 1986 as a document of the Central Committee of the Communist Party of Peru. Reproduced in *Guerra popular en el Perú: El pensamiento Gonzalo*, ed. Luis Arce Borja, 219–304. Brussels.

Habermas, Jürgen. 1987. *The theory of communicative action*. Boston: Beacon.

Human Rights Watch. 1993. *Human rights in Peru: One year after Fujimori's coup*. New York: Human Rights Watch.

Human Rights Watch. 1995. *Peru: The two faces of justice*. New York: Human Rights Watch.

———. 1997. *Presumption of guilt: Human rights violations and the faceless courts in Peru*. New York: Human Rights Watch.

Instituto Nacional de Estadísticas e Información (INEI). 1993. *IX Censo de Población y IV de Vivienda 1993* (CPV). Lima, Peru: INEI.

Isbell, Billie Jean. 1992. Shining Path and peasant responses in rural Ayacucho. In Palmer 1992, 59–82.

Lechner, Norbert. 1998. The transformation of politics. In *Fault lines of democracy in post-transition Latin America*, ed. Felipe Agüero and Jeffrey Stark, 21–39. Coral Gables, FL: North-South Center Press/University of Miami.

Linz, Juan J., and Alfred Stepan. 1996. *Problems of democratic transition and consolidation: Southern Europe, South America, and Post-Communist Europe*. Baltimore: Johns Hopkins University Press.

Llona, Mariana, and Laura Soria. 2004. Presupuesto Participativo: Alcances y límites de una política pública. Paper presented at the first Conference of the Network of Monitoring, Evaluation and Analysis in Latin America and the Caribbean, Lima, Peru, October 20–22.

Lynch, Nicolás. 1992. *La Transición Conservadora: Movimiento Social y Democracia en el Perú, 1975–1978*. Lima, Peru: El zorro de abajo ediciones.

Manrique, Nelson. 1989. La Década de la Violencia. *Márgenes* 5:137–82.

Mauceri, Philip. 1995. State reform, coalitions, and the neoliberal autogolpe in Peru. *Latin American Research Review* 30 (1): 7–37.

Mauceri, Philip. 1996. *State under siege: Development and policy making in Peru*. Boulder, CO: Westview.

———. 1997. The transition to "democracy" and the failures of institution building. In *The Peruvian labyrinth: Polity, society, economy*, ed. Maxwell A. Cameron and Philip Mauceri, 13–36. University Park: Pennsylvania State University Press.

McAdam, Doug, Sydney Tarrow, and Charles Tilly. 2001. *Dynamics of contention*. New York: Cambridge University Press.

McClintock, Cynthia. 1999. Es autoritario el gobierno de Fujimori? In Tuesta 1999, 65–96.

McClintock, Cynthia, and Abraham Lowenthal. 1983. *The Peruvian experiment reconsidered*. Princeton, NJ: Princeton University Press.

Migdal, Joel. 2001. *State in society: Studying how states and societies transform and constitute one another*. New York: Cambridge University Press.

Nieto, Jorge. 1983. *Izquierda y Democracia en el Perú, 1975-1982*. Lima, Peru: DESCO.

O'Donnell, Guillermo. 1993. On the state, democratization, and some conceptual problems: A Latin American view with glances at some postcommunist countries. *World Development* 21:1355–69.

Oxhorn, Philip. 1988. Bringing the base back in: The resurrection of civil society under an authoritarian regime and Chilean shantytown organizations. Paper presented at the 14th International Conference of the Latin American Studies Association, New Orleans, March 17–20.

———. 1995. *Organizing civil society: The popular sectors and the struggle for democracy in Chile*. University Park: Pennsylvania State University Press.

Palmer, David Scott, ed. 1992. *Shining Path of Peru*. New York: St. Martin's.

Panfichi, Aldo. 1997. The authoritarian alternative: "Anti-politics" in the popular sectors of Lima. In Chalmers 1997, 217–36.

Parodi, Jorge. *Ser obrero es algo relativo*. Lima, Peru: Instituto de Estudios Peruanos, 1986.

Pastor, Manuel, Jr., and Carol Wise. 1992. Peruvian economic policy in the 1980s: From orthodoxy to heterodoxy and back. *Latin American Research Review* 27 (2): 83–117.

Pizarro, Risa, Laura Trelles, and Eduardo Toche. 2004. La protesta social durante el toledismo In *Perú Hoy: Los mil días de Toledo*. Lima, Peru: DESCO.

Quijano, Anibal. 1971. *Nationalism and capitalism in Peru: A study in neo-imperialism*. New York: Monthly Review Press.

Reyna, Carlos. 2000. *La anunciación de Fujimori: Alan García 1985–1990*. Lima, Peru: DESCO.

Roberts, Kenneth M. 1998. *Deepening democracy? The modern left and social movements in Chile and Peru*. Stanford, CA: Stanford University Press.

———. 1995 Neo-liberalism and the transformation of populism in Latin America: The Peruvian case. *World Politics* 48 (1): 82–116.

Rospigliosi, Fernando. 1988. *Juventud obrera y partidos de izquierda de la dictadura a la democracia*. Lima, Peru: Instituto de Estudios Peruanos.

———. 1996. *Las fuerzas armadas y el 5 de abril. La percepción de la amenaza subversive como una motivación golpista*. Working Document No. 73. Lima, Peru: Instituto de Estudios Peruanos.

Rubin, Jeffrey W. 1997. *Decentering the regime: Ethnicity, radicalism and democracy in Juchitán, Mexico*. Durham, NC: Duke University Press.

Schady, Norbert. 2000. The political economy of expenditures by the Peruvian social fund (FONCODES), 1991–95. *American Political Science Review* 94 (2): 289–304.

Schmitter, Philippe. 1974. Still the century of corporatism? *Review of Politics* 36 (85): 85–131.

Schönwalder, Gerd. 2002. *Linking civil society and the state: Urban popular movements, the left, and local government in Peru, 1980–1992.* University Park: Pennsylvania State University Press.

Scott, James. 1985. *Weapons of the weak: Everyday forms of peasant resistance.* New Haven, CT: Yale University Press.

Smith, Michael. 1992. Shining Path's urban strategy: Ate-Vitarte. In Palmer 1992, 127–48.

Stepan, Alfred. 1978. *State and society: Peru in comparative perspective.* Princeton, NJ: Princeton University Press.

Stokes, Susan C. 1995. *Cultures in conflict: Social movements and the state in Peru.* Berkeley: University of California Press.

———. 1999a. La opinión pública y la lógica del neo-liberalismo. In Tuesta 1999, 202–30.

———. 1999b. What do policy switches tell us about democracy? In *Democracy, representation and accountability,* ed. Adam Przeworski, Bernard Manin, and Susan C. Stokes, 98–130. Cambridge: Cambridge University Press.

Tanaka, Martin. 1998. *Espejismos de la democracia: el colapso del sistema de partidos en el Perú, 1980–1995, en perspectiva comparada.* Lima, Peru: Instituto de Estudios Peruanos.

Tilly, Charles, Ed. 1996. *Citizenship, identity and social history.* New York: Cambridge University Press.

———. 2003. *The politics of collective violence.* New York: Cambridge University Press.

Tovar, Teresa. 1986. Barrios, ciudad, democracia y política. In *Movimientos sociales y democracia. La fundación de un nuevo orden,* ed. Eduardo Ballón, 143–84. Lima: DESCO.

Tuesta, Fernando. 1989. Villa El Salvador: Izquierda, Gestión Municipal y Organización Popular. Mimeograph. Lima, Peru: CEDYS.

———, ed. 1999. *El juego político: Fujimori, la oposición y las reglas.* Lima: Peru: Fundación Friedrich Ebert.

Webb, Richard. 1991. Prologue. In *Peru's path to recovery: A plan for economic stabilization and growth,* ed. Carlos E. Paredes and Jeffrey D. Sachs, 1–12. Washington, DC: Brookings Institution.

Weber, Max. 1958. Politics as a vocation. In *From Max Weber: Essays in sociology,* ed. and trans. H. H. Gerth and C. Wright Mills. London: Oxford University Press.

Weiss Fagen, Patricia. 1992. Repression and state security. In *Fear at the edge: State terror and resistance in Latin America,* ed. Juan E. Corradi, Patricia Weiss Fagen, and Manuel Antonio Garreton, 39–71. Berkeley: University of California Press.

Weyland, Kurt. 1996. Neopopulism and neo-liberalism in Latin America: Unexpected affinities. *Studies in Comparative International Development* 31 (3): 3–31.

Yashar, Deborah. 1999. Democracy, indigenous movements, and the postliberal challenge in Latin America. *World Politics* 52 (1): 76–104.

Zapata, Antonio. 1996. *Sociedad y poder local: la comunidad de Villa El Salvador, 1971–1996.* Lima, Peru: DESCO.

Checks and Imbalances

Problems with Congress in Colombia
and Ecuador, 1978–2003

FRANCISCO GUTIÉRREZ SANÍN

THROUGHOUT THE ANDEAN REGION, CONGRESSES HAVE at one time or another been a major focus of popular discontent, and opinion polls in Peru, Venezuela, Colombia, Ecuador, and Bolivia consistently show that they are among the least trusted and poorly evaluated of political institutions. These circumstances have opened the way for politicians with authoritarian leanings, and for scandalmongers of various sorts, to advance rhetoric and political platforms that target the legislative branch of government as the root of all social problems. Widespread repudiation of Congress appears linked to the noteworthy deterioration in popular belief in democracy as an appropriate form of rule in the region (Latinobarómetro 2000; see also table 9.1), and it undoubtedly has nourished surprisingly broad levels of support for the military as a legitimate political actor (see, for example, table 9.2 and Freindenberg 2000 for the Ecuadorean case).

At this writing, neither Colombia nor Ecuador has experienced a full-fledged collapse of the democratic system, but Colombia has suffered a slow—and bloody—erosion of democratic governance, while Ecuadorean

TABLE 9.1
PUBLIC PERCEPTION OF DEMOCRACY IN COLOMBIA AND ECUADOR

	1996		1997		1998		1999	
	Colombia	*Ecuador*	*Colombia*	*Ecuador*	*Colombia*	*Ecuador*	*Colombia*	*Ecuador*
Believe democracy is preferable (%)	60	52	69	41	55	57	50	54
Satisfied with democracy (%)	16	34	40	31	24	33	27	23
Believe corruption has increased a lot recently (%)	—	—	76	84	89	93	83	85
Index of democratic perception[a]	38	43	55	36	40	45	—	—

Source: Latinobarómetro (2000).
[a]0, perception that democracy is negligible; 100, that there is a great amount of democracy.

TABLE 9.2
TRUST IN PUBLIC INSTITUTIONS IN ECUADOR

Institution	*December 1997 (%)*	*December 1998 (%)*
Military	69	71
Catholic Church	65	63
Media	54	55
Written press	56	54
Private enterprise	55	53
Police	24	28
Supreme Court	27	21
Democracy	47	49
Government	22	44
Independent movements	39	42
Indigenous leaders	49	36
Congress	32	31
Supreme electoral tribunal	20	18
Trade unions	16	15
Political parties	8	9
Congress members	7	8
Political leaders	8	7

Source: Polibio Córdova (1999).

politics exhibit a permanent climate of instability, punctuated by explosions of sociopolitical confrontation and institutional breakdown. In Colombia and Ecuador alike, Congress has become the epicenter of enormous corruption scandals and has provided the core source of resistance to implementation of crucial policy reforms. The relationship of the legislatures to democracy brings to mind the popular bolero "Ni contigo ni sin ti" (I can't live with you or without you). Stated simply, for democracy to survive, Congress is necessary, yet in Colombia and Ecuador Congress appears so far removed from the common good, and so prone both to corruption and to political obstructionism, as to be rendered an unacceptable luxury in the eyes of many important sectors within the polity.

For the student of comparative politics, the phenomenon is quite a puzzle. Why have processes of democratization launched in the 1970s—Ecuador's democratic transition and Colombia's aperture process, both involving one or more constitutions—failed to generate a place for their legislatures? Any compelling answer must account simultaneously for the common circumstance of congressional instability and institutional survival and the different trajectories of congressional development in the two countries. Liberal modernization—defined as a set of reforms and policies that promote the rule of law and the opening of the economy and society—has failed to create a viable role for parliament in either Colombia or Ecuador. This experience runs counter to the expectations of policy makers, social analysts, and institutional engineers, who believed that liberal reforms would create positive-feedback effects, fostering democracy and stability alike (Carrillo 2001, 4–10; Diamond et al. 1997).[1]

Not only have stronger market institutions, the extension of the rule of law, and the achievement of stable democracy failed to buttress one another, but liberalizing reforms in some areas of social life have unleashed illiberal effects on others. The nonconvergence principle spreads over the whole of public life. The argument is simple enough, and has been presented compellingly elsewhere (e.g., Conaghan and Malloy 1997), but spelling out the concrete mechanisms that prevent convergence, or consistency, can inform analyses of the paradoxical features of liberal modernization both in Colombia and Ecuador and elsewhere.

Analysts of liberal modernization have concentrated on two types of dynamics, generally overlooking a third one that accounts for the peculiar outcomes of recent years in these two Andean countries. Vicious circles have been spoken of, and the story of the way neoliberalism has devastated democracy in several countries is an example. Virtuous circles also circulate adroitly; the social capital metaphor—healthy societies support good institutions, which in turn produce correct outcomes—has its place in the social history of fashion. What seems to have predominated in Colombia and Ecuador in the period analyzed here are, however, home-ostats: local progresses in some part of the system trigger (and are matched by) failures and involutions in other parts, and vice versa, so there is a gradual change in the texture of the system without an obvious directionality toward progress or disaster.

The National Front and the Birth of a Parliamentary Trade Union in the Colombian Political System

From 1948 to 1958, Colombia experienced a bloody civil war between its two main political parties, the Liberals and the Conservatives.[2] The National Front (NF) ended the confrontation through a consociational arrangement (Hartlyn 1993) that, in keeping with Lijphardt's description for such regimes (1989), provided for the planned depoliticization of society and for a system of strong mutual guarantees between the protagonists of the pact. The NF indeed attained several of its key objectives—sustained economic growth, stability, the end of war—but paid two types of costs. The first, as discussed in chapter 2, was political exclusion. The NF established forced rotation in the presidency and a millimetrical division of state bureaucracy between the Liberal and the Conservative parties. Seats in parliament, departmental assemblies, and municipal councils were shared on a fifty-fifty basis, and when members of other parties won a seat they could effectively take it only if they declared allegiance to the Liberals or Conservatives. This meant that non-NF forces could appear in their own name in the electoral arena but not in the parliamentary one.

The second cost was a tendency toward paralysis. Because the Conservative Party was by then already in a situation of semipermanent minority vis-à-vis the Liberals, guarantees were put in place to ensure its ability to block threatening legislation. Thus, two-thirds majorities were required not just to pass constitutional change but also to enact simple legislation. This imposed daunting challenges for the executive branch, which had to assemble wide congressional support to accomplish even minor changes.[3] Because the agenda for the NF emphasized a widely shared commitment to development and modernization, stress soon turned into frustration, especially under the activist presidency of Carlos Lleras Restrepo (1966–1970).

Although it was intended to forestall a new explosion of civil confrontation, the planned depoliticization of society and the taming of inter-party competition generated two unanticipated effects. First, there was a further division of the parties into several factions, with notable regional ramifications. Second, and related, there was an increase in intraparty competition, based on clientelism, patronage, and personalist loyalties. The impact of these trends on congressional performance was twofold. On the one hand, each member of Congress was compelled to fight for more resources for his/her personalist web of relations. On the other, there was a growing independence of individual politicians from their parties. Individual politicians increasingly controlled votes that in the past were attached to the party label, and the parties could no longer discipline politicians with ease.

The combination of the dynamics triggered by exclusion and the tendency toward paralysis gave credibility to the arguments of NF critics who denounced the pact on the grounds that it placed excessive limits on democracy. Thus, they were well positioned to try to repoliticize society by denouncing the very pact that had aimed at the fading out of politics. Factions of the traditional parties as well as anti-NF forces—for example, the Liberal splinter group Revolutionary Liberal Movement and the populist National Popular Alliance—used this strategy to attract a significant portion of the electorate. At the same time, members of the pact had both the incentives (intraparty competition) and the means (super majorities and other prostability arrangements) to trade off public outcomes for individual benefits. The mechanism worked more or less in the following way: Presidents, especially those of an activist and modernizing bent, pressed hard to obtain urgent reforms in Congress. However, they had to win parliamentary votes faction by faction, and since each faction was vitally interested in obtaining resources to fuel its cause against regional and other adversaries, it tried to sell its vote at the best price possible.

The mechanism was self-reinforcing, and can be understood as a particularist loop. Each reform gave more formal power or prebends to Congress and its individual members and created strong incentives for them to ask for more. A good example is the 1968 constitutional reform, promoted by perhaps the most outstanding Colombian modernizer of the past half century, Carlos Lleras Restrepo.[4] The process was so complicated that it forced Lleras to offer his resignation, as a way to confront congressional procrastination. The reasons behind the conflict are easy to identify. Factionalism and lack of party discipline were pervasive, specific congressional representatives made countless particularist demands, and pork barrel politics permeated the legislature as a whole. Moreover, there was a lack of commitment to the reformist thrust, especially in the ranks of the Conservatives. Ultimately, Lleras was able to gain approval for his reform, but only at the price of allowing Congress access to new resources, the so-called *auxilios parlamentarios*, pork barrel money that would subsequently become the source of unending scandals.

Much of the resistance put forth by the Colombian legislative branch reflected the standard practices of democratic political systems. Several of the reforms blocked or hindered by Congress during or after the NF were dubious and could have triggered the concentration of power in excessively few hands. The strong system of checks and balances also protected the health of the economy, as it left Colombian presidents with scant latitude to embark on the sort of pharaonic approach to modernization that emerged so frequently—and catastrophically—elsewhere. The problem was that, given the constraints of the NF, the separation of powers gave rise to a parliamentary trade union, which was characterized by high levels of particularism, oligopolic protection (the arrangement only allowed bipartisan participation), and an esprit de corps, and which thus was structurally biased toward corruption.

Congress and the Traumatic Opening of the Colombian Political System

In 1974 the NF was formally dismantled, although consociational inertia persisted until 1986. The brand-new deregulated alternation in presidency produced the victory of the Liberal Alfonso López Michelsen, another activist president who found it convenient to summon a Constitutional Assembly. The project's merits were more than doubtful, and it was finally blocked by a combination of judicial and parliamentary maneuvers (Archer 1990).

In the late 1970s and the 1980s, the structure of Colombian politics went through three major changes. As the country approached full-fledged partisan competition, the Liberal Party (LP) consolidated its grip on Congress as well as on the departmental assemblies and municipal councils. In the 1980s, the LP acquired a clear majority in Congress. In theory, if it managed to vote as a bloc, the LP not only could pass legislation on its own, which required a simple majority, but could also enact constitutional changes, which required a two-thirds vote.[5] Second, a strong penetration of illegality in politics, and particularly in the LP, developed for reasons that are simple enough to understand: criminals—and not only them—find winners more interesting. Third, the decade's two presidents (Belisario Betancur, 1982–1986, and Virgilio Barco, 1986–1990) shared a quest to modernize the goals of Colombian government, which led them to focus on achieving peace and development and attempting to short-circuit traditional political intermediation. Betancur's was a minority government, and his peace proposals had to tackle savage opposition by the LP. Barco, an LP member himself, had a majority, but in very critical junctures, in which national interests were at stake, he suffered from congressional indiscipline. The emblematic case was the lower house's 1989 vote jeopardizing the extradition treaty with the United States (Matthiesen 2000), despite the severe admonitions of the president and the then director of the LP, Julio César Turbay.

Considered separately, each factor was serious enough, but their confluence was dramatic and generated a widespread conviction that fundamental change was necessary. Both Betancur and Barco responded by promoting decentralization, which formally began in 1988 with the first mayoral elections. Betancur also created a special commission to instigate political opening, linking it to peace processes, but his attempts failed. Barco is justly acclaimed for having mustered the clout to summon a new constitutional assembly, thus unblocking the political system, though this had its downsides: it was based on the manipulation of the fine print of the 1886 constitution and of presidential powers under a state of emergency, and it was obviously directed against Congress.[6] The process ended with the dismissal of Congress under President César Gaviria (1990–1994), with rather tenuous justification. Stated differently, the movement toward a new order that would restore the rule of law was possible because the president decided—after trying conventional channels that respected all the constitutional niceties—to ignore the law or at least to twist it (Palacios 1996).

However, both Barco and Gaviria were scheming against that particular Congress and political class, rather than against parliamentary legitimacy more generally. Indeed, two of the main objectives of the 1991 constitution were to empower Congress, assigning it powers regarding states of exception and enabling it to produce motions of censure against ministers, among various innovations, as well as to clean up politics more generally. Cleaning up politics was the core of a general effort to reestablish legality in Colombian society, which proceeded in various steps. The new constitution created the vice presidency and the run-off elections for the presidency, preventing enduring plurality governments and fostering alternation, blocking in this manner an eventual Liberal hegemony. It created the Fiscalía, a new judicial auditing institution with wide powers that would soon become the protagonist of anticorruption efforts. It also developed a stringent regime of job incompatibilities, limiting members of Congress from holding multiple positions in the public and private sectors. Further, the new charter changed the legal definition of parliamentary immunity,[7] did away with cumulative elected posts, and, at least theoretically, curbed the flow of pork barrel money.

All this is only a sample of a generalized reformist thrust, which was guided by the expectation that opening and democratizing the political system would deconcentrate power and thus destroy the reserved domains that constituted ideal opportunities for corruption. The architects of the 1991 constitution were thus motivated by the notion that it was not only necessary but also possible to pension off traditional politicians. In their view, what Colombia needed was to adjust its institutions to correctly express people's preferences, because the politicians of the past—*el viejo país*—were an anachronism sustained only by corruption, violence, and the manipulation of unfair rules. The president had hailed the new era with a greeting—"Bienvenidos al futuro" (welcome to the future)—that simultaneously expressed all these motives.

Electoral realities frustrated such an optimistic perspective. The reasons behind this failure emerge clearly, albeit in hindsight, and are illustrated aptly by the concrete case of the decentralization process. Decentralization was an important part of the opening of the political system, and of modernization, and corresponded to long-standing social and political demands. It both preceded and informed the 1991 constitution. During the latter period of the NF, and immediately after its ending, a powerful de facto political decentralization already had taken place, as the regional barons were acquiring independence vis-à-vis the political center—the notables of both parties concentrated in Bogotá. This was a result not only of an accumulation of several iterations of the particularist loop intrinsic to the NF but also of the arrival of narcofunding and armed bands in some departments in the late 1970s. When the first mayoral election took place, patronage, one of the last monopolies of the center over key resources, deteriorated, with due consequences. Decentralization simultaneously empowered benevolent expressions of modernity, such as recognition of ethnic minorities, and others that were malevolent, such as regional and municipal clientelist networks related to organized crime. Both types of modernity operated on the small is beautiful principle and were relatively delinked from national elites.

Malevolent modernity was deeply rooted in Colombian electoral traditions and techniques. Thus, the new 1992 Congress seemed as traditional as the previous one, and while institutional engineers were blissfully pursuing the holy grail of renovation, a new process was taking place: the diversity that the 1991 constitution had so cherished as a modernizing force was reinforcing a new and powerful cycle of extreme electoral fragmentation, which in turn sheltered the shadiest of politicians. Moreover, one of the core ideas of the constitutional movement—to force politics back into legality—was an obvious failure. By 1994, the penetration of the Cali cartel in Congress was overwhelming. Then came the presidency of Ernesto Samper (1994–1998), whose government marked a watershed in the trajectory of narcopolitics in Colombia. Samper enjoyed generous funding by narcotraffickers—possibly close to $5 million —in a hotly contested election, and his government survived in the midst of interminable scandals.

Samper's period in office brutally undermined the standing of Congress on four accounts. First, around the same time that Samper was being accused of ties to drug barons, Process 8000, the Colombian equivalent of the Italian Clean Hands Campaign, exposed the degree to which organized crime had infiltrated the political order. As table 9.3 illustrates, such infiltration was not the only source of criminal behavior by members of Congress and other politicians: alongside widespread links to narcotrafficking was the old favorite of embezzlement, and there were even instances of homicide. Notable among these was the case where, in a fit of fury, the president of the Peace Commission of the lower house shot a municipal rival, killing him instantly.

The second way in which the Samper years damaged Congress stems from the fact that Congress itself exonerated the president, on grounds of insufficient evidence. To much of the public, this showed that congres-

TABLE 9.3

TYPES OF CRIME OF MEMBERS OF CONGRESS IN THE 1990S

Motive	Number of accusations
Links with narcotrafficking	41
Embezzlement	9
Violation of the regime of interest conflicts and other crimes against public administration	17
Common homicide	4
Multiple homicide	1
Others	10

Source: Calculations based on the Colombian daily El Tiempo.

sional powers were deployed in a highly unfortunate manner and that members could be bought off if the price was sufficiently high. This had occurred during the NF, only now both the stakes and the incentives for irresponsible behavior were much higher. Third, and more generally, Samper's administration exposed the irresponsibility of a highly particularist—and extremely effective—form of political intermediation, based on the distribution of goods and prebends to a small network of associates (including politicians themselves). Such a clientelist political style was good for winning elections but was indifferent to national interests. It was prepared to trade some of the key variables of the Colombian establishment—for example, the country's strategic relation with the United States—for two or three posts in the state bureaucracy or for a trivial serving of pork barrel money. Worse still, faced with hostile public opinion and skeptical media coverage, Congress tried to restrict public liberties and intimidate journalists with threats of censorship and fines.[8]

A fourth source of congressional disrepute during the Samper administration involved perceptions that traditional politics were hostile to economic liberalism or at least prone to foot dragging to delay implementation of reforms. This latter charge is probably an exaggeration, for while it was no mystery that Samper's government was a rather moderate liberalizer, the economic reforms that were proposed garnered backing from several of the most notorious clientelists, as well as from politicians involved and condemned in the 8000 process. When these figures introduced minor changes in proposed reforms, these amendments were offered not as resistance but as vehicles for paying off supporters in their regional networks.

Together these four factors provoked unprecedented hostility toward Congress among Colombia's socioeconomic elites. A broad sector of the public was also indignant about politicians. The Constituent Assembly had been triggered in part by miserable levels of public confidence in Congress; by the middle of the 1990s, the continuous exposure to scandal had further eroded the image of the institution.

It is ironic, given Colombia's strong legal traditions and the customary absence of space for imposing decisions in top-down fashion, that it was Samper himself, a very controversial figure, who forged the instrument for weakening and confronting Congress. A master of backstage politics, Samper resorted to a distraction, responding to public indignation with calls for electoral reform. The opposition criticized as a mere smokescreen a presidential commission for the reform of political parties, and in retaliation the Liberal majority in Congress floated calls for reforms that would have moved the country in the direction of a parliamentary regime.

In reality, however, Colombia was drifting in precisely the opposite direction. Samper's successor as president, Andrés Pastrana (1998–2002), headed a coalition of Conservatives, independents, and dissident Liberals brought together under the banner of political reform. The leader of the new reformist wave was Íngrid Betancourt, an ex-Liberal who was intent on the dismissal of Congress as an "enemy of the people" (1998, 10). However, since the government was by then assigning priority to another very complicated issue—the peace talks with the country's major guerrilla forces—it opted to seek accommodation with the very congressional opposition (at that point the LP) that was the major target of the reform. In practice, this meant postponing it, though not for long. Some members of Congress had taken the initiative of promoting a so-called *auto-reforma*, in an effort to show that the Colombian legislature was not impervious to popular demands. Yet this all came to nothing, and the stillborn auto-reforma became yet another embarrassment for Congress, once again bringing the issue of reform to the front of the political stage. When two congressional leaders from the progovernment coalition were charged with fraud, the Pastrana administration, which in the past had threatened Congress with dismissal when it showed signs of opposition, reacted immediately and called a popular referendum on a far-reaching proposal for political reform.

Opinion polls revealed widespread support for the referendum, which called for dismissing both chambers of Congress and replacing them with a unicameral body. It also sought to resurrect the politics of notables in the departments and municipalities, requiring candidates to have completed at least a university degree and eliminating salaries for members of local councils and assemblies. This marked a turning point, in that it was the first post-NF proposal based on a discourse that was essentially authoritarian—or at least extremely conservative—and backed by the president and a huge majority of public opinion.[9]

A score of traditional politicians—some of whom had been on the wrong side of corruption scandals in the 1970s and 1980s and even in the 1990s—supported Pastrana. However, the LP opposed the referendum vigorously, presenting its own, so-called social referendum, which also called for the dismissal of the president and for subjecting all elected officials to a new vote. The alternative referendum also put into question the economic policy of the government. The move was perfectly legal, and given that the levels of support for Pastrana were waning, there was a real chance of precipitating a general reshuffle of power in the country. This danger, combined with the veiled threat by the LP to block market-based economic reforms in the event that the government persisted in its proposed referendum, increased Colombia's country risk rating in international financial markets. Pastrana thus had no other alternative than to bargain and both referenda were withdrawn. The initiative had failed.

Álvaro Uribe—a Liberal mentored in Antioquia by one of the great Liberal barons of the 1980s, Bernardo Guerra Serna—won the 2002 presidential election in a landslide, triumphing over the official candidate of his party. Central to his campaign platform was a referendum on a proposal to dismiss Congress, adjust the electoral system to prevent fragmentation, assign priority to fighting corruption, create a small unicameral body in lieu of the existing legislature, and, possibly, curb some of the powers acquired by the judicial system following the adoption of the 1991 constitution.

Uribe's proposal enjoyed broad support, both in public opinion and in the media. However, once in government, he found it difficult to implement his policies. Though his powerful interior minister systematically harassed the judicial and legislative branches during the first year and a half of the administration, there was a gradual tilt toward a more conciliatory tone, and the minister was replaced in Uribe's first major cabinet shuffle. The success of the government's war against the guerrillas represented its foremost priority, and this required national unity. Even though he continued to enjoy majority support, Uribe needed the capacity to reach agreements with the LP, and this necessitated withdrawing proposals to dismiss Congress. New fiscal strains; the control exerted by the constitutional court, which changed critically the formulation of some questions; and the priority given to waging war forced an abrupt change in the agenda behind the referendum, which when it took place in October 2003 proposed modest reductions in the size of Congress and the creation of a new electoral quota. Yet the referendum failed, along with several complementary bills targeting the judiciary and Congress, when low voter turnout failed to produce the minimum number of votes needed for approval. The government has given signs that this defeat marks only a pause in its trajectory, so the story did not end in 2003.

Congress amidst the Comings and Goings of the Ecuadorean Political System

Until 1978, Ecuador hardly seemed fertile ground for democracy. Between 1925 and 1948 there were twenty-seven governments, few of which were able to complete their constitutionally mandated term in office (Pachano 1997, 30). The 1948 Glorious Revolution and the ensuing aftershocks were followed by a short period of stability, which gave way to renewed political turbulence. Only two democratic elections took place during the twenty-year period after 1959. Held in 1960 and 1968, both were won by the populist leader José María Velasco Ibarra, whose influence over Ecuadorean politics spanned more than three decades and whose rejection of political parties was evident in his oft-proclaimed motto, "El mundo no está hecho para partidos" (the world is not made for parties). Given the weight of *velasquismo*, the tendency of the military to intervene in political affairs, and the infrequency of elections, it is no surprise that Ecuador lacked deeply rooted party traditions and identities. The regional cleavages of the country have made it all the more difficult to build a unified national political arena (Freidenberg 2001).

The Ecuadorean military has been interventionist but not necessarily reactionary. Historical and strategic reasons have given the armed forces incentives to craft and foster military-peasant alliances (León 2000) of a sort that has also emerged with some regularity elsewhere in the Andes. With a strong aversion to irresponsible politicians and their tendency to provoke civil strife, the military has maintained an acute sensitivity to the need for a united national front and deep sympathies for social reforms.[10] The regime of General Guillermo Rodríguez Lara, which immediately preceded the transition to democracy, strikingly exhibited these traits.[11] Rodríguez produced an agrarian reform,[12] nationalized oil, entered OPEC, and tried to push other changes to promote inclusion (Isaacs 1993). Levels of repression remained comparatively low, and average gross national product growth during the period was a spectacular 9 percent. When the military finally returned power to civilians, they could declare proudly, "Before the Armed Forces government, the country had a budget of 5 billion sucres. Today, the budget is 27 billion. Our monetary reserves were 600 million sucres; today they reach 15 billion. The GNP was only 47 billion. In 1978 it passed the figure of 190 billion. Exports were on the order of 300 million dollars, in 1978 they were more than 1.5 billion. Per capita income oscillated around 200 dollars, now it is near 1,000 dollars" (General Jorge Poveda, quoted in Cueva 1997, 86). Progress was, or seemed to be, impressive.[13]

To be sure, democratic forces put forth a completely different interpretation of the military's record in power. When the first president of the new democracy, Jaime Roldós, commented that "tenemos que echar a andar un paralítico" (we have to make a paralyzed man walk), he expressed a critique of the military government's legacy that encompassed three key dimensions. First, between 1970 and 1980 Ecuador's debt had grown by a factor of 19 (Pachano 1997, 377), calling into question the country's capacity to achieve sustainable growth. Moreover, while repression had been mild, political exclusion had targeted important sectors, most notably the populists, under whose banner Roldós campaigned with the slogan "We will not forget." Finally, new social advances were urgently needed. Political enfranchisement of the illiterate was an initial and very meaningful conquest of Ecuador's democracy, but the fact that universal suffrage came to the country at such a late date was indicative of the scale of the challenges that remained. An additional strain placed on the nascent democracy stemmed from the fact that it succeeded what might be called a reformist dictatorship. This encouraged people to compare achievements of the two different types of political regime. This comparison has not always been favorable to the proponents of democratic rule.

A Disordered Polity?

Any effort to build democracy confronted a long—and strong—tradition of antiparty sentiment, lack of accountability, fragmentation,[14] and sheer disorder of the public realm. The architects of the 1978–1979 transition were acutely conscious of this set of obstacles and designed a systematic array of institutions to guarantee political coherence and stability. Reforms were enacted to strengthen political parties, curb the tendency toward fragmentation, and guard against the particularly Ecuadorean *velasquista* phenomenon (Isaacs 1993, 122). Among these reforms were many innovations that would be the envy of neighboring institutional engineers intent on fixing the Colombian system.[15] These included a unicameral legislature and the establishment of an electoral quota that was much less benevolent toward small parties than the Hare quota used in Colombia until 2003.[16] Moreover, a severe threshold was established for parties to gain recognition: not only did they have to demonstrate their ability to attract 5 percent of the vote, but they also had to be genuinely national in character, drawing support from no fewer than ten different provinces. In addition, candidates for congressional seats were required to run under a party banner.

As in Colombia, the foundations on which this rather imposing institutional edifice had been erected turned out to be weaker than optimists had anticipated at the outset, but the reasons for optimism in Colombia and Ecuador had been symmetrically inverse. Colombians had sought renewal through the lowering of barriers to new entrants, Ecuadoreans through the strengthening of the parties. The first democratic government reflected a mixed formula, with President Roldós being a member of the Confederación de Fuerzas Populares (Confederation of Popular Forces) and Vice President Oswaldo Hurtado coming from Christian Democracy, but from the outset it had to cope with a congressional rebellion, headed by the powerful populist leader Assad Bucaram (1996–1997), a member of the president's party. And despite the measures introduced to constrain the proliferation of political parties, the number of parties was and remains very high (see table 9.4), exceeding the number found in Colombia, though in Ecuador internal fragmentation is less critical.

Five additional—and interrelated—factors further muddied the waters of Ecuadorean politics, putting enormous stress on Congress. First, there was an endless succession of severe social and institutional conflicts, many of them resulting from programmatic polarization. The first administration of the democratic period experienced three threats of presidential impeachment, two efforts to dissolve Congress, two more of presidential resignation, several attempts to govern through plebiscites, and nearly constant rumors of impending coups d'etat (Sánchez Parga 1998; see also Menéndez Carrión 1991). However, the Roldós-Hurtado period (1979–1984) was smooth sailing in comparison with what followed.[17] President León Febres Cordero (1984–1988) was held hostage by the military and was impeached several times. He resigned and bullied Congress with athletic stamina, enthusiastically launching several initiatives by plebiscite. The 1990s, in turn, made the 1980s appear a paradigm of stability: Presidents Jamil Mahuad (1997–2000) and Bucaram were ousted by civil-military alliances, Sixto Durán Ballén hardly made it

TABLE 9.4
EVOLUTION OF EFFECTIVE PARTIES IN ECUADOR
(CALCULATED OVER SEATS)

Legislature	Effective parties
1979–1984	4,055
1984–1986	5,792
1986–1988	7,669
1988–1990	6,732
1990–1992	6,698
1992–1994	6,094
1994–1996	574
1996–1998	5,369
1998–2003	6,013

Source: Calculations based on Peñaherrera (2002).

through his term (and lost his vice president along the way), and others served for very short periods during the interim and badly defined transition processes between impeachment and new elections. Overall, it seems that parties simply saw no place for their adversaries within the political system; this includes the populist threat that the architects of the democratic transition had wanted to avoid.

Economic liberalism was a second source of strain, directly affecting the coherence of the Ecuadorean polity in at least two ways. On the one hand, the effort to carry out neoliberal reforms sparked huge waves of resistance and opposition that were not easily assimilated by the new democratic institutions. These waves were able to stop specific measures, but they could not overcome the general orientation of economic policies. The stop-and-go nature of the liberal reforms may have canceled their potential benevolent effects, but there was an extraordinary persistence of the neoliberal agenda, which advanced gradually independently of the ideological bent of the government and the dominant parliamentary coalitions (Hey and Klak 1999), including under the administration of Lucio Gutiérrez during 2003–2004. That neoliberalism seemed immune to popular resistance undermined perceptions of the responsiveness of democracy as a system of rule (Przeworski, Stokes, and Manin 1999) and called into question the credibility of the country's political institutions. Responsible politicians had only very limited room for maneuvering to change the agenda of economic liberalism, which offered windows of opportunity to irresponsible agents to enter the fray. In other words, responsibility and responsiveness were at odds at several critical moments.

But the natural discourse of the new entrants was to denounce not only the effect of political unresponsiveness—unpopular policies—but also their cause—the ongoing political equilibriums. Politicians sympathetic to the neoliberal agenda were highly diffident toward the party dictatorship established in Ecuador. Febres Cordero, for one, found it sufficiently noxious as to promote a referendum against it. The discourse of Febres Cordero regarding "partyocracy" is characteristic: "Liberty is for all. In Ecuador we cannot have second class Ecuadoreans; that is why we have asked Ecuadoreans if they want independents to have the same rights as those affiliated to political parties. Voting 'yes' in the referendum is to reestablish the violated right of Ecuadorean independents. Voting 'no' is to play into the hands of the political cliques of the parties" (quoted in Montúfar 2000, 84).

Conservative libertarianism was linked with the effort to build a frictionless state, which needed an isomorphically open and deregulated political system. Pablo Lucio Paredes, a prominent member of the economic staff of the Durán government (1992–1995), questioned whether the corset of partyism was compatible with the logic of a free market economy: "Is the present Ecuadorean political system generating the conditions of efficiency that would allow the political world to adapt dynamically to changing circumstances? The party monopoly prevalent in Ecuador is a system that prevents such adaptation; consequently, we must build a more open one. The possibility of entry of the independents also poses several difficulties that must be studied, but anyway it introduces more competition" (quoted in Sánchez Parga 1993, 72).

Typically, Durán himself initiated an effort to topple, or at least relax, the restrictions on the participation of independents. That effort finally came to fruition with the 1994 referendum, reinforced subsequently by the 1998 constitution. Designed to guarantee the dream of a frictionless state, the 1998 constitution thus separated Congress from key areas of governance. "There is no other Constitution," observed former president Hurtado, one of the main demiurges behind the new constitution, "that cut so much the influence of Congress in the economy, which is now free from instability and crisis. This is the first Constitution that deprived Congress of the powers it used to have: to fire, censure, impeach ministers. In all these areas we had our main governability problems" (quoted in Peñaherrera 2002, 15; see also Pachano 2003).

However, perhaps the most important impact of economic reforms was indirect. Unlike in Colombia, in Ecuador fiscal rigor almost never coincided with steady economic growth, and this motivated a strong bias among broad sectors of Ecuadorean voters against candidates who emphasized macroeconomic discipline. Long before the democratic transition, politicians were careful enough to postpone the most painful decisions whenever an election was approaching (see Schuldt 1994, 50, for an early and colorful example). Politicians were aware of fiscal realities, on the one hand, and of voting patterns, on the other, and this gave them strong incentives to denounce economic liberalism as candidates and to implement it as presidents. This phenomenon is not unique in Latin America (Stokes 1999), but if repeated many times—as it has been in Ecuador—it produces cynicism and fatigue and discredits democratic institutions.[18]

The third factor that has been corrosive of Congress's position is the failure of the democratic regime to fulfill its promise of sociopolitical inclusion. The great innovation of Ecuadorean democracy was to establish universal suffrage; prior to the 1978 constitution, illiterates lacked the right to vote, let alone to be elected. This had severely disenfranchised important sectors of the population, mainly indigenous peoples and peasants. The influx of voters, with their specific styles and interests, changed the political landscape irreversibly. Several mainstream politicians made a bid for the newly available indigenous vote, sometimes simply trying to co-opt a couple of leaders, once in a while working in a deeper and more systematic fashion, with varying degrees of success (Chiriboga and Rivera 1988). The crucial juncture was the Social Democratic government of Rodrigo Borja (1988–1992), who apparently owed his 1988 victory in large measure to having received an important portion of the indigenous vote (Almeida 1992). But as president, the Social Democratic Borja introduced the first serious neoliberal policies (Schuldt 1994), and the result was that he also had to deal with the first indigenous upheavals. Although he did so with success and without resorting to mass repression (Zamosc 2000), the unfriendly reception of some indigenous demands and the persistence of liberal economic policies rapidly eroded the initially pro-Borja sympathies among Indians.

The rupture between the center-left and the Indian movement, headed by the Confederation of Indigenous Nationalities of Ecuador (CONAIE), effectively delinked Ecuadorean parties from the social movements, and this fracture deepened over time. Several corruption scandals—especially the Dahik affair under Durán—combined with the more-or-less open hostility of the populists toward the Indians and the waves of opposition generated by liberal economic reforms to mobilize broad sectors of the population against the political establishment. The contrast between the initial expectations and the final disillusion is dramatized by the following image. In October 1987, the social movements—basically the trade unions—called for a national strike against the anticonstitutional attitudes of the president, who in clear disregard for the powers of Congress had refused to accept the impeachment of one of his ministers and who had confronted the constitutional court, Tribunal de Garantías Constitucionales (Tribunal of Constitutional Guarantees; Bernal and Espinosa 1991). In 2002, those same social movements were the main source of support for Lucio Gutiérrez, whose antiparliamentary rhetoric included having proposed reducing the size of Congress to a purely technical body of twenty-five people.[19]

Disillusion strengthened the alternative, the military-popular alliance. Members of the army who participated in rebellions against civilian neoliberal presidents—Frank Vargas Pazos in 1996, Paco Moncayo as the defense minister that dethroned Bucaram, and Gutiérrez—emerged as electoral alternatives for the Left and the social movements. More deeply, especially after CONAIE withdrew what had been curtly criticized by the government as secessionist issues, several of the social movements aroused sympathies among an important sector of the military, as the army-indigenous takeover of power in 2000 would prove. Though CONAIE was able to create an electoral structure in the 1990s and performed reasonably well at the polls, the popular sectors and other segments of Ecuadorean society harbored an ongoing and deep dissatisfaction with Congress, which was regarded as the epitome of impoverished politics, with its backstage bargaining, its tendency to conciliation, and its frequent corruption scandals (Pachano 1997).[20]

Ecuadorean governments have rarely enjoyed solid parliamentary support, and the persistence of minority governments is a fourth factor undermining the position of Congress. The first democratic administration began with a congressional majority but soon lost it when the president's party rebelled against him, at which point the opposition sought to bring down the government. In 1984, midterm parliamentary elections were introduced, avowedly to increase accountability. Instead, at least in some critical junctures, they increased instability. In the trajectories of subsequent governments that lasted long enough to lose their support, several strategies are evident.

President Febres Cordero tried an openly confrontational approach, creating a vociferous Frente de Reconstrucción Nacional (National Front for Reconstruction) that was contested by the Bloque Progresista (Progressive Bloc) headed by the Social Democrats. For three-quarters of his term, Febres led a minority government (actually, the Bloque Progresista outlived the Frente de Reconstrucción Nacional). Borja started with a broad majority, but his party—Izquierda Democrática (Democratic Left)—lost the midterm elections. Although in his last year he was finally able to build a majority by entering a coalition with several microparties, its very small advantage (three seats) and its heterogeneous character made it hardly operational. Durán was also in the minority, for purely political reasons: he headed a splinter group of the Social Christian Party, which at that time was the main force in Congress. Bucaram, impeached on the grounds of mental incompetence, and Mahuad both operated amidst congressional resistance, and the minority government headed by Gutiérrez had its first brushes with Congress not long after taking office.[21]

Finally, a fifth factor worth noting is that in the eyes of many citizens the performance of democracy in some key domains compares badly with that of the previous regime. For example, on the key issue of corruption, the survey firm CEDATOS reported that 44 percent of respondents believed that democratic governments were more corrupt than dictatorships, 30 percent said the opposite, and 26 percent believed that they were equally corrupt (Polibio Córdova 1999, 119). The main source of dissatisfaction, however, is the lack of economic growth. Ecuadorean politicians recognize that democracy has failed to deliver on this front (e.g., Oswaldo Hurtado, cited in Aguirre 2000, 150). Not only have growth rates been stingy, but the Ecuadorean experience of development has been punctuated by spectacular catastrophes (1983, 1988, and especially 1999).

These factors together guarantee the persistence of a strong antiparliamentary agenda. Confrontation and public denunciation are generously rewarded in electoral terms. Dissatisfaction is widespread, not only with this or that government but with the political system as a whole. Democracy itself is not highly regarded, as opinion polls systematically show. Thus, it is hardly amazing that practically all of the democratically elected presidents have had their pet electoral reforms, the majority of which implied diminishing the role of Congress. The 1998 constitution achieved this objective, but even this seemed insufficient. At the end of his administration, Gustavo Noboa (2000–2003) was calling for a new electoral reform, and Lucio Gutiérrez also campaigned on a strongly anti-Congress platform. Electoral and political reform came to be known as the great myth of the day.

Nonetheless, it would be a mistake to portray Congress as an impotent weakling (or, if it is, as alone in its plight), as highlighted by the executive-legislative conflicts that have taken place since Gutiérrez took office in 2002. Having become president with the backing of the Left and the social movements, Gutiérrez soon saw his alliance split apart, largely over disagreements about further liberal reforms. In response, President Gutiérrez looked for support on the right. Precisely when the opposition was stiffening, and tension mounting, a delicate accusation by the Social Democratic Congress member Guillermo Haro against the army caused an uproar.[22] The army and the government—with the support of the rightist Social Christian Party—called for lifting Haro's parliamentary immunity. There were heated discussions on the niceties of Article 137 of the constitution, which regulated immunity, with each side putting forward its own rationales for its position, but it was more or less clear that what was at stake was the standing of Congress and the right of members of the body to not be prosecuted for their opinions. A new political map appeared, with a Social Democratic–Left–social movement coalition, on the one hand, and a right wing–army–government coalition, on the other. It remains unclear whether this cleavage will be enduring, but it is interesting to note that while the progovernment coalition had a comfortable majority, it backed off at the last moment, dissuaded by opinion surveys showing that the anti-Haro move was highly unpopular.[23]

Confrontation and Accommodation on the Path toward Liberal Modernization

The differences between Colombia and Ecuador, together with the similarity of their antiparliamentary discontent, form a striking contrast. In Colombia, a closed system was opened through a deregulation of the political order, one that implied lowering the barriers to entry into politics. In Ecuador, the system was disordered and was fixed through institutional designs aimed at reversing fragmentation. Yet the remedy did not function in either case: Colombians still find their system closed, and Ecuadoreans deem theirs disordered. Indeed, reforms arguably deepened dissatisfaction with democratic institutions and created new problems.

Not only the contested aspects of modernization, such as economic liberalism, but also relatively consensual ones have lead to outcomes that weaken the standing of Congress. In both countries, there is a dual source of legitimacy. The president is elected in a run-off system, which divides the country into supporters and opponents. Presidents thus represent big programs and broad coalitions. Congress, by contrast, is elected by proportional representation—the Hare quota in Colombia and (at this writing) the D'Hondt quota in Ecuador—and represents a patchwork of small, generally subnational coalitions.

Thus, the checks and balances of both democracies represent not only an institutional safety device but also a territorial one. Checks and balances protect against abuses of powerful actors over weak ones and of the nation over subnational units. Buchanan and Tullock (1962) delineated a useful constitutional terminology: When agents are in a constitutional (original) situation, they trade off between two kinds of costs. Decision costs involve how much time, effort, and money it will take to adopt a decision. Externalities involve how heavy a burden of externalities society can place on particular agents (and therefore, at least potentially, on the voter). In a veto system—where consensus is demanded—decision costs are very high but externalities approach zero, because any actor can block any undesired decision. In a dictatorship, decision costs are near zero—at least in theory—but externalities can grow infinitely, as when the dictator decides to take someone's life. The optimal constitutional decision will be the point of intersection of both curves.

Colombia started rather near the consensus extreme of the spectrum, with its strong guarantees for minorities. This design protected the partners in the consociational pact but at the same time allowed territorial minorities (particularist networks) to charge a toll for decisions, thus increasing decision costs. The additional burden was tolerated so long as consociational designs and antisubversive concerns were all important. Yet two things happened between the end of the NF and 1991: the criminalization of politics led to the toll being increased to intolerable levels, and the Berlin Wall fell, relaxing demands to counter subversives. In the face of high tolls taken by particularist politicians, an effort was made to establish and strengthen the rule of law. Similarly, liberal economic reforms also implied the need to reduce the decision costs. The architects of the 1991 constitution had thought that doing away with consociationalism and the old politics was sufficient, but new politics could be even more particularist. Stated differently, the deregulation of politics increased decision costs even more: if during the NF the president had to negotiate bills on a faction-by-faction basis, today he has to work almost on an individual-by-individual basis.[24] This increases the aggregate toll collection, now in a situation of far more severe fiscal restrictions. The result is a general disaffection with political institutions and the epitome of such institutions—Congress.

Ecuador, by contrast, has not had a consociational experience or a civil war. Problems came in the form of programmatic politics, fomented by institutional engineers intent on modernizing and organizing the political system. The combination of programmatic politics and liberal modernization had three effects. First, a confrontational political style produced continuous conflicts between the president and Congress. This confrontational style was reinforced by the fact that the Ecuadorean polity is built over regional cleavages (Pachano 2003; León 2003). Second, incentives for politicians to switch programmatic positions became strong, because winning a seat and taking state decisions implied two contradictory points of view and sets of incentives. Third, the country was divided, ideologically and regionally, into two extremely unfriendly blocks that did not match well with the small politics of members of Congress.

Thus, for partisans of liberal economic reforms, decision costs were too high, and for adversaries of these measures, externalities were intolerable. In both cases this boils down to a conviction that decision costs were too high, because—given the persistence of minority governments and continuous alternation in power—there was a strong sense of stasis. Both blocks—at the ideological and regional levels—opted for a strong executive, but they did so for diametrically opposed reasons (an analogous argument can be developed for the regional cleavages). As a consequence of this, and of the pattern of divided governments, clashing of powers is a constant.

In both countries, the problem is further complicated by the fact that Congress represents particularist networks that lack an idiom in which to speak of national interests. Political discourse thus juxtaposes national interests and individual interests, and whether the issue at hand is combating corruption, modernizing the economy, or ensuring security, congressional interference is portrayed as a particularly irritating case of the individual trumping the national. As particularist politicians are implored not to meddle, the implication is that Congress should be isolated from all the fundamental areas of social, political, and economic life.

Relations between the executive and legislative branches in Colombia and Ecuador have been full of conflict, but they also exhibit accommodation. Democracy has not collapsed, and in contrast to the experiences of neighboring Peru and Venezuela, the model of strong presidentialism has not yet been imposed.[25]

Tsebelis (1990) considered the conditions through which political parties could achieve cooperation in consociational arrangements. Since his model is a rationalist one, he considers parties—or their leaderships—as self-regarding unitary actors that are striving to acquire the maximum of power. In consequence, they carefully consider two options: strike an agreement or sail to open conflict. They determine which option to take by the relative weight of two arenas: electoral (one could add, popular mobilization), and congressional (bargaining, etc.). Tsebelis shows that when the first arena is more important, elite agreements are unlikely. The critical factor determining which of these strategies prevails is the relative importance of mass or parliamentary politics.

In Colombia and Ecuador, the actors are presidents and legislatures. Disregarding the specifics of each case and focusing only on the mechanisms that drive the dynamics of conflict between both actors, I believe both Tsebelis's assumptions are sensible, as long as the limits of such an operation are specified. Although an executive may reasonably be painted as a unitary actor—at least, no less than a party—Congress is obviously diverse and internally divided. However, in several critical junctures, broad coalitions are formed to defend its existence; the Congress members who side with the executive in such junctures can be considered as part of the other actor, the executive. Furthermore, both in Colombia and Ecuador empirically political conflict has appeared as a confrontation between the executive and the legislature (Sánchez Parga 1998). On the other hand, the model can only help to identify some abstract mechanisms—an important operation, especially when comparing—but cannot offer a full explanation of each case, since it is explicitly setting aside some of its critical variables (regional cleavages, parties, etc.).

In this context, forces that bid for strong presidentialism will play a nested game in two arenas: institutional arm twisting and mass mobilization. The relative importance of each arena, as in the original Tsebelis model, will affect the outcome. Theoretically, in presidential systems the executive and legislative branches will check one another but seldom collide. What is happening, then, if they do so continuously yet somehow manage to coexist? I suggest there is some kind of mechanism analogous to the one Tsebelis studied.

According to Tsebelis, in consociational societies, masses (voters) are radicalized and elites are conciliatory. So when conflict appears, the elites (meaning political elites, following Tsebelis) of the consociational regime play as if they were facing a game of chicken, while masses act as if they were in a prisoner's dilemma (see table 9.5 for a synthesis of the model). The problem is further complicated in that, because consociationalism favors intraelite competition, politicians of the same bloc have to compete for the favor of the masses. If elections are more important than parliamentary bargaining, political leaders will take a radical course, even if subjectively they are convinced of the need for an agreement. In sum, the model takes into account the preferences of the elites and of the masses and the relative weights of the parliamentary and electoral arenas. Adapted to the Colombian and Ecuadorean cases, the dynamic plays out as follows: Elites in the executive branch seek to reduce decision costs and broaden their popular support. They can either appeal to the people to dismiss or emasculate Congress, or they can opt to negotiate with it.[26] If institutional stability is not an important concern, and if the level of disrepute of Congress among the voters is sufficiently high, they will take the first road; otherwise, they will choose the second. Correspondingly, politics unfolds across institutional and plebiscitary arenas that reflect different logics.

In the Colombian case, the model should be able to explain why political reform has been attempted so many times and failed despite popular support. Executive branch elites are influenced by two factors. First, given the consociational and democratic traditions of the country, governing

TABLE 9.5

CONFLICT IN CONSOCIATIONAL SOCIETIES

The game between elites is a game of chicken (Colombia).
Structure of the payoffs: temptation→reward→sucker→punishment.

	Push	Yield
Push	punishment, punishment	temptation, sucker
Yield	sucker, temptation	reward, reward

The game for the masses is a prisoner's dilemma (Ecuador).
Structure of the game: temptation→reward→punishment→sucker.

	Push	Yield
Push	punishment, punishment	temptation, sucker
Yield	sucker, temptation	reward, reward

The overall payoff of each player = k × electoral payoff + $(1-k)$ × parliamentary payoff[a]

[a] k is the parameter that decides which arena is more important. When k is high, direct appeal to the masses is fundamental; when it is low, bargaining between the parties is the basic form of politics. "If elites play only in the electoral arena, then the masses are influential . . . and the game is prisoners' dilemma or deadlock. Dominant strategies exist [push], and choices are clear and unconditional" (Tsebelis 1990, 167).

implies an almost mechanical construction of broad national agreements. Second, war and instability have acted as a de facto substitute for consociational agreements, because they push elites in the direction of risk aversion and concern for institutional stability. Such last-resort restraint is presented as a fact of life that applies to all elites: one cannot issue calls to civil unrest in the midst of a civil war. Thus, even in situations of extreme polarization, Colombian elites are prone to strike bargains.

The plebiscitary arena is much less important, in this sense, than the institutional one. Thus, when their backs are to the wall, members of Congress have sufficient resources to fight back and block government initiatives.[27] At the same time, the president and his supporting coalition have very strong incentives to attack Congress: in doing so, they will win support and simultaneously reduce decision costs. Moreover, as is conventional in such games of chicken, the government prefers to declare that it will not yield in any case, to try to push its adversary into a yielding position. But at the last moment, and responding to the all-important demands of stability, it tends to back off. Another way of interpreting this balance of power in Colombia is to understand the legislature as institutionally strong and politically weak. In synthesis, the executive has the incentives both to attack Congress and to bargain with it: both are playing chicken.

This is the static part of the model. The dynamic part, in brief, consists in the iteration of the loop several times. In each run of the loop, Congress loses political power and widens its disrepute as a staunch opponent of political reform. It is clear that this mechanism cannot last forever. At some moment it will break down, because Congress will have wasted all its resources. The use of democracy does not strengthen Congress but rather weakens it. Here, democracy behaves not as a muscle but as a bank account lacking an influx of new deposits. In a more oblique fashion, each run of the loop creates a prisoner's dilemma among members of Congress themselves. Given the fierce competition resulting from the general fragmentation of the political system, agents are forced to use every available resource to scratch a vote, and the disrepute of Congress is too obvious a resource to be ignored. Thus, at every iteration there are greater incentives for members of Congress to attack the institution and to engage in scandal mongering.

The game in Ecuador is different. There is no consociational tradition, nor is there a war. Here, the mass arena is all important, and in this sense Congress is far more vulnerable than in Colombia. At the same time, the president is also weaker, because of a factor that has largely been absent in Colombia: chronic dissatisfaction with economic policies pursued by elected governments.[28] That both sides are weak has protected Ecuador from authoritarian outcomes; presidents have the incentives, but not the resources, to launch a systematic attack on Congress.[29] Indeed, this balance of power in Ecuador persists because both branches are politically weak, as illustrated so starkly by the Haro case: the government did not hold fire because of institutionalized checks on its power, but rather because its own weakness in the mass arena dissuaded it from assuming the political costs of proceeding further.

The differential behavior of political actors in Colombia and Ecuador can be understood by comparing the importance of retaliatory voting. In both countries presidents end their terms almost completely burnt out, but in Colombia the incumbent party or tendency has a decent (better than 50 percent) probability of winning the following elections. In Ecuador, by contrast, the presidential vote is highly volatile, and there has not been a single consecutive president of the same party: Ecuador suffers an incumbent curse.[30] This, plus the persistence of minority governments, makes of the game a prisoner's dilemma. Collisions are frequent, and the verbal confrontation agenda is transformed in facts; depending on the conjuncture, the government, Congress, or both will be hit. Each collision deepens the public malaise vis-à-vis Congress and thus radicalizes antiparliamentary discourse. But the government remains weak as well (see, for example, table 9.2), so democracy is saved by a low-level equilibrium.

Colombia and Ecuador are not the only countries in the Andes, or in Latin America, where members of Congress and politicians in general are highly unpopular. To the contrary, Congress bashing is a widely practiced sport across much of the hemisphere (for the particulars of the American League, see Hibbing and Theiss 1995), but it is particularly widespread in the Andes. The problem facing presidents in Colombia and Ecuador is that they have incentives to unbid (Elster 1989) and play games against Congress (Elster 1989, sec. 4) and at the same time to remain within the bounds of the democratic regime. This has implied the rise and expansion of coalitions that try to manipulate the rules of the game to obtain correct outcomes (Fleischer 1996). It is not by chance that political reform is the great myth of the decade, both in Colombia and Ecuador. This, by the way, shows that reforming the rules of the game is not simple engineering but endogenous to political change. However, widespread manipulation of the rules of the game has not generated cumulative radicalization, as might be expected, but rather a homeostatic mechanism. In both countries, Congresses somehow have held their own. In Colombia, because of the predominance of the institutional arena, presidents have incentives to attack Congress and to bargain with it. In Ecuador, programmatic polarization exacerbated by the trend toward neoliberalism provides incentives for confrontational speech and behaviors; it also divides the society into two blocs that effectively cancel one another out. Congress is weak, but the president is no stronger. In the end, checks and balances prove more resilient than anticipated. The real problem arises when the loop is repeated many times, given that each iteration expends nonreplenishable democratic resources. Antiparliamentary politics remains a real threat to democracy.

Notes

A preliminary version of this paper was delivered at the March 2003 meeting of the Latin American Studies Association (LASA) in Dallas, Texas. The research results from a project on Democratic Sustainability in the Andes, sponsored by the Crisis State Program of DESTIN–London School of Economics. I thank James Putzel for his valuable remarks and input, the Social Science Research Council for its invitation to LASA 2003, and Eric Hershberg and Paul Drake for their insights and comments.

1. See also the blissfully optimistic paper of Nielson and Shugart (1999) about the effects of the Colombian constitution.

2. The beginning and ending dates of La Violencia are hotly contested by historians. These dates are customary.

3. Several of these rules were relaxed after 1958, especially in the 1968 constitutional reform.

4. Tragically enough, he failed in several of his decisive enterprises.

5. Quantitative substantiation is found in Gutiérrez (1998). The LP is highly factionalized, so this factor must not be exaggerated. Liberals are reputed to rarely vote together, but the evidence is that they are somewhat more undisciplined than U.S. political parties, for example, but much less than generally supposed.

6. A coalition within the Congress had buckled to pressure from narcocriminal elements in attempting to introduce a question about the validity of the extradition treaty into the referendum convening the constitutional assembly.

7. The change was from *inmunidad* proper to *fuero*, or limited protection, which allowed the judiciary to prosecute members of Congress for criminal offenses.

8. Tensions between media and politicians were not new. In 1978 antimedia proposals had been advanced by the president himself.

9. Pastrana (or at least some of his advisers) was trying to play the game of strong presidentialism: weakening Congress, strengthening the executive, and bidding for long presidential periods. The president of the Conservative Party, for example, proposed a measure to allow for the reelection of the president on the grounds that four years was too short a period to cope with the big problems of the nation. These proposals were reintroduced, much more forcefully, after 2002.

10. The emphasis on national unity was no doubt reinforced by the traumatic experience of the 1941 conflict with Peru (Bustamante 1992).

11. I am simplifying here, because the military dismissed Rodríguez in 1976 and practically put an end to the reformist orientation.

12. There are many plausible interpretations of this reform, but I agree with Zamosc (2000), who shows that it cannot be described as mere window dressing.

13. Of course, the military benefited from the discovery of vast oil reserves, which provided the major source of this unprecedented prosperity.

14. Ecuadoreans call this *huasipungo político*, the segmentation of politics into small and autarchic parcels.

15. Valenzuela et al. (1999) propose for contemporary Colombia many of the same design features that were established in the Ecuadorean transition.

16. This was replaced in 1998 by the D'Hondt quota, which is less severe than the previous one but still less benevolent toward small parties than the Hare quota.

17. Roldós was killed in a plane accident while in office.

18. The phenomenon is paradoxical, because each run of this loop—the loop of phony anti-neoliberalism—is castigated by the citizens, who can vote against the incumbent party. In Ecuador, no incumbent party has won the elections, which is a Rikerian indicator of the real power of the voters. On the other hand, the lack of substitutes—in a world in which everybody is a program switcher—can have the effect of making democracy meaningless.

19. After this chapter was written, Gutiérrez himself fell under the attack of social

movements for yielding to international pressures to pursue a liberal economic policy and—attacked on all flanks—was ultimately toppled.

20. But all this is cyclical. The military-popular link may be losing momentum, precisely as a consequence of its electoral victory.

21. See Sánchez Parga (1998). A much more systematic narrative, but with basically the same conclusions, is found in Pachano (2003).

22. Colombian president Uribe had claimed that elements of the Ecuadorean army were selling weapons to Colombian rebels. Gutiérrez demanded hard evidence, and Uribe was unable to produce any. In Ecuador the issue became quite important and had obvious nationalist underpinnings (which the Colombian government, with incredible clumsiness, had failed to foresee). In this context, several political forces considered Haro's accusation to be an antipatriotic provocation against the army.

23. The decision was to neither lift Haro's immunity nor to withdraw the charges: the progovernment coalition expected that this nondecision would technically force the Supreme Court to review the case. But the Supreme Court answered in kind and declared that Haro's immunity was the Congress's jurisdiction.

24. In 2003 there was a political reform and a strong effort by major party leaders to reverse the trend, in which they have apparently been successful. The level of fragmentation, though, remains very high.

25. However, in both countries such a governance model has constituted a temptation for presidents.

26. The situation is not symmetrical, since the Congress is the epicenter of particularism and lacks the ability of acting as a unitary actor and making national appeals.

27. The only possible exception is a situation in which the powers of the president and the Congress are so asymmetrical that there is no credible threat of retaliation by the Congress—an eventuality that should not be discarded.

28. The assumption here is that the sum of the power and legitimacy of the president and the Congress does not amount to a constant.

29. Expressed differently, they do attack it, but soon are overcome by their own problems. As the narrative sketched here, and the study of the 1978–2003 period shows, this is precisely what has taken place.

30. I thank Simón Pachano for kindly supplying me the time series of electoral behavior in Ecuador from the beginning of democracy to 2000.

Bibliography

Aguirre, Milagros. 2000. *Ecuador hoy: Cien miradas*. Quito: Ecuador: FLACSO Ecuador–El Comercio.

Almeida, José. 1992. Los indios del Ecuador y la democracia. *Cuadernos de la Realidad Ecuatoriana* 5:51–70.

Archer, Ronald. 1990. The transition from traditional to broker clientelism in Colombia: Political stability and social unrest. Kellogg Institute, Working Paper 140, University of Notre Dame.

Bernal, Max, and José Luis Espinosa. 1991. Ajuste neoliberal, represión social y oposición laboral. *Revista Idis*, no. 28: 247–86.

Betancourt, Íngrid. 1998. Pueblo versus congreso. *Revista Diners*, October, 10–13.

Buchanan, James, and Gordon Tullock. 1962. *The calculus of consent: Logical foundations of constitutional democracy.* Ann Arbor: University of Michigan Press.

Bustamante, Fernando. 1992. Fuerzas Armadas en el Ecuador: ¿Puede institucionalizarse la subordinación al poder civil? *Síntesis* (January–April): 179–202.

Carrillo, Fernando, ed. 2001. *Democracia en déficit. Gobernabilidad y desarrollo en América Latina y el Caribe, Banco Interamericano de Desarrollo.* Washington, DC: BID.

Chiriboga, Manuel, and Fredy Rivera. 1988. *Elecciones de Enero de 1988 y participación indígena. Ecuador Debate,* no. 17: 181–221.

Conaghan, Catherine, and James Malloy. 1997. Democracia y neoliberalismo en Perú, Ecuador y Bolivia. *Desarrollo Económico* 36 (144) 867–90.

Cueva, Austín. 1997. *El proceso de dominación política en el Ecuador.* Quito, Ecuador: Editorial Planeta.

Diamond, Larry, Marc Plattner, Yun-han Chu, and Hung Mao Tien, eds. 1997. *Consolidating the third wave democracies: Themes and perspectives.* Baltimore and London: John Hopkins University Press.

Elster, John. 1989. *Ulises y las sirenas: Estudios sobre racionalidad e irracionalidad.* Mexico City: Fondo de Cultura Económica.

Fleischer, David. 1996. Las consecuencias del sistema electoral brasileño. Partidos políticos, poder legislativo y gobernabilidad. Cuadernos de Capel (IIDH-Capel) no. 39.

Freidenberg, Flavia, and Manuel Alcántara. 2001. Cuestión regional y política en Ecuador, partidos de vocación nacional y apoyo regional *América Latina Hoy,* no. 27: 123–52.

Gutiérrez, Francisco. 1998. Rescate por un elefante: Congreso, sistema y reforma política. In *Elecciones y democracia 1997–1998,* ed. Ana María Bejarano and Andrés Dávila, 215–53. Bogotá, Colombia: Fundación Social, Universidad de los Andes, Veeduría Ciudadana.

Hartlyn, Jonathan. 1993. *La política del régimen de coalición: La experiencia del Frente Nacional en Colombia.* Bogotá, Colombia: Ediciones Uniandes–Tercer Mundo Editores.

Hey, Jeanne, and Thomas Klak. 1999. From protectionism towards neoliberalism: Ecuador across four administrations (1981–1996). *Studies in International Comparative Development* 34 (3): 66–98.

Hibbing, John R., and Elizabeth Theiss-Morse. 1995. *Congress as public enemy: Public attitudes toward American political institutions.* Cambridge: Cambridge University Press.

Holguín Sardi, Carlos. 1999. Presentation before the first congressional debates on the Acto Legislativo, 01, 03, and 04 of 1999, August 26.

Isaacs, Anita. 1993. *Military rule and transition in Ecuador: 1972–1992.* London: McMillan.

Latinobarómetro. 2000. http://www.mori.com/latinobarometro2000.htm.

León, Jorge. 2000. El contexto y el sistema político en el movimiento indígena ecuatoriano. Mimeograph. Quito, Ecuador: CEDIME

———. 2003. . . .y el Estado se volatilizó. In *Ecuador en crisis: Estado, etnicidad y movimientos sociales en la era de la globalización,* ed. Víctor Breton, 103–22. Barcelona, Spain: ICARIA.

Lijphart, Arend. 1989 *Democracia en las sociedades plurales: Una investigación comparativa.* Buenos Aires, Brazil: Grupo Editorial Latinoamericano.

Matthiesen, Tatiana. 2000. *El arte político de conciliar*. Bogotá, Colombia: FESCOL-CEREC-Fedesarrollo.

Menéndez Carrión, Amparo. 1991 *Ecuador, la democracia esquiva*. Quito, Ecuador: Instituto Latinoamericano de Investigación.

Montúfar, César. 2000. *La reconstrucción neoliberal: Febres Cordero o la estatización del neoliberalismo en Ecuador 1984–1988*. Quito, Ecuador: Abya-Yala.

Nielsen, Daniel, and Matthew Shugart. 1999. Constitutional change in Colombia: Policy adjustment through policy reform. *Comparative Political Studies* 23 (3): 313–42.

Pachano, Fernando, ed. 1997. *La ruta de la gobernabilidad*. Final report of the CORDES-Gobernabilidad project. Quito, Ecuador: CORDES-CIPIE.

Pachano, Simón. 2003. El tejido de Penélope: La reforma política en el Ecuador. Mimeograph. Quito, Ecuador: FLACSO.

Palacios, Marco. 1996. La gobernabilidad en Colombia. *Análisis Político*, no. 26:1–23.

Peñaherrera, Blasco. 2002. *Trazos de democracia: 22 años de elecciones (1978–2002)*. Quito, Ecuador: Imprenta Mariscal.

Polibio Córdova, Ángel. 1999. Opinión pública y realidad nacional: Los últimos 25 años. *Ecuador Debate*, no. 46: 95–122.

Przeworski, Adam, Susan Stokes, and Bernard Manin, eds. 1999. *Democracy, accountability and representation*. Cambridge: Cambridge University Press.

Sánchez Parga, José. 1993. El gobierno estatal y la gobernabilidad: Entrevista a Mario Ribadeneira y Pablo Lucio Paredes. *Ecuador Debate*, no. 30: 54–66.

———. 1998. *La pugna de poderes: Análisis crítico del sistema político ecuatoriano*. Quito, Ecuador: Abya-Yala.

Schuldt, Jorge. 1994. *Elecciones y política económico en el Ecuador 1983–1994*. Quito, Ecuador: ILDIS.

Stokes, Susan. 1999. What do policy switches tell us about democracy? In Przeworki, Stokes, and Manin 1999, 98–130.

Tsebelis, George. 1990. *Nested games: Rational choice in comparative politics*. Berkeley, Los Angeles, and Oxford: University of California Press.

Valenzuela, Arturo, Josep Colomer, Arend Lijphart, and Matthew Shugart. 1999. *Sobre la reforma política en Colombia*. N.p.: Georgetown Analytics.

Zamosc, Leon. 1994. Agrarian protest and the Indian movement in the Ecuador highlands. *Latin American Research Review* 29 (3): 37–68.

Sowing Democracy in Venezuela

Advances and Challenges in a Time of Change

MIRIAM KORNBLITH

THE STUNNING RECENT UPHEAVALS AND CONFLICTS in Venezuela demonstrated that even a robust democracy (1958–2004) was vulnerable to the Andean crisis. As in the rest of the region, the severe breakdown of relations between the state and society began with the economic downturn of the 1980s. Social protests erupted, moreover, when governments attempted to respond to worsening economic conditions with market-oriented structural adjustments. Feeling betrayed by institutions and leaders that either converted to neoliberalism, as did President Carlos Andrés Pérez, or failed to revive the economy by any means, as did President Rafael Caldera, protesters rejected the political establishment altogether.

As in Colombia, dissidents blamed their economic plight on the two elitist political parties that had dominated national politics since the democratic pact of 1958 had ended military rule. Venezuela's catchall parties could not channel this popular discontent because they no longer had the oil revenues required to sustain the clientelist relations between the state and society. They were unable to reinvent or replace themselves as the leaders of a consensual national development project because such a project was predicated on "sowing the oil" through the populist state. At the same time, they proved incapable of devising new policies that would satisfy both the international economic order and their impoverished citizens. They could offer the voters neither attractive economic packages nor fresh political options. As with the two-party system in Colombia, their support eroded, and as elsewhere in the Andes, an unstable multiparty system emerged.

As in the other Andean nations, elites in Venezuela responded to the disintegration of the political order in three main ways: authoritarianism, institutionalism, and personalism. When repression and coup attempts, on the one hand, and institutional innovations such as decentralization, on the other hand, failed to restore political normality, Hugo Chávez took power in 1999 with his personalized national project of a Bolivarian republic dedicated to the dispossessed. However, like other charismatic leaders in the Andes, his popularity rose and fell along with the economy. As Chávez and his adversaries became more heavy-handed, electoral politics became less participatory, representative, and integrative. Instead of curing the disconnection between the state and society, Chávez aggravated it, although his mobilization of the lower classes reversed the groups who felt most excluded from the government.

As a result, Venezuela joined its Andean neighbors in over two decades of frustrated political experiments to overcome the public's alienation from failed socioeconomic policies. Despite disappointments, the country's leaders maintained its precarious and poorly functioning economic and political models. They did so because it would have been even more costly to defect from the liberal international regimes emphasizing markets and elections. Since full-blown military takeovers were rarely acceptable, Venezuela struggled valiantly to solve the crisis principally through democratic means, above all elections. Although some political actors preferred authoritarian remedies, most Venezuelans, like most Ecuadoreans and Bolivians, tried to find legal means of shortening presidential terms without relying on traditional coups d'état. These efforts climaxed in the impeachment of Pérez and the effort to secure a popular referendum against Chávez. The electoral evolution from the 1980s to the present shows how democratic institutions have struggled to mediate social conflicts and the complex process through which the 2004 showdown between Chávez and his opponents was reached. Although Chávez defeated his adversaries once again in the 2004 referendum, whether that continuing polarization is ultimately settled through democratic or authoritarian means could have a profound impact on the future of Andean democracy.

Since 1958, Venezuela has had a pluralist political order based on a systemic and populist conciliation of elites (Rey 1989, 1991) that is commonly known as the *Puntofijista* democracy, in reference to the Punto Fijo Accord, signed in October 1958 by the three major political parties—Democratic Action (AD), the Catholic Comité de Organización Política Electoral Independiente (COPEI; Committee of Independent Electoral Political Organization), and the Unión Republicana Democrática (URD; Democratic Republican Union). During its early decades, the accord enabled political stability, consensus among the elites, alternation in power, and extension of the benefits of the country's model of development to the population. Starting in the 1980s, however, the country entered a period of socioeconomic, political, and institutional instability and change that continues to this writing. Its most recent phase—the Chávez administration—has been marked by conflict and confrontation as a result of the administration's project to reestablish the republic. Chávez's political program has led to the imposition of rules, actors, and institutions that are different and even in conflict with those that have ruled Venezuelan society since 1958.

As in the rest of the Andean region, the achievements and limits of the Venezuelan model of democracy and its associated electoral processes may be evaluated according to their ability to express collective preferences, enable changes in the established leadership, promote coalitions in tune with the expectations of the population, and guarantee representational arrangements that are both inclusive and expressive of social diversity. During times of confrontation, such as the current period in Venezuela, democratic practices and democratic culture face particularly acute challenges, precisely at a moment when these must confront the authoritarian and antidemocratic pretensions of diverse actors lacking strong knowledge of or commitments to democratic values and institutions. At this critical juncture in Venezuelan sociopolitical development, it is important to evaluate the country's democratic order, particularly with regard to the ability of post-1959 democratic institutions to counteract the authoritarian and hegemonic pretensions of those currently in power and at the same time correct the distortions and obstacles that in recent years have cultivated the frustration of millions of Venezuelans.

The Crisis and Transformation of the Venezuelan Political System

In February 1989, the recently elected President Carlos Andrés Pérez announced a draconian economic adjustment program. Only a few days

later, on February 27 and 28, there was an unprecedented social uprising—known as the Caracazo (Caracas Event)—which according to official
numbers left approximately three hundred dead, countless wounded, and
scores of businesses looted and destroyed. These events led to a declaration of a state of emergency and to the mobilization of the armed forces to
put a stop to the uprising. The Caracazo and its aftershocks dealt a severe
blow to the legitimacy of the recently elected president and his administration. It also shook the foundations of the Puntofijista democratic order.

Beginning with Black Friday in February 1983, which saw a sharp
devaluation of the national currency following several decades of stable
exchange rates, there were numerous and inconsistent attempts to redefine the country's model of economic development. Despite these efforts,
however, it was not possible to reverse the tendency toward social and
economic decline. Poverty rates continued to grow, fiscal difficulties
become more acute, and there was growing evidence that the oil-depend-
ent model was incapable of generating well-being for the population.
Since the mid-1980s, social welfare indicators had been declining steadily,
reversing the gains made in previous decades in the well-being of the
population. There was also a growing criticism of the institutions, actors,
values, and outcomes of democracy Venezuelan style, particularly about
corruption, impunity, and the role of political parties.

Analysis of these events and trends inevitably points to the undeniable
sociopolitical decline of the model inaugurated in 1958. The late 1980s
were marked by a pronounced popular disaffection with the socioeconom
ic model and the existing political, social, military, entrepreneurial, and
union leadership. As the coup attempts of February and November 1992
demonstrated, one of the key pillars behind the Puntofijista order had been
undermined—the subjection of the military to civilian authority.

During this period, however, there were also important attempts to
implement institutional changes that would change the rules, actors, and
institutions in question. Among these was the program for political and
administrative decentralization—perhaps the most important political
reform undertaken in recent years—as well as the organizational reform of
electoral processes. Yet despite these attempts, many of which achieved
their desired outcomes, it was not possible to reverse the crisis of legitimacy and the sociopolitical and economic decline facing the very leaders who
were pushing for these reforms. Perhaps most importantly, these reforms
were not able to generate a viable new cohort of leaders from the traditional elite circles with the intensity and celerity that public opinion demanded.
Nevertheless, they have endured over time and have played an important
role in maintaining a democratic order in highly adverse conditions.[1]

New Political and Electoral Trends in the 1990s

The tensions and transformations affecting Venezuelan society have had an important impact on political and electoral dynamics. Institutional reforms played a fundamental role in the channeling of new realities and expectations into innovative representational schemes as well as in the emergence of new sociopolitical articulations.

The Opportunities of Decentralization

The direct election of governors and mayors in 1989, 1992, and 1995 generated new patterns of behavior and new articulations of power in Venezuela's political and electoral landscape. These elections fostered the expansion of inter- and intraparty competition and created opportunities for the emergence of new leaders and alternative political organizations.

The 1989 regional election was the first time that governors and mayors were directly elected, and it marked the first step in the implementation of political and administrative decentralization, a process that continued with regional elections in 1992, 1995, 1998, and 2000. Since the first direct election for governors and mayors, important changes were set in motion both in the electoral landscape and in the voting behavior of Venezuelans. During the first three such elections, abstention rates were high, reaching 54 percent in 1989, 50.72 percent in 1992, and 53.85 percent in 1995. Despite the novelty of these regional electoral processes as well as the fact that Venezuelans were participating in the election of authorities who were very proximate to their everyday lives, these races were unable to generate a significant mobilization of the electorate.

From the first election in which regional and local authorities were elected independently, there were important achievements for the decentralization agenda, such as the incorporation of regional leaders into positions of power, the expansion of the spectrum of political party representation, and a more balanced representation of the different political parties. The regional arena also gained greater visibility and autonomy. Parties such as Movement toward Socialism (MAS) or La Causa R (LCR), which under the previous electoral framework had been unable to gain a national presence, achieved important victories when their gubernatorial and mayoral candidates were elected to office. There were also new party-oriented collectivities, such as Project Carabobo, that emerged in particular states and were able to gain national recognition.

The 1993 Presidential Elections

The 1993 elections revealed an important turning point in the bipartisan politics that had characterized electoral processes since 1973 and demonstrated even more forcefully than the regional elections that the preferences of Venezuelans were shifting toward newly emerging electoral options (Sonntag and Maingón 2001). In the 1988 and 1993 presidential elections, the four leading contenders advocated reform and questioned the conventional rules and institutions of the nation's sociopolitical order. Claudio Fermin of AD, the former mayor of Caracas, and Oswaldo Alvarez Paz of COPEI, the former governor of the state of Zulia, both belonged to the new generations within their respective political parties and had emerged by challenging the traditional party leadership. Their economic platforms included neoliberal policies, and they both supported further decentralization. A. Velasquez, the former governor of Bolivar, was also a proponent of decentralization, despite being a member of LCR—a party that at the time was espousing radical critiques of the political status quo.

Caldera, who went on to win the elections, positioned himself in open opposition to COPEI (the party of which he was a founding member) and to President Pérez's adjustment policies, riding on the popular sympathies toward the military officers who staged the attempted coup on February 4, 1992. In that election, Caldera ran as the candidate of the Convergence Party with the support of a broad coalition of fifteen other parties, which included left collectivities such as the MAS, the People's Electoral Movement, the Venezuelan Communist Party, and others. His victory in that election was the first time since 1958 that a candidate from a party or coalition outside of AD and COPEI was elected to the presidency.

Abstention rates increased dramatically in the 1993 presidential election, jumping from 12 percent in 1988 to 39.84 percent of eligible voters. While the combined number of votes obtained by the AD and COPEI candidates in 1988 had reached 93.29 percent of all votes cast—a percentage that had remained relatively consistent from 1973 onward—the combined votes of these two parties in the 1993 election barely reached 46.33 percent. The votes cast for the antisystemic candidacies represented by Caldera and Velasquez totaled 52.41 percent.

The Caldera administration may be understood as the final attempt to conserve the rules of the political order established in 1958 and as the last opportunity that the electorate gave the traditional political elites to lead the country. Yet the shortcomings and failures of the Caldera administration demonstrated to that same electorate that the traditional political elites were increasingly unable to lead the country successfully in the context of an increasingly complex and tense national reality.

At the same time, organizations and individuals from the political Left, which were part of the coalition that supported Caldera and which for the first time contributed sufficient votes to influence the outcome of a presidential election (MAS support brought Caldera almost six hundred thousand votes), generated new possibilities for traditionally marginalized political groups and parties. In this context, such groups gained public visibility that contributed to the amelioration of the public's misgivings about their role in the national political arena. This would prove to be a crucial factor for the Chávez candidacy in 1998.

In the parliamentary arena, there was a similar shift in the preferences of the electorate and thus in the balance of power in Congress. While in 1988 AD and COPEI controlled 81 percent of the seats in the Chamber of Deputies, and the MAS 9 percent, in the 1993 election AD and COPEI were able to retain only 53.2 percent of those seats, with LCR winning 19.7 percent, Convergence 12.8 percent, and the MAS 11.8 percent of all seats.

The Rupture between the Traditional Leadership and the Population

A series of critical political events between 1989 and 1993, the sustained deterioration of the pillars of the democratic order established in 1958, and the new political and electoral possibilities enabled by decentralization explain the deep and rapid changes in collective perceptions and preferences evinced in the 1993 elections. There is little doubt that the electorate was searching for new options through which to overcome the crisis. Despite repeated warnings of public impatience and disaffection, political elites were unable to satisfy the collective expectations of the population and chose instead to rehearse old formulas or—in the best of circumstances—to promote innovations that were unable to generate sufficient traction.

Adverse socioeconomic conditions intensified criticism and collective discontent. Since the early 1980s, sustained socioeconomic deterioration had sharply accentuated existing inequalities and marginalized vast sectors of the population, leading to rising rates of poverty and extreme poverty. The traditional leadership, however, appeared not to notice the profound impact this was having on Venezuelan society or the new divisions and political alliances that this situation was generating.[2] Traditional elites, including political party leaders as well as those from labor and entrepreneurial sectors, continued to operate as if the traditional accords and the ability to produce and maintain them through abundant oil rents and conventional arrangements were still intact. This communicational breakdown between the leadership and broad sectors of the population further convinced the electorate that it was futile to continue supporting traditional power elites, thus making alternative options more attractive.

The Ascent of Chávez and the Displacement of the Traditional Leadership

As a result of their participation in the failed coup attempt of February 4, 1992, Hugo Chávez and the leaders of his movement were sent to prison. In early 1994, during the Caldera presidency, they were released and expelled from the armed forces. While Francisco Arias Cardenas and other freed leaders chose to incorporate themselves into democratic politics, with Arias going on to win the 1995 Zulia gubernatorial election with the support of LCR, Chávez chose to abstain. He changed his political strategy in 1997, however, aligning himself with several civilian organizations and individuals and entering the electoral arena. Soon afterward, the Movement for the Fifth Republic (MVR) was founded and awarded legal status, and Chávez began his ascent in the public opinion polls. The Patriotic Pole was created to serve as the umbrella organization for the recently founded MVR party and several traditional organizations, such as the MAS, the Venezuelan Communist Party, the People's Electoral Movement, and other small new groups such as Nation for All (PPT; Ellner 2003; Hellinger 2003; Roberts 2003).

The COPEI party selected independent Irene Sáez, a former Miss Universe and the popular mayor of Chacao, as its presidential candidate. AD, by contrast, chose its most senior party leader and secretary general, Alfaro Ucero, whose first forays into national politics dated back to the 1940s. The recently formed Project Venezuela (PV), a national extension of the regionally based Project Carabobo, nominated the popular former governor of Carabobo, Henrique Salas Romer, as its candidate. LCR initially supported Irene Sáez but later decided to run its own candidate, Alfredo Ramos. Sixteen candidates registered for the election, although that number decreased to eleven as a result of withdrawals and other circumstances.

Because both regional and national elections were to take place in December 1998, in May of that year Congress decided to separate them. It was decided that elections for Congress, governorships, and the legislative assemblies would take place in November 1998 and that the presidential elections would be held in December of that year, leaving the elections for municipal councils and neighborhood associations for the second half of 1999. Thus, 1998 was the first time since 1958 that a presidential election was separated from other elections, and the first time that two elections were held in the same year.

The schedule proposed by Congress served the interests of the dominant political parties in consolidating positions of power in the parliamentary and regional arenas in the face of the growing consolidation and popularity of the Chávez candidacy, which they perceived as a menace to the stability and continuity of the democratic order as well as a threat to their own survival. It was thought that if the presidential election took place first, a Chávez victory could lead to a sweep of the congressional and regional elections by Chávez supporters, generating a favorable balance of power for Chávez throughout the country's political and administrative institutions. If the parliamentary and regional elections were held first, on the other hand, voters would be better able to separate the candidates from the presidential contest, and would thus be more likely to support the traditional leadership.

Another unusual development took place only a few days before the presidential election, when AD and COPEI withdrew their support from their respective candidates and decided to back Salas Romer, whom they had bitterly opposed only weeks before. This created widespread confusion and irritation among the electorate, which eventually threw its support behind Chávez. These events were a vivid expression of the confusion and deterioration of the traditional political organizations and parties and of the significant challenge that the emerging alternatives posed. Public opinion polls revealed a consistent and growing support for candidates who represented a break from the past.

The Regional and Parliamentary Elections of November 1998

Several aspects of the 1998 legislative elections merit close examination. The first is the rapid growth and positioning of the PV party and the MVR party. For both of these organizations, it was their first participation in a national election. Also important was the drop in the total percentage of the votes and legislative seats captured by AD and COPEI, which received a combined 36.1 percent of the votes and as a result of the electoral rules, 43.5 percent of the legislative posts. These elections also revealed the fragility of electoral support for LCR and Convergence, both of which registered a sharp decline from their performance in 1993.

In the legislative election, the combined votes for AD and COPEI reached 36 percent, while the vote for MVR (19.9 percent) and PV (10.4 percent)—the recently formed political parties—together surpassed 30 percent of all votes cast. Although these percentages did not directly translate into seats in Congress, they did reveal the growing displacement of traditional political organizations by emerging electoral alternatives. As Molina Vega (2001) and Molina Vega and Pérez Baralt (1996) have pointed out, this suggests the emergence of an unstable and unconsolidated multiparty system—vastly different from the stable bipartisan system that characterized party dynamics between 1973 and 1988—as a result of a volatile electorate and widespread party deidentification. It also confirms a tendency toward the displacement and substitution of traditional parties, which first became visible in the 1989 regional elections and was again seen in the presidential election of 1993.

There was a similar realignment at the gubernatorial level. Of a total of twenty-three governorships, AD candidates captured eight, their COPEI counterparts won four, and a joint AD/COPEI candidacy won in one state. The parties affiliated with the Patriotic Pole won seven gubernatorial races, with one going to MVR and three each to the MAS and PPT. PV repeated its victory in the state of Carabobo, Convergencia retained its governorship in Yaracuy, and Arias won again in Zulia, supported by a broad alliance that included MVR, COPEI, and LCR.

The results of both elections point to the emergence of a new political-electoral landscape in which positions of power are equitably shared by traditional parties and emerging groups, with a rapid rise of the latter and the decline of LCR and Convergence, the two emerging groups that had figured prominently in the 1993 election. Although these results did not produce a definitive consolidation of the Patriotic Pole or a clear displacement of the traditional parties, they augured a dramatic change in the balance of power and sent a strong message to traditional sectors about the ascendancy of Chávez and his coalition.

The Presidential Elections of December 1998

Numerous developments, including the rapid ascendance of the Patriotic Pole, the weak showing of the PV party, the solid support for the Chávez candidacy in public opinion polls, the withering support for Irene

Sáez, Alfaro Ucero's lack of traction with the electorate, and the sharp polarization in the political arena created an unusual atmosphere between the November and December elections. AD and COPEI decided to withdraw support from their own candidates and backed Salas Romer. They calculated that the total votes for the parties and candidates aligned with those organizations would surpass the votes for Chávez. Although this was not an unreasonable calculation, the outcome proved quite different. Their last minute decision to support Salas Romer—an acerbic critic of the AD-COPEI bipartisan arrangement whom they had confronted even more aggressively than they had confronted Chávez—generated confusion and rejection among much of the electorate, which threw its support behind Chávez. The rise in voter turnout, moreover, with the abstention rate dropping from 46 to 37 percent from one election to the next, mainly benefited Chávez.

The result was a highly polarized election in which the two most popular candidates, both representatives of the emerging sectors, obtained 96.17 percent of the votes. As in the 1993 elections, voters strongly favored the candidacies critical of the status quo, with Chávez—the candidate with the most radical platform—winning 56.2 percent of the vote from a total of 3,673,685 voters, making him the preference of 33.43 percent of all registered voters.[3]

The defining characteristics of Venezuelan electoral behavior had become its high level of volatility and eroding support for the AD-COPEI formula, the emergence of new political actors, the appeal of antisystemic candidates, and a sharp rise in abstentions. This new electoral landscape persisted throughout the 1990s and continues today. In this context, last-minute political maneuvers were not only unsuccessful but also counterproductive.

Loyalty to traditional political parties and corporatist groups diminished as they became increasingly incapable of meeting the needs of their constituents, in part because declining oil revenues made it increasingly difficult to maintain the clientelist relationships that sustained them. The emergence and intensification of socioeconomic differences created the conditions for the realignment of political preferences according to the interests of different socioeconomic groups. Economic decline, accompanied by increasing unemployment and the informalization of the economy, generated high levels of poverty and extreme poverty, excluding vast sectors of the population from the formal networks of economic activity as well as from labor union activity, social services, and education. The growing number of abstentions and of eligible voters who did not register to vote (an estimated 3 million)—particularly among youth and people from lower socioeconomic strata—were the electoral corollary to the growing socioeconomic disarticulation facing the country since the mid-1980s. In this context, Chávez and his allies positioned themselves as the voice of the excluded, who no longer trusted the traditional political leadership.

The Constituent Process and the Legitimization of Powers

The victory of Chávez and his supporters brought rapid changes to Venezuelan sociopolitical dynamics. These emergent forces captured state power with a political program that they had been developing for some time, dating back to their conspiratorial days within the armed forces. A National Constituent Assembly (NCA) to "reestablish the republic" was Chavez's central campaign promise, and as soon as his administration came to power, the mechanisms to convene it were set in motion.[4] On January 19, 1999, in response to two motions filed before it, the Supreme Court of Justice had upheld the legality of using the referendum mechanism stipulated in the electoral law to convene a National Constituent Assembly, even though the 1961 constitution did not explicitly establish the notion of such an assembly. On the same day that the Chávez administration officially assumed power—February 2, 1999—the newly inaugurated president issued a decree mandating a consultation of the electorate with regard to the convening of an NCA. Ironically, this decree was issued only hours after Chávez had formally accepted the responsibilities of his post, swearing to uphold the "moribund" constitution of 1961.

Elections and the Constituent Process

The constituent process was implemented in three phases: the referendum of April 25, in which the electorate was asked whether to convene an NCA; the election of representatives to the NCA, which took place in July 1999; and the December 15 referendum in which the electorate was asked to approve or reject the constitution elaborated by the NCA. Each of these electoral processes added its own particularities to the country's sociopolitical landscape, and each served both to strengthen support for Chávez and his program and to shape the character of the opposition.

In the referendum to approve convening of the NCA, voters were asked two questions. The first was, "Do you call to convene a National Constituent Assembly with the purpose of transforming the state and creating a new juridical order that allows for the effective functioning of a social and participatory democracy?" The second concerned the electoral mechanism through which the members of the NCA would be elected. This was the first nationwide referendum in Venezuela's history. The abstention rate was unprecedented, reaching 62.3 percent, yet low voter turnout did not derail or delegitimize the constituent process. The yes votes confirmed the electoral support captured by Chávez in December 1998, with 3,630,666 positive responses to the first question and 3,275,716 to the second and only 300,233 negative responses to the first question and 512,967 to the second. As these numbers reveal, the opposition was still reeling from its defeat in the December elections and opted to abstain rather than mount a campaign to reject the convening of an NCA. Neither in this election nor in those that followed in 1999 and 2000 was the opposition able to equal or surpass the number of votes captured by the Salas Romer candidacy. Nor was it able to sustain the support it had received in the 1998 regional elections, although its performance began to improve in subsequent contests.

The July 25, 1999, election of representatives to the NCA took place through an electoral mechanism adopted by the Chávez administration that ensured its ability to retain control of the assembly. The system was based on majorities and consisted of one national district with twenty-four delegates and twenty-four regional districts with a variable number of delegates based on population. It also included three indigenous representatives selected according to "their ancestral uses and customs." The outcome was an extreme overrepresentation of the majority, with the Patriotic Pole accounting for 95 percent of the members of the NCA, although they only captured 65 percent of the votes cast. Thus, of the 131 members of the NCA, 122 were from the Patriotic Pole list and 3 were indigenous representatives also associated with the Patriotic Pole. The abstention rate reached 54 percent.

The Chávez administration operated with great efficacy in this referendum, maximizing its electoral possibilities by presenting a unified list of 124 candidates distributed over two large electoral zones. This strategy allowed the administration to maximize the benefits from the electoral system and from its existing electoral base. The process, however, was also characterized by what has today become the standard practice of those in power—the abusive and unregulated use of public resources for electoral purposes.[5]

Winning political control of the NCA represented a major victory for the governing coalition and enabled it to define the text of the new constitution in accordance with its political project. Hegemonic control of the process, however, had negative consequences for relations within the coalition as well as for popular acceptance of the resulting charter. The deliberations of the NCA created disagreements within the Patriotic Pole rather than between the governing coalition and the opposition (Viciano and Martinez 2001). The lack of representation of vast political sectors, moreover, led to a perception that the text of the new constitution was a direct expression of Chávez's political project rather than a reflection of the aspirations of Venezuelan society as a whole. In contrast to the 1961 constitution—which was the longest-standing constitution in the country's history and the result of a broad consensus between divergent political sectors—the duration and acceptance of the 1999 constitution appears to be tied to the stability and the vicissitudes of the Chávez government.

Starting during the electoral campaign, the constituent process was framed by debates about the reach and limits of the NCA, disputes as to whether it would have a founding or derivative character, and arguments over the definition of the roles of different state institutions vis-à-vis the constituent process. Although the Supreme Court of Justice ruled on the limits of the NCA in several cases, the NCA declared itself a founding power after it was constituted, thus freeing itself from the restrictions placed on it by the 1961 constitution and such existing institutional structures as the court.

The NCA vigorously assumed its founding character. From the outset, it became clear that the constituent process and the reach of the NCA were conceived as mechanisms to produce changes in the balance of public powers that emerged after the November 1998 elections, with the goal of consolidating its results and broadening the electoral support that the governing coalition received in the election of December 1998. The NCA was also used to promote the emergence of hitherto unknown public figures that would become part of the new political class (Martinez Barahona 2002). The process afforded high visibility and a central role to an emerging new leadership, thus further displacing traditional political elites.

The NCA was a powerful political instrument. It served several different functions, which were astutely conceived and implemented by the governing coalition. It served as a mechanism with which to restructure the state even before the promulgation of the new constitution; it also served to influence the balance of power in public institutions and to strengthen emerging sectors; it was employed as well to promote new political leaders and displace the traditional ones; and finally, it was used to generate a new constitution, with the objective of engendering a new set of rules, values, actors, and institutions with which to transform Venezuelan society. The elaboration of the new constitution was rushed through, at the expense of systematic discussion and of the consistency of the text itself. This led to the publication of several different versions of the constitution on different dates, each revealing both formal and substantive changes (Combellas 2001).

The third election of the constituent process took place on December 15, 1999, coinciding with the tragic landslide in the state of Vargas and torrential rains in other parts of the country. Once again, the results were highly favorable to the governing coalition, but on this occasion the opposition effectively organized itself, improving its results over those of the April election. The question submitted to the electorate was, "Do you approve the project for a Constitution elaborated by the National Constituent Assembly?" The results yielded 3,301,475 affirmative responses, equivalent to 71.78 percent to the total valid votes, and 1,298,105 negative votes, equivalent to 28.22 percent. The abstention rate was 56 percent.

The culmination of administration efforts to use the constituent process to occupy public institutions came in the final weeks of 1999, during the period of juridical limbo that came after the electoral ratification of the constitution but before the date of its official promulgation and publication in the *Official Gazette*. Late in December, the NCA dismissed all the leaders of the institutions of the state (with the exception of the president), including the attorney general, the legislative branch, the judicial branch, and the National Electoral Council (NEC), and replaced them with individuals associated with the governing coalition. The NCA also designated the director of the recently formed Public Ministry (Defensoría del Pueblo).

The Constituent Phase

Emerging political forces positioned themselves quickly and aggressively in the political arena, taking advantage of their initial popular support to consolidate and extend their capacity for capturing positions of power beyond those afforded by the November and December elections. In one year, they had secured approval of a new constitution and had displaced traditional political sectors, transforming themselves into a new political class. What the Patriotic Pole did not accomplish through the electoral processes of 1998—such as the quasi suspension of the Congress and its intervention in the judiciary—it accomplished through the constituent process. This period was also marked by the acute confusion and disarticulation of traditional actors in the face of the irruption of these new forces in the political arena.

The audacity, novelty, and questionable legality of many of these actions disconcerted traditional political actors. Combined with the broad support that Chávez and his supporters still enjoyed during this period, these measures generated a climate of encroachment and confrontation among traditional sectors that were facing the onslaught of these emerging forces. The alignment of public institutions behind the political project of the Fifth Republic led to several decisions that significantly aided the implementation of Chávez's program. In this context, the politics of consensus that had characterized the Puntofijista democracy was replaced by an exacerbation of differences, political exclusion, and a sharp division between sectors associated with Chávez and those associated with the traditional leadership. This growing disjuncture became visible not only in the political arena but also in economic, religious, military, and educational arenas as well as in labor unions and the media.

The electoral path taken by Chávez and his supporters was highly effective in generating legitimacy for the governing coalition from the outset, and its popular support served as an effective rationale for pushing beyond discursive and institutional limitations as well as legal obstacles. During 1999, the foundations were laid for a long-term sociopolitical project that drew upon a desire for change that had existed among the electorate for at least a decade. This same sentiment, however, also led to the acceptance of excesses and distortions that were not necessarily part of the popular aspirations for change.

The Relegitimization of Public Institutions

The idea of calling for new presidential elections was being considered by the ruling coalition even before the approval of the new constitution. From a legal and constitutional standpoint, the decision was justified by the argument that the periods and mandates of elected officials needed to be reconciled with the dispositions of the text. Parliamentary structure had to be changed, for example, from a bicameral to a unicameral format, and changes needed to be made to guarantee indigenous representation. There was also much debate about extending the presidential term, which would give Chávez six more years in office.

In this context, there were also other important considerations related to the possibilities for implementing the sociopolitical transformations of the governing coalition. While the December 1998 elections had produced an executive branch dominated by Chávez and his supporters, traditional political forces had won a considerable presence in the parliamentary and regional elections held in November of the same year and still wielded significant power in those arenas. The disjuncture between the executive and municipal authorities was even greater, since the latter had been elected in 1995. Given these circumstances, the call for a general election—the so-called relegitimization of powers—was justified by the need to align the balance of power in public institutions and in central, regional, and local administrative structures to ensure the predominance of the Patriotic Pole within them.

There were also debates about the electoral support for the governing coalition. In all of the elections held in 1998 and 1999, those registered for Chávez and those associated with the Patriotic Pole composed approximately a third of the electorate. The votes obtained by the Chávez candidacy totaled 3,673,685, equivalent to 33.4 percent of the total electorate. In December 1999, the votes cast for the yes option in the referendum represented 30.2 percent of all registered voters. While the totals were higher than those captured by the other options on the ballot, they appeared low for a political program with the goal of reestablishing the republic and transforming the architecture of the Venezuelan social order. This created a need to maximize the potential of those votes to transform that 33 percent of electoral support into the control of close to 100 percent of public posts. From the perspective of the new administration, it was necessary to act quickly to take advantage of their popular support, which, although steady, was also quite modest in relation to the magnitude of the project. The Chávez administration was also aware that this support could erode with time, leading to a strengthening of the opposition.

To implement a radical transformation of society, Venezuela's new leaders had to control the key decision-making mechanisms both in the horizontal structures of power—the political-administrative bureaucracy—and in the vertical structures of power—the different elected bodies at the national, regional, and local level. The first was accomplished by the NCA in December 1999 when it appointed Chávez supporters to all the nonelected public posts (attorney general, national comptroller, public prosecutor, judges of the Supreme Court of Justice, and members of the NEC). With the new elections, the administration sought to fill the elected posts, hoping to match or surpass the results obtained in 1998.

The organization of this new electoral process began in December 1999 with the NCA's appointment of all the members of the NEC, all of whom were supporters of the Chávez administration. On February 3, 2000, the

NCA issued the Electoral Statute for Public Institutions and set the date for the elections—May 28, 2000. The stage was now set for the mega-elections, in which 6,241 national legislative and local posts would be decided. The electoral statute also modified the existing electoral rules, adopting a mixed electoral system for legislative bodies in which 60 percent of the posts would be defined by majority vote and 40 percent by proportional vote. This was intended to generate an overrepresentation of the majority, although it would not be nearly as skewed as the governing coalition's overrepresentation in the NCA. The Chávez administration's concern with maximizing its electoral support early on also influenced the decision to convene the mega-election, which undermined important agreements about the need to separate regional and local elections from national electoral processes to promote the autonomy and visibility of the former.

These decisions were quickly challenged before the Supreme Tribunal of Justice (STJ), established by the 1999 constitution, with arguments about their illegality and unconstitutionality. In its response, the STJ used the controversial argument of transitoriality, which required that the process contemplate an established period—the transition—during which the institutional order could be adjusted to meet the dispositions of the new constitution. This meant that full applicability of the rules governing the elections and public institutions would have to wait until the creation of the National Assembly (Tribunal Suprema de Justicia 2000). The notion of transitoriality, like the notion of supraconstitutionality, which was employed by the NCA, was used to justify decisions that were favorable to the new regime—much to the detriment of the equality and impartiality of the electoral process.

The elections were marked by multiple risks and problems. There were important ruptures within the governing coalition, including the departure from the coalition of Arias, Urdaneta Hernández, and Joel Acosta Chirinos—three of the four commanders who along with Chávez had led the coup attempt in February 1992. Arias launched his own presidential candidacy, and there was a temporary distancing of PPT from the coalition as well. The election was also an opportunity for the articulation of an opposition, though this was not fully taken advantage of by key opposition actors still reeling from their recent electoral defeats. The most dramatic event of all, however, was the suspension of the balloting three days before it was to take place.

The combination of the inherent complexity of the election, the operational incompetence of the leaders of the NEC, and the political intervention of the ruling coalition led to the election's collapse. When it became clear that the election could not take place, two groups from civil society filed an oral injunction before the STJ requesting its suspension. On May 25, only three days before the elections, the STJ ordered that they be suspended and that new elections be immediately convened. Never before in the country's electoral history had such a disaster occurred.

The National Legislative Commission—the so-called Little Congress that was appointed by the NCA after it suspended the regular legislature—appointed a new steering committee for the NEC. This time they decided to separate the elections, scheduling the presidential, parliamentary, gubernatorial, state legislative, mayoral, and municipal council elections for July 30, 2000, and the remaining contests for December 3, 2000.

The Elections of July 30, 2000

The results of these elections were overwhelmingly favorable for the Chávez administration. There were only three candidates in the presidential contest: Chávez, who was supported by nine organizations; Arias, who was supported by six; and Claudio Fermín, who was supported by only one. This presidential election had the fewest candidates since 1958. Chávez captured 3,757,773 votes, 2.2 percent more than in the 1998 election and equivalent to 59.8 percent of the valid votes cast and 32.06 percent of all registered voters. Arias obtained 2,359,459 votes, equivalent to 37.5 percent of the votes cast, and Fermín received 171,346. The abstention rate reached 43.7 percent of the 11,720,971 registered voters. Chávez's support was approximately the same as in the last presidential election in both absolute and relative terms, while the opposition was unable to match the support it had received in 1998, although it surpassed its 1999 results.

The most important outcomes were in the parliamentary and state gubernatorial elections, which were key arenas in the Patriotic Pole's overall strategy. The governing coalition obtained a solid majority in the National Assembly, and within it, MVR captured 44.3 percent of the votes, making it the biggest single delegation within this legislative body. The traditional parties, AD and COPEI, suffered a significant decline, obtaining 16.1 percent and 5.1 percent of the vote, respectively, and the new parties saw similar results, with PV capturing 6 percent.

The combined number of MVR, the MAS, and indigenous representatives in the assembly reached 102 seats, which was greater than a simple majority although less than the two-thirds (110) required for important decisions, such as the appointment of ministers and other heads of public institutions. The governing coalition systematically employed this major-ity to further its political project. In the early days of its mandate, the administration was easily able to generate the alliances and negotiate the agreements needed to secure two-thirds of the vote in the assembly, and it was already guaranteed simple majorities. Yet political changes within the coalition, including the withdrawal of the MAS and of a group of MVR congressmen, significantly reduced the size of its delegation in the assembly, making winning coalitions increasingly difficult to achieve (Kornblith 2003) and in some cases even jeopardizing its simple majority.

In the regional arena, the elections were also favorable to Chávez, gen-erating a shift in the balance of power in favor of MVR, which won eleven gubernatorial contests. In the states of Bolivar, Cojedes, Merida, Nueva Esparta, Tachira, and Trujillo, MVR candidates displaced governors from AD and COPEI, in some cases by very small margins and amidst contro-versies over the transparency of the electoral process. PV once again won in the state of Carabobo, COPEI triumphed in Miranda, and Convergence won in Yaracuy. The MAS captured four governorships, and in Zulia the office went to a new regional organization called A New Time.

The governing coalition was able to fully realize its objectives in these elections. The traditional parties were further weakened and displaced, losing important positions within the legislature and a significant number of governorships. This generated a new balance of power that was clear-ly favorable to the Patriotic Pole and to Chávez's political project.

The Municipal Council, Neighborhood Associations, and the Labor Union Referendum of December 3, 2000

To complete the electoral process that had originally been scheduled for May 2000, representatives to the municipal councils and neighbor-hood associations still had to be elected. These elections took place on December 3, 2000. Given that these were the seventh elections in three years, it is no surprise that they elicited very little enthusiasm. This was compounded by the fact that the authorities to be elected were not consid-ered very important by the already weary electorate and by the fact that by this point political organizations and candidates lacked the resources to mobilize visible campaigns, since these had been spent on the May 2000 campaign. In short, this time around there was barely a campaign. The results yielded an abstention rate of 76 percent, the highest in Venezuela's electoral history, and 35.5 percent of the councilmen elected were mem-bers of MVR.

The labor union referendum was also held on that date. Its objective was to renew union leadership throughout the country with the expectation that the voting would yield a balance of power more favorable to the government. In the election, the yes option obtained 1,632,750 votes, equivalent to 62.02 percent of valid votes cast, and the no option captured 719,771 votes, equivalent to 27.34 percent, with null votes totaling 10.64 percent. During the second half of 2001, union elections were held across the country, and while the governing coalition succeeded in displacing the existing leadership through the referendum, the results of these elections were highly favorable to the opposition, making this the first electoral event in which opposition to the Patriotic Pole was able to articulate itself successfully.

The Relegitimization of Public Institutions

Despite the tensions and ruptures experienced within the new ruling coalition, the net result of its effort to relegitimize public institutions was undoubtedly favorable to Chávez and his supporters. The administration was able to harmoniously realign the entire political and administrative structure behind its project through electoral processes. Once the new National Assembly was finally established in late 2000, it appointed the heads of the civil and judiciary powers, taking advantage of the majority enjoyed by the governing coalition as well as its ability to broker agreements within that body. Through these appointments, the governing coalition was also able to secure majorities in each of these institutions. With these last elections, the political-electoral phase of the refoundational program had successfully come to a close.

Hegemony versus the Popular Will

Following the advances and electoral victories of President Chávez and his allies, the political landscape continued to change. Numerous surveys and public opinion polls began to show evidence of popular disaffection with the president and increasingly negative evaluations of his administration's policies. Beginning in the second half of 2001, an opposition to Chávez and his sociopolitical project began to emerge, particularly around the recently formed Coordinadora Democrática (Democratic Coordinator), which brought together a broad and heterogeneous array of old and new political parties as well as old and new organizations from civil society. Unfortunately, after December 2000 there were not opportunities for these changing collective perceptions to gain electoral expression, and they therefore had little impact on the balance of power.

Despite several important changes, such as the attenuation of the administration's legislative majority, the balance of power that emerged from the electoral processes of 2000 now appeared anachronistic, a static arrangement out of sync with a clearly shifting public opinion. Many of the political struggles that have taken place since the second half of 2001 have entailed efforts to change this situation, to achieve a political order more representative of these new collective aspirations. Given the skewed concentration of power and leadership in the figure of Chávez, and the highly personalist character of the political order that he has put in place in Venezuela, it is no surprise that both his staunchest supporters and his fiercest detractors have focused their efforts on the president himself. Indeed, opposition has focused on removing Chávez from power.

The Referendum as a Political Strategy

Since the failed coup against Chávez in 2002, one of the main democratic strategies used by the opposition to remove him from power has been the referendum. From 2002 to 2004, three separate attempts were made to convene referenda. The first took place in November 2002, when the opposition submitted a petition to the NEC requesting a referendum on Chávez's permanence in power, accompanied by close to 2 million signatures of citizens on the electoral rolls. Although the NEC approved the request, the Electoral Court of the STJ rejected it in late January 2003, arguing that the petition was not valid given the irregular composition of the NEC's steering committee.

On the same date as the referendum had been scheduled to take place, the opposition organized the Firmazo (signing), during which the diverse opposition groups in the Coordinadora Democrática and an organization known as Súmate mobilized to collect signatures for several issue-specific referenda. These included a referendum on a constitutional amendment that would abrogate a set of forty laws, and a referendum on whether Chávez should remain in power, among others. On August 20, 2003, the Coordinadora Democrática once again submitted the petitions to the NEC, this time with more than 3.2 million signatures, requesting a call for a referendum to revoke Chávez's mandate.[6] This second initiative also failed as a result of a 3–2 decision adopted against it on September 12, 2003, by the newly appointed steering committee of the NEC, which argued that the petition did not satisfy certain "essential formalities" such as the supposed extemporaneousness of the collection of signatures and the lack of mention of the NEC in the text of the petitions.

Despite these setbacks, the referendum continued to be the main strategy employed by the opposition to oust Chávez from power. On September 26, 2003, the NEC approved a set of norms for referenda that were highly restrictive and limited popular expression. Nevertheless, the opposition was able to deliver 3,467,050 signatures to convene a referendum on the presidency. These signatures were collected between November 28 and December 1 in an operation known as the Reafirmazo (reaffirming). According to the constitution, the minimum number of signatures required must equal 20 percent of all registered voters, which in this case amounted to 2,452,179.

The signatures were submitted to a rigorous verification process. In March 2004, the pro-Chávez majority in the NEC declared that there had not been enough valid signatures collected and that it was necessary to ratify the validity of numerous allegedly dubious signatures, citing evaluation criteria that were not part of the original rules (such as the so-called flat ballots and signatures with similar handwriting). After an undecipherable manipulation of the numbers, the NEC ruled that more than 1.1 million signatures needed to be "ratified" through a process of "restoration," which took place at the end of May. In the meantime, 375,000 signatures were arbitrarily invalidated. To the surprise of many Chávez supporters, the opposition was able to overcome this new obstacle and submit the required number of valid signatures to convene a presidential referendum, which was set for August 15, 2004, by the NEC. Yet much like the collection, submission, and verification of signatures, preparations for the referendum were plagued by delays, improvisation, artificial obstacles, and widespread doubts about the impartiality of electoral authorities and the transparency of their procedures. This entire process was closely monitored by representatives from the Carter Center and the Organization of American States, which since mid-2002 have served as mediators in Venezuelan political affairs, because of the high levels of tension and polarization.

The three attempts to collect signatures became a crucial part of the opposition's efforts, increasing its organizational capacity and consolidating its democratic credentials. The millions of signatures collected during the Firmazo and the Reafirmazo surpassed the electoral support that the opposition had obtained since 1998. And while these numbers are not exactly comparable to an election, they do evince changes in collective preferences and the growing ability of the opposition to mobilize the electorate.[7]

The perseverance and determination of broad sectors of the population during this period were notable. Large numbers of Venezuelans patiently struggled against arbitrary decisions that attempted, time after time, to undermine the expression of their will. Rather than undermining this collective spirit, recent difficulties appear to have strengthened the determination and democratic aspirations of this segment of the population.

Despite the tenacity of the opposition, the 2004 recall lost by 59 to 41 percent, tracking the vote shares that Chávez had garnered in his two presidential victories (56 percent in 1998 and 60 percent in 2000). He triumphed thanks to the government's control over the electoral institutions, its social assistance programs fueled by rising oil revenues, the strength of the president's support (solidified by a massive registration drive among lower-income groups), and the weakness of the intimidated opposition coalition. While fortifying Chávez's rule, the referendum also entrenched the intense polarization of the electorate, with nearly half of society severely alienated from the state.

Reestablishing the Republic versus Sowing Democracy

Paradoxically, the presidential recall referendum and the other eight national or regional elections that Venezuelans witnessed between 1998 and 2004 have served to consolidate the power of figures who burst on the political scene as a result of the failed military coup of February 1992 and whose commitment to representative democracy and the voting booth is, to put it generously, utilitarian at best. Chávez's political project is built around the triad of strongman plus army plus people and not around a system of institutionalized parties, separated powers, and impartial respect for the rights and liberties of all citizens. The so-called participatory democracy enshrined in the 1999 constitution devalues representative democracy. In this model, elections are instruments to be used at the service of a personality cult and a sociopolitical model with long-term hegemonic aspirations, deeply tied to politicized armed forces and connected to a population mobilized by means of plebiscites and patron-client mechanisms. It is a bitter irony that elections have served so often and so well to promote the ambitions of a group and a political project that oppose democracy, its principal institutions, and its crucial values. In the process, some Venezuelans who are committed to liberal democracy believe less each day in the effectiveness of elections as mechanisms to articulate collective preferences and to produce power relations that can adequately express collective sentiment.

The accomplishments and limitations of Chávez's political project were both a product of the new socioeconomic reality that emerged with the economic decline during the 1980s. Yet they must also be understood within a longer history, of the evolution of democratic experience in Venezuela, which goes back to at least 1958. It is to this temporal frame that I refer with the term sowing democracy. This democratic experience has been a source of inspiration for the struggles against the hegemonic and authoritarian pretensions of the current regime, which, although born with strong popular and electoral support, has progressively revealed that its commitment to democratic values and institutions was only a strategy to gain and consolidate power, rather than a commitment to a pluralist order and democratic institutions.

As in the rest of the Andean region, precarious socioeconomic conditions, institutional deterioration, widespread poverty, and the isolation of the elites have created the conditions for the emergence of atavistic personalisms, authoritarian schemes, and demagogic appeals that, far from satisfying collective aspirations, create more problems than they solve. The Venezuelan case illustrates the dramatic decomposition of a democratic order produced by a combination of changing socioeconomic conditions and the inability of elites to respond effectively and in a timely manner. Yet it also underscores the benefits of a long-term and well-consolidated democratic experience, however imperfect, for confronting the authoritarian pretensions of a populist leadership that capriciously and irresponsibly uses institutions and public resources for its own benefit. The intense challenges of the past few years have led to the creation of new kinds of organizations, removed from both the distortions of the past and the aberrations of the present. We hope that these new strategies can take root and contribute to the reorientation of Venezuelan society, as well as to the resolution of the common problems that plague the countries of the Andean region.

Notes

An earlier version of this paper was presented at the Forum on Latin America: Turbulent Democracies, sponsored by the Department of Political Science, University of the Andes, in Bogotá, Colombia, September 11–12, 2003.

1. This section draws heavily from Kornblith (1998). See also Hidalgo (2000).

2. For analysis of the relationship between socioeconomic deterioration and sociopolitical realignments in Venezuela, see Ellner (2003), Hellinger (2003), and Roberts (2003).

3. After these and the 2000 elections, claims were made that Chávez had received the highest number of votes of any presidential candidate in the nation's history. In

fact, and without diminishing the importance of the large number of votes obtained by Chávez in the 1998 and 2000 elections, it is relevant to note that in 1983 Jaime Lusinchi received 3,773,731 votes, equivalent to 56.72 percent of the vote, with an abstention rate of 12.25 percent. In 1988, Carlos Andrés Pérez captured 3,868,843 votes, equivalent to 52.89 percent, with an abstention rate of 18.08 percent. In relative terms and as a result of the high abstention rate, the absolute number of votes captured by Chávez represented 33.43 percent of all registered voters, while Lusinchi obtained 49.77 percent and Pérez 43.32 percent.

4. Reestablishment of the Republic (Refundación de la República) was the campaign slogan that condensed the idea of transforming the basic institutional structures of Venezuelan society.

5. The situation reached such extremes that the National Electoral Council fined President Chávez for violating regulations that prohibit public officials from using their posts for partisan/electoral ends.

6. The minimum number of signatures required was 2.4 million, equivalent to 20 percent of registered voters.

7. According to estimates by Súmate, close to 4.7 million people participated in these events.

Bibliography

Carrasquero, J. V., T. Maingón, and F. Welsch, eds. 2001. *Venezuela in transición: Elecciones y democracia 1998–2000*. Caracas, Venezuela: CDB Publicaciones-RedPol.

Combellas, R. 2001. *Derecho constitucional: Una introducción al estudio de la Constitución de la República Bolivariana de Venezuela*. Caracas, Venezuela: McGraw-Hill Interamericana.

Ellner, S. 2003. En la búsqueda de explicaciones. In Ellner and Hellinger 2003, 19–42.

Ellner, S., and D. Hellinger, eds. 2003. *La política venezolana en la época de Chávez: Clases, polarización y conflicto*. Caracas, Venezuela: Editorial Nueva Sociedad.

Hellinger, D. 2003. Visión política general: La caída del puntofijismo y el surgimiento del chavismo. In Ellner and Hellinger 2003, 43–74.

Hidalgo Trenado, M. 2002. Liderazgo, reforma económica y cambio político in Venezuela, 1989–1998. In Ramos Jiménez 2002, 77–129.

Kornblith, M. 1998. *Venezuela en los noventa: Las crisis de la democracia*. Caracas, Venezuela: IESA.

———. 2003. Elecciones y representación in tiempos turbulentos. In *Esta Venezuela: Realidades y nuevos caminos*, ed. P. Márquez, and R. Piñango, 375–402. Caracas, Venezuela: IESA.

Kornblith, M., and Levine, D. 1995. Venezuela: The life and times of the party system. In Mainwaring and Scully 1995, 37–71.

López Maya, M. 2003. Hugo Chávez, su movimiento y presidencia. In Ellner and Hellinger 2003, 97–120.

Mainwaring, S., and Scully, T., eds. 1995. *Building democratic institutions: Party systems in Latin America*. Stanford, CA: Stanford University Press.

Martínez Barahona, E. 2002. La formación de una nueva clase política in Venezuela: ¿Un cambio para seguir igual? In Ramos Jiménez 2002, 131–162.

Molina Vega, J. E. 2001. Comportamiento electoral in Venezuela 1998–2000: Cambio y continuidad. In Carrasquero, Maingón, and Welsch 2001, 188–213.

Molina Vega, J. E., and C. Pérez Baralt. 1996. Los procesos electorales y la evolución del sistema de partidos. In *El sistema político venezolano: Crisis y transformaciones*, ed. A. Alvarez, 193–238. Caracas, Venezuela: UCV-IEP.

Ramos Jiménez, A., ed. 2002. *La transición venezolana: Aproximación al fenómeno Chávez*. Mérida, Venezuela: Centro de Investigaciones de Política Comparada.

Rey, J. C. 1989. *El futuro de la democracia in Venezuela*. Caracas, Venezuela: Colección IDEA.

———. 1991. La democracia venezolana y la crisis del sistema populista de conciliación. *Revista de Estudios Políticos*, no. 74:533–78.

Roberts, K. 2003. Polarización social y resurgimiento del populismo in Venezuela. In Ellner and Hellinger 2003, 75–95.

Sonntag, H., and Maingón, T. 2001. Cambio político y resultados de las elecciones de 1998. In Carrasquero, Maingón, and Welsch 2001, 101–122.

Tribunal Suprema de Justicia. 2000. *Bases jurisprudenciales de la supraconstitucionalidad*. Caracas, Venezuela: Colección de Estudios Jurídicos TSJ.

Viciano Pastor, R., and Martínez Dalmau, R. 2001. *Cambio político y proceso constituyente en Venezuela*. Caracas, Venezuela: Valencia, Vadell Hermanos Editores.

CONTRIBUTORS

JEREMY ADELMAN is chair of the Department of History at Princeton University.

JO-MARIE BURT is assistant professor of political science at George Mason University.

PAUL W. DRAKE is dean of social sciences at the University of California–San Diego.

ANN MASON is director of the Department of Political Science at the Universidad de los Andes, Bogotá, Colombia.

FRANCISCO GUTIÉRREZ SANÍN is director of the Instituto de Estudios Políticos y Relaciones Internacionales (IEPRI) at the National University of Colombia, in Bogotá.

ERIC HERSHBERG is a program director at the Social Science Research Council and adjunct associate professor at Columbia University. He has been elected to serve as vice president and president-elect of the Latin American Studies Association (LASA).

MIRIAM KORNBLITH is a professor and researcher at the Institute for Political Studies at the Central University and at the Institute for Advanced Administration Studies (IESA) in Caracas, Venezuela.

ARLENE TICKNER is professor of international studies at the Universidad de los Andes, Bogotá, Colombia.

JOHN SHEAHAN is professor of economics at Williams College.

DONNA LEE VAN COTT is associate professor of political science at Tulane University.

DEBORAH J. YASHAR is associate professor of politics at Princeton University.

INDEX

Page numbers in *italic* type refer to figures or tables.